STUDIES IN EVANGELICALISM
edited by
Kenneth E. Rowe &
Donald W. Dayton

The Holiness Revival Of The Nineteenth Century

by

MELVIN EASTERDAY DIETER

Studies in Evangelicalism, No. 1

The Scarecrow Press, Inc.
Metuchen, N.J., & London
1980

Library of Congress Cataloging in Publication Data

Dieter, Melvin Easterday.
    The holiness revival of the nineteenth century.

    (Studies in evangelicalism ; no. 1)
    Bibliography: p.
    Includes index.
    1.   Holiness churches--United States--History--19th
century.   2.   Holiness churches--Europe--History--19th
century.   3.   Revivals--United States--History--19th century.   4.   Revivals--Europe--History--19th century.   5.
United States--Church history.   6.   Europe--Church history.   I.   Title.
BX7990. H6D53   269'. 24'0973   80-17259
ISBN 0-8108-1328-9

To Hallie,
for love, wisdom,
and a lot of hard work

CONTENTS

EDITORS' NOTE

The current resurgence of Evangelical religion has highlighted the important role of Evangelicalism in the formation of American culture. This series will explore its roots in the Evangelical Revival and the Awakenings of the 18th century, its 19th century blossoming in revivalism and social reform, and its 20th century developments in both sect and "mainline" churches. We will be particularly concerned to emphasize the diversity within Evangelicalism--the search for holiness, the Millennial traditions, Fundamentalism, Pentecostalism and so forth. We are pleased to publish Melvin E. Dieter's study of the holiness revival in 19th-century America as number one in the series.

Following undergraduate studies with honors at Muhlenberg College, Professor Dieter studied theology first at Eastern Pilgrim College and then at Temple University where he also took the doctorate in 1973. He is a regular contributor to several theological journals, has published essays in two books and is currently working on a new history of the Wesleyan Church. The former General Secretary of Educational Institutions of the Wesleyan Church is now Professor of Church History and Historical Theology at Asbury Theological Seminary in Wilmore, Kentucky.

Donald W. Dayton
Northern Baptist Theological
   Seminary
Lombard, Illinois

Kenneth E. Rowe
Drew University
Madison, New Jersey

PREFACE

This journey through the nineteenth century began almost thirty years ago at a small college near Boston, Massachusetts. There, at a chance meeting, two fledgling history professors shared their common interest in someday writing the history of the American perfectionist revival movement.

Both men eventually used their doctoral research projects to that end. In 1957 Dr. Timothy Smith's thesis on revivalism and social reform brought the movement to the attention of the academic and religious world. That volume quickly took its place as one of the crucially definitive interpretations of nineteenth century religious and social history.

The other young man, after long involvement in academic administration, finally got back to his own commitment to contribute to the history of the holiness revival; his doctoral research is summed up largely in the volume which follows. One of the joys of that research was to share the journey again with Tim Smith, now director of studies in American religion at Johns Hopkins University. Dr. Smith served on the doctoral committee.

Many others have shared in the venture. Dr. Franklin H. Littell graciously adopted a doctoral candidate at a critical point in his study. Dr. Earnest B. Stoeffler, whose loving concerns for pietism shaped not only that candidate's teaching but his life, and Dr. Elwyn Smith, who encouraged the original research, were good guides.

The kindness of the many librarians who shared the dusty recesses of their nineteenth century collections was always an encouragement. Special thanks go to Lawrence McIntosh and Kenneth Rowe of Drew University and to the librarians at Pasadena Nazarene College (now Point Loma College) who were especially helpful.

And all along the extended journey, Hallie was there encouraging, prodding, typing,--sharing good time and bad. Very near to the beginning Judy padded along--Judy, who is now following her own research and teaching paths.

All of us, who have experienced the pleasures of the unexpected discoveries as well as the humdrum plodding which a professionally-honed venture demands, hope that all who join us through the account which follows will share the joy of discovery and find little "humdrum plodding." It has been a purposeful journey, an attempt at a balanced and reliable view of a small but significant segment of life; it has all been con amore.

Melvin E. Dieter
Wilmore, Kentucky
June 6, 1980

CHAPTER I

INTRODUCTION: THE SPECIAL PROMOTION OF
HOLINESS, A NEW FORCE IN AMERICAN REVIVALISM

It is a commonly accepted truism in American church history that from the time of the Great Awakening until the close of the nineteenth century revivalism was the dominant force in the shaping of American Protestantism. [1] The first issue of a new religious magazine in Boston in July 1839 announced the presence of a struggling, new force within the American revival tradition. Claiming a certain novelty for the venture, the Rev. Timothy Merritt, founder and editor, noted that his Guide to Christian Perfection was the "first publication of its kind ever commenced." [2] Merritt was a New England Methodist minister already well prepared for editorial work through his extensive service to the publishing interests of his church. [3]

The title of an introductory editorial, "What Shall Be Done to Revive the Work of Holiness in the Church?", [4] spoke directly to the special purpose of the venture. It rooted the then incipient American holiness revival, which the paper soon came to represent, in the revivals of the experience of entire sanctification in certain Methodist societies in England in 1760 and 1762. Merritt noted that John Wesley, convinced of the religious validity of the professions of those who had then testified to being made "perfect in love," had predicted that the time would come when "sanctifications would be as common as conversions." [5] In eager anticipation of that day, the editor concluded,

O, what a day that will be! What shall be done to hasten it? [6]

The publication of the Guide indicated the editor's determination to hurry Wesley's hopes on to reality within nineteenth-century American Methodism. Merritt had prepared the paper particularly for the "encouragement" of the "many" who were becoming involved in a renewed interest in the experience of Christian perfection within the Methodist Episcopal Church about that time. "God was advancing the work in many circuits, stations, and classes,"[7] he noted.

The Zion's Herald for February 22, 1837, reported that at a recent Methodist preacher's meeting at Stafford, Connecticut,

> there was a thorough conviction on the minds of the preachers present of the importance and necessity of a revival of holiness both in the ministry and in the membership of our church; and it was a matter of rejoicing that the subject of entire sanctification not in theory only, but in experience and enjoyment had occupied the ... attention of preachers and people more fully, for a few months past than for some time previous. [8]

The next month the same paper carried a report of the Maine Conference of the Methodist Episcopal Church to the editors of the Christian Advocate and Journal which indicated that

> there is an interest in the distinguishing doctrine of evengelical holiness, greatly increased from former years.... An unusual number of witnesses of sanctifying grace have been raised up in different parts of the state.... [9]

By fall of the year, at the close of the camp meeting season, camp reports such as that from Derry, New Hampshire were common:

> Many [were] sanctified and cleansed from all sin. The work of holiness seems to be advancing in a powerful manner on many circuits and stations on this district. [10]

Aware of this immediate interest in the doctrine, the first edition of the Guide urged Methodist pastors to make the revival of the work of Christian holiness a particular concern of semi-monthly "special meetings of the church." It insisted that, "the importance of the subject demands special attention and extra effort at this time" [emphasis mine]. The Guide was to become a special vehicle for publishing the per-

sonal testimonies to those new experiences of Christian perfection which were being made with increasing frequencies
in such meetings. [11]

A NEW BLEND: HISTORIC PIETISM,
AMERICAN REVIVALISM, AND
WESLEYAN PERFECTIONISM

What Merritt could not know was that in his call for
"specialty" he was most accurately defining a new emphasis,
a factor which lent uniqueness to the American holiness revival.   As the story of the succeeding history seems to dem-
onstate, it produced shades of distinction which set it apart
from earlier holiness movements within the Christian church
in general and from the promulgation of the experience of
holiness by the Wesleys in particular.   It also set the pattern
for a movement which developed special organizations dedicated to the promotion of entire sanctification; this eventually
led to the creation of "holiness churches" and other religious
organizations which made this "specialty" their priority concern. [12]   Merritt's publishing venture represented a particular sense of purpose and logical procedure in the pursuit of
Christian holiness unparalleled in the history of the tradition
which preceded it.   It marked the wedding of the American
mind, prevailing revivalism, and Wesleyan perfectionism in
as widespread a popular quest for the beatific vision as the
world had known.

The Holiness Message

The adherents of the revival, which was gathering
momentum and developing its character in the quarter century prior to the Civil War, were rooted deeply in the same
Biblical orientation as that of the Pietists, Spener and Zin-
zendorf.   They shared in John Bunyan's Bedford jail dreams
of a Christian existence on the borders of heaven itself--a
spiritual plateau beyond "the Valley of the Shadow ... out of
the reach of the Giant Despair ... [and] out of sight of
Doubting Castle. "[13]   They claimed to have found a spiritual
highland where "they heard continually the singing of the
birds, and saw every day the flowers appear on the earth
and heard the voice of the turtle ... [they were called] holy
people. "[14]

But they were also planted firmly in the midst of unique

religious soil, part of the very pragmatic American experiment. Their vision of holiness was not a mystical one.
They were guarded from such tendencies by their largely
Methodist roots. Their pietism was a Wesleyan pietism oriented much more towards Christian activity than pietistic in-
trospection. These American perfectionist revivalists appro-
priated Bunyan's pleasant "highlands" of his Christian's pil-
grimage not for the "then" of death but for the "now" of life.
They claimed that "pleasant" country as their earthly spiritual homeland; its Biblical language and rich imagery they
adopted as their mother religious tongue. A present possibility of a life of practical holiness, a "Beulah land" within
the reach of every Christian, became the rallying cry of the
movement's evangelism. [15]   To "spread Scriptural holiness
over these lands" was the watchword of all who were involved. [16]

        Claiming Biblical authority and experiential authentica-
tion for what they believed was Wesley's own teaching on
Christian perfection, they preached the necessity for a second crisis of evangelical faith in the life of every Christian.
This "second blessing," subsequent to the crisis of evangelical conversion, as understood in the revivalistic tradition,
involved the Christian's utter consecration of himself to God
through Jesus Christ in the faith that God would free him
from the inner disposition to willful sin and fill him with divine love. The holiness adherents always denied that this produced a state of absolute perfection or of non posse peccare;
they did maintain that, as long as the entirely sanctified individual did not consciously and willfully transgress this new
relationship, he would continue in the Christian life with an
undivided love for God as he developed the graces of Christian maturity; there could be an enduring relationship, they
said, of posse non peccare. Wesley gave this definition:

> Entire sanctification or Christian perfection is nei-
> ther more or less than pure love; love expelling sin,
> and governing both the heart and life of a child of
> God. The Refiner's fire purges out all that is con-
> trary to love. [17]

The American Context

        The American milieu in the nineteenth century compre-
hended certain cultural and religious moods which encouraged

the revival's attempt to adapt Bunyan's dreams to everyday Christian experience. The expansive thrust of American revivalism accompanied by its emphasis on the universal call of the Christian Gospel made every man a prospective citizen of "Beulah Land"; burgeoning American Methodism with its basic commitments to Wesleyan Arminianism was influencing religious life. [18]

A transcendental thrust was also shaping American thought patterns. It "represented an intellectual effort to overcome the base material world," and "created a tendency in American Christianity ... [to emphasize] the spiritual and ideal side of life...."[20] A perfectionist trend was inherent in transcendentalism itself. When the trancendentalist wrote that the "absolute or natural religion" is that which produces "the normal development, use, discipline, and enjoyment of every part of the body, and every faculty of the spirit; the direction of all natural powers to their natural purposes,"[21] he was setting out concepts, the connotations of which, were very near to those expounded by the Wesleyan perfectionist who proclaimed that the experience of entire sanctification would free a man to be all that a loving God originally had intended him to be.

Another factor in the total milieu was the idealism which inspired the American national destiny--a divine destiny whose goal was to create a new society, free from the ills which had plagued the societies left behind when immigrants set out for America. The conviction of the New England pioneers that their colony was "the place where the Lord ... [would] create a new Heaven and a new Earth in new Churches and a new commonwealth together" had fixed itself generally within the American mind. [22] In their new land they were part of a new Israel; this vision infused both politics and, later, technology. [23] The inherent optimism in this American dream was readily assimilated with the optimism of perfectionism in the holiness movement; the two were to be regular traveling companions throughout the nineteenth century--each undoubtedly helping the other along the way. For the holiness advocate it was all a part of a grand, divine plan to usher in the "most glorious and last dispensation"-- the dispensation of the Holy Spirit. [24]

In the midst of these, often mutually serving, religious, social and political currents, those who professed this "second blessing" witnessed everywhere to the new depths of spiritual reality they believed the experience of "perfect love" had opened for them. They zealously invited all Christendom to share in their discovery. With unbounded expectation they proclaimed the advent of a new dispensation of spiritual power. In this experience, Christians who felt increasingly threatened by the rapidly altering culture in which they lived, might discover new resources for personal endurance and collective counter-attack upon the evils which these changes represented to them.

The power and the victory promised in the optimism of the holiness message, therefore, may be seen, from this aspect, as a natural and significant consequence of developing revivalism among individuals in whom the principles of perfectionism, puritanism and pietism were at work.[25] It was a response to an urgent desire for some effective, counter-revolutionary, spiritual force which could enable the individual Christion, other Christians, and through them the Christian church to cope with the disturbing changes in society as a whole. They were certain that this formula for Christian action promised a "panacea" for "all" their evils. It could "solve all the religious, social, and political problems of mankind."[26] Regardless of whatever other bastions of traditional Christianity might fall before the increasing onslaughts of its critics, they believed that as long as "Pentecostal effusions" continued to manifest themselves, "primitive Christianity survives in one of its chief characteristics and will ... vindicate its reality and potency...."[27]

THE SIGNIFICANCE OF THE MOVEMENT IN CHURCH HISTORY

The story of the holiness movement is not, consequently, a story of unique twists of unorthodox patterns of theology or of Christian life; it is rather an account of a movement at the center of an accelerating current of some of the steadily flowing streams of Christian tradition. The quest eventually resulted in bringing thousands of new converts into the Christian faith and churches, but its main thrust was to reform the church itself.

In the Christian reform tradition which sought to assert the claims of apostolic Christianity as the pattern for determining the nature of the church and its life, the movement, like Wesley and the Anabaptists before him, generally considered the church far gone from original Christianity.

Its professed primary aim was to bring the fallen church
back to primitive New Testament standards. The revival
call to the church to experience again the outpouring of the
Holy Spirit, as received by the Apostles themselves on the
day of Pentecost, was the focal point of this effort to restore
the church to its pristine power and purposes. It gave the
movement a compelling sense of mission; the goal was to
"Christianize" Christianity. When one relates that goal to the
prevailing concepts of American idealism, mentioned above,
which cast Christian America in her role as the destined
leader in the Christianizing of all society, he can better understand why the holiness advocated saw their own role as
very crucial. The pages which follow will demonstrate that
this challenge to Christians to discover higher levels of personal holiness and new sources of spiritual power in a second personal religious experience as definite and critical as
their initial Christian conversion left a telling and permanent
impact upon Protestant evangelicalism in both America and
Europe. [28]

The Methodist Context and Influence

The preaching of the doctrine often created sharp division in congregations and denominations just as general revivalism, itself, had done throughout history. The Methodist oriented churches were most deeply influenced; they eventually suffered the greatest loss of members to the churches
which were organized out of the revival activity at the century's close. At the same time, the revival's influence continued to make itself felt within that church through the large
number of adherents of the movement who chose to remain
with the church in the welter of conflict on the "church question" in the course of the institutionalizing of the holiness
revival.

This intimate relationship with the Methodist movement in America, undoubtedly accounts, in some degree, for
the fact that until recently the significance of the movement
in American church history has largely gone unnoticed. [29]
Because the early leaders were Methodists, their efforts
were comprehended within the Methodist denominational col-
losus or in the smaller churches which circled like orbiting
satellites around its strong Wesleyan-Arminian theological
center of gravity. Historical views of American revivalism
and evangelism have often majored in revivalists and revival
movements from the viewpoint of Calvinistic revivalism. The

leaders of these were commonly more independent of intense
denominational involvements, thereby developing a personal
ministry more easily indentifiable in historical analysis of
revivalism.

This involvement in the revivalism of a large, highly
organized, revival church may account, in part, for the fact
that we have heard more about the Moodys, Chapmans, and
Sundays than we have about the Caugheys, Palmers, and Inskips. Yet the latter group, in the history of American revivalism, represent holiness evangelists who not only set the
stage for, or strongly influenced the main emphases of the
former group, but also contributed directly to the American
revivalist and evangelical traditions in a degree not yet ade-
quately represented in American church history. In their efforts to reform the churches and bring them back to primitive holiness with all of its ethical implications, they were
typically puritanistic: in that they were working within the
structure of the church and not as independent or charismatic
prophets, they were typically pietistic. They were puritan-
pietists, but not separatists.

The holiness movement, which was fostered by them
and their successors, today claims a regular membership of
approximately 1,250,000 in the United States and several thousand more in other countries around the world.[30] The effective constituency, however, numbers at least double that figure. Restrictive standards for membership in its component
churches make it difficult to account accurately for thousands
of non-members, actively involved in the institutional life, who
in more latitudinarian churches would have been received into
full membership.[31] In addition to the regular members of the
organized holiness churches, one must include in the movement's statistics the supporting constituencies of the non-denominational and interdenominational agencies which draw support, not only from members of the holiness churches, but
also from a less readily identified, but equally committed, holiness constituency within the older churches, expecially within
Methodism.[32]

The largest of the organized holiness groups is the
Nazarene, with a world-wide membership of 600,000; the
smallest is probably a splinter group of ten or twelve members started yesterday, unrecorded in any statistical tables,
yet clearly claiming allegiance to the theological and historical
tradition under consideration. The majority of the organized
bodies and many of the individual supporters within the United

Methodist Church maintain cooperative holiness promotion
through the Christian Holiness Association, formerly the National Holiness Association.

A CASE STUDY IN THE DEVELOPMENT OF THE
AMERICAN CHURCHES

In the degree that these groups vary in size and influence, so they also bear the demonstrable imprint of a variety of religious traditions. Quaker, Mennonite, Baptist, and
Presbyterian influences all blended emphases of spirituality,
simplicity, freedom and piety into the mainstream of Methodism to shape modern holiness life. The richly varigated
design which one sees when he views these diverse threads
of American evangelical tradition which have been woven into
the fabric of the religious life of the holiness churches, may
scarcely be found in any other clearly identifiable segment of
American Christianity. A study of this mix and its major ingredients constitutes another central purpose of this dissertation. This heterogeneity has always given the whole complex
a strong interdenominational flavor. Variety is a hallmark
of the movement; it has tended to keep the movement more
open and flexible in its responses to other religious movements than it might have been without such a multiplicity of
religious inputs. However, at the same time, these inputs
from so many traditions have consistently created differences
of viewpoint which have hindered efforts to extend the organizational unity of the movement.[33]

One may find, then, in the holiness movement, a unique
and distinct composite of the development of American evangelicalism of the past one hundred years. It is replete with
instructive comparisons which can contribute to a more objective understanding of the movement itself, its place in
American religious history and, therefore, to that history itself. The loose organization of the movement allowed the
cultural and social forces which were shaping American religious life during that time to impinge upon, influence, penetrate and shape its component groups to a degree scarcely
possible in the other orthodox, but already more highly structured churches of the nation. The resultant microcosm of
American religious life demonstrates all of the forces which
Sidney Mead identifies as factors active in the development of
American denominationalism: historylessness, voluntaryism,
mission, enterprise, revivalism, flight from reason, and the
concomitant triumph of pietism and competition among the denominations.[34]

SUMMARY

The history which follows is a study in the "dynamic"
orientation which H. Richard Niebuhr saw in American Protestantism[35]--the dynamic of a "creative" religious force "in
the process of passing over into custom and habit."[36] The
pre-Civil War story demonstrates the creativity of the movement in its development of a new emphasis in American revivalism by applying the logic of revivalism to the special
promotion of Wesleyan perfectionism; the history of the post-
war revival in America and Europe outlines the significant
success of holiness revivalism in permanently placing this emphasis in the thought and life of all of evangelical Protestantism around the world. The final section relates and analyzes
the "process of passing over into custom and habit,"[37] or the
institutionalization of a spiritual movement into holiness churches
and other holiness organizations,--a study which, in conjunction with the preceding sections, contributes to the movement's
self-understanding, to its understanding by others, and to an
understanding of nineteenth-century religious history, particularly in the revivalistic tradition.

NOTES

1.   See H. Shelton Smith, Robert T. Handy, and Lef-
ferts Loetscher, American Christianity: An Historical Inter-
pretation with Representative Documents (New York: Charles
Scribner's Sons, 1963), I, 194; The Shaping of American
Christianity, ed.   James Ward Smith and Leland A. Jamison
("Princeton Studies in American Religion: Religion in Life,"
Vol. I, No. 5; Princeton, N.J.: Princeton University Press,
1961), II, 194.

2.   "Editorial Remarks, "Guide to Christian Perfection, I (July, 1839), 23.   Merritt rightfully limits the uniqueness of the publication to those of American and British Methodism; the Oberlin Evangelist, representing the perfectionist
views of Charles G. Finney and others had begun publication
in 1837.   Future references to the Guide to Christian Perfection which became the Guide to Holiness in 1864 are cited
hereafter as Guide.

3.   For résumés of Merritt's life and work see Abel
Stevens, History of the Methodist Episcopal Church in the
United States of America (New York: Carlton and Lanahan,
1867), III, 504ff.; "The Rev. Timothy Merritt," Advocate of

Christian Holiness, XIV (July, 1882), 193-95; George Hughes,
Fragrant Memories of the Tuesday Meeting and Guide to Holiness (New York: Palmer and Hughes, 1886), pp. 167ff. For
a brief time in 1838 Merritt's name was carried as associate
editor of Zion's Watchman, the abolitionist periodical published
by La Roy Sutherland, also a Methodist minister. Because
of failing health, Merritt never served the paper. See Edward D. Jarvey, "La Roy Sutherland: Zion's Watchman,"
Methodist History, VI (April, 1968), 21.

4. Guide. I (July, 1839), 13.

5. Ibid.

6. Ibid.

7. Ibid., p. 23. Merritt had considered the publication of such a periodical as early as the spring of 1825;
see "Revival of Holiness in New London in 1824," Zion's Herald and Wesleyan Journal, XX (February 28, 1849), 33; this
paper is cited hereafter as Zion's Herald. Sarah Lankford
Palmer, who began the "Tuesday Meeting for the Promotion
of Holiness," finally induced him to start the Guide; see Delbert Rose, A Theology of Christian Experience (Minneapolis,
Minn.: Bethany Fellowship, Inc., 1965), p. 38.

8. Zion's Herald, VIII (February 22, 1837), 30.

9. Ibid. (April 12, 1837), p. 60.

10. Ibid. (October 4, 1837), P. 158.

11. Guide, I (July, 1839), 13. Merritt had first urged
such efforts two and one-half years earlier; see Zion's Herald,
VIII (January 25, 1837), 16. The interaction between this
Methodist revival movement and the parallel movement in the
Congregationalist churches chiefly centering in the work of
Charles G. Finney and Asa Mahan at Oberlin College is al-
ready evident. Merritt's publishing partner, D. S. King, pub-
lished Mahan's Scripture Doctrine of Christian Perfection
(Boston: 1839). Merritt quoted it in the first issue of the
Guide, loc. cit.

12. Infra, Chap. VI.

13. As quoted by the Guide, X (July, 1846), 20. Also
see Advocate of Christian Holiness, VI (September, 1875), 63.

14.   Guide, loc. cit.

15.   Ibid. A footnote to the Guide's article illustrates
the movement's common interpretation of this imagery from
Bunyan's Pilgrim's Progress: "The pleasant country of Beulah,
where the pilgrims 'solaced themselves for a season before
they passed the river of death, seems to shadow forth the
highest state of spiritual enjoyment attainable in the present
life...." The name, "Beulah," is taken from Isa. 62:4; it
means "married." The theme was widely used by the holiness movement in its songs, literature, and testimonies; see,
e. g. , Hughes, op. cit. , pp. 49-50; Harriet Beecher Stowe's
"Review of Thomas Upham's Interior Life," Guide, VII (July,
1845), 14; and I. N. Kanaga, "Visions of Beulah," Bible
Standard, XII (August, 1880), 8.

16.   Minutes of Several Conversations between The
Rev. Thomas Coke, L. L. D. , The Rev. Francis Asbury and
Others ... in the Year 1784. Composing a Form of Discipline for the Ministers ... of the Methodist Episcopal Church
in America (Philadelphia: Chas. Cist, 1785), p. 4. This
slogan represented Methodism's understanding of its mission
as a church.

17.   Thomas Jackson (ed.), The Works of John Wesley
(Grand Rapids, Mich. : Zondervan Publishing House, 1959),
XII, 432. It is not possible here to outline the varying in-
terpretations of Wesley at this point; however, the summary
in the text represents the traditional understanding of Wesley
that prevailed in the American holiness movement. Harald
Linström, Wesley and Sanctification: A study in the Doc-
trine of Salvation, tr. H. S. Harvey (London: Epworth
Press, 1946) and George Allen Turner, The More Excellent
Way: Scriptural Basis of the Wesleyan Message (Winona Lake,
Ind. : Light and Life Press, 1951) are two scholarly works
that come to conclusions defending this general stance. W.
E. Sangster, Methodism Can Be Born Again (New York: The
Methodist Book Concern, 1938), p. 86, said that Wesley admitted that in all the points in this complex question he could
not "split the hair." Sangster commented: "Nevertheless,
the ... centrality of this teaching to Wesley's mind, it would
be difficult to exaggerate. In the hour when he was least satisfied with his exposition, he was most positive about the experience. "

18.   Timothy L. Smith concludes in his Revivalism and

Social Reform in Mid-Nineteenth Century America (New York:
Abingdon Press, 1957), p. 92, that by mid-century all the
Calvinistic churches in the country except for the Scotch Presbyterian. Antimission Baptist, and German Reformed denominations "had moved decidedly to free will." Many of the former were also susceptible to the invasion of perfectionism.
Also see William Warron Sweet, The American Churches, an
Interpretation (New York: Abingdon-Cokesbury Press, 1947),
pp. 130ff.

  19. James E. Johnson, "Charles G. Finney and a
Theology of Revivalism," Church History, XXXVIII (September, 1969), 357, notes that "optimism was the order of the
day with an emphasis on the ultimate perfection of society
through progressive movement in mankind." Also see Winthrop Hudson, Religion in America (New York: Charles
Scribner's Sons, 1965), p. 342, and John B. Bury, The Idea
of Progress: An Inquiry into Its Origin and Growth (London:
Macmillan, 1928).

  20. Jerald C. Brauer, Protestantism in America (Philadelphia: The Westminster Press, 1953), p. 160.

  21. Theodore Parker, Autobiography, Poems, and
Prayers, edited with notes by Rufus Leighton; his Works
(Centenary ed.; Boston: American Unitarian Association,
1910), XIII, 335, as quoted in Sidney F. Mead, The Lively
Experiment: The Shaping of Christianity in America (New
York: Harper and Row Publishers, 1963), p. 92. T. Smith,
op. cit., p. 113, says that the transcendental "revolt" and
the "quest for Christian holiness" were different expressions
of the same "strivings."

  22. Edward Johnson, A History of New England or
Wonder-working Providence of Sions Saviour (London, 1654),
as quoted by Willard Sperry, Religion in America (Cambridge:
At the University Press, 1948), p. 249.

  23. Ibid., p. 250.

  24. Lewis R. Dunn, The Mission of the Spirit: Or
the Office and Work of the Comforter in Human Redemption
(New York: Nelson and Phillips, 1871), p. 299. Dunn, a
Methodist minister in New Jersey, was deeply involved in the
post-war holiness revival. For further discussion on the
"Age of the Spirit," see infra, p. 110.

  25. It is difficult to distinguish sharply between Pur-

itanism and Pietism because, as Ralph Bronkema says in The
Essence of Puritanism (Goes, Holland: Oosterbaan and Lecointre, n. d.), p. 76, they are "religious tendencies." Their
historical origins can be readily identified. Both were reac-
tionary movements--Puritanism against impurities in the
Church of England and then against immorality, and Pietism
against the "dead orthodoxy" of the German Reformation
churches. Both were reformatory. Both had the ability to
combine with other systems, even systems opposed to one another such as Calvinism and Anabaptism. Both were able "to
combine with different confessions and take root in different
countries"; ibid. , p. 77. Bronkema maintains that "it is impossible to draw a sharp line of demarcation between them,
for they assimilated influences from each other." He notes
that W. A. Visser't Hooft says that in America "the age of
revivalism or pietism followed on the age of original Puritanism and in that sense the two can be distinguished, but the
two eventually were fused and confused so that 'through revivalism, Puritanism became Pietism....' "; ibid. , p. 78.
In this study, therefore, pietism is the predominant term and
is used within the definition given to it by F. Ernest Stoeffler
in his recent study, The Rise of Evangelical Pietism (Leiden:
E. J. Brill, 1971), p. 13-23; in summary, the four characteristics which he uses to identify the tradition are: (1) the essence of Christianity, a Pietist believes, is to be found "in
the personally meaningful relationship of the individual to God."
It is "inward" and "experiential." (2) He is committed to religious idealism or perfectionism; sanctification and a Christian life of good works follow conversion; the goal is Christian maturity. (3) His central focus is on the Bible with a
consequent Christian ethic based squarely on the New Testament. (4) An "oppositive" or "over-against" element is always essential for the Pietist. Prevailing religion must be
ignoring the views to a measure which calls out sufficient expression of protest by those who hold the above emphases to
be able to identify a movement. These characteristics, Stoeffler maintains, may be used to identify an on-going "experiential tradition" in Christianity which should be a valuable
tool in interpreting church history along with other categories
commonly used such as the Anglican, Roman, Lutheran, or
Reformed traditions. It has been especially neglected, he
says, in efforts to understand the American pietistic churches
and movements; ibid. , pp. 6-7.

The present work recognizes the validity of such an
"experiential tradition" as most critical to proper understanding of the holiness movement in America. It may be best

identified, perhaps, as a "puritan-pietist" movement with the
"puritan" element generally used to denote the revivalist's
concerns for morality, conduct, and the reform of the church
and society according to the laws of God; "pietist" is utilized
to refer to their concern for individual Christian experience,
centering in both conversion and sanctification--all under the
direct and personal guidance and power of the Holy Spirit.
If revivalism tended to fuse the two in America as Visser't
Hooft claims, then perfectionism with its concern for personal sanctification and its larger optimism for reform of
the church and the world through the church infused new meaning into both puritanism and pietism.   Perfectionism kept the
puritan dream alive in the former's preachments concerning
the new age of the Spirit and the coming millennium; at the
same time, it put new emphasis upon the pietistic doctrines
of experience in its insistence that only as each Christian realized the fullness of the blessings of the baptism of the Spirit
in his own life could the age of the Spirit become a reality.

26.   As quoted from The Methodist Times in "Timely
Words for all the Churches," Divine Life and International
Expositor of Scriptural Holiness, IX (May, 1886), 305.   Here-
after cited as Divine Life.

27.   "Revivals of Religion, How to Make Them Pro-
ductive of Permanent Good," Philip Schaff and S. Iranaeus
Prime (eds.), History, Essays, Orations, and Other Documents of the Sixth General Conference of the Evangelical
Alliance Held in New York, October 2-12, 1873 (New York:
Harper and Brothers Publishers, 1874), p. 351.   It is interesting to note the emphasis which was given to revivalism
and perfectionism at this Alliance meeting; Philip Schaff was
the organizer of, and dominant figure in, this general conference; see "Evangelical Alliance," The New Schaff-Herzog Encyclopedia of Religious Knowledge, ed. Samuel Jackson et al.
(New York: Funk and Wagnalls Co., 1909), IV, 221-23.   Yet
he was no friend of revivalism.   Apparently, at this point the
subject demanded attention.

28.   The inscription on John Wesley's tombstone states
that he revived, enforced, and defended "the pure Apostolic
doctrines and practices of the Primitive Church."   Quoted in
Zion's Herald, XX (February 14, 1849), 25.   For the development of the importance of the concept of the fall of the church
and restoration teaching among early Anabaptists, see Franklin
H. Littell, The Anabaptist View of the Church: A Study in
the Origins of Sectarian Protestantism (Boston: Star King
Press, 1958), pp. 46-108.

29. Merrill E. Gaddis, "Christian Perfectionism in
America" (unpublished Ph. D. Dissertation, University of
Chicago, 1929), constituted the earliest attempt to evaluate
the movement and provided the best source of general information until the forties. General surveys now have begun to
recognize the movement as a distinct part of the history of
American religion; see, e. g. , Hudson, op. cit. , pp. 341-50
and Martin Marty, Righteous Empire: The Protestant Experience in America (New York: Dial Press, 1970), pp. 216,
226, 247; Smith and Jamison, op. cit. , IV, 327ff.; Sperry,
op. cit. , p. 98, was one of the earliest to do so.

30. Hudson, op. cit. , p. 345, places the membership
of the holiness bodies in 1960 at 1,500,000.

31. The statistics which the General Secretary-Treasurer of The Wesleyan Church reported to the Second General
Conference of that church held at Lake Junaluska, N. C. , in
1972 would be typical for most of the holiness churches. They
show that while that denomination had a full membership of
only 74,049, those churches which reported average attendance for the Sunday morning service listed 111,794 worship-
ers. Average attendance in the same churches on Sunday
evenings was given as 66,961--only slightly less than the regular membership--while the average Sunday school attendance
was listed as 135,030 out of a total enrollment of 219,497;
"Statistical Report of the General Secretary-Treasurer of The
Wesleyan Church to the Members of the Second General Conference of The Wesleyan Church," Statistics section, pp. 8-9.

32. The largest of these in the field of missions are
The Oriental Missionary Society and the World Gospel Missionary Society. In higher education the largest non-denominational holiness colleges are Taylor University, Upland,
Indiana; and Asbury College, Wilmore, Kentucky; Asbury Theological Seminary at the same place is one of the largest independent accredited seminaries in the United States. All of
these, together with the other independent holiness oriented
organizations, are active with the holiness denominations,
associations, and individual members mainly from Methodistic
larger bodies, in the Christian Holiness Association. The latter serves more as a point of common communication and fellowship than as an instrument of joint action.

33. These tensions surfaced most dramatically as the
movement began to move into firm organizational patterns in
the closing decades of the nineteenth century. See infra,
Chap. VI.

34. Mead, op. cit. , p. 21.

35. H. R. Niebuhr, "The Protestant Movement and Democracy," Smith and Jamison, op. cit. , I, 22, 24.

36. Anton Boisen, Religion in Crisis and Custom: A Sociological and Psychological Study (New York: Harper Brothers, 1955), p. 93.

37. Ibid.

CHAPTER II

1835-1865: THE DEVELOPING SYNTHESIS

AMERICAN REVIVALISM AND WESLEYAN PERFECTIONISM

To understand the essential character of the American
holiness movement as a phenomenon in American and world
religious history, it is as necassary to look back to Jonathan
Edwards as it is to look back to John Wesley. It may seem
to be enigmatic to refer to Jonathan Edwards before one mentions the name of John Wesley in searching out the origins of
a modern perfectionist movement, for most historians of Protestant "holiness movements" of recent times would agree with
W. E. Sangster that all of them in some way "stem down"
from the founder of Methodism.[1] American believers in the
doctrines of Christian perfection have consistently recognized
such a debt. The movement always has struggled hard to
maintain the label of "true Wesleyanism" in defense of its
theological position. But the American holiness movement
was just that--both "American" and "holiness." The implications of the latter have been recognized almost universally
by those who have written about it; but the implications of the
former have had less attention until recent years.

Thus Jonathan Edwards! For to speak meaningfully
of the history and significance of the rise and development of
the holiness movement in the United States is to speak of revivalism; to speak of revivalism is to speak of Edwards' revival theology and methods. They have become the principles
which in fuller development, under successive New England
revivalists, have shaped American revivalism. Robert Baird
had already pointed this out in 1844 to his European readers.[2]
The basic principle of Edwards' evangelistic practice was
the stress on repentance as the "immediate duty' of every
sinner. "Now" became the moment of salvation for every
non-Christian within the range of the urgent Gospel appeal of
the American evangelist. "Responsibility" in the "old Calvin-

18

ism" was matched with "ability" in the "new Calvinism." "The
days of half way convenants were numbered when New England
divines established their doctrine of natural ability."[3] Revival activity became the hallmark of the American Church.
It was not only essential because of the responsibility of the
church to disciple all men, but in America it became equally
essential to the structure of the voluntary church system which
became the pattern everywhere after regular church establishment was no longer the rule in the United States. The win-
ning of men to the voluntary support of the churches centered
in revivalism.[4]   Under the broadening influences of Jacksonian
politics and this voluntarism, revivalism consistently developed.
strong Arminian tendencies.   Its opponents often labeled them
Pelagian.[5]

By 1839, when Merritt put out his call in The Guide
to Christian Perfection for special efforts for the revival of
holiness in the Methodist Church. Arminian revivalism was
well on its way to becoming the accepted and essential mode
of evangelism and populating the churches.   It was heartily
accepted by certain churches such as the Methodist and Baptist; it became the cause of schism in others such as the
Congregationalists and the Presbyterians.   Very few American churches were able to completely reject these "new methods" and the Arminianization of theological thought which accompanied them.   Holiness advocates' hearts were gladdened
to read in the Beauty of Holiness that Albert Barnes, a leader
of the "New School"   Presbyterians, was saying that he held
"no doctrine which will seem to be inconsistent with the free
and full offer of salvation to every human being...."[6]   The
pattern was so widespread that Methodist Bishop Morris could
challenge the 1864 General Conference of the Methodist Episcopal Church to name any church at that time "where the five
points of Calvinism ... [were] plainly and pointedly and fully
taught."[7]

                        The Pietistic Impetus

To the Wesleyan perfectionists who believed that the
sinner's response to the revivalist's appeal for justification
by faith still left him, as a Christian convert, short of a life
of uninterrupted love for God and man; it was but a short step,
given the prevailing mood and methods of American revivalism,
to move in with the "second blessing" message.   The appeal
to the spiritual advantage of a second crisis in the Christian's
life was an extension of the basic revival call in every respect.

The invitation was a universal one. Every convert was a candidate. The sense of immediacy was also there; the time to enter into the "higher life" was "now."

Just as Edwards and his successors pressed upon the sinner the decision to forsake sin, so those who shared the sense of urgency expressed in Merritt's call for "special efforts" in the promotion of holiness, pressed upon the unsanctified Christian a decision to consecrate himself entirely to God and be entirely sanctified. Harriet Beecher Stowe took note of the parallelism in a tract favorable to this new development in revivalism. She wrote:

> It has been found, in the course of New England preaching, that pressing men to an immediate and definite point of conversion produced immediate and definite results and so it may be found among Christians that pressing them to an immediate and definite point of attainment [i. e. entire santification] will, in like manner, result in marked and decided progress. [8]

The dynamic in both crises was the grace of God.

The application of the revivalist's methods to the promotion of this particular doctrine and the adoption by revivalism of the experiential goals and possibilities of a "higher Christian life," marks a change both in revivalism and the advocacy of Christian perfection. Those who look for the differences between original Wesleyanism and the tone and teaching of the American holiness movement will probably discover that there were no radical differences in theology and belief, but rather, they will find subtle differences in emphases that derive from the application of all that was America in the nineteenth century to the promotion and practices of the Wesleyan emphasis. Perfection in love or a "Divine fullness" was the remedy for the church's fitful periodic piety, ... [its] disgraceful alienation of revival and declension...." It would make the Christian church "as steady as Niagara."[9]

The pietistic essence of American revivalism also helped to create a religious and social climate favorable to the rise of a holiness revival during this period. Whatever else pietism has represented in its history of consistent influences on the Protestant churches, it has symbolized religious emphases which favored experience over theology and the call to individual commitment to a Christian life of witness and charity. It was not enough to be a "formal" Christian,

One had to know for himself that he was a "born-again" Christian. The logical goal of such a life was individual Christian perfection. [10]

    The dominance of this pietistic view of the nature
of salvation and the Christian life in the early nineteenth century revival tradition and revival churches is a
"commonplace' among church historians. [11] That this bent
was especially evident in the Methodist Church with its
own emphasis on experiential religion and perfectionist ideals,
is also "a commonplace." [12] If the Great Awakening indeed
ushered in "the Pietist or Methodist age of American Church
History," [13] as Robert Thompson concluded, then the special
efforts to revive the pietistic, peculiarly Methodist doctrine
of Christian perfection marked the high point of both these
pietistic and Methodist tendencies; it was the "radical and
popular expression of the new evangelism." [14]

Oberlin Perfectionism: Finney Bridges the Gap

    The Methodization of the Calvinistic wing of the revival
tradition which culminated in a "New Theology" and "New
Methods" reached its fullest expression in the revival efforts
of Charles Grandison Finney. He, more than any other leading revivalist out of the Calvinistic churches, repudiated classical Calvinism's ideas of the inability of man to exercise
himself in any degree for his conversion. Finney chided those
in the churches who waited for salvation to come to them.
He saw it following as a natural result of obedience to certain
spiritual laws, laws just as fixed as the physical law of seed-
time and harvent. The only impediment which hindered the
sinner in responding to the Gospel invitation lay in the failure
of his own volition to declare, "I will believe and be saved." [15]
Obvious success in the practical application of these con-
victions concerning revival possibilities and methods to his
own ministry gradually overcame most of the opposition to
Finney's approach; the response to his appeals proved as effective in metropolitan New York City as in the "burned over"
territory surrounding his home area in rural, western New
York. [16]

    In 1835, with the promise of substantial support from
the wealthy Arthur Tappen of New York, Finney went west to
take up the position of professor of theology at the newly founded Congregational college at Oberlin, Ohio. [17] Prior to that
move, he had already considered Christian perfection and

its possibilities in several sermons in his New York City
church. [18]

Finney's agitation over the possibilities for the attainment of a higher experience of Christian life than he then enjoyed intensified with his move to his new post in Ohio. In
his treatise on sanctification which was published in 1840, he
summarized the basic issue:

> Whether the provisions of the Gospel are such, that
> did the Church fully understand and lay hold upon
> the proffered grace, she might attain this state [En-
> tire Sanctification]? [19]

During the first year at Oberlin, he, with President Asa Mahan,
began to look eagerly for an answer to that question. In 1836,
both Mahan and Finney professed to experience a second spiritual crisis as radical as the latter's dramatic initial conversion experience. [20] The importance of these "second conversions" of the Oberlin leaders was that they constituted an ex-
plicit admission by prominent revivalists of the non-Methodist
tradition of the inherent impulses within revivalism towards
more intense Christian experience. [21]

The Oberlin evangelists' promotion of a perfectionist
experience as the epitome of evangelical Christian life, brought
a parallel impulse toward perfectionism into play along side
the special efforts of Merritt and his friends to revive the
testimony to the experience within its more familiar Methodist
environment. Concurrent efforts of the two forces gave rise to
a new movement which introduced change into both sides of the
house; American revivalism gave perfectionist promotion new
and effective methods, and Methodist perfectionism provided
American revivalism with enlarged vision of the possibilities
of normal Christian life. [22] "Beulah Land" was coming into
view! On that common ground a new "higher life" movement
was born. This advocacy by both Calvinist and Methodist revivalists assured a larger hearing and more vigorous leadership for the doctrine than it had ever enjoyed before.

In 1840 Finney wrote a widely read book setting forth
his new views. [23] His critics maintained that these attempts
to systematize the theology of his new relationship were never
entirely successful. He attempted to retain distinctions from
the purely Wesleyan view which he felt were consistent with
his theological roots in Calvinism, but in true revivalist and
pietistic fashion his experiental confessions proved more per-

suasive than his formal apologetics. The result was that he
was probably closer to his Wesleyan sympathizers than to the
theological turns which Oberlin perfectionism later took under
the aegis of William Cochrane and President Fairchild. [24]

Mahan tended, even more than Finney, toward Methodist interpretation of the "higher Christian life" doctrines.
He quickly entered into the growing controversy which the
Oberlin revival had generated in Congregational circles. In
the course of one of these exchanges with those who were
questioning the propriety of the new turn at Oberlin, Mahan
laid down the gauntlet for this arm of the new movement by
declaring that

> the Church is now rising to ask of her spiritual
> guides, what degree of holiness she may rationally
> hope to attain in view of the commands of God, her
> natural powers, and the acknowledged provisions and
> promises of the Gospel? Till this question receives
> a specific answer, she will not and ought not to
> rest. [25]

Wesleyan perfectionism would attempt to give the "specific"
answer. A new rising class of holiness evangelists in the
revival tradition was to attempt to give what it believed to
be specific answers; both were to give the Church no rest until there was some kind of decision.

Radical Reform and Radical Perfectionism

Whether revivalism in its constant and essential activity in the American churches was at ebb or flow during these
years, is difficult to determine. It is certain that from the
middle of the third decade of the century until the Layman's
Revival of 1858 there was no general surge of popular revival
similar to the flood-tide resulting from Finney's preaching
immediately prior to that period. [26] There were major di-
versions; financial panic, war, and a multiplicity of reforming
movements weighed heavy on many men's minds. The reform
movements of the 1840's in particular made a strong appeal
to the puritan revivalistic mind, attracting to themselves much
of the dynamic which commonly went into traditional revival
religious activity. [27]

These reforming efforts were laced through and through
with revivalistic impetus and ideals, particularly with a dynamic,

perfectionist idealism which contributed significantly by the
end of the century, to the rise of the social gospel. [28] They
represented a turning outward of the concept of individual
freedom from sin to the creation of a society free from evil
as well. Emerson reported to his friend, Carlyle, during
the 1840's:

> We are all a little wild here with numberless pro-
> jects of social reform. Not a reading man but has
> a draft of a new community in his waistcoat pock-
> et. [29]

Among these reform movements were some which centered in a mystical perfectionism. The most publicized of
these experiments which commonly involved radical expression
of new social organization and inter-personal relationships
was that of John Noyes and his Oneida community. The community's modification of the monogamous marriage relationship was first among a number of innovations which agitated
Noyes' neighbors and the religious community in general. [30]
Soon after Noyes finally located in Oneida, New York, the
Guide complained that one could no longer use the term, "perfectionist" in its regularly accepted sense, because of a new
class who are "wild fanatics ... who have nothing in common
with us except it be a few scriptural expressions. "[31] This
reference may have comprehended a number of lesser cele-
brated perfectionist groups as well as Oneida. The existence
of all of them testified to the perfectionist longings moving
through society during these decades. These groups were
unrelated to the mainstream movements in orthodox Christian
channels, except for their use of the term perfectionism and
claims to its concomitant idealism. The relationship, mutually disclaimed and minimal as it was, was nevertheless,
a source of concern for the perfectionist of the holiness movement. Any guilt by association which the Guide feared the
Wesleyan perfectionist cause may have suffered from these
associations, however, was more than compensated for by the
encouragement which had come from Oberlin. [32]

A reforming thrust more amenable to the Wesleyan
concepts of perfectionism permeated the abolitionist's crusade
against slavery. Abolitionism was absolutist or ultraist in its
moral perceptions; it was most natural for perfectionism to
head that way. In its religious expression perfectionism demanded complete consecration to the known will and purposes
of God. This level of dedication provided a ready springboard
for insistence upon ultimate answers to moral and ethical
questions. The relationship between perfectionism and the

anti-slavery crusade, therefore, was not coincidental. "Converts of revivalism saw that the law of love ... was being vitiated by slavery. They had to act against it" (emphasis his). [33] John Noyes, the Oneida perfectionist, warned William Lloyd Garrison that the abolitionists could be successful in their efforts only if such efforts were closely related to perfectionist ideals. Garrison ultimately espoused perfectionism, but according to Benjamin B. Warfield it paralleled that of the more Wesleyan Asa Mahan, than that of the mystical Noyes. [34] Garrison's steady inclination toward revolution rather than reform, ultimately created a rift between himself and evangelical abolitionists. [35]

The defection of the Wesleyan Methodists, from the mainstream of the Methodist Episcopal Church in 1843 is another example of the interworking of the principles of Wesleyan perfectionism doctrines and the campaign to extirpate slavery as a moral evil. Declaring their complete frustration in their efforts to move the official stand of the church to a more positive stance against slavery, Orange Scott and other outspoken anti-slavery advocates in the Methodist Episcopal Church ultimately called a convention on the issues at Utica, New York in 1843 [36] which resulted in the organization of the Wesleyan Methodist Connection of America, sometimes known as "True Wesleyans." [37] Their perfectionist leanings were formalized in the adoption of an article of faith on Christian perfection in the 1848 Discipline; they were the first Christian community ever to do so explicity. [38]

The Perfectionist Revival in Methodism: The Tuesday Meeting.

There is strong indication that at the very time that perfectionist impulses were surfacing in these patterns that traditional Methodist revivalism and its witness to the doctrines of sanctified Christian experience were at low tide, John Peters, in his definitive work on the relationships between American Methodism and the doctrine of Christian perfection, marshalls evidences of the fact. [39] According to the 1832 General Conference Episcopal Address the experience was "rarely met with" within the church at that time. [40] Bishop Peck looked back on the 1830's as a period in the life of the doctrine in Methodism in which it "received less and less attention ... [and was in] danger of being regarded as a novelty...." [41] This period, then, witnessed a strange paradox in relation to Christian perfection in the American revival

churches: at the very moment that non-Methodist revivalists
were joining themselves to the doctrine it was suffering neglect in its native home.

    If that point, however, marks the nadir of the decline
of the doctrine in Methodism, it necessarily marked as well
the starting point for holiness revival. In fact, from 1835
to 1858 the revival of the promotion of the doctrine and the
number of those who professed personal enjoyment of the experience appears to have expanded at almost unbroken pace.
In 1851 George Peck wrote the "within the last twelve years
... [men had] appeared in increasing numbers as open and
fearless advocates of entire sanctification ..." (emphasis
his).[42]

    The most effective promotion of the doctrine centered
in the activities of Methodist laymen in New York City. Sarah
Worrall Lankford, one of the principals involved there, in a
manner reminiscent of the testimony of the famed Blaise Pascal, dated her entry into the experience of holiness as of
"half past two p.m., the twenty-first day of May, 1835 ..."
(emphasis mine).[43]   Both experiences were datable.   Her
continuing account of the event, however, bears little resemblance to the emotion-packed record which the brilliant French
scientist left us of his own spiritual encounter. Aware of the
spiritual ecstasy which many of her Methodist forebearers
had testified to at the moment they believed they had entered
into the perfection in love, she had anticipated a similar surge
of intense feeling of her own; but none came. Mrs. Lankford,
like Pascal, however, witnessed to the continuing realities of
that crisis during the rest of her life:

         All was calm and stillness; I had none of the ex-
         pected emotions. I arose from my knees fully de-
         termined to rest in God, ... if I had not a joyous
         emotion in forty years.
             Since that ... May 21st., 1835, I think there
         has not been an hour in which my soul has not
         been ... resting in the ... atonement.[44]

    In August of the same year, Mrs. Lankford transferred
the meetings of certain prayer groups which she was sponsor-
ing at the Allen Street and Mulberry Street Methodist Episcopal Churches to the parlor of her home at 54 Rivington Street
in New York City. There the combined meetings soon became
known as the "Tuesday Meetings for the Promotion of Holiness";
they came to be the movement's focal point.[45] Sarah Lankford's

vivid religious change which she had just experienced, probably helped to establish the continuing emphasis of the meeting upon the instruction, attainment, and testimony to the
higher Christian life of heart holiness. The subsequent revival of the influence of this doctrine within its home soil of
Methodism and out to all of evangelical Christianity in America
and around the world flowed chiefly from this "house-church";
it constitutes one of the most unusual phenomena of American
religious history.

A new approach to holiness
evangelism: the "altar theology"

        Soon after the move to 54 Rivington Street, the sister
of Mrs. Lankford, Phoebe Worrall Palmer, also testified to
a similar "rest of soul."[46] She wrote that it had come after
severe and prolonged inner struggle. Mrs. Palmer emphasized
three aspects of that experience: (1) entire consecration, (2)
faith, (3) confession. Out of these elements of her experience
and her understanding of the Scriptures, she developed what
has become known as her "altar" terminology or theology.
It constituted a scala sancta, for the achievement of entire
santification and the personal assurance of the reality of that
experience. An understanding of its formulation and application supports the thesis that the holiness revival represented
a new blend of religious forces.

        Mrs. Palmer believed that the Scriptures taught that
Christ was both the sacrifice for her sin and the altar upon
which she could offer up her whole heart in consecration to
God. She reasoned that the divine promise of fullness of
spiritual life, release from self-will and the habit of sinning
could be realized in every Christian through entire consecration of the self offered as a gift of faith upon the "Altar,
Christ." The New Testament, she said, told her that, "the
altar sanctifieth the gift." She declared that in the sanctifying efficacy of Christ as the Christian's altar, the exercise
of faith was certain to secure to the individual an experience
characterized by a freedon from any inclination which did not
spring from love. This remained constant as long as the
individual continued to exercise faith and obedience.[47] She
wrote:

                On everyone who will specifically present himself
                upon the altar ... for the sole object of being
                ceaselessly consumed, body and soul in the self-
                sacrificing service of God, He will cause the fire

> to descend. And ... he will not delay to do this
> for every waiting soul, for He standeth waiting, and
> the moment the offerer presents the sacrifice, the
> hallowing, consuming touch will be given. [48]

Or again, if one should ask, "How soon may I expect to ar-
rive at this state of perfection?", she replied,

> Just so soon as you come believingly, and make the
> required sacrifice.... When the Saviour said, 'It is
> finished!' then this full salvation was wrought out
> for you. All that remains is for you to come com-
> plying with the conditions and claim it ... it is al-
> ready yours. If you do not now receive it, the de-
> lay will not be on the part of God, but wholly with
> yourself. [49]

On this straight-forward appeal to immediate commitment rode
much of the widespread response which Phoebe Palmer and
others enjoyed in the special promotion of a second crisis in
personal Christian experience which lay at the heart of the
holiness revival.

The significance of the "altar theology"

It is difficult to define the subtle differences which
were involved in this critical re-statement of the Wesleyan
theology of entire sanctification from Wesley's own statements.
Phoebe Palmer was a woman who always denied any inclination to theological hairsplitting. In that she stood squarely
in good American religious tradition. [50] What she had done
was to use her proven ability for concise, convincing expression to definitively record her own experience. She ver-
ified it, in true Wesleyan fashion, by what she believed to be
the settled message of Scripture upon the subject and then
called upon other Christians to walk in the light of that truth.

Nathan Bangs, one of her closest friends and regular
attendant at the Tuesday Meetings in his later years, directly
challenged Mrs. Palmer on her "altar terminology." Bangs
feared that emphasis on the reliance upon a sinple statement
of faith by an individual as the basis of his claiming the experience of entire sanctification endangered the concept of the
"witness of the Spirit" which constituted the ground for assurance of spiritual life in historical Wesleyanism. Bangs, in
essence, said one cannot claim to have believed until God witnesses the same to him; Mrs. Palmer, on the other hand,

said God cannot witness to one until he has believed and re-
fuses to waiver until the witness is given. [51]   Two articles
in the January 1857 issue of the Beauty of Holiness illustrate
the tension on the question which prevailed within the movement.   In a letter to Mrs. French, the editor, Dr. Bangs
insisted that

> until this [work of entire sanctification] is done for
> me and in me, I have no right to believe I have
> complied with the condition, for he has promised
> that the moment I do this, he will receive and give
> me the spirit of adoption and, therefore, if I have
> not the spirit of adoption, I may rest assured that
> I have not believed with the heart unto righteous-
> ness.... [52]

In her "Editorial Sketches," Mrs. French took up the very
phraseology which Bangs was criticizing by saying:

> If you do by grace now claim that promise, confess
> that you claim it, that it is yours.... Your faith
> cannot go beyond the promise, power, willingness
> of God.... [53]

Those who defended the steps which Mrs. Palmer outlined for personal attainment of Christian perfection were able
to match each of them with definite parallels in the regular
teaching of John Wesley.   In her book, Incidental Illustrations
of the Economy of Salvation, she drew on Wesley's works to
support her own positions on the immediacy of the experience,
the distinction between the experiences of conversions and entire sanctification, the place of faith in acquiring the experience and the necessity for public testimony if one is to retain the experience. [54]   As a result of this congruity, the terminology and the steps she outlined for attainment of the traditional Wesleyan experience of perfect love were finally commonly accepted in Methodism.

The acceptance was not total, however.   The main
point of concern for most of those who hesitated to fully endorse the implications of this "altar theology," was the fear
that the demand for "naked faith in a naked promise," too
readily, inferred a kind of auto-suggestion or self-deception
concerning spiritual attainment, which somehow was in conflict with, or was an unacceptable substitute for, the Methodist doctrine of definite assurance and the witness of the Spirit.
Her own life and writings give no hint that she herself, suffered any problems at this point. [55]   In an earlier conflict

over the question in 1848, however, Mrs. Palmer had written to Mrs. L. L. Hamline that

> the entire Scriptures are the voice of the Holy
> Spirit.... The promises of God are fulfilled the
> moment the waiting one relies fully upon the Prom-
> isor, after having complied with the stipulations
> laid down in His word. [56]

It was because of her insistence on the qualifying limitations
of the compliance, called for in the final clause of the preceding statement, that she denied ever having taught "only
believe you have it and you have got it." Such phraseology,
she contended, is not scriptural...." Wesley, himself, after struggling with the issue, had decided that his own difficulty in trying to explicate the question arose out of the tension between his earnest conviction that every man could believe "if he will"; and his equally earnest denial that every
man could believe "when he will"; he finally relegated the
matter to a condition of permanent tension, and concluded
that,

> there will always be something in the matter which
> we cannot well comprehend or explain. [57]

Abel Stevens, editor of the Christian Advocate and
Journal, was very sympathetic to the Palmer movement; in
his biography of his close friend, Nathan Bangs, he concluded
that Bangs, in spite of the strong remonstrance on Mrs. Palmer's "altar terminology," referred to above nevertheless,
had

> pronounced her teachings substantially orthodox, and
> Wesleyan, and in his opinion he had the concurrence
> of many of our [Methodism's] best minds. [58]

Eventually the "altar theology" set the common, but not exclu-
sive, pattern as well for further formulation of the experience
in the theology and preaching of what became the holiness
movement. [59]

Both Charles Jones and John Peters agree that the
"altar theology" introduced new emphases in Wesleyan perfectionism which produced permanent changes in Methodist teaching
and in that of the developing movement. [60] Ivan Howard, in a
recent monograph, maintains that Phoebe Palmer was really
struggling with a contradiction in Wesley's own definition of

the witness of the Spirit and his doctrine of assurance; he
wavered, Howard contends, in defining the permanence and
persistence of his subjective "inner persuasion" in the heart
of the believer. Mrs. Palmer's approach, he concludes, appears to be more consistent in that she laid the greater em-
asis on the individual's more objective reliance upon what she
considered to be the clear Scriptural truths of the possibilities of personal holiness. [61]

The newness then, essentially was a change in emphasis resulting from a simple, literal Biblical faith and the prevailing mood of revivalism combined with an impatient, American pragmatism that always seeks to make a reality at the
moment whatever is considered at all possible in the future.
Edwards' "immediateness" and Finney's "directness" joined
with Wesley's claim to full release from sin to create a powerful logic for the new perfectionist movement's challenge to
Methodism and the whole Christian church. If one accepts
the conclusion of William Warren Sweet that the new revivalism of Finney "made salvation the beginning of religious experience in contrast to the older revivalism which made conversion the end,"[62] then one could contrast Mrs. Palmer's
view of the attainment and meaning of entire sanctification
with the prevailing tone of Wesley's teaching in similar terms,
and that in spite of Wesley's use, at times, of the "now" element in the experience. For the Palmer movement, perfection in love was the beginning of days for the Christian
and, therefore, an urgent necessity of the moment; in the
English Wesleyan Revival it obviously had carried less urgency and might not become a reality until the end of the
Christian's days. The understanding of this distinction is fundamental to the understanding of the American revival in relation to its original Methodist roots. [63]

There is little question that some who sought to follow
the Palmer path too literally, failed to achieve her own balance at these points. Those who accused her of setting up
a theological syllogism were not completely in error, for one
of the patterns into which the theology and preaching of the
ensuing holiness movement often fell, was to press upon seekers after holiness too simplistic a stereotyped formula for the
promised attainment of so existential a spiritual experience.
Henry Clay Morrison, a leader in the southern holiness movement at the turn of the century, took note of this tendency toward what he, with Bangs before him, felt was spiritual pre-
sumption. He said:

> I sometimes meet people who say when asked if they

are sanctified, "Yes I have taken it by faith," Well
where is the witness? "Brother you have no right to
stop crying to God until the baptism consciously
falls. "[64]

There is evidence, on the other hand, however, that
other holiness preachers, in an exactly opposite tack, used
the failure to accept the experience within the terminology
and pattern of the Palmers' revivalistic formulation of it, as
de facto evidence of willful unbelief on the part of a halting
hearer; they then concluded that such indecision threatened to
keep the conscientious, but confused, individual not only out
of the experience, but out of heaven itself. Granted the urgency which characterized the revivalistic message, it was
not difficult for some to take up such a statement by Mrs.
Palmer as, "if you delay presenting the sacrifice from any
cause whatsoever, you make food for repentance. God demands present holiness,"[65] and press it unduly into a pattern of "holiness or hell" preaching which appeared early in
the movement; it maintained that those who die without a personal conscious crisis experience of entire sanctification would
not be saved. Mr. Wesley's admonition to avoid "harshly
preaching perfection" and to always place it in "the most ami-
able light"[66] was sometimes lost sight of.

The spectre of separatism

Probably sensing an essential shift in emphasis, some
of her contemporaries charged that her promotion of entire
sanctification represented a position a step beyond that of
Wesley, himself. They continued to maintain outspoken opposition in spite of strong protestation by Mrs. Palmer, herself and her prominent friends in the church who defended
her as being strictly Wesleyan. [67] One who expressed fear
was Professor Hiram Mattison, of Falley Theological Seminary in Fulton, New York, who became a severe critic of
Phoebe Palmer and her terminology and promotion of Christian perfection. He bitterly chided her for her "new theory"
and her "shorter way," and he charged in the Christian Advocate and Journal that she was the cause of the controversy
of "the last ten years" in the Methodist Church.

The developing holiness movement in the churches, he
said, was an exact parallel to the disruption created by
George Bell and Thomas Maxfield in Wesley's day. They
too, he said, "began to preach sanctification as a specialty
with great zeal and vehemence. " His judgment of Mrs. Palmer and her followers as theological separatists who claimed

to possess superior knowledge and refused criticism and instruction, raised all the ghosts of that old heresy in Mattison's Methodist mind.   All this bode nothing but ill for the
church, he contended, unless one of several things happened;
either Mrs. Palmer had to change her position, withdraw
from it altogether, or be properly disciplined. [68]

Mattison's concerns for the separatism potentially inherent in the extraparochial nature of Mrs. Palmer's meetings were shared by some more friendly to the movement
than he.   Jesse Peck, upon hearing of efforts to establish a
special organization for the promotion of holiness in New
Brunswick, Maine, quickly sought to lay any such ideas to
rest.   He saw nothing but schismatic possibilities in such a
move.   But the atmosphere was too charged with concern for
the doctrine for such fears to slow down the momentum.   The
Tuesday Meeting soon became the pattern for holiness meetings both inside and outside of the churches. [69]

In the course of the ongoing holiness revival, the
struggle to resist the divisive tensions feared by the movement's friend and foe was to prove long and valiant but only
partially successful; those Methodists who defended the growing popularity of these special meetings often held outside of
the church and, therefore, generally free from direct ecclesiastical supervision called upon the societies which the Wesleys
themselves had established within the eighteenth century Anglican Church as the prime witnesses to the integrity and re-
gularity of their own efforts. [70]   Others, however, remembered that, regardless of the integrity of Wesley's motives,
his movement finally led to schism in the Anglican ranks and
the formation of the Methodist Church. [71]

There is no proof that the early promoters of special
means and meetings for Christian perfection in the Methodist
Church had any schismatic intentions or even tendencies; they
did everything to avoid any such accusations.   At the same
time, there is ample proof that those who harbored real fears
about the ultimate divisive consequences of such efforts were
accurate prophets of future possibilities.   As early as 1845
Thomas Upham, a Tuesday Meeting convert, was warning the
holiness people that in spite of the difficulties they might encounter in their efforts to live and promote their experience
within their denominations and the consequent tendency to division and separation, they should remain within their local
fellowships and bear patiently with the infirmities and even
the sins of others in the churches. [72]

The beginning, then, of the long road at the end of
which lay the loss of many holiness adherents to the church,
was part of the microcosm which was the Tuesday Meeting.
The close personal relationship between Dr. and Mrs. Palmer
and their friends, high in the Methodist bureaucracy, along
with the restricted response to the more restrained promotion of holiness doctrine in these early stages of the movement, tended to restrict the tendencies to divisiveness which
both the movement's friends and foes had already identified.

In the post-war movement and beyond, other persons
with less influential relationships in a rapidly changing ecclesiastical climate would not allow similar viability to those
who carried on the mission of these pioneer meetings.   It
was Mrs. Palmer's hope that "this church in the house" would
be "one of the nurseries of the general church."73   The un-
folding history of the holiness revival and the holiness churches
will reveal the fulfillment of that dream, but in a way quite
different from what she, herself, may have anticipated.   Her
death, in 1874, prevented her involvement in the struggle
between movement and church which began to demonstrate
more definite patterns of conflict and even separation only
a short time thereafter.

Most of these fears concerning the Palmer movement,
however, eventually were apparently pushed aside by a massive outflow of spiritual activity.   The age was increasingly
pressed with problems which, many Christians seemed to feel,
challenged the church and individual Christians to seek for
more dynamic inner resources than they then commonly enjoyed.   This, the movement's message promised.   The quiet
discourse and boundless activity of a woman who felt she had
found the means of making these resources available to all
Christians now, by a single act of consecration and faith,
became the major impetus in setting off a worldwide movement.   Whether the seeker for holiness was a Methodist
bishop or the most ordinary camp meeting attendant, her
directness seemed to work, and to the pragmatic American
mind, that was what really mattered.74

By 1867, both the Christian Advocate and Journal and
the Northern Christian Advocate were promoting Phoebe
Palmer's major book on her concept on entire sanctification, Faith and Its Effects; the former commented that
in that work, the author

exposes and corrects the errors into which some

have fallen, points out the good old ways of attain-
ing this state of grace and supports all she advances
by direct and incidental appeals to the Word of God.
(Emphasis theirs.)[75]

The ensuing prominence of the "altar" theology or terminology in later Methodist, holiness and other higher life movements is the major, but not sole, indicator that the promotion of holiness by the Lankfords and Palmers in their Tuesday Meeting, represents a pivotal point for the understanding
of these movements and revivalism as a whole. The patterns
of the Tuesday Meetings portray a rather stark microcosm
of the holiness revival and institutions which followed after
the Civil War and beyond to the present. Much that continued to shape the character of the expanding revival forces
found its roots here. It will be shown that it also left telling influences on the general concepts of evangelical Protestantism as well.

Although Mrs. Palmer never replied directly to the
assaults made by Mattison, her friends stoutly defended her
position.[76] Nathan Bangs said, "The prejudices which have
existed against her have arisen chiefly from misapprehension
of her opinions."[77] Phoebe Palmer apparently evaluated the
situation in a similar fashion, for she held to her positions
and by extensive publication sought to explain them not only
to doubting Methodists, but to the whole world.

The testimony controversy

Another feature of the Tuesday Meeting, prophetic of
future traits of the American holiness movement, was the
prominence given to public, personal testimony to the work
of God in the individual's heart. Much of the journalistic
reporting in the holiness periodicals which publicized the
weekly proceedings of the "holiness meetings" consisted of
verbatim accounts of individual experiences of the higher life.
The Guide had been established mainly for that purpose.[78]
Compilations of personal accounts of individual experiences
of sanctification were widely circulated in promotion of the
doctrine.[79] Here also, it would be difficult for one to define any major break with the traditional position of Wesley.
Although Wesley, himself, nowhere leaves a specific testimony to his own perfection in love, he did overcome, in
principle, his natural reticence to open up his inner experiences to others by encouraging guarded, humble testimony by
those whose experiences he estimated to be genuine. In fact,

his whole system of discipline in the band and class meetings
was dependent, in a great part, upon the individual's subjective, public evaluation of his own state of grace and Christian
experience. This critical reality of Methodist history was
perhaps the strongest refutation of the position taken by those
opponents, who in the heat of often futile argument, set up
the absence of any recorded personal public confession by
Wesley over against the often exuberant public witness of those
of his spiritual descendants who felt that a whole new world
of spiritual victory had been ushered in for them through this
"second blessing. "[80]

With mass evangelism and mass response there was
additional opportunity, however, for modification or advance
on the Wesleyan position, choose as one will. Even in Mrs.
Palmer's time there were hints of a hardening of the line on
this question which seemed to be such an essential part of
the whole higher life experience and its effective promulgation. Her emphasis on public testimony usually took the form
of varying degrees of insistence that testimony was not only
essential to the promulgation of Christian holiness, but even
more essential to the personal retention of that grace. One
had to give public testimony in order to be "clear in his experience. " Indeed if personal testimony lagged, it was one
of the most certain signs of a lack of religious life which
would finally culminate in complete apostasy. [81] The narrow-
ing down of this position runs concurrently with the ongoing
development of the holiness tradition within the total context
of revivalism; that revivalism encouraged public profession of
grace and religious attainment. Some degree of public confession was required to become a member of every revivalistic church. In reply to the critics, the movement also
attempted to validate its basic claims concerning the essential nature of public confession in the life style of evangelical
Christians by appealing to non-Methodist authorities as well
as to Wesley. [82]

Such testimonies of certainty and affirmation of personal experience, even in their moderate forms, frequently
produced reaction against "euthusiastic" religion. Extrav-
agance of expression afforded unsympathetic critics ample
excuse to write off the genuiness of it all. Examples of public, personal testimony, which at times seemed to smack of
hypocracy, often made the most sympathetic, yet honest, observer cringe and draw away. Nevertheless, a movement
such as this, which made a strong appeal to Biblical authorities and to primitive Christianity in justification of its practices, easily identified itself with the early Christians, who,

when asked to relent in their propagandizing, replied, "We
can but speak of the things we have seen and known." In
its strong emphasis on public testimony and spiritual assurance, the American holiness movement was a normal child
of the pietistic, revivalistic, Wesleyan tradition. [83]

Interdenominationalism

Another important facet of the Tuesday Meeting which
demonstrates a dominant characteristic of American revivalism and which also permeated the holiness movement was
the strong interdenominational influence which it exhibited in
spite of its predominantly Methodist origins. The centrality
of the Methodist relationship was always evident in the support which the special efforts for the promotion of holiness
enjoyed among the highest circles of that church's leadership.
Less than a decade after the Tuesday Meetings commenced,
Phoebe Palmer recorded in her diary that she had " ...
witnessed the ordination of Rev. L. Hamline and E. S. Janes
to the office of Bishop of the M. E. Church." "They are,"
she said, "in no ordinary degree, lovers of holiness...."[84]
These new bishops joined two others of its supporters who,
in that year, 1844, were already serving the church in its
highest office--Thomas Morris and Elijah Hedding.

Bishop Leonidas L. Hamline and his wife became the
Palmer's closest friends. Both the bishop and his wife were
instrumental in spreading the doctrine and the literature of
the holiness movement throughout the mid-west prior to the
Civil War. [85] Nathan Bangs, one of Methodism's most highly
honored leaders, was a stout friend of the doctrine. [86] So
too, was Stephen Olin, who was one of the most influential
delegates in the founding of the Evangelical Alliance in London
in 1846, and was a former president of Wesley University. [87]
The Methodist educators, Wilbur Fisk and John Dempster,
were also strong proponents of Wesleyan holiness. [88] The
former served as president of Wesleyan University, Middle-
town, Connecticut, the oldest Methodist college in the United
States; the latter founded both Concord and Garrett Seminaries
for the Church. Most of these men were among the growing
number of the top Methodist leadership who frequently shared
the Tuesday Meeting with the Lankfords and the Palmers;
some came to be personally instructed more perfectly "in the
way of holiness." All came because they were concerned for
its revival throughout the Church which historically had practically claimed it as its unique glory.

But all of this Methodist influence apparently did not

exclude from the movement the many non-Methodists, who in
their own way, and sometimes utilizing their own terminology,
were seeking the same blessing in their own religious communions. [89]   Thomas Upham, a Congregationalist professor
from Bowdoin College, claimed to be sanctified as a result
of attending a Tuesday Meeting in 1839. [90]   Henry Belden, a
Congregationlist, was a regular attendant; William Hill, also
Congregationalist, who with Belden, was removed from the
Presbyterian ministry because of his espousal of the holiness
revival, came before his untimely death. [91] William E. Boardman, author of The Higher Life, was frequently there; Asa
Mahan, colleague of Finney, and Oberlin College president,
was a close friend, as was the Rev. Isaac M. See of the
Dutch Reformed Church. [92]   Boston evangelist, A. B. Earle,
and the Rev. Dr. Levy of Philadelphia, both prominent Baptist leaders, were frequently involved in the services. [93]   Dr.
Charles C. Cullis, of the Episcopal Church, a Boston physician, participated in the New York Tuesday Meetings and
promoted interdenominational holiness conventions over the
northeast and England. [94]

Phoebe Palmer noted that "the time is past for the
doctrine of holiness to be characterized as the doctrine of
a sect.   It is the crowning doctrine of the crowning dispensation. "[95]   Experiences such as that which she related to
her friend, Mrs. Hamline, during the Palmer's pre-war
ministry in Toronto, seemed to her to substantiate such conclusions.   She wrote that she had attended one of the "Conventions of Holiness" held at "an old established Episcopal
Church." It had been "a season of Holy Ghost power ...
[in which] Congregational, Episcopal, Baptist, Presbyterian,
and Methodist ministers as one [were] witnessing the great
salvation." She added, "The Tuesday Meeting seems to be
the general rallying point with these...."[96]   The Palmer home
and the weekly meetings for the promotion of holiness, thus
became the nerve center of a general holiness movement outside of Methodism and a developing international holiness revival.

The contributions of Phoebe Palmer and other holiness
promoters to the fostering of the growing unity movement
among the denominations in the two decades prior to the Civil
War, have gone largely unrecognized.   But given her strong
feelings on the direct relationships between the doctrine and
experience of holiness and Christian unity and her widespread
influence in evangelical Christianity through her personal
evangelism publications, the views which she promoted through

these channels and the Tuesday Meeting are worthy of note.

References are sprinkled all thoughout her accounts
of her evangelism in which she and other reporters relate
her work and that of the movement as a whole to the ecumenical spirit which was then most prominently represented by
the Evangelical Alliance founded in London in 1846. One of
the most extensive descriptions of her hope for Christian unity
and the role of holiness promotion in achieving it, is given
in an 1857 report on the characteristics of the Tuesday Meetings written for the Beauty of Holiness. Their "unsectarian
character" was one of the "crowning excellences" of these
meetings, she said. The common experience of holiness
united "Presbyterians, Baptist, Methodist, Episcopalians,
Quakers, United Brethren in Christ, Jews and proselytes" in
a single language of praise and a common desire for "free,
full perfect, immediate salvation"[97] To her mind, in such a
fellowship lay the answer to the sectarian evils so strongly
lamented by so many. She wrote:

> We may long to see the happy, glorious era when
> God's people shall see eye to eye-- ... all united,
> heart, and hand, and soul, in the worship and serv-
> ice of God; all laboring ... to do away the super-
> abounding evils that curse the world ... ! But
> will this happy, glorious, joyful period ever be, till
> gospel holiness prevail. [98]

In describing the founding of the "Christian Alliance
[Evangelical Alliance] in London when more than thirty different sects were represented to devise means and measures
for a heavenly union on earth," as a "marked success," she
said:

> Every soul present, at one time, was cemented in
> love ... The room seemed filled with the Holy
> Spirit. It was a truly pentecostal season. Souls
> were on fire!--and they spoke as it were with other
> tongues as the Spirit give them utterance. [99]

The secret of the successful union of the churches, she continued, is the promotion of the experience of holiness which
will leave no room for "selfishness or sectarianism." Granted
this, she inquired,

> Are not these meetings for holiness ... the germs,
> the dawnings of millenial glory? Are they not strik-
> ingly imitative of the pentecostal? ... Is not this the

> baptism now called for, ... ere the world blos-
> soms as a rose. 100

If the union of the churches and consequently the salvation
of the world and the ushering in of the millenium depended
upon the promotion of the holiness of the churches,

> how vastly important then that meetings for this
> special object should be established in every city,
> village, country, place, throughout the land and
> world, by every church and people ... ?101

This natural relationship between a doctrine which heralded the conquest of selfish interests through the promotion
of perfect love and the overcoming of the sectarian interests
by the infilling of the Holy Spirit as outlined here by Phoebe
Palmer continued to remain prominent in the life of the movement. It especially haunted the leaders of the nineteenth century holiness forces as they sought to organize the divisive
elements among the revival's converts into a common holiness
force. The implication for modern ecumenical efforts of this
appeal to a common spiritual language of perfect love which
might overcome the babel of sectarian interests are yet to be
fully explored. The influence of holiness revivalism which
helped to give impetus to the beginnings of efforts toward
Christain unity along with other evangelical input into the
thrust for Christian unity was muted somewhere along the
way. 102

Along with this persistent impetus toward unity which
was inherent in the doctrine of perfect love and the experience
of entire sanctification, the common meeting of this heterogeneous group, with their diverse theological and religious backgrounds, also displayed, in miniature, the future pattern of
the breadth of the coming post-war revival. It also heralded
a still more distant diversity of thought which would be introduced into the later movement, often to plague its efforts
to unify under a single banner. Many of the "side issues,"
which the aging Methodist leadership of the late nineteenth
century movement fought hard to keep in the background at
national holiness conventions, were channeled into significant
sections of the movement through men who represented or at
least were strongly influenced by non-Methodist traditions
which were rooted in the broader evangelical currents flowing
outside of institutional Methodism. 103

<u>Lay involvement</u>

An additional point at which the Tuesday Meetings
participated in a developing current of American religious
life was the manner in which they contributed to a growing
consciousness of a new role for the laity in the church. The
Palmers and the Lankfords, at whose common residence the
meetings were held, were all laymen. Both ministers and
laymen were always in attendance after the meetings were
opened to men in 1839. Long before the great lay-evangelist,
Dwight L. Moody, gave leadership to the revivalism of the
last quarter of the century, these lay evangelists were de-
monstrating the potential for such leadership in the renewal
of the church.

The promoters of holiness who gathered at Dr. and Mrs.
Palmer's house every Tuesday met in a fellowship in which as
an observer noted, "the ministry does not wait for the laity;
neither does the laity wait for the ministry."[104] This blurring
of the lines of the usual pattern of preacher-leader, layman-
follower was not an entirely new thing in American religious life.
As Howard Grimes points out in his essay on the place of the
layman in the American churches, laymen have assummed "considerable control" from earliest times. [105] It was fostered
mainly by the voluntaryism which formed the basis of the American churches, especially the Disciples of Christ movement.
Alexander Campbell insisted that the "Protestant priesthood ...
stood between the people and the Bible." In addition to the Disciples of Christ, the other two large revivalistic churches also
played a major part in the laicizing of the American religious
life--the Baptists in their radical lay orientation and the Methodists with their lay preachers, class leaders, and exhorters.
To these must be added the transplanted "Free Churches"--the
Brethren, Dunkers, Mennonites, etc. [106]

The added significance of the Palmer's lay movement,
however, did not relate to the question of the layman's place
in church government, but rather to that of his personal responsibility for the mission of the church. To these individuals the position of the professional minister was, to borrow
Spener's terms, one of "director and elder brother" along
side the lay member. [107] Both were responsible for the
evangelization of the world and the work of the church.

One can distinguish in this development another example of how Methodism and revivalism both permeated with

Biblicism and Pietism, in combination with American democracy and activism tended to produce new emphases in revivalistic Protestantism.   Singularly prominent in this theology
of the layman's place was the concept of the work of the Holy
Spirit who cleansed and equipped each sanctified Christian,
minister and layman, alike, for Christian vocation.   This
sense of responsibility and ministry of each spirit-filled individual believer was the dynamic which lay behind the ministry of the Palmers and other laymen.   Their lay activity
constituted a dominant contribution to the outburst of revival
activity in the Lay Revival of 1858 around the world and in
the revivals of the last half of the century.   Like its earlier
counterparts in Europe had done, it released a massive flow
of zeal for foreign missions and social reform as well. [108]

The role of women

     The leadership role exhibited by Phoebe Palmer and
Sarah Lankford in the Tuesday Meetings and subsequent holiness evangelism came at a time when the whole question of
women's rights was being newly agitated.   Lucy Stone made
her first public address in 1847, and Antoinette Brown was
refused the right to speak at the World Temperance Convention in New York City in 1853.   This milieu may have contributed to their role. [109]

     However, the greater freedon which commonly has
been given to women to witness and exercise their spiritual
gifts in lay and pietistic revival movements must be looked
to to account for the fact that these women leaders of the
early holiness movement could hold the effective places of
leadership which they and others who followed them held.   It
was the theology of the movement and the essential nature of
the place of public testimony in the holiness experience which
gave many an otherwise timid woman the authority and the
power to speak out "as the Holy Spirit led her. "[110]

     To those who allowed the theology, the logic was irrefut-
able.   Although Mrs. Palmer never claimed to have preached,
she wrote a widely read book in which she took to task anyone
who would deny the rights of public testimony to any woman
on purported scriptural grounds.   She herself, probably "testified" more frequently to more people than many of the leading ministers of the day.   One of the most outstanding consequences of her own ministry was the encouragement which
she have to Catherine Booth, wife of the founder of the Salvation Army, to begin her public preaching ministry. [111]

The camp meeting preachers of the post-war movement commonly advanced similar arguments. One of them
chided a Presbyterian minister who refused to attend a camp
meeting love feast because a woman was to preach by insist-
ing that

> She may - she will speak for the cross. We will
> listen to her testimony and profit from her experi-
> ence. But not alone from potency of influence or
> dignity of her nature, but because of Pentecost. [112]

William G. Godbey, a fiery evangelist of the Methodist Episcopal Church South, the nineteenth century holiness movement's most prolific author, prosaically summed up the persistent feeling of the movement; he took exception to the ancient Hector's address to his wife, Andromeche:

> My wife, go back to your home to quid the spindle
> and direct the loom
> Me, Glory summons to the martial plains; ...

Godbey commented:

> That will do for a heathen warrior on whom the
> "Sun of Righteousness" never shone. Not so in
> the army of the Lord.... [113]

Given this persistent tradition within the revival from
Phoebe Palmer's time on, the new holiness churches, which
were organized out of the movement in the closing decades
of the century, were among the first to grant full ministerial
rights to women. In the mid-1880's the Mennonite Brethren
in Christ, a peace church group associated with the holiness
movement, made full provision for women ministers. [114]
After a visit to Phineas Bresee's Church of the Nazarene in
1899, H. C. Morrison, editor of the Pentecostal Herald,
wrote that "women are ordained to preach, and may sit in
yearly conventions as delegates." [115]

Seth Cook Rees, a Quaker evangelist and co-founder
with Martin Wells Knapp, of the Apostolic Holiness Union and
Prayer League at Cincinnati, Ohio in 1897, wrote more directly about the question of women's place in a "Pentecostal
Church";

> Nothing but jealousy, prejudice, bigotry, and a
> stingy love for bossing in men have prevented

> woman's public recognition by the church.   No
> church that is acquainted with the Holy Ghost will
> object to the public ministry of women.... 116

At the same time, at least some of the holiness advocates
who were active members in the Methodist Episcopal Church,
lent their influence toward the attainment of similar status
for the women of that church.   Bishop Gilbert Haven, a friend
of the holiness movement, defended the rights of Maggie Van
Cott to her evangelistic ministry within the church; in her
interests he questioned the judgment of Methodism's most able
Bible commentator, Adam Clarke.   But Methodism and others
were not ready to ordain women. 117

Phoebe Palmer's Biblicism

Phoebe Palmer claimed to have found her way out of
spiritual confusion and weakness to an assurance of perfection
in love because of the testimony of the Word of God to her
soul.   Her Biblio-centricity reveals another fundamental root
of this early holiness revival which continued to feed the ongoing movement.   In discussing what she considered the primary characteristics of her Tuesday Meetings, she said her
theological and experiential foundation was not on "Wesley,
not Fletcher, not Finney, not Mahan, not Upham, but the
Bible ... [which is] first, last and in the midst always."118
She rooted her own experience in that fact:

> I ... covenanted with God that I would be a Bible
> Christian and most carefully seek to know the mind
> of the Spirit as recorded in the written Word, though
> it might lead to an experience unlike all the world
> beside....   My highest and all consuming desire
> was to be a Bible Christian. 119

This strong commitment to the written Word undoubtedly served to lend intransigence to some of her positions
when more capable theologians sought to caution her on some
of her expressions of her experience; but it also guarded her,
just as it had her spiritual forebearer, John Wesley, from
the many radicalisms so common to spiritual movements in
the history of the church.   Later on, the formalization of
holiness theology often tended to restrict this immediate reliance on Biblical reference with the result that stereotypes,
with their attendant proof texts, became the common authoritative staples which the faithful were fed.   Nevertheless, following Mrs. Palmer's pattern, the movement became basically

a fundamentally Biblical movement in that it sought its experiences and spiritual motives in the experiences of the Biblical New Testament Church and tested both its theology and experience by what it felt was the most accurate interpretation of the Scriptures. [120]

The interpretations on the essential nature of certain aspects of spiritual truth were not always uniform, however. Varying theological and historical pre-dispositions brought into the movement from other than Methodist traditions were not always overcome by the appeal to Biblical authority. The differing views concerning the sacraments illustrate the fact. There is no indication that Phoebe Palmer, herself, held anything other than the prevailing view of the sacraments in the Methodist Church of her day. Other holiness adherents, however, held views which ranged from the traditional Quaker position which spiritualized the question to the views of some of the smaller groups who elevated foot washing to sacramental status. [121] Neither common insistence upon Biblical authority nor the spiritualizing impulses of the doctrine of the Baptism of the Holy Spirit to which the varying groups in the movement have been mutually committed, have been able to submerge these differences sufficiently to provide an adequate basis for their complete organic union. Their continued close association in their common commitment to the authority of Scripture and the promotion of Christian holiness, in spite of the tensions created by differences in other areas, produces a community in diversity which affords a unique opportunity to explore variations both in faith and practice among groups which, with such differences, ordinarily would be opposed to one another, not only in concept, but in context as well.

The Fire Spreads

It was not long before many of those who had received personal benefits from the "social religious company" at the Palmer home were seeking to reproduce its usefulness in the promotion of Christian perfection in their own localities. Professor and Mrs. Upham of Bowdoin College established a weekly meeting for holiness at Brunswick, Maine very soon after Upham had testified to sanctification under Phoebe Palmer's influence. [122] By the 1850's such meetings were common to a majority of the major cities of the east and midwest. All of them had one particular purpose:

... 'Holiness unto the Lord.' These meetings were

not for debate, controversy, or speechifying, but
for holiness. Everyone that enters these consecrated halls is expected to conform strictly to the
objects and purport of the meeting.... [123]

The format of the meetings was usually that of informal religious dialogue:

Many inquirers after the 'Way of Holiness' gather,
and it is not unusual for the meeting to assume
something like the form of an inquiry meeting. [124]

It is certain that the attractiveness of these Tuesday
Meetings and similar holiness meetings was enhanced by all
the religious and psychological benefits recognized in the
"small group" and "neighborhood group" methods being used
by churches as well as sociologists and political propagandists
today.

When one analyzes the fellowship patterns of those holiness meetings by utilizing the categories suggested by Raymond J. Corsini and Bina Rosenberg in their studies of the
psychotherapeutic values of small group dynamics, namely:
acceptance, altruism, universalization, intellectualization,
reality testing, transference, interaction, spectator therapy,
and ventilation, he can identify the forces at work. [125]

In such interplay, communication was possible which
was not possible under the more formal atmosphere of the
larger meetings held for either religious or political purposes;
prejudices were more easily overcome; the subjective feelings of those who were involved were more readily opened
up to the common concern of the group, and unity of purpose
and action were more easily achieved. Theological concerns
were subsumed within a common experience; moreover, considerable inprecision of theological expression could be tolerated in the small, intimate situation such meetings tended to
create. These were "family gatherings"; one could patiently
overcome tensions in the family, where communication might
result as readily from non-verbal understanding, which otherwise might be sources of conflict. In this kind of context there
was also an interaction at work which made ordinary people often
quite extraordinary. [126]

These small group meetings for the promotion of holiness
teaching and the encouragement of the spiritual life of Christians parallelled in many significant ways both the purpose

and practice of the "house churches" of the "spiritualists" or "sectaries" in the Lutheran and Reformed Churches of Germany of the Reformation period, and the religious "cells" of the Pietists which followed them. The service to the Christian community was similar. They generally represented a concern for the quality of Christian life rather than purity of doctrine and often served as centers of Christian lay activity. Bishop Willard Mallilieu's description of the character of the meetings at the Palmer-Lankford home, illustrates the parallelism: "It has not been a school where great skill and wisdom have been displayed in analytical definition of terms .... It has not been a place of controversy, but a place where ... a really new ... life commenced. "127

The Tuesday Meeting and the class meeting

But the pattern and meaning of these meetings must be related even more directly to the Methodist class meetings. The successful use of the small holiness meeting represented one positive effort, all unconscious as it may have been, to find a substitute to fill the spiritual and social void which was being created in the changing Methodist religious community by the declining significance of the class meeting. The latter served Methodism as an organizational unit which provided the opportunity for the small group dynamics discussed above. The consistent appearance of similar evangelical "cells" within the larger structures of formal church organizations throughout church history indicates their proven utility and possibly their basic importance to religious life. The Tuesday Meetings and similar holiness meetings, therefore, fulfilled many of the functions of Wesley's "special societies." Bishop John P. Newman called the class meeting "the nursery of Scriptural Holiness" (emphasis his). In his mind, Phoebe Palmer was "following the example of ... Wesley. "128 However, in the later movement, gathered together in a home as frequently as in a church, and a step removed from official pastoral care, instead of contributing to the unity of the denomination while they were filling the small group role, they tended to become centers of separate interests rather than instruments for strengthening the church itself. All that was needed was to take the holiness meeting to the masses, and that is essentially what the revived camp meeting movement, which became the leading edge of the tide of post-war holiness revival, was to do. 129

The importance of the Guide

The Tuesday Meetings and their patterns of holiness

promotion could not have become the revival force they did
become in Methodism and certainly not beyond it, without the
instrumentality of a "special voice." As has already been
noted, Timothy Merritt's Guide to Christian Perfection became that voice. [130]   Its inception was a part of the special
nature of the new methods to promote Christian holiness. Its
pages provided the means to broadcast accounts of revival
activities and, more particularly,

> Accounts of such as have attained the enjoyment of
> this blessed state, especially such as have died in
> the possession of it.... And let not modesty of any
> stand in the way of their complying with our re-
> quest. [131]

In 1853 the Beauty of Holiness, printed at Delaware,
Ohio, joined the Guide in the field of holiness journalism. In
1864 both the Guide and the Beauty were acquired by the
Palmers, eventually becoming known as the Guide to Holiness.
By 1870 circulation had jumped to thiry-seven thousand. It
tied the movement together until the official house organs of
rapidly developing holiness associations began to enter the
field. That competition from more strongly based organizational strength and interest might have forced it out of competition were it not for an endownment fund for its continued
publication created by Mrs. Joseph Knapp, wife of the president of the Metropolitan Life Insurance Company, and daughter of Dr. and Mrs. Palmer. It survived until early in the
next century. [132]

Conflict in Methodism

The years following the beginnings of the Tuesday
Meeting and the Guide were "a period of unusual trial" according to the report of the statistical committee to the New
England Centenary Convention meeting in Boston in 1866. It
indicated that the decade from 1840 to 1850 had produced an
increase of only one-half percent in that conference's membership. The committee attributed this inertia to "the reaction
and deadness which followed the Millerite excitement, the
losses of the Wesleyan secession, and the violent controversies connected with the Church South...."[133]   From Massachusetts to Kentucky the same conditions prevailed. The
historian of Methodism in Kentucky has indicated that although
from 1835 to 1844, the churches had experienced revival
growth in that state, by the latter date, "the agitation over

the subject of slavery sapped the spiritual vigor and brought
about an actual decrease of 1500 members. "[134]   The preval-
ence of these conditions across the church caused William
Warren Sweet to call this period leading up to the Civil War
"the tragic era" of American Methodist History. [135]

In the midst of this milieu the effects of the activities
of the Palmers, the Lankfords, and the Merritts began to
make themselves felt.   The pattern of the growing revival is
a checkerd one.   However, the general conclusion of men
like Sweet and Gaddis that the doctrine was in decline during
the two decades before 1860 is open to question. "[136]   The
reasons for their conclusions undoubtedly lie in such testimony as that of E. A. Hazen, a Methodist minister, who
recounted that when he was a student at Indiana Asbury University in 1846 he "seldom" heard the experience of entire
sanctification "referred to in a sermon," heard anyone give
"clear testimony to its possession," or saw anyone "invite
Christians ... to seek the great blessing. ... "[137]

Even as late as 1856 S. H. Platt noted that,

> with a single exception the fundamental doctrines
> of the Bible are still retained by our [Methodist]
> people.   The exception is Christian perfection!

He said that the doctrine is still retained in standard authors,
and preachers are required to emphasize it.

> But unless appearances greatly deceive, there are
> thousands upon thousands ... who utterly ignore it
> or regard it of little consequence as to be unworthy
> of their attention. [138]

On the other hand, there are many indications that
although the fortunes of the doctrine were low they were definitely responding to the new revivalists' thrusts.   In 1841
George Peck wrote that "the subject of entire sanctification
is exciting great, great interest. ... "[139]   In 1850 Nathan
Bangs, a consistent proponent of Wesleyan perfectionism, reported that within the space of six or seven years there were
more people than before professing "the blessing of perfect
love"[140]

Moreover, a review of the many Methodist publications
of antebellum years indicates the increasing frequency with
which articles emphasizing the centrality of the experience to

the Methodist's mission and the necessity for its revival began
to appear. The Christian Advocate and Journal, Methodism's
official voice; the Zion's Herald, one of the church's oldest
publications; the Methodist Quarterly Review, and many other
area publications took notice of the growing emphasis. Not
all of the new attention was favorable, but it was publicity
in any case. [141]

In addition to the periodicals within the church, which
publicized the developing revival of Methodist perfectionism,
books defending the doctrine, published during this period,
indicated that some of the most forceful voices in American
Methodism were showing a new concern for the subject. George
Peck, editor of the Methodist Quarterly Review (1840-1852)
lectured and wrote in its cause. [142] His younger brother,
who later was elected bishop in 1872, published The Central
Idea of Christianity in 1856. [143] Another influential spokes-
man was Randolph Foster, whose views were heard widely
throughout the church through his book, Christian Purity, and
through his work at Garrett Biblical Institute, Evanston, Illinois and Drew Theological Seminary at Madison, New Jersey;
he served as president of both of these institutions. He, too,
became a bishop in the church in 1872. [144]

At the close of the forties, Bishop Hamline, also an
active proponent of the new holiness cause, foresaw the potential for conflict which the revived interest in that doctrine
would create. He wrote to a friend:

> I am more than ever convinced that a conflict im-
> pends over the M. E. Church on the doctrine of
> holiness, but the results will be glorious. Where
> no war rages, no victories await her. If her foes
> are still, it is because her friends are idle.... [145]

He was writing about the time of the controversy in the church
over Phoebe Palmer's "altar theology" and "the shorter way"
to holiness; it was obvious that the "friends" had not been
idle and the "foes" had not been still. The conflict was to
prove an enduring one.

The opposition to the attempt to restore holiness in
its traditional Wesleyanism to the church developed a two-
fold thrust by mid-century. The one already referred to of
the Mattison variety attacked the new revival efforts as un-
Wesleyan; the second front against the holiness revival was
opened up by a succession of men[146] who openly or by infer-

ence turned to a Zinzendorfian concept of sanctification which
undercut the restoration efforts on theological grounds.   In
the developing conflict within the church, the holiness proponents generally suffered as much from the shift of the church
away from Wesley as they did from those who tried to deny
that they were his rightful followers.   The dual lines of opposition created strange bedfellows in the anti-holiness camp
in the Methodist Church.   Men who considered themselves
Wesleyan perfectionists, but not of the new "variety" found
themselves joined in their opposition by a school which denied Wesley at the very point of the holiness conflict.

        The controversies developing around the renewed in-
terest in the subject were sufficient to command a warning
from the Methodist bishops at the 1852 General Conference
of the church.   They urged all the protagonists to

            avoid both new theories, new expressions and new
            measures on this subject, and adhere closely to
            the ancient landmarks. [147]

Hamline's prediction of impending conflict was a reality.   The
tensions were real and would not go away even at the bishop's
command.   Both the "new theories" and the "new measures"
persisted throughout the developing history of the movement
in Methodism.

        Whether the results of such controversy were as "glo-
rious" as Bishop Hamline had anticipated in his remarks noted
above, must be judged in the light of the bitterness of the
polemics which tended to produce weariness with the question
in the church; this noise of persistent rejoinder undoubtedly
produced waning concern for the whole matter among many,
who under other circumstances, may have given a more
sympathetic ear to the appeal which to thousands of others
appeared so winsome.   It is certain that the debate, which
continued with greater or lesser intensity for the balance of
the century, indicated the strength of the movement and the
centrality of the issues it was raising in Methodism.

The Free Methodist separation

        As the year 1859 began, the Guide took notice of a
developing crisis in the Genesee Conference of the church.
It reported that it was apparent that "a struggle [was] going
on, not in the Genesee Conference merely, but in the churches
of the land, between a modern phase of piety and the spiritual

element for which our fathers contended.... "[148] The Rev.
Benjamin T. Roberts, a pastor of the Genesee Conference,
stood at the center of the controversy because of his leadership among a group of pastors and laymen who protested a
"New School Methodism" which had become dominant in the
conference. Among other charges against this "New School,"
Roberts noted the new theological trends mentioned above,
and claimed that they held that "justification and entire sanctification or holiness are the same.... "[149] This concern
for what Roberts and his sympathizers believed to be the
Wesleyan doctrine of perfectionism, together with the closely
related concerns for the abolition of slavery, and the enforce-
ment of a more stringent discipline in the churches became
the dominant theme of the protest of the new movement. When
Roberts and others associated with him were eventually disciplined and forced out of the Methodist Episcopal Church,
they took the name of Free Methodists because of another
issue in their expressed discontent with the church--the growing tendency to build more elaborate church edifices financed
in part by rented pews; this practice, they claimed, kept the
common man out of the congregation and out of reach of the
church's message. The Discipline of the new sect which was
formed in 1860 out of a union of dissenters in the Genesee
Conference and others who had expressed similar opinions
in other sections of the Methodist Episcopal church, uniquely
tied them to the Wesleyan perfectionism promoted by the
growing Palmer movement. It has played a significant continuing role in the advancement of the post-war revival and
the organization of its converts. [150]

Wesleyans Outside the Methodist Camp

New literature in the perfectionist camp outside of
Methodism, which fanned the fires of the revival interest in
the experience, added other converts to the "second blessing"
forces. Both Finney and Mahan contributed treatises in defense and explication of the Oberlin revival. [151] It was more
natural that their writings should produce negative reactions
among their fellow-ministers than those of the Methodist proponents produced in their circles. But, as the impetus to
general revival once more was generating strength in the
nation prior to the Panic of 1857, the opposition to their perfectionism in Presbyterian and Congregational churches di-
minished. As Smith has shown, even where the "second conversion" concept was rejected, many ministers in these circles espoused a strong emphasis on the place of Christian

holiness in Christian conversion. [152]

The influence of Thomas Upham

During this same period several books by Professor Thomas Upham of Bowdoin College, substantially enlarged the perimeters of the new movement's influence in the churches.

His wife's urgent insistence that he seek the help of Phoebe Palmer, in his spiritual quest, led him to the Tuesday Meeting at the Palmer's residence in New York in 1838. That visit marked the opening of those meetings to men as well as to women. Following the pattern of consecration, and immediate faith, and public testimony, which she taught, Upham finally professed to enter a new state of Christian experience and became an ardent member of the movement. [153]

His Congregational background, his scholarship and his irenic spirit gained an entrance for his essentially Wesleyan perfectionist teaching where normal prejudice would otherwise have excluded it. This was particularly due to the historical relationships in which he saw the American movement. Upham believed that what was being experienced in the holiness meetings in America in the 1840's was part and parcel of a long tradition in Christianity which reached back, not only to Wesley and the Pietists before him, but beyond the Reformation to Catholic traditions of piety as well. His book on the life and experiences of Madame Guyon, the French Catholic mystic and friend of Fénelon, received wide-spread publicity and review. [154] Together with his other writings on the Christian life, all of which delved heavily into the relationship of the life of Christian perfection and classical mystical concepts, particularly those of the Catholic Quietists, he permanently infused into the holiness tradition in America a deep sense of experiential kinship with these.

Upham's sympathetic emphasis on the importance of the inner, contemplative, devotional life of holiness possibly reminded some Methodist friends of John Wesley's warnings concerning the quietistic character of Catholic perfectionists. [155] Even Phoebe Palmer warned her close friend that he was moving beyond the clear teachings of the Scriptures in some of his teaching concerning the possibilities of "divine union. "[156] A careful reading of Upham's writings does not seem to bear out the intensity of these fears or the continuing charge of "heresies. " The reaction may have been intensified by the fact that his emphasis on the inner life of holiness was in

quite direct contrast with the radical perfectionism which was
then expressing itself in the reform movements of the same
period.

Harriet Beecher Stowe defended Upham's strong appeals to inner holiness and a life of devotion. She felt they
afforded an essential balance to the activistic mood of the
times. She noted in a review of the book in the New York
Evangelist that in spite of some difficult metaphysical and
philosophical principles in the book,

> the Christian may ... rejoice that such a work has
> been given to the church.
> The whole state of the times seems to call forth
> an effort to bring back the Christian mind to a deeper
> internal scrutiny.... 157

The church, she said, was finding out that the mere organization of a voluntary movement to correct evils in society
or the church did not automatically mean that "Satan was ...
outvoted." The book was a reaction to an age whose spirit
was conveyed in the following:

> Only keep on acting for Christ and your heart will
> keep right....
> But while the church has been ... enabled to
> do great and glorious work in ... developing a
> system of efficient energetic action, are there not
> signs which show that she must turn her attention
> again within? ... The experience described in Pro-
> fessor Upham's work may be looked upon as utterly
> hopeless as a mark of personal attainment. Yet
> the history of the church in all ages shows instances
> how it has been attained [emphasis hers]. 158

Through the pages of the Guide, Upham also called attention to other Christian traditions which he considered to
be in the vanguard of the revival of holiness during his time.
John Arndt's pietistic classic, True Christianity, appeared to
him "to be everywhere favorable to the doctrine of evangelical
holiness." Noting its influence upon the origins of Pietism,
he concluded that,

> the great power and charm of the work ... con-
> sists in the prominence which it gives to the doc-
> trine of entire sanctification. Not in a formal way,
> it is true, but in such a way that there can be no

mistake as to the views; the desires and aims of
the author. [159]

This type of interpretation led Benjamin Warfield to severely
criticize Upham. Of the rapport which the latter established
with the Catholic Quietists, Warfield said: "He undertook ...
nothing less than the amazing task of evangelizing ... [them]."
He had really assimilated Quietism to Wesleyanism. He
further said that Upham used "Miguel de Molinos to Antoinette
Bourignon" adapting them to his own purposes "with utmost
freedom, not to say violence. "[160] Upham's writings were
published widely in England as well as America. They prepared the way for the English holiness evangelism of the
Palmers during the way; their influence moved on into the
seventies opening doors for the holiness revival of the Smiths,
Mahan and Boardman. They continue on the active lists today. Through them Madame Guyon, Molinos, St. Catherine,
Fénelon, Catherine Adorna and others in the Christian mystical tradition remain on the active list of holiness "saints"
as well.

Harriet Beecher Stowe's sympathetic review of Upham's
work indicates the growing desire among a significant number
of people at that time for a different quality of Christian experience than that which the churches were then experiencing.
Her brother, Henry Ward Beecher, too, expressed similar
perfectionist sentiments:

> Now this steadfastness of God's presence is both
> to be prayed for and possessed. There is provis-
> ion in the Gospel for that very blessing. It is the
> promise of the Father.... It is made to be the
> Christian's duty to pray for it and expect it [empha-
> sis mine]. [161]

Favorable, if not entirely approving, reviews of Upham's
works also appeared in the Biblical Repository. Henry T.
Cheever said of Upham's two-volume work on The Life and
Writings of Madame Guyon:

> These volumes make their appearance as the legit-
> imate demand and offspring of the times, because
> there is arising in the religious mind of the evan-
> gelical Christendom generally a strong desire to
> know more of that form of holiness, or phase of
> religious experience....
>   The important truths wrapped up in mysticism,

> Quietism, Pure love, or Perfectionism so-called
> should be carefully unfolded. ... [162]

Cheever rejoiced in what he felt was divine purpose in allowing "the ideas that have revolutionized the world ... [to orig-
inate] in the cells of obscure enthusiasts. ... " In the new
interest in these subjects he saw a potential for greater religious discoveries than the church had realized to that time.
The Harvards, the Oxfords, and the Sorbonnes would have
to systemetize it all, he admitted, but it will originate "in
the conscious wants ... and fulfilled aspirations of everyday
Christians."[163]

In the same journal in January 1848, the Rev. Erskine
Moore struck a note which was not unrelated to Cheever's
encouragement to the churches to give the perfectionists a
hearing. Erskine anticipated that

> as we draw near to the consummation of all things,
> ... we may expect more wonderful spiritual achieve-
> ments and more magnificent results, than the world
> has ever seen. [164]

This expectation of expanding Christian experience and spiritual achievements fitted hand-in-glove with the prospects
promised by the holiness evangelists.

William E. Boardman's influence

These rising religious aspirations of the 1840's did
not wane with the approaching shadows of the Civil War conflict which was to test the very existence of the nation. They
found a measure of fulfillment in the Revival of 1858. Their
continued persistence in the life of the churches right up to
the outbreak of the war in 1860 is best indicated by the enthusiastic response to the publication of a new book on Christian holiness in 1858, William E. Bordman's The Higher
Christian Life. [165] This book opened the doors of non-Methodist churches to the revival's teachings more widely than
any volume which had preceded it. It had none of the sophis-
tication of the books of the scholarly Upham. Denying any
pretentions to systematic statements of theology and drawing
upon his own experience and spiritual longings, Boardman
apparently caught up in significant measure all the religious
longings which were coursing through the popular temper of
much of Christendom in America, Canada and Europe at the
time. [166]

Boardman, a Presbyterian, had had intimate contact
with the mainstream of Wesleyan and Oberlin perfectionism.
The writings of Finney and Mahan had been given to him by
an itinerant Methodist minister. His first glimpses of the
experience of the higher Christian life had come to him while
he was reading the life of James Brainerd Taylor. He finally
professed to enter his own "second conversion" through Methodist influences. This conbination of both Methodist and Oberlin teaching and expression flowed through his work to produce
a statement of the nature and reality of the life of holiness
which was more widely received than the expositions in the
more classic traditions.

The book enjoyed unusual popularity. It went through
repeated editions in England where it was one of the chief
influences in stirring up the religious awakening of 1859 and
following. Within the movement and beyond, only Hannah
Whitall Smith's later classic, The Christian's Secret of a
Happy Life[167] sold so quickly.

In spite of his efforts to stay away from the traditional
Wesleyan terminology, Boardman was essentially a part of
the Wesleyan holiness movement. He was a frequent attendant at the Tuesday Meetings and for a time was the leader
of Union Holiness Conventions in conjunction with other holiness advocates. He participated, although only in a lesser
public role, with Robert Pearsall Smith in the famous English holiness conferences at Brighton and Oxford in 1874 and
1875. After a brief return to America, he returned to England in December of 1885 to make his permanent home there.
The later years of his long life were spent in a healing ministry. [168]

A. B. Earle's profession of the experience of holiness
in 1859 also secured a hearing for the doctrine in non-Methodist circles, especially among members of his own Baptist
faith. His books on the subject emphasized the central idea
of the doctrine as a "rest of faith. "[169]

The Palmer's Widening Revivalism

The widespread preparation for holiness revival was
not due only to these effective instruments of publicity, or
the small group fellowships such as the Palmers promoted.
The rooms where the groups met for mutual encouragement
in the experience, were too small, and the circulation lists

of the periodicals devoted to its publications were too limited
to accomplish all of that.   The use of larger public mass
meetings to emphasize the doctrine added their influence in
this preparatory period.   Methodist camp meetings and holiness conventions everywhere gave new attention to the teaching.   Accounts by the camp meeting reporters of sanctifications reported along with the more usual conversions became
increasingly common at the mid-point of the nineteenth century. [170]   Pre-war holiness associations and their public
meetings in the churches already predicted the later pattern of
more extensive organization within the post-war movement. [171]

As it is shown in a later section, the Methodist camp
meeting, though much larger than the Tuesday Meetings, was
able to keep alive many of the latter's small-group commu-
nicative and therapeutic values within its own structure; however, its more public nature necessarily brought charges
which tended to a more rigid formulation of theology, practice, and standards by which the orthodoxy of true holiness
faith and life were measured. [172]

During the 1850's the Palmers moved the experience
and the teaching of the Tuesday Meeting out into this arena
through their evangelistic activities.   Aided by the growing
acceptance of inter-denominational evangelism by the churches
and the generally prevailing longing for some new trancenden-
tal word, they were invited to many non-Methodist as well
as Methodist churches and conventions to speak to eager audiences about the way of faith into the higher Christian life.
Together with the books already listed, Phoebe Palmer's own
popular works had gone through edition after edition creating
a ready audience for these two laymen throughout Canada and
the United States, and beyond.   Edwin Orr who chronicles
the worldwide revival which ensued in 1858 as the Second
Evangelical Awakening roots the beginnings of the revival
movement in the work of Dr. and Mrs. Palmer in Canada
in 1857. [173]

Toward the end of the latter year, letters from Phoebe
Palmer to Mrs. French, co-editor of the Beauty of Holiness,
were filled with glowing reports of the revival upsurge which
they were seeing in their work among Canadian Methodists.
From a camp meeting at London, in then Canada West, she
wrote:

> The meeting we have just attended has been one of
> the most remarkable for the displays of saving

> mercy, of any we have ever attended....
> Perhaps we have never before been quite so
> abundant in labors. Meetings have been kept up
> with scarcely any intermission.... [174]

The usual response to the Palmer's ministry continued from
the September of the incident above on into the winter. The
very last page of the Beauty for 1857 carries a hurried in-
sert of a two line note:

> Glorious News From Hamilton, C. W. too late for
> insertion; 700 converted and sanctified. [175]

This was the eve of what Timothy Smith calls "Annus Mira-
bilis, "[176] the year of the well publicized revival of 1858. The
revival had strong perfectionist tendencies; it marked the beginning of a decade of renewed revivalism which was interrupted
briefly in America by the spiritual barrenness born of war.

However, the eruption of the civil strife in America
did not bring revivalism to a complete standstill. There
were significant revivals in both the Northern and Southern
armies during the war period. Some holiness adherents,
mostly Methodist ministers, served as military chaplains.
William E. Boardman served as Executive Secretary of the
United States Christian Commission early in the war. [177]

Revival in England

The Palmers were in England during much of the war;
their attitude, and that of other holiness movement leaders, toward the issues of the day may rightfully be criticized for its
inclination to follow rather than to lead the public mind as the
Wesleyan Methodist perfectionists had. The former were too
closely linked with the leadership of the Methodist Episcopal
Church to follow an activist line. The Methodist bureaucracy,
on the whole, saw the slavery issue as a threat to the institutional
organization; they wanted mainly to keep antislavery controversy
from rending the fabric of the church. The Wesleyan Methodist
schism in 1843 and the separation of the Southern church a little
while thereafter, showed how unrealistic this approach was under the temper of the times. [178]

If the revival progress in America was at least tem-
porarily delayed by the war, the same was not true of holiness evangelism in England and Scotland during that period.
After their successful public ministry in the United States and

Canada, the Palmers went to England and Scotland to participate in the 1859 awakening of the religious interest there
which was encouraged by the revival upsurge in America the
previous year. They remained there for most of the Civil
War period ministering in those Wesleyan Churches which
chose to ignore the general ban put on the Palmers' work by
the main English Methodist body. The constant flow of reports on their successful campaigns and the length of their
stay indicated that the official Methodist apprehensions were
not widely shared by local church congregations. The ecumenical character of the slowly rising English revival movement undoubtedly assured them their wide hearing. [179]

Influences upon the Salvation Army's founders

        Both the Palmers and Caughey had considerable in-
fluence on the beginnings and temper of the Salvation Army
movement during their visits. William Booth was converted
as a young man under Caughey's revival ministry in an earlier English campaign; in the Civil War period revivals, the
Booths, Palmers, and Caughey worked closely in cooperative
or alternating campaigns in England and Northern Ireland.
It was at one such series of meetings that Booth's "Hallelu-
jah Band" was first formed out of his converts; these lay
organizations were one of the first concretizations of Booth's
conviction that Christianity could be communicated to the
common man most effectively by his own kind and through
cultural media he naturally understood. [180]

        But perhaps the most important influence of the Palmer-
Caughey holiness evangelism in connection with the founders
of the Salvation Army was that in these associations Phoebe
Palmer's widely accepted and effective revival preaching
overcame whatever reluctance Catherine Booth may have retained in following her husband into the public Christian ministry. She began her preaching career in the wake of the
Palmer meetings. [181] The current work of the Salvation Army
testifies to the significance of these contacts of early responsible representatives of the American holiness movement with
the founders of the Salvation Army during its formative years.
The influences of the Americans for the strengthening of the
Army's Wesleyan holiness position fed back into the American
movement with strength and vigor when the Army began its
American work in 1880; the Army's active influence within
the movement continues to this day. [182]

        Finney, another representative of the American per-

fectionist movement, also took part in the British revival.
He was old and his stay was brief, but the accounts of evangelistic successes he leaves in his <u>Memoirs</u> are generally
supported by local contemporary reports. [183]

According to James Orr this "second evangelistic
awakening" effected every county in Ulster, Scotland, Wales
and England, adding a million members to the evangelical
churches, accomplishing a tremendous social uplift, and
giving an effective impulse to home and foreign missionary
enterprise. [184] The presence of the American holiness evangelists as part of the English revival activity proved to be
part of the preparation for the influence of the movement in
the later surge of revival in which holiness evangelists such
as the Robert Pearsall Smiths, Asa Mahan and William E.
Boardman joined Moody and Sankey in the 1870's. In 1864
the Palmers came home to a war-weary America, longing
"for the dawn of peace." The initial ground swells of the
post-war revival which moved to high-tide within ten years
of the close of the conflict were already being felt in the
nation's churches.

SUMMARY

The preceding chapter has attempted to outline the
developments by which American revivalism, in the tradition
from Jonathan Edwards to Charles Finney, and Wesleyan perfectionism, in the tradition of the Amercan Methodists, each
took up the emphasis of the other to form a new blend of
American revivalism and Wesleyan perfectionism. One can
maintain that to properly understand either revivalism or the
holiness movement, thereafter, he must take into account the
results of the wedding of these two forces.

Given the American voluntaristic church system, which
encouraged revivalism, and given pietistic revivalism's inherent tendencies towards perfectionism, the continuum was
a very natural one. The call of the revivalist to the sinner,
for an immediate faith decision for his evangelical conversion,
was paralleled by the holiness evangelist's call to the Christian for an immediate faith decision for his entire sanctification. Out of this new urgency in perfectionist revivalism,
reinforced as it was, by the transcendentalism, the progres-
sivism, and the optimism which were seething in the national
mind at the time, a new holiness movement arose in the
American churches. At its heart, it was a puritan-pietist

movement which lived very comfortably, by the nature of
those tendencies, in its predominantly American-Methodist,
perfectionist environment.

The main focal point for these dynamic elements, in
their initial interaction, was the holiness promotion of Phoebe
Palmer; her family, and friends. The practice, promotion
and teaching of holiness, as developed in the Tuesday Meetings at her home and in her ministry, became normative for
the movement. It is difficult to overestimate the importance
of a proper understanding of the nature of that incipient history to all further efforts to interpret the ensuing movement,
or its proper place in the history of revivalism. Within its
activities, the Palmers' Tuesday Meeting best comprehends
the religious, cultural, and social forces which fed their
input into the structure, teaching, and methodology of the
holiness revival.

Phoebe Palmer's Biblical orientation carried strong
Methodist and, therefore, pietist overtones, as also did her
insistence upon the centrality of personal experience, and
the individual's witness to it, as the essence of the Christian life. The movement's contention that the ministry must
be "fully sanctified" to be effective and fruitful, the emphasis
upon the priesthood of every believer, as demonstrated in the
common ministry of laymen and ordained ministers, the place
given to the ministry of "Spirit-led" women, the ease with
which men of differing creeds promoted a common concern
within the non-theological context of the small group meet-
ings--all categorize the whole as highly pietistic. It is not
suprising that all of these should come out so boldly in a
revival which had as its goal, the goal of all pietism--the
sanctification of the Christian, and that, "entirely." Nor is
it surprising that the movement should arise in Methodism,
under the leadership of a woman whose father was a personal
convert of John Wesley. The perfectionist, the pietist, the
puritan elements--all were part of him also. These were
ingredients that went into the dynamics of the special promotion of holiness, as fostered by its pre-Civil War proponents.

The terminology, the methodology, and the praxis pie-
tatis which were fixed on the movement during the first thirty
years, were both used and abused. Whichever way it may
have been, they strongly determined the future course and
nature of the post-war revival and the holiness sects and
other institutionalized forms of the movement which followed.
Out of the same ingredients, the ongoing movement demonstra-

ted, at various times and in various sectors, most of the
well-known weaknesses, characteristic of pietistic traditions.
Inherent in the Palmer emphases, were the tendencies to
deemphasize any theological definition, to overemphasize the
validity of subjective experience as the norm of the Christian
life, and to become introspective and quietistic. Phoebe
Palmer, herself, maintained a better balance in these areas
than did some of her followers in the later movement.

With all of the above, Phoebe Palmer and her friends,
in the special promotion of holiness prior to the Civil War,
set the patterns of a new evangelical pietism, commonly
known as "the higher Christian life." Its essential dynamic
was the one word heard most at the Tuesday Meetings--"definite." That was the keynote; from that platform a new revivalism had been launched.

NOTES

1. W. E. Sangster, The Path to Perfection (London:
Epworth Press, 1943), p. 7.

2. Robert Baird, Religion in the United States of
America (New York: Arno Press and the New York Times,
1969), p. 459. Baird's work, originally published in 1844,
noted that Edward's principles had prevailed from 1735 to
that time. Martin Marty, op. cit., pp. 84-85, outlines the
development of these principles in such men as Nathaniel
Taylor, probably the most effective advocate of the "New
School"; Timothy Dwight, President of Yale University; Samuel Hopkins; and men who followed a similar pattern in Pres-
byterianism such as Albert Barnes and Lyman Beecher. On
Edwards' principles also see C. C. Goen, "The Methodist
Age of American Church History," Religion in Life, XXXIV
(1965), pp. 564-65 and C. C. Goen, Revivalism and Separatism
in New England, 1740-1800 (New Haven: Yale University Press,
1962), pp. 13-14.

3. Daniel T. Fiske, "New England Theology, "Bibliotheca Sacra, XXII (July, 1865), 512.

4. Franklin H. Littell, From State Church to Pluralism:
A Protestant Interpretation of Religion in American History (New
York: The Macmillan Co., 1971), p. 55, notes that the American
churches often violated this pattern of voluntaryism by seeking aid from the state. Voluntaryism also required a reviv-

alism which would win men to the churches. In this sense
Littell also maintains that the American churches essentially
paralleled the mission churches more closely than their European conterparts; ibid. , pp. 57-8; the call to Christian perfection was closely related to the success of the revivalists
in flooding the churches with new, but at best, immature
Christians.

5. T. Smith, op. cit. , pp. 25-33, 88-92; also see
Jackson, Church History (September, 1969), p. 357.

6. Beauty of Holiness, VIII (February, 1857), 36.
Goen, Religion in Life (1965), p. 565, discusses the developments from Edwards down to the Methodization of revivalism.

7. Journal of the General Conference (New York:
Carlton and Porter, 1864), p. 283.

8. Harriet Beecher Stowe, Primitive Christian Experience as quoted by Jacob Hoke, Holiness: or the Higher
Christian Life (Dayton, Ohio: United Brethren Printing Establishment, 1870), p. 38. Henry Ridgeway, the biographer
of Rev. Alfred Cookman, attributes this sense of definiteness
which pervaded holiness promotion not to "New England preaching, but to Methodism; in the course of its history, he said
that that tradition held "that when an object ought to be effected,
there is a way to effect it, and that this way is usually the
one that goes straight to the object and deals specifically with
it. " See Ridgaway, The Life of Rev. Alfred Cookman (New
York: Harper and Brothers, 1873), p. 321. That same definiteness was carried into the English movement later by American holiness evangelists. Hannah Whitall Smith advised Lady
Cowper-Temple that to have a successful holiness conference,
"the call to it must be very definite. " (emphasis hers.) She
continued, "It has been proved a thousand times that meetings
held expressly for the definite purpose of the promotion of
holiness or the Higher Christian Life are infinitely more
blessed than the same people meeting indefinitely. " As quoted
in J. C. Pollock, The Keswick Story (London: Hodder and
Sloughton, 1964), p. 20.

9. Divine Life (July, 1879), p. 3. Thirty years
earlier Henry T. Cheever had looked to the renewed interest
which Thomas Upham had excited in the experience of Christian Holiness by his book, The Life, Religious Opinions, and
Experience of Madame Guyon (London: H. R. Allenson and
Co. , Ltd. , 1961 [originally published in 1846]), in almost

exactly the same light. "This good book," he said, "[would accelerate] the pulse of the church, without the intermittent fever ... of revival and declension; enlarging its faith, ... and adding to its ... momentum in the onward movement for the world's evangelization, until the Kingdom is given to the People of the Saints of the Most High, and the conquest of the world is accomplished for Christ." "Life and Writings of Madame Guyon," The Biblical Repository and Review, IV (October, 1848), 642.

10. See Smith, Handy, Loetscher, op. cit., II, 312-14, 421-22; Jamison, op. cit., II, 202, says that revivalism "dynamically stimulated ... the desire for absolute perfection...." Wm. Warren Sweet sees this combination of individualism, German pietism, and interior moralism as the factors which produced the American spiritual awakenings, and eventually, the social gospel. See Wm. K. Anderson (ed.), Protestantism: a Symposium (Nashville, Tennessee: Commission on Courses of Study, the Methodist Church, 1944), pp. 99-109. Stoeffler, op. cit., pp. 3-6. R. Newton Flew, The Idea of Perfection in Christian Theology: an Historical Study of the Christian Ideal for the Present Life (London: Oxford University Press, 1934), p. 275.

11. Mead, op. cit., p. 115.

12. See A. W. Nagler's Pietism and Methodism (Nashville, Tennessee: Publishing House of the Methodist Episcopal Church South, 1918). Ibid., pp. 35-36, has a summary of the perfectionism of Jacob Spener, one of the fathers of Pietism; he acknowledged that a wholehearted service to God in this life did allow for a relative Christian perfection. Nagler also demonstrates, ibid., p. 128, that the connection between perfectionism and pietism is indicated by the fact that the latter's opponents in Germany always considered that perfectionism was the one common ground on which the otherwise quite diverse pietistic groups stood together. See Stoeffler, op. cit., p. 17.

13. Robert Ellis Thompson, A History of the Presbyterian Churches in the United States (New York: Charles Scribner's Sons, 1895), p. 34.

14. Smith and Jamison, op. cit., IV (Parts 3, 4, 5), 679. Glenn C. Atkins, who was no sympathetic critic of revivalism in his Religion in Our Times (New York: Round Table Press, 1932), p. 19, claims that "if one adds the

influence of Wesleyanism in England to the force and outcome
of evangelism in America, one has the religious dynamic of
almost two hundred years among the English-speaking peoples." The holiness movement was most representative of
that combination of forces and the resultant dynamic.

15.   Charles G. Finney, Views on Sanctification (Oberlin: James Steele, 1840), p. 59: "It is self-evident that entire obedience to God's law is possible on the grounds of
natural ability." James E. Johnson, op. cit., p. 342, observes that neither A. T. Swing's claim that Finney's theology was developed independently of "New Haven Theology"
made in Bibliotheca Sacra, LVII (1900), 465, nor R. H. Foster's indictment of it as "pure Taylorism" in A Genetic History of New England Theology (Chicago: University of Chicago Press, 1907), p. 457, is entirely accurate. Johnson,
loc. cit., claims it was probably both. Finney did have contact with Nathaniel Taylor. See Sidney E. Mead, Nathaniel
Taylor, 1798-1858: A Connecticut Liberal (Chicage: The
University of Chicago Press, 1942), p. 167. Cf. also James E.
Johnson, "Charles G. Finney and Oberlin Perfection," Journal
of Presbyterian History (March, 1968), 42-57 and ibid. (June,
1968), pp. 128-38. Finney's Revivals of Religion (New York:
Fleming H. Revell Co., n. d.), his most extensive treatment
of his revivalistic methods, is still widely read in holiness
circles.

16.   This in spite of the fact that his followers had
feared he would be shorn of his strength in the city. Whitney R. Cross, The Burned-over District; the Social and Intellectual History of Enthusiastic Religion in Western New
York, 1800-1850 (Ithaca, N. Y.: Cornell University Press,
1950), p. 147. For Finney's early work see ibid., pp. 151-
69.

17.   Tappan offered to give all of his annual income of
"about a hundred thousand dollars a year" (except what was
needed to provide for his own family) if Finney would go to
John Sheperd's new college at Oberlin, Ohio. Tappan was
unable to fulfill his promise because of the financial panic
which set in soon after Finney had made the move. Charles
G. Finney, Memoirs of ... (New York: Fleming H. Revell,
1908 [originally published in 1876]), pp. 334, 336-37. Finney
was president of Oberlin from 1851-1866.

18.   Ibid., pp. 340-41.

19.   Finney, Views on Sanctification, p. 193.

20. For accounts of the Oberlin revival, see Finney, Memoirs, pp. 336-41; 349-51. Asa Mahan, Out of Darkness into Light or the Hidden Life Made Manifest (Louisville: Pickett Publishing Co. , n. d. [originally published Boston: Willard Tract Repository, 1876]), pp. 180ff. Zion's Herald, VIII (March 15, 1837), p. 42, rejoiced that Finney had "recently come out in favor of Christian perfection as taught by Mr. Wesley. " (emphasis theirs.)

21. Ibid. (September 13, 1837), p. 146, noted that "many Calvinists [were] thinking favorably of the doctrine as held by the Methodists and some ... [were] publically teaching it. " In 1837 the Oberlin Evangelist was begun to promote the doctrine from that center. In 1839 Mahan published his Scripture Doctrine of Christian Perfection (Boston: D. S. King, 1839), and in 1840 Finney published Views on Sanctification cited above.

22. See supra, p. 20. James H. Fairchild, "The Doctrine of Sanctification at Oberlin," The Congregational Quarterly, LXX (April, 1876), 238-39, notes that the desire was to find an establishment in Christian experience beyond the ups and downs of the revivalistic pattern. George Highes, The Beloved Physician, Walter C. Palmer, M. D. ... (New York: Palmer and Highes [ca. 1884]), pp. 239ff. , speaks of Oberlin and the beginning of the holiness revival; also see T. Smith, op. cit. , pp. 103-113.

23. Finney, Views on Sanctification cited above.

24. George Peck, editor of the Methodist Quarterly Review, commented that Finney did not express himself "Methodistically" in his work on sanctification, but Peck was satisfied that, "the thing which we mean by Christian Perfection is truly set forth in that work. " (emphasis his); "Methodist Quarterly Review, XXIII (April, 1841), 308. Paul Rader, "A Study of the Doctrine of Sanctification in the Life and Thought of Charles G. Finney" (unpublished B.D. thesis, Asbury Theological Seminary, 1959), p. 103, concludes that the Wesleyans and Finney are in "substantial agreement" on the doctrine and experience. T. Smith, op. cit. , pp. 108-111, gives a concise summary of the fluctuations in Finney's emphases on faith and natural ability. James H. Fairchild, op. cit. , pp. 252-59, outlines the shades of difference within the views of the Oberlin men themselves.

25. Guide, III (January, 1842), 156. Ibid. , pp. 153-86, gives the whole of Asa Mahan's reply to the criticism leveled

against the Oberlin School by Professor Woods of Andover
Seminary. See Mahan, Out of Darkness, pp. 245-48, for
Mahan's observations on some of the distinctions between
Finney's and his views on perfectionism. Smith, Handy,
Loetscher, op. cit., II, 42-48, is a ready source on Mahan's
perfectionist persuasions. The Zion's Herald, XX (July 25,
1849), 118, commends Mahan to Methodist pulpits as a preacher
of entire sanctification, for "he differs but slightly from the
Wesleyan view of the subject...." Smith's comment on Mahan's
standing as an example of Christian perfection in Revivalism and
Social Reform, p. 11 could be expanded by the feelings of the
Wesleyan Methodists toward Mahan after he was influential in
moving the Michigan Union College in 1859 from Leoni, Michigan to a new campus in Adrian, Michigan. The library of
the Leoni school was moved to Adrian by ox-cart at night to
escape the wrath of the local populace who had supported
Michigan Union College. Mahan, who served the new Adrian
College as a Wesleyan Methodist, left the college after five
years, although his title of president continued into the spring
of 1864. The trustees at last decided that his absence during the 1864-65 term, together with his attachment to the
Methodist Protestant Church and one of their colleges, war-
ranted a call for his resignation. He was replaced in 1865.
Adrian College became a Methodist Protestant College in
1868. For the fullest account of these events see Willard
Garfield Smith, "The History of Church Controlled Colleges
in the Wesleyan Methodist Church" (unpublished Ph.D. thesis,
School of Education, New York University, 1951), pp. 47-53.
Also Ira Ford McLeister, History of the Wesleyan Methodist
Church, ed. R. S. Nicholson (Rev. [i.e., 3rd ed.]; Marion,
Ind.: Wesley Press, 1959), pp. 334-36; and Fanny A. Hay,
Rugh E. Cargo, and Harlan Freeman, A History of Adrian
College, The Story of a Noble Devotion (Adrian, Mich.: Adrian
College Press, 1945), p. 21.

    Mahan probably became acquainted with Wesleyan Meth-
odist leaders even before their separation from the Methodist
Episcopal Church in 1843; the Guide, III (September, 1841),
pp. 70-71, reports on a "convention of those interested in the
doctrine of entire sanctification." Mahan and other Oberlin
leaders joined with Upham and Methodist perfectionists in
these, the very first conventions for the promotion of holiness.
See also Cross, op. cit., pp. 261, 278-81; and T. Smith,
op. cit., pp. 116-17.

    26. Clifton E. Olmstead, History of Religion in the
United States (Englewood Cliffs, N.J.: Prentice-Hall, 1960),
p. 90; James Edwin Orr, The Second Evangelical Awakening

(London: Marshall, Morgan and Scott, 1955), pp. 11-40;
William Warren Sweet, Methodism in American History (New
York: Abingdon Press, 1953), p. 254.   All of these general
conclusions comparing this period with previous revival surges
must be modified by the fact that during the whole time revivalism was far from dead as evidenced by the continuing
work of Finney and Mahan together with the activities of
Caughey and the Palmers.

27.   Reviews of these reform movements can be found
in: Alice F. Tyler, Freedom's Ferment: Phases of American Social History from the Colonial Period to the Outbreak
of the Civil War (Minneapolis: University of Mineapolis
Press, 1944) and Cross, op. cit. , T. Smith, op. cit. . pp.
148-237, treats extensively with revivalistic or evangelical
reform efforts.

28.   Sidney F. Mead, The Lively Experiment, pp. 92-
98, describes the mind of the National Period: "Central was
the figure of the free individual, ..." Ibid. , p. 92.   Therefore, a perfect society was created by free individuals volun-
tarily developing organizations which in turn could exert reform pressure to produce a "paternalistic response" from
those who would have to make reform possible; ibid. , p. 97.
William Warren Sweet, Protestantism in American History,
p. 108, observes that "it was out of this background of emphasis upon the practical and experiential [in revivalism] that
the social gospel arose." Cf. Winthrop Hudson, op. cit. ,
p. 343, for the relationship of perfectionism and reform.
Also see Johnson, Religion in Life, p. 357.   Sweet, American
Churches, pp. 121ff. , traces much of this social action back
to Jonathan Edwards' concept of "disinterested benevolence."

29.   As quoted by Ray Strachey (ed.), Religious Fanaticism: Extracts from the Religious Papers of Hannah
Whitall Smith (London: Faber and Gwyer, 1928), p. 74.
Strachey reviews some of the more bizarre reform efforts
of the period.

30.   See Tyler, op. cit. , pp. 184-95.

31.   Guide, VI (December, 1844), 131.   Noyes was
just as careful to dissociate himself from the more orthodox
perfectionists whom he called "semi-perfectionists." See
Benjamin Warfield, Perfectionism (New York: Oxford University Press, 1931-1933), II, 252-53; Cross, op. cit. , pp.
238-51; and Asa Mahan, Scripture Doctrine of Christian

Perfection, pp. 7-13. Noyes' career is portrayed in Robert
A. Parker, A Yankee Saint: John Humphrey Noyes and the
Oneida Community (New York, 1935).

32. The views of Antinomian Perfectionists at New
Haven, Conn. in The Perfectionist originally raised the perfectionist questions at Oberlin; they were rejected, but applied
differently in the context of "natural ability." See James
Fairchild, The Congregational Quarterly, p. 238.

33. Brauer, op. cit., p. 179.

34. Garrison was a friend of Noyes. Warfield, op.
cit., II, 331, refers to the Liberator (December, 1839).

35. For general treatments of the antislavery crusade
and the churches, see T. Smith, op. cit., chap. xii; Brauer,
op. cit., chap. xi; G. H. Barnes, The Anti-Slavery Impulse:
1830-1840 (New York: Appleton-Century-Crofts, Inc., 1933),
passim.

36. That the perfectionist mind did not necessarily
lead on to abolitionism is demonstrated by the lively debate
between holiness advocates such as Wilbur Fisk and Bishop
Hedding vs. Orange Scott and Timothy Merritt in the pages
of the Zion's Herald. See ibid., VIII (1837), passim. Scott
was charged with leaving the main "business" of the church
which was "to save souls"; ibid. (February 22, 1837), p. 30;
and with a "manifest exchange of the gospel for politics...";
ibid., p. 32. Fisk in replying to Merritt, ibid. (March 1,
1837), p. 33, prophesied that the issue would "rend the
church." Scott replied to Fisk, ibid. (March 8, 1837), p. 38:
"I despise that time-serving, cringing policy which can sacrifice millions of human beings on the altar of peace; and which
is less affected by the groanings of the prisoner than with a little
excitement and agitation...."

37. See Orange Scott, The Grounds of Secession from
the M. E. Church (New York: Arno Press, 1970 [originally
published in 1848]).

38. Arthur T. Jennings, American Wesleyan Methodism
(Syracuse, N.Y.: Wesleyan Methodist Publishing Association,
1902), pp. 189-90, closely relates the struggle against slavery
with the perfectionist leanings of the Wesleyans. "The essence of liberty," he says, "is found only in perfect conformity to the will of God, hence we find the Connection, early in

its history, adopting an article of faith on the subject of entire sanctification.... The doctrine ... was as much a logical necessity for a church which would be free from bondage
to their fellow man as any logic ever noted among men."
Also see Peters, op. cit., pp. 124-27; Cross, op. cit., pp.
263-267. The holiness emphasis was prominent in the early
conventions and conferences. The "Pastoral Address" to the
Utica Convention in 1843 concluded with it: "But above all,
brethren, we exhort you to make holiness your motto; it is
holiness of heart and life that will arm you against every
assault.... It is holiness that will assure success in our
enterprise.... 'And may the very God of peace sanctify you
wholly.... ' "; "Record of the Wesleyan Convention," original
copy in The Wesleyan Church archives, Marion, Ind. An
article on entire sanctification was also presented to the same
convention but not acted upon; ibid. The General Conference
adopted a statement on the doctrine and sent it to the conferences for approval; it was subsequently placed in the Discipline cast in language strongly favoring a perfectionist
stance; "Record of the Minutes of the Proceedings of the
First General Conference of the Wesleyan Methodist Connection in the United States of America Held in Cleveland, Ohio
... October 2, a.m., 1844," pp. 7, 10, original copy in the
same archives. Mead, The Lively Experiment, confirms the
relationship; "Central," he said, "was the figure of the free
individual.... The perfect individual was the fully free individual.... "

39. See Peters, op. cit., pp. 99-101 and T. Smith,
op. cit., pp. 114ff.

40. Journal of the General Conference of the Methodist
Episcopal Church, 1832 (New York, 1832),

41. Guide, XX (August, 1851), 2.

42. Peck, ibid., pp. 1-7, outlines this progress; ibid.,
p. 3; "The doctrine is preached more than for at any period for
probably the last thirty years, ibid., p. 4. Nathan Bangs,
Prospects and Responsibilities of the Methodist Episcopal
Church (New York: Lane and Scott, 1850), p. 288, confirms
this conclusion: "[The] work of holiness ... [has] revived in
the six or seven years past, more people than before seeking
and finding 'the blessing of perfect love. ' "

43. Guide, LXXVI (July, 1880), p. 11 of "Supplement."
Pascal recorded his experience in these words: "In the year

of Grace, 1654, on Monday 23d of November ... from about
half past twelve, FIRE, God of Abraham, God of Isaac, God
of Jacob, not of philosophers and scholars." Emile Calliet,
Pascal: The Emergence of Genius (New York: Harper and
Brothers, 1961), p. 131.

44. Guide, III (July, 1841), 13; John A. Roche, The
Life of Mrs. Sarah A. Lankford Palmer, Who for Sixty Years
Was the 'Able Teacher of Entire Holiness' (New York: George
Hughes [1898]), pp. 32-33. For further details of her life
see ibid. and George Hughes, Fragrant Memories of the Tues-
day Meetings and Guide to Holiness (New York: Palmer and
Hughes [1886]).

45. See ibid., pp. 10-13; Roche, op. cit., pp. 105-
129; R. Wheatley, The Life and Letters of Mrs. Phoebe Palmer (New York: W. C. Palmer, Jr., 1876), pp. 238-57.
The meeting was a ladies' meeting until 1839. In that year
Professor Thomas Upham, professor at Bowdoin College, was
allowed to attend; thereafter, the meetings were open to everyone. Ibid., p. 238; Roche, op. cit., p. 111.

46. Wheatley, op. cit., pp. 36ff. Wheatley's work is
as much an apology for Mrs. Palmer's teachings as a biography. Her description of her experience reminds one of the
moment of enlightenment of the mystics: "O! into what a
region of light, glory, and purity was my soul at this moment ushered. I felt I was lost as a drop in the ocean of
infinite love, and Christ was all in all." Ibid., pp. 43-44.

47. Ibid., pp. 15-26. For typical summaries of the
"altar theology" see Phoebe Palmer, The Way of Holiness
(New York: Palmer and Hughes, 1867), pp. 52ff.; the same,
"The Act of Faith by which the Blessing Is Obtained and Retained." in J. Boynton, Sanctification Practical: a Book for
the Times (New York: Foster and Palmer, Jr., 1867), pp.
115-130. "We Have an Altar," Guide, XXIII (May, 1853),
158-59.

48. Ibid. (June, 1853), p. 176.

49. Phoebe Palmer, Faith and Its Effects: or Fragments from My Portfolio (New York: Published for the Author
at 200 Mulberry St., 1854), pp. 52f.

50. See Sweet, The American Churches, pp. 110ff.

51. See Beauty of Holiness, VII (January, 1857), pp.

1-3. Also see John L. Peters, Christian Perfection and American Methodism (New York: Abingdon Press, 1956), p. 113, and T. Smith, op. cit. , pp. 126-127. Abel Stevens, Life and Times of Nathan Bangs, D. D. (New York: Carlton and Porter, 1863), pp. 396-402.

52. Beauty of Holiness, VIII (January, 1857), 3.

53. Ibid. , pp. 14ff.

54. See Phoebe Palmer, Incidental Illustrations of the Economy of Salvation, Its Doctrines and Duties (Boston: Henry V. Degen and Son, 1860); she draws directly on Wesley to support her positions on the immediacy of the experience, the distinction between the experiences of conversion and sanctification, when it may be received, its reception by faith, and the necessity for testimony for the retention of the experience. Ibid. , pp. 37-41. Also see Wesley's sermon on "The Scripture Way of Salvation," The Works of John Wesley (Grand Rapids, Mich. : Zondervan Publishing House, n. d.), VI, 53; Wesley says, "If you seek it [entire sanctification] by faith, expect it as you are and expect it now." (emphasis his.)

55. See Wheatley, op. cit. , p. 583: "Neither would she tolerate for a moment the phrase, 'Believe that ye have it, and ye have it. ' "

56. Ibid. , p. 516; also see Palmer, Faith and Its Effects, p. 190.

57. As quoted by Peters, op. cit. , p. 113.

58. Stevens, Life of Nathan Bangs, p. 351.

59. J. Wesley Corbin, "Christian Perfection and the Evangelical Association through 1875," Methodist History, VII (January, 1969), 41, says that her phraseology and methodology were "almost taken as normative...." After 1869, Phoebe Palmer's "altar theology" became the means by which the holiness teaching of the denomination was expressed; ibid. , 39. Abel Stevens recommended it sympathetically in the Christian Advocate and Journal which he edited; see ibid. , XXXIII (December 30, 1858). By this time the Wesleyan Methodists were also recommending Mrs. Palmer's books and utilizing her terminology; see The Wesleyan, XVII (March 21, 1885), 7; "hundreds all over the land are testifying that the altar, Jesus, sanctifies their gift, and the blood of Jesus

Christ cleanseth from all sin." On this terminology the
holiness message was introduced into the mainstream of
European evangelicalism; Record of the Convention for
the Promotion of Scriptural Holiness Held at Brighton,
May 29 to June 7, 1875 Brighton: W. J. Smith, n. d.),
p. 370.

60. Charles E. Jones. Perfectionist Persuasion:
The Holiness Movement and American Methodism, 1867-
1936 (Metuchen, N. J. : Scarecrow Press, 1974), p. 5;
Peters, op. cit. , pp. 112-13.

61. Ivan Howard, "Wesley Versus Phoebe Palmer:
Extended Controversy," Wesleyan Theological Journal, VI
(Spring, 1971), 31-40.

62. Sweet, The American Church, pp. 126-27.

63. Jones, op. cit. , aptly makes this point by
contrasting Charles Wesley's hymn, "Jesus Thine All-
Victorious Love," with Phoebe Palmer's "Cleansing Wave."
The former speaks of the relationship in terms of "Till
... all renewed I am," the latter in terms of "now"
with all verb tenses in the present. See Robert G. Mc-
Cutchan, Our Hymnody: A Manual of the Methodist Hymnal (2nd ed. : New York: Abingdon Press, 1937), pp.
279-80.

64. Byron Ress, Halleluyahs from Portsmouth
Camp-meeting, Number Three: A Report of the Camp-
meeting Held at Portsmouth, Rhode Island, July 29 to
August 8th, 1898 (Springfield, Mass. : Christian Unity
Publishing Co. , 1898), p. 53. Morrison was only re-
peating what R. S. Foster had said in 1851 when he
wrote in his Nature and Blessedness of Christian Purity
(New York: Lane and Scott, 1851), pp. 130-31: "Persons seeking the blessing have been told that they must
believe they are sanctified, and they will be sanctified.
What a misfortune that so great, so dangerous an error
should be taught in connexion with so important a subject. . . . I trust it will no more find place in the language of the friends of this glorious doctrine."

65. Palmer, Faith and Its Effects, p. 104. Corbin, Methodist History, p. 31, notes that already in 1856
the Botshafter, a German holiness periodical of the

Evangelical Association, carried an article by "An Old
Evangelical," which held that the view of the Association
was that those who die without entire sanctification will
be lost. Wm. Nast, the leader of German-American
Methodism in an article of the Catechism of the Methodist Episcopal Church and its teachings sanctification,
commented: "Then to refuse to be cleansed from all filth-
iness of the flesh and spirit, is to imperil one's justification"; see the Christian Advocate and Home Journal,
VIII, No. 41, 321.

66. Richard Watson, The Life of the Rev. John
Wesley, A. M. , Sometime Fellow of Lincoln College,
Oxford, and Founder of the Methodist Societies (New
York: G. Lane and C. B. Tippett, 1847), p. 159. Jack
Ford, In the Steps of John Wesley: The Church of the
Nazarene in Britain (Kansas City, Mo.: Nazarene Publishing House, 1968), p. 228, in speaking of the groups
which formed the Church of the Nazarene in Britain said
that "in all three movements the alternative of 'Holiness
or hell' was sometimes vigorously put.... In so far as
these movements made fear a motive for seeking entire
sanctification they departed from the counsel of Wesley."

67. See supra, p. 30; other than such men as
Abel Stevens and Nathan Bangs, Bishops Matthew B.
Simpson, Willard F. Mallilieu, and John P. Newman, all
testified to the essential soundness of her Methodism;
see Wheatley, op. cit. , p. v; Hughes, op. cit. , p. iv;
and Roche, op. cit. , p. 11. Bishop E. S. Janes tied
it to "the Pauline doctrine of sanctification, as defined
by Wesley...." See the same, Sermons on the Death
of Nathan Bangs (New York: Carlton and Porter, 1862),
p. 27.

68. Hiram Mattison, "Deceived Professors of Sanctification," Christian Advocate and Journal, XXX (August
2, 1855), 121. Mattison's heaviest attack fell three months
later; see ibid. (November 29, 1855), 189. Wheatley,
op. cit. , pp. 93ff. , discusses the controversies and Mrs.
Palmer's reactions to them. She tells of having a terri-
fying nightmare-dream in which he was viciously attacked
by a lion immediately before the first attack was published. Also see ibid. , 115ff.

69. Guide, XXI (April, 1852), 113; ibid. , XXII

(July, 1852), 5; ibid., XXIII (May, 1853), 153, encourages
the expansion of such meetings in spite of the criticism
of some; ibid., p. 157, gives an account of one in Ves-
try, N.Y., attended by representatives from thirty churches. Ibid. (June, 1853), p. 175, calls for one in Cincinnati; also see ibid., XXIV (October, 1853), 126-27; and
ibid., XXV (April, 1854), 125-28.

70. Bishop Newman saw them in this relationship.
Speaking of Sarah Lankford Palmer, he said, "following
the example of the illustrious Wesley, this Christian lady
maintained for years the Tuesday meeting...." Roche,
op. cit., p. 11.

71. Guide, XXI (April, 1852), 112-14, announced
that a Brunswick, Maine "Christian Union" had been
formed for "those desiring a more thorough knowledge
of the theory and experience of Scriptural Holiness...."
Jesse Peck, then president of Dickenson College, Carlisle,
Pa., came out with a strong warning against "any organization of the friends of holiness as a distinct work...."
He labeled it "undesirable and highly dangerous." He
said that he was not against special meetings but as far
as holiness organizations were concerned the Methodist
Church was an adequate institution dedicated to those interests. See the same, "To Professors of Perfect Love,"
Guide, XXII (July, 1852), 5-6.

72. Guide, VII (November, 1845), pp. 97-101.
Also see Thomas Upham, "Peculiar Dangers Attending
A State of Holiness, "Advocate of Christian Holiness,
III (July, 1872), 13.

73. Wheatley, op. cit., p. 243.

74. By 1867 both Northern Christian Advocate and
New York Christian Advocate and Journal were commend-
ing her Faith and Its Effects: "The author clearly shows
that it is the will of God that believers should be wholly
sanctified." See Phoebe Palmer (ed.), Pioneer Experiences (New York: [Walter C. Palmer,] 1867), advertise-
ments at end of volume. The pragmatism and practicality
of the "New methods" continued to prove themselves in
the later movement. See a very clear defense of the
terminology and its practical effects in E. F. Walker,
"The Altar Sanctifieth the Gift," Nazarene Messenger,

XIV (March 3, 1910), 2. Walker notes that when the
altar terminology was presented to a group of people
who were seeking holiness "the effect was electrical. At
once victory came to a number of seekers. Thus did
God approve, as he constantly has done, the application
of the text to personal sanctification and most clearly
and emphatically condemn opposition to it." Walker, loc.
cit., claims support of such non-Wesleyan scholars as
Alexander Cruden, William Milligan, and Matthew Henry
to the defense of the terminology. In Ibid., (February
24, 1910), p. 3, he also quotes Dr. Lightfoot in its
defense.

75.   Palmer, loc. cit.

76.   See infra, p. 133.   Stevens, Life of Bangs,
p. 352, commented: "It may indeed be doubted whether
any one occasion of social devotion ... has in the last
twenty years had more profound and wider influence in
favor of the special doctrines of Christian experience
as taught by Methodism.... At no place have those doctrines been more thoroughly and devoutly discussed...."

77.   Ibid.

78.   Supra, p. 2.

79.   Phoebe Palmer's Pioneer Experiences became
the best known of these.   As well known in the later
movement was S. Olin Garrison (ed.), Forty Witnesses
Covering the Whole Range of Christian Experience (Freeport, Pa.: The Fountain Press, 1955 [Reprint of 1888
ed.]).

80.   Wesley's "Plain Account of Christian Perfection," The Works of John Wesley, XI, 399, cautions all
who testify to their religious experience to "avoid all
appearance of boasting." The most complete essay on
the question of Wesley's own direct testimony to a personal experience of entire sanctification is in Peters,
op. cit., pp. 201-215. George Croft Cell, The Rediscovery of John Wesley (New York: Abingdon-Cokesbury Press,
1946), p. 181, believes that Wesley "must have set an
example of that sharing of Christian experience which he
inculcated in season and out of season upon all his followers and was the dynamic of early Methodism. To

suppose that he stood outside and aloof from the exper-
ience-sharing [emphasis his] into which he labored ende-
fatigably to draw every member, ... would render the
Wesleyan Reformation historically unintelligible." Cell refers particularly to Wesley's Rules of the Band Societies
drawn up in December, 1738. Also see J. Peck, The
Central Idea of Christianity (Boston: H. V. Degen,
1856), pp. 289ff. , for a basic Methodist defense of the
place of public personal testimony. See Jack Ford, op.
cit. , pp. 230-31, for a general summary of the same
in the modern movement.

     81.   The experience of Bishop L. L. Hamline il-
lustrates this emphasis. In early life he had failed to
testify to the experience of entire sanctification; he says,
"For some eighteen months I was like Sampson [sic]
shorn, because I didn't fully confess God's goodness
towards me." As quoted in Walter C. Palmer, Life and
Letters of L. L. Hamline, D.D. (New York: Carlton
and Porter, 1866), p. 101. Hamline advised his ministers to not neglect public testimony. Ibid. , pp. 206-
212. The 1901 General Holiness Assembly at Chicago
encouraged testifying "moderately and unassumingly" but
also warned that the withholding of testimony can lead
to "darkness and relapse." S. B. Shaw (ed.), Echoes
of the General Holiness Assembly Held in Chicago, May
3-13, 1901 (Chicago: S. B. Shaw Publisher [1901]), p.
32.

     82.   See Phoebe Palmer (ed.), Pioneer Experiences,
pp. vii-viii; she defends the strong emphasis on testimony by calling on men from the non-Methodist camp
such as Matthew Henry and Dr. Thomas Scott. The latter is quoted: "I likewise learned the use of experience
in preaching, and was convinced that the readiest way to
reach the hearts and the consciences of others was to
speak from my own!" Ibid. , p. vii. Bishop Latimer is
also called as a witness.

     83.   Mead, The Lively Experiment, p. 136, says
that the nation was given over to pietistic emphases on
experience with a strong holiness appeal. He quotes Bushnell, who spoke of a heart secure from "speculations of
the philosophers and the literati"; loc. cit. The more
the movement became inbred, the less caution was given
to "bold" testimony; e. g. , one can note a difference in

tone and semantics between the testimonies as published
in the Guide, passim, and those in the Revivalist, published by Martin Wells Knapp, one of the founders of
the Apostolic Holiness Union and Prayer League. See
God's Revivalist and Bible Advocate, XIII (September 9,
1901), pp. 4-5. This is an ever-present danger in pietistic groups. See Emil Brunner's caution on the Oxford Movement in Sangster, Methodism Can Be Born
Again, p. 54. This pietistic emphasis exerted a strong
influence on the psychology of William James according
to Sperry, op. cit., p. 152. Sperry says: "The importance which he attaches to experience ... matches an
emphasis which is wholly familiar to us. Admission to
membership in most of the congregationally ordered denominations has always traditionally seated upon the can-
didates ability to give satisfactory proof of his own spiritual state."

84.   Wheatley, op. cit., p. 61.

85.   Melinda Hamline wrote to Phoebe Palmer from
Mt. Pleasant, Iowa, December 30, 1864: "Both our
preachers here receive subscriptions for Guide and Beauty.
I have written to many friends abroad to enlist them in
this good cause." "Hamline-Palmer Letters," Drew University Manuscript Collection, Madison, N. J.   Also see
Walter C. Palmer (ed.), The Life and Letters of Leonidas L. Hamline, D. D. (New York: Carlton and Porter,
1866).

86.   Wheatley, op. cit., p. 252.   Janes, op. cit.,
p. 27, says that Bangs, during his "late years" presided
over the Tuesday Meetings.   Also see Matthew Simpson
(ed.), Cyclopedia of Methodism (Philadelphia: Everts and
Stewart, 1878), p. 86.

87.   Phoebe Palmer recorded in her "Diary," Oc-
tober 27, 1844: "Dr. Olin now enjoys the blessing."
Quoted by Wheatley, op. cit., p. 244.   Also see the
Methodist Quarterly Review, XXXIII (1851), 654.   Ibid.,
XXXVI (1854), 17-18.

88.   Wm. McDonald said that Wilbur Fisk was
sanctified and lay five hours under the power of the
Holy Ghost under a sermon preached by Timothy Merritt.
E. Davies, Illustrated History of Douglas Camp Meeting

(Boston: McDonald, Gill and Co., 1890); also see Simpson, op. cit., p. 363; ibid., p. 285.

89. Cf. Palmer, Pioneer Experiences, p. vi; Wheatley, op. cit., pp. 196-98, 247, 248, 250; and Beauty of
Holiness, VIII (December, 1857), 364, for the interdenominational influences of the Tuesday Meeting.

90. Wheatley, op. cit., pp. 238-39. Phoebe Palmer had made a vow that if the Lord would sanctify Upham, she would make it a special subject of praise. Upham testified that in response to that vow he considered
himself "consecrated and pledged forever!" Ibid., p. 241.
See complete statement on his experience in Garrison,
op. cit., pp. 226-36.

91. Wheatley, op. cit., pp. 66-67, indicates Mrs.
Palmer first met Belden and Hill at a camp meeting:
she described the two ministers, then still Presbyterians,
as "flaming torches filled with the Spirit." In 1844 both
men were deposed from the Poughkeepsie, N.Y. presbytery. They then became Congregational pastors, although
Hill died soon thereafter. Cf. also ibid., pp. 578-79;
Guide, XX (January, 1847), pp. 5-6; Divine Life (July,
1879), pp. 12-13. The Rev. J. A. Wood, later one of the most
prominent men of the National Camp Meeting Association, took
his ministerial apprenticeship under William Hill.

92. See's volume on Christian Holiness, The Rest
of Faith (New York: W. C. Palmer, 1871), was reviewed
in the Guide, LX (July, 1871), 35.

93. Levy joined "the sanctificationists," as he once
called them, while he was preparing a sermon to oppose
them. When he informed a deacon in his church of his
intention, the layman replied, "I think any minister has
mistaken his calling when he preaches against anything
that has for its only object the making of people better."
Adam Wallace (ed.), A Modern Pentecost: A Record of
the Sixteenth National Campmeeting for the Promotion of
Holiness Held at Landisville, Pa., July 23 to August 1st,
1873, (Philadelphia: Methodist Home Journal Publishing House,
1873), p. 201. Levy also claimed to have been instrumental in having Charles Wesley's holiness hymn, "Love Divine," with its phrase, "take away the bent to sinning,"
placed in the Baptist Hymnal, ibid., p. 72. Levy was
pastor of the Berean Baptist Church.

94. Guide, LXXV (March, 1880), 94; The Christian Standard and Home Journal, VIII (September 6, 1874), 311.

95. Palmer, Pioneer Experiences, p. vi.

96. Wheatley, op. cit., p. 57.

97. Phoebe Palmer, "Meetings for Holiness--Sectarianism," Beauty of Holiness, VIII (December, 1857), pp. 364-65. Mrs. Palmer sometimes used a verse to express her hopes for Christian unity:
"Names and sects and parties fall,
And Christ alone is all in all."
See Wheatley, op. cit., pp. 197-98.

98. Beauty of Holiness, loc. cit.

99. Ibid., p. 365.

100. Ibid.

101. Ibid.

102. The institutionalization of the revival particularly in the second generation tended to create a "turning inward" and isolationism. Timothy Smith, Called Unto Holiness: The Story of the Nazarenes, the Formative Years (Kansas City, Mo.: Nazarene Publishing House, 1962), p. 297, notes that "the denominationalism which the founders [of the Church of the Nazarene] thought inappropriate for men seeking a reformation of American Christianity became for their successors the hallmark of orthodoxy."

103. E.g., faith healing, prudentials of Christian life and conduct, millennialism.

104. Wheatley, op. cit., p. 254. See Phoebe Palmer, "A Laity for the Times," ibid., pp. 554-57, for a full treatment of her views. See T. Smith, Revivalism and Social Reform, pp. 66, 80ff. Orr, op. cit., pp. 95ff.

105. Howard Grimes, "The United States: 1800-1962," in Stephen Charles Neill and Hans-Ruedi Weber (eds.), The Layman in Christian History: a Project of the Department of the Laity of the World Council of Churches (Philadelphia: The Westminster Press, 1963), p. 240; Grimes notes that

exceptions must be made for "Lutheran bodies, ... Roman
Catholicism [and] ... Eastern Orthodoxy; ibid.

106.   Ibid. , pp. 245-46.

107.   Ibid. , p. 166.   William Arthur's Tongue of Fire
or the True Power of Christianity (New York: Harper and
Brothers, 1880) is one of the most reasoned treatises in the
movement on the characteristics of the Spirit-filled church.
He says on this point, "A church wherein, from the pulpit
down, every man in his order ... is called to exercise his
gift ... can alone answer to the New Testament ideal of a
Church." Ibid. , pp. 128-49.   Also see ibid. , p. 87: "The
greater should never attempt to extinguish the less, and to
reduce the exercise of spiritual gifts within the limits of the
public and ordained ministry.   To do so is to depart from
primitive Christianity."

108.   E. g. , see Ladies Repository, XXVI, No. 5, 66,
et passim, for Mrs. Palmer's involvement in social work,
particularly in New York City.   T. Smith, Revivalism and
Social Reform, pp. 169-73. gives an excellent summary of
these; Mrs. Palmer, through her own projects and participation in those of others, took a place of leadership in such
agencies as The New York Female Assistance Society for the
Relief and Religious Instruction of the Poor, and more particularly in the founding of the Five Points Mission.   Smith
indicates that the latter represents the beginnings of Protestant institutional work in the slums.

109.   Tyler, op. cit. , pp. 424-62.

110.   See Phoebe Palmer, The Promise of the Father,
or a Neglected Specialty of the Last Days (New York: Foster
and Palmer, 1866); Lewis R. Dunn. The Gospel in the Book
of Numbers (New York: Hunt and Eaton, 1889), pp. 264ff.;
Dougan Clark and Joseph H. Smith, David B. Updegraff and
His Work (Cincinnati, Ohio: Published for Joseph H. Smith
by M. W. Knapp, Revivalist Office, 1895), pp. 219-26; all
these deal with the question on this premise.   The subtitle
of Palmer's book speaks directly to it; the "last days" were
upon them; the Holy Spirit was inspiring both the "sons and
the daughters."   See also the Beauty of Holiness, XI (July,
1860), p. 379, "Women Prophesying," a column of news items
on women who were speaking out in the churches of Europe
and America.   William A. Clebsch, From Sacred to Profane
America: The Role of Religion in American History (New
York: Harper and Row, 1968), p. 192.

111. Bernard Watson, A Hundred Years' War: The
Salvation Army, 1865-1965 (London: Hodder and Stoughton,
1964), p. 30, says that Mrs. Booth was so stung by a Methodist paper's attack on Phoebe Palmer that she wrote the
first of her numerous pamphlets on the subject of women's
ministry and their rights to preach the gospel. See Orr,
op. cit., p. 121; however, in her own account of how she
began to preach she said that her husband had been urging
her to do it for ten years and that she had had strong im-
pressions to do so since she had been fifteen or sixteen
years of age; Catherine Booth, Aggressive Christianity (Boston: McDonald and Gill, 1883), pp. 126-32.

112. Amos P. Mead, Manna in the Wilderness: or the
Grove and Its Altar (Philadelphia: Perkinpine and Higgins,
1860), p. 242. Advocate of Bible Holiness, I (August, 1882),
on the inside of the back cover carried the notice of "A
Holiness Compmeeting, LED PRIMARILY BY WOMEN
of the Various Christain Denominations, who believe in EN-
TIRE SANCTIFICATION as a distinct work...."

113. William B. Godbey, The Woman Preacher (Atlanta:
Office of the Way of Life, n.d.), p. 12.

114. Jasper Abraham Huffman, History of the Mennonite
Brethren in Christ Church (New Carlisle, Ohio: Bethel Publishing Co., 1920), pp. 150ff.; Everck Richard Storms, History of the United Missionary Church (Elkhart, Ind.: Bethel
Publishing Co., 1958), p. 251. Storms says that one out of
every eight churches in the denomination was started by women preachers. Ibid., p. 253.

115. H. C. Morrison, "Editorial, The Church of the
Nazarene," Pentecostal Herald, XI (January 25, 1899), 8.

116. Seth Cook Rees, The Ideal Pentecostal Church
(Cincinnati, Ohio: Revivalist Office, 1897), p. 41.

117. The American Lutheran Church was among the
latest to grant full ministerial rights to women. See "Lutherans Ask New Standards," Chronicle-Tribune [Marion,
Ind.] (October 6, 1972), p. 11. The Methodists gave full
rights to women ministers in 1956. Exactly seventy years
before that, Bishop Gilbert Haven, a "holiness" bishop, had
written in the "Introduction" to Maggie Van Cott's The Harvest and the Reaper: Reminiscences of Revival Work (New
York: N. Tibballs and Sons Publishers, 1876), p. xix, that
women should have such full rights although he did not expect

many of them to exercise them. He held up Susannah Wesley as an example, within Methodism, who had exercised
practically every ministerial right except that of the pulpit
in assistance to her son, John; "her silver treble" chimed
in with "his manly bass." He chided Adam Clarke, the Methodist Biblical commentator, for allowing such rights to women
in his exegesis and then qualifying it in its application in order to throw "a sop" to the men whom he may have offended.
"Offset the demon Woodhull with the saintly Palmer and Van
Cott," he cried; ibid. , p. xxvi. It was "time," he said, "to
fight fire with fire." Mrs. Van Cott was licensed by a local
church; she evangelized extensively.

118.   Wheatley, op. cit. , p. 257; see an almost identical statement in the Beauty of Holiness, VIII (December,
1857), 365.

119.   Hughes, op. cit. , p. 16. Mrs. Palmer exercised
this principle in her sharp judgment of Professor Upham,
who, she felt, was becoming too mystical in his writings on
holiness. Warning him about the implications of his thoughts
on "Divine Union," she said: "Surely the excellency of a
religious experience is only to be treated by conformity to
the Word of God." Wheatley, op. cit. , p. 522.   Bishop
Matthew Simpson had had some fears that Mrs. Palmer may
have "imbibed something of that mysticism which affects
Madame Guyon." Wheatley, op. cit. , p. v.   But he found
that "her constant effort was to persuade friends to trust ...
the simple Word of God. This preserved her, on the one
hand, from wild fanaticism, and on the other from the depths
of mysticism." Ibid. , p. vi.

120.   This was true to the Methodist tradition. See
Umphrey Lee, The Historic Backgrounds of Early Methodist
Enthusiasm (New York: Columbia University Press, 1931),
chap. vi, "Methodist Enthusiasm."

121.   One of the largest groups in the movement, The
Salvation Army takes a position very similar to the traditional
Quaker position. Milton S. Agnew, Manual of Salvationism
(n. p. : The Salvation Army, 1968), p. 61, says, "It is the
Salvation Army's firm conviction that the ceremonies commonly known as 'the sacraments' are not necessary to salvation nor essential to spiritual progress...." Religion is
spiritual and inner and "in spirit and in truth." The revival
elements of the movement were strongly affected by this.
Even George Hughes, the Methodist editor of the Guide, could

ask, "Is it right to deprive a congregation for twelve Sabbath mornings in a year to hold sacramental services?"; ibid. , CIII (November, 1898), p. 158. The Mennonite elements in the movement favored foot washing; see Walter L. Fleming, "The Religious and Hospitable Rite of Feet Washing," Sewanee Review, XVI, No. 1, pp. 1-13; especially see p. 11 on the River Brethren and the Brethren in Christ who were part of the holiness movement.

122.   Advocate of Christian Holiness, XI (April, 1880), 77-78.

123.   Hughes, Fragrant Memories, p. 39   See Guide, XXIII (May, 1853), 156-57; ibid.   (June, 1853), 175; ibid. , XXIV (October, 1853), 126-27; ibid. , XXV (April, 1854), 125-28, for the spread of the Tuesday Meeting's influence.

124.   Hughes, Fragrant Memories, p. 40.

125.   Raymond J. Corsini and Bina Rosenberg, "Mechanisms of Group Psychotherapy: Process and Dynamics," in Group Psychotherapy and Group Function, ed. Max Rosenbaum and Milton Berger (New York: Basic Books, 1963), pp. 340-48.   Jerry Sproul used the above to study the Methodist class meeting. The same, "The Methodist Class Meeting: a Study in Its Development, Dynamics, Distinctions, Demise, and Denouement," (Unpublished Master's thesis, Asbury Theological Seminary, 1967).   Also see J. L. Morento (ed.), Sociometry Reader (Glencoe, Ill. : Free Press, 1960), pp. 15-16, et passim.

126.   Guide, XXIII (May, 1853), 156-57; the same, VII (December, 1857), 364-65. Wheatley, op. cit. , pp. 238-57. This has been a common result of such small spiritual groups. W. E. Mann, Sect, Cult, and Church in Alberta (Toronto: University of Toronto Press, 1955), pp. 3-4, observes that two premiers of Alberta had been active members of the small Prophetic Bible Institute. Neill and Weber, op. cit. , p. 165, also take note of this phenomenon in the "spiritualist" tradition of the sixteenth and seventeenth centuries in European Protestantism.

127.   Hughes, Fragrant Memories, p. iv.

128.   Bishop John P. Newman, "Introduction," Roche, op. cit. , p. 10. Also see Janes, op. cit. , p. 27.

129. See chap. iii. The problems were not uniquely American or limited to the Palmer Movement in Methodism. See the dispute at this point between Karl Barth and Emil Brunner over Buchman's Oxford Movement in Sangster, Methodism Can Be Born Again, pp. 52-53. Barth felt they could not be integrated. Brunner felt they could be.

130. Supra, pp. 1-3.

131. Guide, I (July, 1839), 23.

132. Jones, op. cit., p. 19. Hughes, The Beloved Physician, p. 259; the same, Fragrant Memories, pp. 167ff. Publication was finally discontinued in the fall of 1901.

133. A Phonographic Report of the Debates and Addresses together with the Essays and Resolutions of the New England Methodist Centenary Convention Held in Boston, June 5-7, 1866 (Boston: B. B. Russell Co., 1866), pp. 159ff., "Report on Committee of Statistics," Rev. D. Dorchester, Chairman.

134. W. E. Arnold, A History of Methodism in Kentucky (Louisville: Ky.: Herald Press, 1936), I, 310.

135. Sweet, Methodism in American History, p. 254 Also see Orr, op. cit., p. 11; Olmstead, op. cit., p. 90.

136. Sweet, op. cit., p. 340; Gaddis, op. cit., pp. 375-76. Gaddis probably reads too much of the trends of post-war Methodism into the pre-Civil War Period. See ibid., pp. 384-97.

137. E. A. Hagen, Salvation to the Uttermost (Lansing, Mich.: Darius D. Thorp, Printer and Binder, 1892), p. 40.

138. Smith H. Platt, The Gift of Power: or the Special Influences of the Holy Spirit, the Need of the Church (New York: Carlton and Porter, 1856), p. 95. Platt felt that the tendency toward stationed rather than itinerant ministers was isolating local congregations in the face of increasing social evil, leaving each one to fight alone; the danger was great enough "to prevent us from preserving our ancient purity."

139. George Peck, "Christian Perfection," Methodist Quarterly Review, XXIII (January, 1841), p. 123. Ibid. (April,

1841), 307: "The discussion of the subject of Christian Perfection ... is a matter of no small interest to the church of
Christ in general."

140. See supra, n. 42. Also Palmer, Life and Letters
of Hamline, pp. 184, 207. The question of the evaluation of
spiritual activity in the churches is such a relative one that
one consistently meets very contradictory conclusions concerning the revival activity at any given period. See Paul
A. Carter, The Spiritual Crisis of the Gilded Age (DeKalb,
Ill. :   Northern Illinios University Press, 1971), pp. vii-ix;
expecially note the statement of William R. Hutchison to the
author concerning the religious faith of the end of the century: "Faith was both growing and declining; the point is to
figure out the special form (if any) in this age, of perennial
paradox." Ibid. , viii. The same may probably be said of
the 1840's and the revival of holiness.

141. A review of the Zion's Herald during this period
reveals the tensions mentioned above, n. 140. A letter to
the editor in ibid. , VIII (January 25, 1837), 13, asks "why
so few of our vast church have experienced this work [entire
sanctification] ... ?" But in ibid. (February 8, 1837), p.
21, L. Pierce writes that "the time is not far distant when
the cry will become general in the ministry and the membership, 'O Lord,' cleanse me from all sin.'" A similar review
of Zion's Herald for 1849-1850 reveals the same contrast.
The editor, Abel Stevens, consistently carries reports of
revival of interest in holiness; yet these first-page reports
are followed by an editorial decrying the fact that "revivals
are occasionally reported, but they are seldom, and seem not
to be extensive and profound." Ibid. , XX (September, 1849),
134. Articles on entire sanctification in the Christian Advocate and Journal appeared in increasing numbers especially
during the Revival of 1858, e. g. , ibid. , XXXII (February
18, 1858), 25; ibid. (March 18, 1858), p. 41; ibid. (April
8, 1858), p. 53; ibid. (May 13, 1858), p. 72; et passim.

142. George Peck, The Scripture Doctrine of Christian Perfection (New York: G. Lane and P. P. Sanford,
1842). Simpson, op. cit. , p. 698.

143. Jesse Peck, The Central Idea of Christianity (Boston: H. V. Degan, 1856). Simpson, op. cit. , pp. 698-99.

144. Randolph Foster, Nature and Blessedness of Christian Purity (New York: Lane and Scott, 1851). Simpson, op.
cit. , pp. 371-72.

145. Beauty of Holiness, VIII (May, 1867), p. 154.

146. For a concise summary of these controversies see Peters, op. cit. , p. 122, and T. Smith, Revivalism and Social Reform, pp. 127-29.

147. Journals of the General Conference of the M. E. Ch. , 1848-1856 (New York: Lane and Scott et. al. , 1848-1856), p. 160.

148. Guide, XXX (January, 1859), 31.

149. B. T. Roberts, Why Another Sect: Containing a Review of Articles by Bishop Simpson and Others on the Free Methodist Church (Rochester, N. Y. : "The Earnest Christian" Publishing House, 1879), p. 91.

150. In addition to Roberts, op. cit. , see F. W. Conable, History of the Genesee Annual Conference of the Methodist Episcopal Church, 1810-1872 (New York: Nelson and Phillips, 1876), pp. 618, 620-21, 635-36; Ray Leslie Marston, From Age to Age a Living Witness: a Historical Interpretation of Free Methodism's First Century (Winona Lake, Ind. : Light and Life Press, 1960). Simpson, op. cit. , pp. 379-80; it was Robert's reaction to Simpson's Cyclopedia article on the Free Methodists which prompted him to write Why Another Sect. Ibid. , pp. 15-21.

151. Supra, p. 22.

152. See T. Smith, Revivalism and Social Reform, p. 113.

153. Thomas C. Upham, The Christian Experience of Thomas C. Upham, D. D. (of the Congregational College, Brunswick, Maine, America) in Reference to Entire Sanctification and the Full Assurance of Faith (Liverpool: W. Sanderson, 1858), is a pamphlet relating his experience; the copy at Drew University is personally autographed to Dr. and Mrs. Walter Palmer. Also see Advocate of Christian Holiness, XI (April, 1880), pp. 76-78.

154. Thomas C. Upham, The Life ... of Madame Guyon. See reviews: Henry T. Cheever, "Life and Writings of Madame Guyon," The Biblical Repository and Review, IV (October, 1848), 608-44; and George Peck, "Upham's Works," Methodist Quarterly Review, XXVIII (1846), 248-65. Peck's

article, loc. cit. , also reviews other books by Upham: Principles of the Interior or Hidden Life ... (New York: Harper
and Brothers, 1854 [originally published in 1843]); The Life
of Faith ... (Boston: n. n. , 1847 [originally published in
1845]); Life of Madame Catherine Adorna ... (New York:
Waite, Pierce and Co. , 1845); later came his Treatise on
Divine Union ... (Boston: Charles H. Pierce & Co. , 1852).
He also published a book of poems, Christ in the Soul (New York:
Charles H. Pierce, 1872).

155. See Cell, op. cit. , chaps. iv and v, for a summary of Wesley's stance in regard to the Catholic mystics
and mysticism. Wesley "acquired his interest in Christian
perfection from [them] ...," ibid. , p. 113, but accepted
the state and goal only, not the means. "Among all of Wesley's antagonisms in religion [antinomianism, predestination,
etc.] the opposition to mysticism is easily the strongest...."
Ibid. , p. 117; this in spite of some modifications in later
life. Regardless of this strong Methodist tradition, the New
York Christian Advocate and Journal defended Upham's perfectionism and recommended his works to Methodists; see
"To Ministers and Others. Upham--Faith--Perfect Love,"
ibid. , XXXIII (September 23, 1858), p. 149. J. Agar Beet,
Holiness, Symbolical and Real (London: Robert Culley, 1910),
pp. 167-68, agreed that there was a "profound agreement"
and "a similarity of phrase" between Madame Guyon, Molinos,
Fénelon, and Wesley, which "suggests that he learned this
great truth of holiness, in part, from them." Dean Inge's
conclusion in W. R. Inge, Mysticism in Religion (Chicago:
University of Chicago Press, 1948), final chapter, that
"Blessed are the pure in heart" is the essence of religion
is also instructive here. The goal was Christian perfection
and thereby the relationship between the Mystics and American perfectionism was established. See also Anne Freemantle (ed.), The Protestant Mystics (London: Weidenfeld
and Nicolson, 1964); she includes Wesley and Hannah Whitall Smith in the book. Stephen Hobbhouse, Wm. Law and
18th Century Quakerism (London: George Allen and Unwin,
Ltd. , 1927), also has a good section on Wesley and Law's
mysticism--chap. xi.

156. Wheatley, op. cit. , pp. 518-523. Nevertheless,
she herself had had a mystical experience described in ibid. ,
pp. 96ff. Of it she said, "I never felt before in such blessed
unity, the unity of Godhead.... No voice issued but love--
infinite love. " Thus the unio mystica of the Catholic mystical tradition in its evangelical expression through a faith

experience rather than a scala sancta filtered into American
experience just as it had into the Pietists' beforehand.

157. Harriet Beecher Stowe, "A Review of The Interior Hidden Life," Guide, VII (May, 1845), p. 114.

158. Ibid. , pp. 114-15.

159. Guide, VIII (September, 1845), p. 49-51; ibid.
(October, 1845), 73-76; ibid. , IX (January, 1846), 6-7. Upham undoubtedly was reading Arndt differently from what Warfield did below. The former was reading him existentially
as a man who had come through an experience of sanctification similar to his own. Arndt was "testifying" to him from
his heart "as the 'father of Pietism,' who transformed the
doctrine of the Word, as Luther understood it, into an ethical doctrine, and thereby changed the experience of justification into one of sanctification." As quoted by Stoeffler,
op. cit. , p. 203, from R. Friedman, Mennonite Piety
Through the Centuries (1949), p. 24. This is a good example of the necessity for using Stoeffler's concept of an experiential tradition in any analysis of the development of American pietistic churches.

160. Benjamin B. Warfield, Perfectionism (New York:
Oxford University Press, 1931-1932), II, 373, ibid. , 342;
Warfield concludes that it was all "just Wesleyan doctrine...."
Ibid. , p. 360. Ronald Knox, Enthusiasm: a Chapter in the
History of Religion with Special Reference to the XVII and
XVIII Centuries (New York: Oxford University Press, 1961),
pp. 235-38, also claims that Upham misread Madame Guyon
completely. Both missed the experiential tie which existed
between them in the "emphasis on inner identification with
God." Stoeffler, op. cit. , p. 15, says this is why mysticism
infiltrated Pietist ranks. See Flew, op. cit. , p. 277.

161. Beauty of Holiness, VIII (February, 1857), 48.

162. Henry T. Cheever, "Life and Writings of Madame
Guyon," The Biblical Repository and Review, IV (October,
1848), 608-609.

163. Ibid. , pp. 610-11.

164. Ibid. (January, 1848), pp. 84-85.

165. William E. Boardman, The Higher Christian Life
(Boston: Henry Hoyt, 1858).

166.   Jacob J. Abbott in a negative review of The Higher Christian Life in Bibliotheca Sacra and Biblical Repository, XVII (July, 1860), pp. 508-35, ridicules the optimism and the sense of expectation which the book exudes. "The air and tone told us all along ... that the author was almost beside himself under the inspiration of a new and extraordinany discovery which he was trying to make known." Ibid. , p. 511. "His theory claims to be a new and grand discovery, the time having come now for this morning star of the millennium to rise." Ibid. , p. 529. Regardless of Abbott's feelings, the mood of the book was much closer to the mood of the day than his own.

167.   Warfield, op. cit. , II, 465, attributes the rise of the whole "Higher Life" revival to its influences. That statement is too broad in that Warfield was not well informed on the work of the Palmers, but it does reveal the impact of the work. Warfield, loc. cit. , quotes Mark Guy Pearse on the importance of Boardman's book: "[It was] perhaps the first popular treatise on the subject that has won its way among all denominations; and its vast circulation, both in America and England, not only melted the prejudice of hosts against the subject, but made it possible for other writers to follow in the paths which he opened...." Mrs. William E. Boardman, Life and Labors of the Rev. W. E. Boardman ... (New York: D. Appleton and Co. , 1887), p. 105, gives her own rather enthusiastic account of the demand for the book.

168.   Ibid. , 136-37, 156-60.

169.   See A. B. Earle, Bringing in the Sheaves (Boston: James H. Earle, 1870), for an account of his revivalism. Chap. xviii defends his union meetings; chap. xxviii, "The Rest of Faith," outlines his own religious experience.

170.   See continuous flow of reports in Beauty of Holiness, VIII (1857), passim; the New York Christian Advocate and Journal, XXXIII (October, 1858), 161.

171.   See, e. g. , Zion's Herald, XXI (February 6, 1850), p. 18.

172.   Infra, p. 112ff.

173.   Orr, op. cit. , p. 62.   A report from Canada says, "The whole of 'Faith and Its Effects' was published in successive numbers of the Christian Guardian, the official organ

of the Church. Her other works were scattered broadcast
through every part of our country.... The popularity of these
works ... created ... an earnest desire to become personally
acquainted with their author." Beauty of Holiness, VIII (November, 1857), 321. Ibid. (September, 1857).

174. Beauty of Holiness, VIII (December, 1857), 366.

175. Ibid. , p. 368.

176. See T. Smith, Revivalism and Social Reform,
chap. iv, for an account of the 1858 Revival, often called
the Layman's Revival because of the dominance of a rising
lay leadership. For the relationship of the financial panic
of 1857 and the course of the revival, see Timothy Smith,
"Historic Waves of Religious Interest in America," Annals
of the American Academy of Political and Social Science
(1960), No. 332, pp. 9-19. Olmstead, op. cit. , p. 90, says
that "the revival of 1858 bore powerful indications of the influence of perfectionist doctrines...." T. Smith, Revivalism
and Social Reform, p. 69, notes that the revival "evoked support from Old School Presbyterians, Episcopalians and even
Universalists and Unitarians." E. g. , The Church Journal,
the Episcopalian High Church paper, urged revival methods
upon its pastors because people were not attending services
which were not "manifestly ... of a character more or less
extraordinary.... Crowds will everywhere attend a definite
series of special services when no persuasion will get them
to come to Daily Prayer." [emphasis theirs]. As quoted
by the New York Christian Advocate and Journal, XXXIII
(March 25, 1858), 46. Also see Wm. C. Conant, Narratives of Remarkable Conversions and Revival Incidents ...
(New York: Derby and Jackson, 1858); John Hall (ed.),
Forty Years' Familiar Letters of James W. Alexander, Con-
stituting with notes a Memoir of His Life ... (2 vols.; New
York: Scribner, 1860); James Waddell Alexander, The New
York Pulpit in the Revival of 1858: a Memorial Volume of
Sermons (New York: Sheldon, Blakeman and Co. , 1858);
James Waddell Alexander, The Revival and Its Lessons (New
York: Anson D. F. Randolf, 1859). The Christian Advocate
and Journal for 1858 carries especially interesting accounts
of the revival and commentaries by Nathan Bangs and others
on its implications for the Wesleyan doctrine of Christian
perfection. See ibid. , passim.

177. See Wm. W. Bennett, A Narrative of the Great
Revival which Prevailed in the Southern Armies ... (Phila-

delphia: Claxton, Remsen, and Haffelfinger, 1877); J. William Jones, Christ in the Camp, or Religion in Lee's Army (Richmond, 1887); Harrison W. Daniels, "A Brief Account of the Methodist Episcopal Church South in the Confederacy," Methodist History, VI (January, 1868), 34. A. B. Earle, the Baptist evangelist, continued his meetings throughout the war; see Earle, op. cit., pp. 100-106, 187-97.

178. The divided house which existed among Methodist holiness adherents in the New England Conferences (see pp. 20-21) also existed elsewhere. Alfred Cookman and John Inskip, both founding members of the post-war National Camp Meeting Association for the Promotion of Holiness, stood for a time on opposite sides of the antislavery debate in the church. Cookman favored antislavery legislation in the church. Ridgaway, op. cit., pp. 218-21. Inskip "felt averse to the discussion of slavery by ecclesiastical bodies...." That was 1844; by 1858, he was calling himself "a thorough abolitionist...." Wm. McDonald and John E. Searles, The Life of Rev. John S. Inskip, President of the National Association for the Promotion of Holiness (Chicago: The Christian Witness Co., 1885), p. 49; ibid., p. 130.

179. Walter and Phoebe Palmer, Four Years in the Old World Comprising the Travels, Incidents and Evangelistic Labors of Dr. and Mrs. Palmer in England, Ireland, Scotland and Wales (New York: Foster and Palmer, Jr., 1867), is the most complete account of the Palmers' efforts. Orr, op. cit., pp. 62-77 et passim, is a more modern English account of the revival. Strangely enough, Orr admits to having little information available to him on the Palmers themselves. Ibid., p. 12. See Orr, op. cit., p. 121. B. T. Roberts, still smarting from his own battles with the Methodist Episcopal establishment, noted that the English Wesleyan Methodist Conference of 1861 called on its superintendents to keep the Palmers out of their chapels, and that the Conference of 1862 prohibited "all continuous revival services by visitors from America or elsewhere; President Prest ... reprobated the spirit, teaching, and services of Dr. and Mrs. Palmer as being fraught with immense mischief to the interests of Methodism." The Earnest Christian, IV (December, 1862), 185. The Palmer Meetings were often called "Evangelical Alliance Revivals." See Palmer, Four Years in the Old World, p. 105; Orr, op. cit., p. 63. Caughey also took part in this revival during the American war years. Orr, op. cit., p. 73. The opposition was not so strong as it had been earlier when the English Methodists had complained to

the American Methodist Episcopal Church in an official letter
"against the unofficial visits of American ministers to the
European Connection." "Methodism in Earnest," Zion's Herald, XXI (March, 1850), 37. For a brief summary of Caughey's earlier English revivals (1841-1847) see Daniel Wise,
"Sketch of the Life of Rev. James Caughey," James Caughey,
Earnest Christianity Illustrated; or, Selections from the Journal of the Rev. James Caughey ... (Boston: J. P. Magee,
1855), pp. 9-19. Also see James Caughey, Methodism in
Earnest: Being the History of a Great Revival in Great Britain ..., ed. R. W. Allen and Daniel Wise (Boston: C. H.
Pierce, 1850).

180. Orr, op. cit., pp. 58, 71, 103, passim; Ford,
op. cit., p. 29.

181. F. de L. Booth-Tucker, The Life of Catherine
Booth, the Mother of the Salvation Army (New York: Fleming H. Revell Co., 1892), pp. 117-23, 343ff. "Prejudice
and lordly usurpation" may be limiting the "sphere of women's
religious labors," and imposing "restrictions upon the operations of the Holy Ghost." Ibid., p. 22. Also see supra,
p. 42.

182. The Salvation Army in one of the largest and most
active bodies in the Christian Holiness Association whose annual meetings bring together representatives of the holiness
denominations and other holiness institutions.

183. Finney, Memoirs, chap. xxxv; Beauty of Holiness,
XI (December, 1860), 379; Orr, op. cit., pp. 47-66.

184. Orr, op. cit., p. 81, says 200,000 members were
added to the English Methodist Churches alone; but the Baptists and Congregationalists gained even more. Orr attributes
this to the fact that neither of them "troubled to pass resolutions of exclusion against free lance revivalists." Loc. cit.
This may explain, in part, why the Keswick or non-Methodist
holiness movement became the more dominant force in England and Europe. Orr concludes that the Roman Catholic
Church was the only English religious body unaffected by the
revivals; ibid., p. 125. However, see Palmer, Four Years
in the Old World, p. 663; the Roman Catholic Church at Wal-
sall along with the revival churches and the Church of England announced special services continuing daily for four weeks
with five services every Sunday. A Catholic revival bill declared: "A mission is a message from ... God to His people

to put them in mind that 'one thing' is necessary, ... the
salvation of their souls.... What must I do? ... I must
prepare to make a good confession. 'Behold now is the accepted time; now is the day of salvation' "

CHAPTER III

1867-1877: THE POST-WAR HOLINESS REVIVAL

REVIVAL AND THE AMERICAN DREAM

Abraham Lincoln's prayer at Gettysburg for a new
birth of freedom for the American nation helped to establish
the post-war mood.   William Clebsch concludes that "a
cleansed nation now greeted this worldly, millennial dawn
for which all history had been preparing."[1]   For some, this
"millennial dawn" became the occasion for unscrupulous ven-
tures into materialism--a quest for individual wealth and the
power which polarized around it.[2]   To many others, however,
the deep religious overtones of Lincoln's own concerns were
a new challenge to begin again on the American utopian dream.
It was a perfectionist dream which involved an optimistic
anticipation of individual, national and world redemption which
would usher in a Christian millennial order.   The bustling
activity in every area of national life provided a ready ration-
alization for the bitterness of the recent conflict; it was a
catharsis for four years of fevered illness.   These post-war
aspirations were "palpably religious, for in most cases they
appealed to a divine vocation laid upon Americans through
their peculiar experiment in human freedom."[3]

This religiously oriented dream of national destiny
was already firmly fixed in the American mind in the perfectionist revivalism of pre-war years.   In 1856 Nathan Bangs
regarded America's "future greatness and consequent responsibility" as,

> a pleasing acticipation to the believing Christian
> and the zealous patriot, of the rising glory of our
> country, and the important part she is to take in
> the emancipation of mankind from the thralldom of
> sin.[4]

96

If the Christians of his day would persist, he said,

> in striving after pure and perfect love ... they
> may look forward ... and joyfully anticipate the
> day when the knowledge of the Lord shall cover the
> earth.... [emphasis his][5]

This dream of the divine restoration of man and his world
has lived in most movements which have emphasized the work
of the Holy Spirit. Bangs' sentiments could be duplicated
again and again from the literature of the revival movement
from 1840 to the end of the century. In his Sermons, Speeches
and Letters on Slavery and Its War, Bishop Gilbert Haven,
also a strong proponent of the need for holiness revival in
Methodism, forsaw the same remedy for the pressing problems of the nation and "the nations";

> Let Christ abolish sin from your souls ... Labor to
> make all other hearts equally perfect. Strive to
> bring the laws of society into subjection to His
> control.... Root up the gnarled tusks of prejudice ...
> toil cheerfully ... to bring in the Grand Sabbatic
> Year.... [6]

This prevailing mood, as it was projected by such
perfectionist advocates, was bound up with a secular cast
provided by the growing materialism and humanism. This,
by the end of the century, was to produce a tragic gap in
society between barons of wealth and the masses of the poor
as well as an earthward turn of mind which looked less to
transcendental roads to the "Grand Sabbatic Year" and more
to innate power of man to gradually perfect his own state.
Darwinism, developmentalism, and a mystique of progress-
ivism were all seething in mid-century America in what
Martin Marty calls the "metaphysics of Progress."[7]

The tenor of it all strongly permeating post-war
American society provided fertile soil for holiness revivalism.
Holiness advocates were aware of this although they often
expressed the issues in more negative tones. In response to
a charge that the sense of urgency which characterized the
movement was only an annoying "hobby," the editors of the
Beauty of Holiness replied that

> it is high time that all concerned should wake up
> to the idea that the spread of Scriptural holiness
> is the only thing that can save the church from

utter apostacy.   Indeed it is the only instrumentality that can save the world from ruin. [8]

    The triumph of holiness constituted the instrument of
the world's salvation in each of the references noted above;
the last one, however, carries the seeds of the apocalypticism
which tended to become increasingly prominent in the movement as the century wore on, expecially as pre-millennialism
became generally dominant in American evangelicalism. [9] This
element kept dwelling on the first step of the perfectionist
formula as expressed by both Bangs and Haven--the sanctification of the indivdual to save the church from apostacy.
A second group, out of the same perfectionist visions, fastened on to the hope for societal redemption which interlaced
these mid-century dreams.   The eventual result was the development of the social gospel. [10]   Each element carried off
with it a part of the dream of perfectionist revivalism into
the twentieth century.   The adoption of pre-millennialism
allowed the holiness movement to live with its postponed dream.
Prevailing optimism, centered in progressive and evolution-
ary activism, buttressed by technological progress, fed the
hopes of the social gospel.   Two majoy world wars and modern technology "made perfect" in atomic destruction were to
bring both up short.

The Rise of the National Camp Meeting Association

    As noted above, the four years of the war dampened
the revival interest which had been fanned into a blaze so
shortly before the start of the conflict. [11]   The "Pastoral
Address" of the Methodist bishops to the 1864 General Conference decried a loss of spirituality in the church and called
for revival.   Even before its formal ending, however, signs
of the renewal which was coming were breaking out across
the north.   In April of 1865, while Lee and Grant were holding their fateful rendevous at Appomatox Court House, Methodist Episcopal papers were reporting spiritual awakenings
all through the church.   The editor of the Western Christian
Advocate, Dr. J. M. Reid, wrote that within the circulation
area of his paper, mainly Indiana, there had been eleven
thousand, four hundred and ninety four converts in a six
weeks period. [12]

    The enthusiasm which the Palmers and Caughey, fresh
from unprecedented revival activities in England, brought back
to the war-weary nation the year before the "stillness at
Appomatox" added impetus to renewal. [13]   The expanding cir-

culation of the Guide to Holiness and the Beauty of Holiness,
now combined under the Palmers' editorship, broadcast the
success of their English missions.

The rapid expansion of organized meetings for the
promotion of holiness also helped to generate growing interest in the doctrine. The 1865 issues of the Guide and Beauty
contained long lists of these; most of them were held in the
larger urban centers, and in many of those, at several loca-
tions. [14] New York, Philadelphia, and Boston were the homes
of the Palmers, the Inskips, the Levys and the McDonalds.
The fact that the holiness movement began and for two generations was fostered mainly in the larger urban centers of
the northeast raises serious doubts about the common gen-
eralization that this movement attracted chiefly the poorer
and uneducated classes.

New leadership: John S. Inskip

The Rev. John S. Inskip was one of the leading young
pastors of the Methodist churches in New York City at the
end of the war. His sometimes critical attitudes toward the
special efforts to revive the experience of entire sanctification in his denomination up until 1864 scarcely predicted any
possibility of the central leadership role he was to play in
the post-war revival. They were not atypical of the feelings
of many another Methodist pastor at that time: "his denominational pride led him to tenaciously contend for the doctrine,
while he virtually discarded the experience." [15]

In 1832, while a student at Dickinson College in Carlisle, Pennsylvania, he appears to have accepted the doctrine
and briefly professed the experience. He attributed his loss
of that new life to his "failure to confess frankly what God
had done for him...." Again in 1853, now a Methodist pastor, he testified to an experience similar to that of his student days; but for the second time, he felt that a lack of
public confession of it dissipated its effects on his life. [16]

For the next twelve years his interest in the higher
life movement centered mainly in complaints against those
who presumed to actively promote it within the church. In
Methodism Explained and Defended, published in 1851, Inskip
acknowledged the Methodist doctrine of "the more excellent
way." [17] However, he charged many of the higher life advocates in the church with being "wild and deluded enthusiasts,"
full of "practical inconsistencies." This type of holiness

adherent, he maintained, could not "endure the least contradiction, [but] in the most uncharitable manner possible pass
judgement upon all who do not happen to be as he is."[18]
His own subsequent demands, once he had moved inside the
movement, for discipline and moderation, together with the
policy of avoiding public controversy over any personal criticism directed against the members of the National Committee
may have been influenced by these early concerns.

Martha Inskip was the critical agent in her husband's
religious turnabout in 1864. Dissatisfied with the level of
her Christian experience, she went to the Methodist camp
meeting at Sing Sing, New York in August of 1864, with the
definite intention of finding a more stable and satisfying inner
life. On Friday, August 19, 1854, she claimed "the blessing" by consecration and faith in the manner taught by the
Palmers. The spiritual erraticisms of his wife greatly "af-
flicted and mortified" the rising young minister.[19]

From that time, however, his anti-perfectionist stance
began to weaken. The desire for "more religion," "a deeper
work of grace," and a "baptism of the Spirit" began to appear
in his diary. The convincing manner in which Mrs. Inskip
related the effects of her camp meeting experience to a
prayer meeting congregation in his church, pressed him further; the occasion, he wrote, was a "glorious" one.[20]

Only nine days after his wife's spiritual crisis, John
Inskip confessed his own complete commitment to the religious
experience urged upon the church by the holiness advocates.
On Sunday morning of August 28, 1864, the "South Third
Street pastor" was strongly exhorting his congregation with
a vigor even beyond that for which he was commonly noted;
his text was Hebrews 12:1. He urged his hearers to consecrate their lives totally to God. With Methodistic enthu-
iasm, he exhorted:

> Brethren, lay aside every weight! Do it now.
> You can do it now, and therefore should do it. It
> is your privilege and therefore your duty at this
> moment to make a consecration of your all to God,
> and declare you will henceforth be wholly and for-
> ever the Lord's.[21]

In these terse phrases, Inskip captured the essence of the
synthesis of American revivalism, Wesleyan perfectionism,
and even evangelical pietism which formed the heart of the movement.

He later asserted that while he was emphasizing the
<u>now</u> and the need for immediate, personal commitment, that
a voice within him seemed to say, "do it yourself!" He
hesitated; the voice said again, "Do it yourself, and do it
now." Calling upon his members to follow him, he made
his way to the altar rail at the front of the chancel of the
Methodist church; surrounded by his parishoners, he cried
out, <u>"I am, O Lord! wholly and forever thine!"</u> [emphasis
his.]22

Too much must not be read into or out of this account
of John Inskip's personal espousal of the holiness cause.
But, in the attempt to trace out the development of the movement, the record left by him at the time does merit comment;
one may note here many of the emphases which put Inskip
in the Palmers' succession; he in turn, during the next twenty
years, deepened the impression of these on the movement as
a whole. The urgency of the now, the call for entire commitment, the provision become a duty, all were already part
of revivalistic holiness preaching. They called for the Christian to fix his attention on Christian perfection and seize it
by faith at any cost.

Very soon thereafter, Inskip attended the holiness
meeting at the Palmer's home; he told the group of his recent experience. The next day, he visited the Palmers to
invite them to hold special meetings for the promotion of
holiness in his church. Later in reviewing that visit, he
admitted that his "mind had been prejudiced against the efforts made by a few ... to keep this flame alive in [the]
church." He knew the doctrine was "of God. But their
manner of promoting it," he confessed, was "a rock of of-
fence." "It pleased God, however, to reveal his grace to
me...." he concluded. 23

Inskip was destined to general the main forces of that
post-war movement in its challenge to the churches to recognize not only the validity of the Palmers' call to holiness,
but also the necessity for a broader response to that call;
this alone could guarantee the reform of the church, the
nation and the world. The changes which the new phase was
to bring would be, in the main, advances or enlargements
upon the new promotional methods of the earlier phase. The
intimate Tuesday Meetings in the parlor, became "National
Camp Meetings" with their clouds of dust or seas of mud
stirred by the feet of the thousands in attendance; the informal lay emphasis fostered by the Palmers as lay leaders was

to be overshadowed by the more formally organized efforts
of the ardent ministerial advocates who maintained a loosely
structured, but tight control over the movement for thirty
years after the way.

The winsome, yet urgent appeal of personal testimony
in the earlier parlor meetings which invite men of widely
differing creedal stances to personal dialogue on the deeper
Christian life was often to be replaced in the approaching
camp meeting promotion by a more polemical, definitively
dogmatic proclamation of the doctrine in terms which tended
to become stereotypes. At its extremes this zeal lent itself
to the appearance of driving men into an experience of perfect love with the naked alternatives of holiness or hell. Beulah Land was often lost sight of.

The terms, the theology, the process would not change
significantly from that of the Palmer period, but the tone and
the tempo would vary. Furthermore, in spite of the best
efforts of sincere leaders, the irregular meetings which
spurred on the revival tempo as that leadership began to lose
its grip on the movement were to encourage the irregularity
of schism. Here were the beginnings of the conflicts which
eventually led to the reorientation of loyalties for thousands
of Methodists and members of other established churches.

These proponents of Christian perfectionism developed
a sense of homelessness as the popularization of church membership, through the very success of revivalism itself, brought
masses into the American churches for the first time in the
nation's history. As Franklin Littell points out, "converts"
were often received into the Christian fellowship without a
sense of Christian commitment and without concern for the
basics of Christian life, much less a higher Christian life;
these masses had little time for spiritual zealots who in their
puritanism and pietism insisted that the church was a fellowship of believers and Christian experience comprehended every
aspect of a man's existence. [24]

Furthermore, the theological tolerance which the more
intimate atmosphere of the smaller group meetings could practice without diversion from the main issue also suffered in
the midst of larger meetings and the later institutionalization
of the revival; differences of terminology were to become
points of issue as Calvinist and Methodist wings of the movement began to define the higher life more definitively within
the context and terms of their own theological biases.

All of these trends and potentialities were there in
embryo in John Inskip's expression of his own mind and experiences as he turned himself without reserve to the holiness cause.   It was a holiness crusade which participated in
all the strengths which other moral crusades in America have
generated by the unswerving dedication of their members to
the achievement of an all consumming goal; it also shared
in many of the weaknesses which result from the tendency to
create imbalance of view and misunderstanding and intolerence
of those who do not see the issues in so narrow a framework.

The strengths and the weaknesses tended to show their
full potential in this movement which was not alone a crusade
against the evils of alcohol or other social ills which have
often caught the attention of a particular group; this was a
crusade against the last vestiges of evil itself in the hearts
of men.   Holiness revivalists sought to redeem them from
that inner evil and bring them to the possibilities of the grace
of Christian perfection; this would restore the power of primitive Christianity to the churches and through them the Holy
Spirit would redeem the whole of mankind.   It was, at heart,
a reexpression of enduring Christian faith, in the adequacy
of divine grace for the complete moral redemption of men
now; but that expression was often clothed with the accoutre-
ments of its nineteenth-century milieu.

Inskip joined the "revival" in the closing months of
the war.   He had served as a chaplain in the Northern Army,
but he now confessed that he was excited "very little" by the
dying struggle.   After his August 28 experience, he wrote:

> I am interested in the government of my country
> ... nevertheless, I do not feel myself particularly
> called to that work: my business is of a different
> character entirely....   This business will occupy
> all of my time and call out all my energies. [25]

Vineland: the first National Camp Meeting

A brief notice in the Philadelphia Public Ledger, "Local
Affairs" section for Thursday, June 27, 1867, carried news that:

> a meeting of Methodist ministers from New Jersey,
> New York, Baltimore and of this city, was held a few
> days since at 1018 Arch Street, and it was agreed
> to hold a camp meeting at Vineland, New Jersey
> commencing July 17th. [26]

The Methodist ministers who met at Philadelphia on
June 13th, were there in response to a call to help to plan
a camp meeting, "the special object of which should be the
promotion of the work of entire sanctification."[27] This concept of devoting an entire ten-day camp to the preaching of
that doctrine was undoubtedly as unique to the camp-meeting
tradition as the men who met seemed to consider it to be.[28]
Special services in camp meetings had sometimes been set
aside for particular instruction on the experience, but never
had it been made the central goal of the entire meeting.

A conversation between the Rev. J. A. Wood and Mrs.
Harriet Drake of Wilkes Barre, Pennsylvania, in August 1866,
had sparked the June 13, 1867 meeting which planned the
Vineland National camp meeting. While the two were traveling to a small camp near Red Bank, New Jersey, Rev. J. A.
Wood had observed that the holiness cause often was ignored
or ridiculed in the camp meetings of the day. In response,
his parishoner, a member of one of the leading families in
her home community, offered to pay for half of the expenses
for a camp meeting devoted especially to that cause if one
could be arranged. During the Red Bank camp, John Wood
relayed the concern to Rev. William B. Osborn, an ardent
supporter of holiness doctrine within Methodism in southern
New Jersey; the latter carried the idea to John Inskip at his
New York church. Inskip received the suggestion enthusiastically and prepared for the June meeting in Philadelphia.[29]

The men who conceived this "new method"[30] for holiness promotion were well-known pastors in their home conferences in the New York and Philadelphia areas of the Methodist Episcopal church. Rev. A. E. Ballard, a presiding
elder, was active in the planning. Dr. George C. M. Roberts,
Baltimore, Maryland, served as president of the ad hoc committee. Rev. J. A. Wood, Wilkes Barre, Pennsylvania pastor, suggested that the special camp be held at Vineland,
New Jersey from July 17 to July 26. Rev. Alfred Cookman,
revered by the church for his piety and irenic spirit,[31] wrote
out the call for the camp, addressed to the "friends of holiness,"[32] which appeared in the church and secular press.
It invited

> all, irrespective of denominational ties, interested
> in the subject of the higher Christian life, to come
> together and spend a week in God's great temple
> of nature.[33]

The call to this "National Camp Meeting for the Promotion of

Holiness" was careful to point out that although the meetings
would seek for the conviction and conversion of sinners, its
special object would be

> to offer united and continual prayer for the revival
> of the work of holiness in the churches; ... to
> strengthen the hand of those who feel themselves
> comparatively isolated in their profession of holi-
> ness; ... to realize together a Pentecostal baptism
> of the Holy Ghost--and all with a view to increased
> usefulness in the churches of which we are mem-
> bers. [34]

The call for the Vineland camp produced a reaction
indicative of the mixed fortunes of the movement in the Methodist Episcopal churches in the summer of 1867. The old
fears for the unity of the church first raised two decades before by a friend of the movement, Jesse Peck, and later by
many others less sympathetic to it, were resurrected in the
face of this most dramatic suggestion for special holiness
promotion. Appeals were made to Presiding Elder Ballard
to withdraw his sanction of the special camp meeting. Like
Peck before them, these Methodists still looked upon their
church itself, as a great holiness church. Its declared purpose was the proclamation of Christian perfection and they
saw little need for these urgent special measures within the
church structure. Many of them took affront at any such
intimations of the declension of the purpose or the effectiveness of the denomination. [35]

These critics failed to turn the mind of the Vineland
committee, however; the latter seemed to be confident that
they were advancing a theme whose time had come. They
appear to have been convinced that there was a special desire in the land for a deeper spiritual answer to the problems the post-war nation was facing; and that Methodism, in
particular, because of her high pretentions, was the first to
require renewal. Statements from the upper echelons of the
church's leadership reinforced their concerns. In 1866 during Methodism's centenary year, Rev. John McClintock, one
of the church's most respected scholars, had warned American Methodism that the measure of its success was its dedication to the preaching of holiness. "And that," he urged,
"in the face of any who would choose to call it 'fanaticism'."
He concluded that this was Methodism's "glory; ... [and]
power ... and there shall be the ground of our triumph. [36]

The critics of the special efforts were correct in

looking on the Methodist Church as a holiness church; that
was its commitment and message.   But the "friends of holiness" proved to be equally correct in maintaining that there
was something lacking in the response of that church and
others to the rising tide of demand for a quality of Christian experience beyond that which the revivalism of the past
hundred years had produced in the church.   They shared
deeply in the national sense of expectancy released by the
change from war to peace.   For them the proposed meeting
at Vineland promised to serve as an effective new measure
for advancing Christian experience and preparing the people
of the nation for whatever personal and collective challenges
the realization of that expectation might produce. 37

        Thousands of people poured into Charles Landis's
model town in the pine flats of southern New Jersey, for the
beginning of the Vineland camp on July 17, 1867. 38   Crowded
trains stopped at the Cape May Railroad station; long lines
of buggies thronged the roads which led to the forty-acre
public park on the edge of town which served as the camp
site.   Overnight the town's population swelled to almost double its 10,000 regular inhabitants as hundreds of tents sprang
up around the speaker's stand on the camp ground.   For ten
days the campers listened to sermons and exhortations on
the theme of Christian holiness by members of the organizing
comittee and Bishop Matthew Simpson.   The camp closed
with the observance of the Lord's Supper.   The meeting had
more than met the expectations of the organizers.   The Philadelphia Public Ledger's earlier prediction that the camp
meeting would be the largest ever held in the area was accurate. 39   The enthusiastic pastor of the Spring Garden Methodist Episcopal Church of Philadelphia wrote to his sister
that it "had only one disadvantage--it made every other service seem tame by comparison."40

The organization of the National Association

        The enthusiastic response to Vineland led to the de-
mand that another special holiness camp meeting be held the
following year.   During the meeting of a committee called
for that purpose at the close of the Vineland camp, the decision was made to create the National Camp Meeting Association for the Promotion of Holiness. 41   Its object was "to
glorify God in building up the church in holiness and saving
sinners."42   The nature of the almost impromptu inception
of the organization and the fact that it operated without a
constitution or by-laws for the three decades during which it
was most influential in the holiness movement, both left their

own impact on the movement.   It was publicized widely that
the organization had been born while the committee was on
its knees in prayer and the idea had come not through any
human planning but by the inspiration of the Spirit. [43]   This
example of non-structure and Spirit guidance combined with
the consequent success of the association, often set a pattern
for the approach of holiness groups to the organization of
meetings, rituals of service, and institutional planning as
well.   There was a consistent tendency to keep definition of
organization and duties loose and fluid.   Tensions frequently
arose between the strong commitment to openness, to spiritual
leadership, and the necessity for some kind of human initiative
in programming and, above all, internal discipline. [44]

        This formation of the National Camp Meeting Associ-
ation for the Promotion of Holiness in Vineland, after the
close of the camp there, marks the formal opening of a new
phase of activity and influence for the movement within the
American churches and evangelical Christianity around the
world.   John S. Inskip was chosen as president of the new,
loosely structured, but extremely durable, organization of
Methodist ministers dedicated entirely to holiness revivalism.
Its leadership in the movement was practically unquestioned
for the next fifteen years.   Its structure was a significant
prototype in the organization of American evangelism.   It
was possibly the first team of revivalists working jointly in
extended revivalistic efforts in the history of modern evangelism.

Manheim and Round Lake: the success of the
"new methods" for holiness promotion

        Six hundred tents dotted the camp ground near Man-
heim, Pennsylvania at the start of the second National Camp
Meeting in the summer of 1868.   Alfred Cookman, to whom
the Association had given the responsibility of selecting the
site for the camp, had decided to engage these grounds in
Lancaster County, Pennsylvania for the camp because of his
own familiarity with that area.   Representatives had come to
this "Pennsylvania Dutch" country from most of the states
of the union.   More than 300 ministers and 25,000 other
attendants crowded into the camp area for the Sunday services.
Twelve thousand pressed around the preaching stand to hear
the morning sermon by Bishop Simpson.   A reporter noted
that, "the weather was oppressively hot; dust was abundant,
water scarce, and board most miserable. "[45]

        The Manheim meeting was significant to the American

holiness revival, not only because of the large crowds who
gathered there, but also because of the interdenominational
influences. In one of the meeting tents Presbyterians, Methodists, Baptists, Dutch Reformed, Congregationalists, and
Quakers all gave testimony to a common experience of a work
of God in their hearts which knew no denominational distinctions. The site of the camp was central to the churches of
the Evangelical Association, already strongly conditioned by
Methodist influences in their early history. A renewed emphasis on Wesleyan perfectionism in the denomination followed
Manheim through the influence of the large numbers of Evangelical Association ministers and laity who attended the meetings. Reuben Yeakel, prominent editor and leader of the
holiness movement in the Evangelical Association, says that
the National Camp Meeting Association rescued camp meetings in America and "the result [of Manheim and successive
meetings] was a great improvement in holding and conducting
camp meetings through the Evangelical Association beyond
her borders. "[46] The Wesleyan perfectionist views which
were beginning to develop in small segments of the Mennonite
people of the area of eastern Pennsylvania also received new
impetus from the camp. [47]

The National Camp at Manheim ranks as one of the
largest convocations in American nineteenth century religious
history, perhaps the greatest in number of attendants at a
single meeting until the Moody-Sankey revivals which followed
it by a decade. In these holiness meetings the extreme physical manifestations which had marked the first Great Awakening and the early camp meeting movement, were almost non-
existent; nevertheless, the atmosphere was packed with emotion, typically Methodist enthusiasm, and spiritual expectancy.
As two thousand people bowed in prayer after a sermon by
the Rev. John Thompson on Monday afternoon, Dr. G. W.
Woodruff began to pray aloud,

> when, all at once, as sudden as if a flash of light-
> ening from the heavens had fallen upon the people,
> one simultaneous burst of agony and then of glory
> was heard in all parts of the congregation; and for
> nearly an hour, the scene beggared all description. . . .
> Those seated far back in the audience declared that
> the sensation was as if a strong wind had moved
> from the stand over the congregation. Several in-
> telligent people, in different parts of the congrega-
> tion spoke of the same phenomenon. . . . Sinners

stood awestricken, and others fled affrighted from
the congregation.[48]

The people were convinced they were "face to face with
God."[49]

Although the leaders of the National Committee always
took special note of the presence of members, particularly
ministers of other denominations at the meetings, the difficulties of ordering so diverse a crowd of non-Methodists as
appeared at the Manheim encampment may have given them
second thoughts about the possible complexities of setting up
and administering their own camp meetings; there was also
the additional concern that too much broadening of the movement might carry them too far into an irregularity of program
which could excite further reaction from their already vocal
critics in the Methodist Church. Subsequent to the 1868 camp,
the members of the National Association, therefore, decided
to take their holiness ministry only to regular Methodist camp
meeting grounds upon invitation from the local camp meeting
administrators.[50] Furthermore, since the members of the
association were full-time pastors, the summer vacation times
which they devoted to those efforts did not allow time for both
evangelism and the organizational details involved in administering camps teeming with thousands of campers and visitors.

The 1869 camp was held at Round Lake, New York.
Spiritual response still ran at full flood. Although the Committee had stipulated that no trains should be run to the camp-
site on Sunday, no less than twenty thousand people were reported to be on the grounds. Bishop Peck was there and
preached "a most powerful sermon."[51] Following the Bishop's sermon, one of the ministers present declared:

> I am glad that I was not born before I was ... I
> have a big programme before me for I begin to
> see how God is going to spread His work by the
> instrumentality of a holy church.... This is a
> wonderful meeting. It seems I could afford to
> stay out of heaven for this. This meeting has
> rolled the world a hundred years towards the millen-
> ium.... This is the outflow of heavenly influence,--
> God's great Amazon,--which is to flow around the
> globe. Let the nations make way for the coming
> of God.[52]

The remark was typical of the optimistic enthusiasm which

often swept the crowded camp grounds. These happy participants gave further proof of the persistent belief within the
movement that the rising holiness revival was sweeping the
world toward the dawn of the millennium with quickened pace.
Even close-communion Baptists were carried along by the tide
and shared in the closing communion service conducted by
Bishop Simpson. [53]

The American Camp Meeting and the
Special Promotion of Holiness

American church historians who contend that revivals
and camp meetings were fading in influence in the religious
life of America after the Civil War have been challenged to
reconsider their thesis as the full extent of the national and
worldwide enlargement of Christianity in the latter half of
the nineteenth century comes into clearer historical focus.
Actually, both revivalism and camp meetings were both very
much alive and drowing. As Timothy Smith points out, they
had moved from rural to urban American. [54] In spite of a
continual undercurrent of doubt on the part of some as to
their further usefullness[55] and questions as those which Hor-
ace Bushnell raised concerning the quality of the Christian
life which their methods produced[56] there was no slackening
of the revival pace. [57]

If camp meetings were not fading out as a religious
institution, many of them were changing, nevertheless. The
changes were disconcerting to those who looked upon these
gatherings as the main evangelistic arm of the church, particularly the Methodist Church. To these individuals such innovations as the Chautauqua program of popular education, patterned after the camp meeting idea, but varying from its
spiritual purposes, represented a radical departure. [58] This
deviation was not so alarming, however, as was the inclination to make camp meetings as much recreational as evangelistic centers. To those who were already fearful for the
quality of Christian piety within the church this represented
another step backward--a concession to an increasingly non-
committed church membership. Harper's Weekly took note
of the changing conditions as 1873 summer camp season
approached:

> The fervent Methodists are all through the month
> of August holding their camp meetings. Near the
> great cities their once primitive assemblies have

> changed their form.   The camp is sought for its
> sanitary as well as religious advantages....   Boat-
> ing, bathing, fishing, have a place with religious
> worship in the round of occupations. [59]

The use of camp meetings for holiness promotion

Such changes in some camps, together with the out-
right opposition to, or neglect of, specific promotion of the
doctrine of entire sanctification in others, concerned the
leaders of the post-war Methodist revival.   Their decision
to utilize the institution as a special instrument for the promotion of holiness was a significant factor in the continued
growth of the American camp meeting as an evangelical instrument.   Indeed, the American camp meeting movement became
dominantly a higher life movement thereafter.   Many existing
camps and the hundreds of new, specifically holiness, camps
which the movement spawned all across the country became
centers of holiness evangelism. [60]

When one reads the history of the movement it becomes evident that a more suitable instrument for such evangelism than the open air meetings of the camp meeting groves
could scarcely by conceived.   The wedding of the two was
another step in the specialization of the promotion of the
holiness which makes up so large a part of the development
of Christian perfection in America.   Through the institution
of the camp meeting, then mainly Methodist dominated and
well established, though never recognized in the Discipline of
the church, the holiness revivalists were able to get their
message out to larger numbers of church and non-church
people than otherwise ever would have been possible in the
face of the opposition which developed within the structure of
the churches themselves.

The pre-war evangelism of the Palmers in the camps
of Canada and the United States had already proven the potential for holiness work in such summer gatherings.   As has
already been noted, the glowing success of their ministry in
Canadian camps in the summer and fall of 1857 had marked
the first signs of the 1858 Layman's Revival in the United
States and its counterparts in other parts of the world, especially England.

Shortly before her death in 1874, Phoebe Palmer had
had to remind George Hughes, one of the leaders of the National Camp Meeting Association of this history.   His review

of the first five years of the promotion of holiness cause
through camp meetings held especially for the purpose, Mrs.
Palmer indicated, drew too dark a picture of the fortunes of
the cause and the pre-war relationship of the doctrine to the
work of Methodism's camps. She charged that the contrasts
were drawn much too sharply to suit the facts. Her editorial
went on to note that pre-war editions of the Guide had carried frequent reports of camp meetings which had served as
centers of holiness promotion, not by special design, but
because of the place of the doctrine within Methodist tradition
and preaching. She further pointed out, that as early as
1853, she had observed that "the Spirit had never before
been so largely poured out upon the churches." It was this
history, she added, which had prepared the way for the obvious success of the National Camps in which she too rejoiced. [61]

Post-war life and the post-war
camp meeting

        The continued effectiveness of the camp meeting after
the Civil War as an instrument for holiness revivalism was
probably abetted by the milieu of post-war American life.
Little has been said about the relationship of these outdoor
tented grounds and the potential nostalgia related to other
encampments, under other circumstances, which undoubtedly
attracted many war veterans and their families to the country
groves. The families who "roughed it" through a ten-day
camp meeting may have heard many a tale of camps at Vicks-
burg, Harper's Ferry, Richmond, or even Andersonville.

        The American view of nature, one of the dominant
ideological patterns in the development of American history,
also clearly played its part in the camp meeting mystique.
Nature was "a splendid system of signs."[62] American society
was also still a rural one--tied to the open sky, the trees,
the earth. [63] The growth of large camps, close to urban
centers, attended mainly by residents of rapidly expanding
cities supports this. When the editors of the holiness journals
called these people to come,

        away to the tented grove! Away from the busy
        scenes, from the din and conflict of earthly strife!
        Away to the place of holy convocation.... [64]

most of the people to whom they were appealing were city
residents who had either recently left their rural homesteads
or older residents who still maintained strong ties with rural

residents and friends. The camp meeting was the time to
annually renew these relationships. A camp meeting advocate
wrote long before the post-war rush to the cities that "without some such meeting, the members of a large city church
will, to a great extent, remain strangers to each other and
though they might be seated side by side in heaven, would
need the angel Gabriel to give them an introduction." He
noted further that given such surroundings it was easy to see
the campers became "one happy family."[65] Charles Jones
concludes that "to the nostalgically satisfied believer, fellowship in the suburban camp meeting communities seemed like
reaching Beulah Land."[66]

The strong and enduring relationship between the camp
meeting and the holiness groups was not only due to their
historical use in Methodism and the rural posture of American life, however; just as important to the union was the
easy meshing of the setting of the meetings and the transcendental and spiritual elements of the theology and experience
of perfectionism. They were convinced that the same God
who created and controlled the natural settings in which they
met was also able to order their inner lives in a way which
would create a world of peace and harmony. The introduction to a book of camp meetings sermons observed that,

> there is a peculiar charm about camp meetings.
> We worship in God's great Cathedral, in nature's
> magnificent temple, arched over with brilliant
> heavens, and floored with beautiful green earth--
> under the foliage of the trees planted by God's own
> hand. There is a kind of grandeur about such a
> temple that accords with man's own noble origin
> and lofty destiny [emphasis mine]. [67]

Andrew Manship, frequently engaged in Methodist camp
meetings of the Civil War period, reported to the Christian Advocate and Journal, in 1858 from a camp meeting he was attending
that

> the stately trees afford a delightful shade; the beau-
> tiful vallies [sic] that environ the "holy mount" af-
> ford places suitable for the members of the Church
> in the wilderness to "steal away awhile" for secret
> prayer. The numerous springs and running brooks
> were well calculated to remind us of the well of
> salvation and the "springs that never run dry."[68]

The "noble origin and lofty destiny" of man and the "springs

that never run dry" were dominant themes in holiness message; they blended easily and effectively with the natural
setting of this semi-urban revival of the frontier camp.

The "Church in the wilderness" concept also carried
special meaning with it. Many of the campers did not feel
fully at home in their home churches, particularly those in
the cities; their enthusiastic holiness promotion often struck
a discordant and lonely note in the fellowship of urban congregations moving toward more liturgical patterns of worship.
As Jones has pointed out, the holiness revival was strongly
based among the people who were migrating from rural to
urban centers in the latter half of the nineteenth century. The
camp meeting was more like the church "back home." "The
camp meetings encouraged the non-liturgical, subjective bent
of American Methodist worship...."[69]

The campers met in God's free fields; there was room
to breathe and room to move. As has been noted above, the
extreme physical demonstration of the early frontier camps
and revivals was generally absent; however, traditional Methodist enthusiasm was commonly expressed. In defense of
such spiritual zeal, the Methodists reminded their detractors
that "you could not endure to see men laboring to save im-
mortal souls from unending death with the cool gravity of a
Turk sipping coffee."[70]

Camp meeting experience could range all the way from
the high emotionalism of a whole congregation, one moment
on its feet waving handkerchiefs in ecstatic praise, and the
next lustily singing as it marched around the tabernacle, to
the awesome solemnity of a midnight communion service with
a thousand communicants.[71] Musical selections ranged from
the staid hymn to the latest revival song; the musical accom-
paniment may have been by "professor Mitchell, educated in
music in Germany and now filled with the Holy Ghost in Rhode
Island," or by an "old colored brother" who "rattled a tam-
borine in a most marvelous way."[72] The campers also
tolerated such typical camp meeting eccentrics as a "Crazy
Elisha," "Shouting Harris,"[73] or the little Jewish convert who
showed up year after year in his black mohair suit, poking
every piece of litter on the camp ground with his long, ever-
present umbrella and challenging every minister he could
corner with his superior knowledge of the Bible--usually successfully.[74] The whole, at times, constituted a "glorious
confusion."[75] At camp, the evangelist and the people were
in a community of life and worship which was ordered to
their own religious and cultural commitments. It provided

identity, meaning, and purpose. This milieu was the most favorable one in which the holiness evangelists could find a platform with relative freedom to proclaim their message to the membership of the churches as opposition to the movement increased among many pastors and local congregations. One reporter declared:

> We thank God in these days of ecclesiastical bondage and pastoral despotism there are camp meetings ... , where the children of God can seek, find, and bear witness, to the Scriptural experience of entire sanctification without having their shoulders lashed by self-constituted bosses. [76]

If one allows that the camp meeting freed the worshipper from the lashes of "self-constituted bosses," he cannot allow that there were not any "bosses" at all. A recognized authority figure, be he evangelist or platform manager carrying either charismatic or administrative credentials or both, generally kept a firm, if not dictatorial hand on all activities. The observations of Wallace concerning Inskip at the National Camp at Landisville, Pennsylvania in 1873 are not atypical of the prevailing camp meeting patterns. Obviously giving personal acknowledgment to the charisma of the leader of the National Committee, he said:

> The management is a depositum. Everybody and everything must bow to the control of one master mind. That mind infused by a fervor extraordinary and guided by a supernatural wisdom and power, holds the congregation in a steady unrelaxing grasp. To rebel in any case, is to mar the grand end in view, so far as it relates to the individual and the universal good to be attained [emphasis his]. [77]

The same author notes that the day to day camp life outside of the actual meetings were more obviously regulated by "arbitrary" rules, which made the encampments, "models of management, good order, and the highest social privilege.... Obstinate, or narrow-minded men [who] ... found them too exacting ... [should] either stay away or yield at once and move with the mighty current as it flows onward...."[78]

An account of the daily schedule at the 1875 National Camp Meeting on the Newburgh District of the New York Conferences of the Methodist Episcopal Church lists the typical camp routine. [78]

> The bell rang at five in the morning for the
> benefit of the sleepy.   Half-past five a prayer meet-
> ing was held in the pavilion; after breakfast, at
> eight o'clock, prayer and experience meeting; half-
> past two, preaching from the stand; after tea, a
> six o'clock prayer meeting; and then the closing
> public service at seven o'clock.   At ten the bell
> rang for all to retire. [79]

Only the Holy Spirit could interrupt the regimen.   Rowdyism,
less a threat than in the frontier camps, was not tolerated. [80]

The religious mystique created out of these elements
combined with the psychological and spiritual intensity generated by ten days of direct spiritual exercise was readily felt
by the friends of holiness who annually responded to the summer call to local and national camp meetings.   The air of
the camps sometimes was recognized even by disinterested
observers.   A newspaper reporter gave the following account
of his visit to a Texas holiness camp meeting:

> The increasing years see no diminution of the num-
> bers of so-called holiness people as they answer to
> the roll call of the great annual assembly on the
> thither side of the Brazos....
> Whatever may be said of the beliefs of the
> Holiness people or of their relations to other wor-
> ship, the simplicity of their nature, their profound
> belief in the actual presence of the Spirit of God
> in their midst, the intensity of their piety, and it
> may be safely said the integrity of their lives, make
> them a pleasing study and the hours spent with them
> are profitable ones.   To escape from the arid doubts
> and sneers and materialism of daily life and sit
> among a people who whether in reality or imagina-
> tion walk and talk with God, is, as if one, lost
> in an arid desert, should suddenly find himself on
> the banks of a great river, amid the umbrageous
> shade of laughing trees and the aroma of singing
> flowers.
> The exercises of the first day or two ... are
> devoted to prayers for the appearance of the Holy
> Ghost....   There is hardly a moment when from
> the quivering voice of holy women, grizzely good
> men and even children, the throne of God is not
> dynamited with burning and fiery supplications, all
> of one tenor and one purpose, that of the coming

> of the Holy Ghost. It seems as if heaven could
> not stand the bombardment. "The kingdom of heav-
> en suffereth violence and the violent take it by
> force."
> The Holy Ghost does come or seems to come.
> There is no doubt of the presence of an afflatus,
> weird, powerful and overwhelming. It comes as
> the sound of a mighty rushing wind.... The pre-
> sence lasts for days in a mad, spiritual, but al-
> ways beautiful revel and one so full of bliss and
> rapture and inexpressible glory that, if it be God,
> one day with God is worth a thousand years of
> mundane life.

The reporter concludes:

> To the curious in recondite and abstruse studies
> the phenomena of the Holiness camp meeting is
> worth going a thousand miles to observe.[81]

Few people came a thousand miles to observe the
phenomena of the holiness camp, but many a holiness camper
went a thousand miles, even in the post-war era to attend
and take part in the religious activities. Dr. William Godbey, one of the most prominent holiness evangelists of the
last quarter of the century, tells of his visit to the Texas
camp grounds referred to above, when four thousand tenters
were on the grounds and sixteen thousand people were in attendance at the meetings.[82]

The adoption of the camp meeting by the National Committee as centers of higher life evangelism broadened the
utility and influences of the camps. They became focal points
for personal communication between areas of the movement
which were otherwise out of contact with one another;[83] such
communication became very critical to the progress of their
common cause. The broad spectrum of representation from
practically every state in the country in the first National
Camp Meetings, established a means by which the movement
stabilized around certain pivotal patterns of faith and order
in spite of geographical discontinuity. Traveling evangelists
moved from camp to camp spreading the propaganda of the
cause from point to point; the camp meeting circuit became
more than a round of meetings, it became a communication
and fellowship circuit by which the fluid movement found
coherence and a measure of informal but very effective inter-
group discipline. Timothy Smith, in reviewing a portion of

the later history of the movement in the Church of the Nazarene, the largest of the "camp meeting churches," says:

> Here in the tented grove they [the Nazarene fathers]
> forged the unity, the interdependence, and the com-
> mon front against "worldliness" out of which a new
> denomination was born. [84]

The High Tide of the Revival

The Methodist pastors who formed the National Camp
Meeting Association for the Promotion of Holiness were as
ardent Methodists as they were holiness advocates.   They
were completely honest in their consistent denial that there
was anything schismatic in their adoption of the Methodist
camp meeting for their own special purpose.   They were sure
that here was the most suitable platform for the sounding of
the call to bring that church back to its central message and
the only insurance of its continued blessing and usefulness.
What they were really accomplishing, was to transplant a
revivalistic doctrine and way of life with strong roots and
vigorous new shoots into the structure of the only established
institution congenial enough to the doctrine to nurture and
preserve it through the tumultuous late nineteenth centruy.
Meetings in the camp meeting pattern also produced vigorous
transplants of the movement which found root and flourished
among non-Methodist churches of America, England and
Europe.

By 1870 the tempo of holiness evangelism through the
camp meeting medium was rapidly increasing.   Three National
Camps were held that year.   The reports of the first one
at Hamilton, Massachusetts indicate that the revival activity
at Hamilton excited "Unitarians and others" to hold special
meetings, but probably the most significant work done for
the promotion of the cause of holiness was the large number
of ministers who professed to enter into the experience of
perfect love. [85]

The reports of success at the second 1870 camp meeting at Oakington, Maryland, indicate that the relation between
the pleasant surroundings of the open grove and the Beulah
Land experience of the campers was not an absolute one.
The weather there was unbearably hot; the preachers preached
with the temperatures above one hundred degrees, but with
"mental clearness, propriety of utterance, and far-reaching

power. The people were in high spirits; no wearing, no sign
of exhaustion; ..."[86] By 1871, the summer editions of the
Guide to Holiness were filled with reports of holiness camp
meetings within Methodism and beyond. [87]

A New Evangelism

In the spring of that year, Inskip, leaving the pastorate, toured the Methodist conferences of the southwestern
states at the invitation of and in company with Bishop Ames.
At Council Bluffs, Iowa, Inskip was joined by other members
of the National Committee who, together with other friends,
traveled to California where the pattern of successful evangelism, which had marked the summer camps, was now repeated in smaller, but equally successful, meetings in Methodist churches and conferences. [88]

John Inskip and Brigham Young

The high point of the return trip was the meeting held
at Salt Lake City at the invitation of Rev. C. M. Pierce,
Methodist missionary on station there. Brigham Young and
most of the other Mormon leaders, as well as the territorial
officials, crowded into the large tent for the closing service.
According to the National Association's reporter, the converts
in this center of Mormonism were few, but significant. The
wives of Bishop Hunter, president of the board of Mormon
bishops, and of the leader of the Mormon Godbieite sect,
together with the wife and daughter of Orson Pratt, one of
the able prophets of Mormonism, responded to the call. [89]

The account of the stay of the National Committee in
the capital of Mormonism, indicates that the holiness evangelists did not stay as close as usual to their commitment to
the particular promotion of holiness as their central theme.
The evangelists seem to have been too much aware of where
they were and who was present. The preaching was almost
exclusively directed to Brigham Young and the evils of Mormonism; the record clearly indicates that the cause of Christian holiness was scarcely advanced. The participants and
some other contemporary observers saw it differently, however. Inskip's biographers who also took part in the meetings conclude that,

> Mormonism has never recovered from the terrible
> bombardment it received from the batteries of the

National Camp Meeting Association. The authority
and influence then lost by the Mormon rulers, have
never been regained, and never will be. [90]

The Rev. Dewitt Talmage agreed with them; to The Christian
at Work he wrote,

> We have never seen the brethern of that religious
> storming party but we hail them ... for the glori-
> ous work that they have accomplished in Salt Lake
> City. [91]

In spite of the overtones of the Salt Lake City meeting which was the last of the 150 public meetings of the seven
thousand mile tour, the revival results had been good; but
more significantly the pattern had been set for the peripatetic
holiness evangelist who, in their own way, would become the
new circuit riders of Methodism, spreading the holiness message and literature across the spiritual wilderness of the
church just as the Methodist circuit rider had done across
the unchurched wilderness of the American frontier. [92]

Continued interdenominational influence

Although the work of the National Committee was distinctively Methodist in its background and its organization,
the interdenominational element which has always been a distinct feature of the revival movement continued to involve
other communions in the developing holiness revival. Reports of holiness revivals among Quakers, United Brethren,
Moravians, Mennonites, Lutherans, and from evangelical
missionaries in China and India appeared in the Guide. [93]
Henry Belden and William E. Boardman and others who were
regular attendants at the Palmer's Tuesday Meeting continued
their ministry of the Wesleyan holiness emphasis in the post-
war period into numerous Baptist, Congregational, Presbyterian, Episcopal, and Lutheran churches and especially through
Union Holiness Conventions. The May 1842 issue of the Guide
announced that the two of them were going to enter evangelistic work on a full-time basis. [94] In Philadelphia, the Baptist, Dr. Edgar Levy, maintained his active position in the
Friday meetings held at the headquarters of the National Association on Arch Street. [95] In the fall of 1871, Finney, now
an elder statesman of perfectionist revivalism, preached before the National Congregational Council, representing three
thousand churches, on "the baptism of the Holy Ghost." [96]

The growing use of the camp meeting service, as special
means for promoting holiness doctrine, allowed ministers and
laymen from non-Methodist churches much greater freedom
to participate in perfectionist gatherings, than would have
been possible to them in meetings held for a similar purpose
in the denominational churches themselves; there was less of
the sectarian emphasis in the former.

Influences upon the Evangelical Alliance

The presentation of two papers to the international
meeting of the Evangelical Alliance in New York City in 1873,
further demonstrates the fact as well as the extent of the
penetration of the general evangelical community by the revival's doctrines of higher Christian experience. In one of
them, the speaker, Richard Fuller, directing his remarks to
the quality of Christian life required by dangers threatening
the Church of that day, called for a total response throughout Christendom to a new piety; the nature of that piety, the
means for its achievement and the terminology used to describe it were completely within the patterns of Wesleyan
perfectionism then being utilized by the holiness movement. [97]

The address was important because it spoke particularly to the relationship between Christian activism and the
quality of the life of the Christian who engaged in that activism. He observed that one of the most "remarkable features"
of the age was the energy with which men in that day were
combining "their efforts in every sort of enterprise" in both
the religious and secular worlds everywhere forming special
societies to do whatever "they wish to do...." As a result
of this constant doing, he concluded, the peril in religion is
"the mistaking what we do for what we are and consequently
the neglect of our spiritual health ... while we engage in
the diversified systems of concerted movements which inces-
santly claim our attention" (emphasis his). Fuller then
launched into a lengthy appeal to the Christian church to dis-
allow its traditional excuses for a lack of consistent Christian life and to promote a piety whose "fruit" was "holiness."
The church "can scarcely adopt a system which ... mocks
the highest, holiest aspirations of the 'new creature,' " he
continued. One genuine "act of faith," he said, "[was] ...
worth a whole lifetime of attempted faithfulness, in subduing
the depravities which diluted the quality of usual Christian
life" (emphasis his). The question he was raising, he observed, was a most critical one at the moment because the

"state of the world" indicated to him such a rapid expansion
of Christianity that nothing less than the quality of Christian
piety he had described would be demanded of Christians themselves. [98]

Thus the pietistic thrust of the movement again raised
the question of the quality of devotion required for effective
Christian action. It had been raised before by Harriet
Beecher Stowe as a consequence of the strong emphasis upon
the "interior life" raised by Thomas Upham's works. Both
Beecher and Fuller concluded that the revival's call to the
inner life of the Christian in a perfection and purity of love
was a necessary antidote to the tendancy of the social activism of the churches to divorce both its content and methods
from its "Christianess." The tragedy for the Christianity
of the latter part of the century was that the viable tension
between Christian devotion and Christian activity frequently
broke down under the pressures which the churches faced as
part of a revolutionary social order.

The tragedy for the holiness revival in America was
that it let its pietism, some elements of which tended toward
pious passivity, overcome its Wesleyan perfectionism, which
inclined toward activity rooted in the inherent optimism of
its broad universal concepts of the designs of divine redemption for man and society. Neither was ever completely submerged, but the scales commonly tipped toward _being_ rather
than _doing_. Its activism centered in evangelism and such
efforts at social reform as contributed to that end; the goal,
as has been already noted, was to "Christianize" Christianity,
to prepare the church for whatever activity it put itself to. [99]

The second holiness address to the Evangelical Alliance was by William Nast, father of the German Methodist
work in America, and an active participant in the development of the Methodist Church in Germany as well. Nast, at
this time was a member of the National Association for the
Promotion of Holiness. His sermon, typical of that of the
National Association for the Promotion of Holiness evangelists,
reinforced the conclusions drawn by Fuller concerning the
desire and demand for higher, more potent, Christian experience which was abroad in the churches. [100]

It is impossible to ascertain what elements of these
appeals may have been carried home by the European delegates present at the meeting. In both England and on the
continent the Palmer's work had left its influence. The

Methodist churches of England and the newly developing Methodist movements in Germany contained active holiness elements.   These together with the influences of the movement's
literature and periodicals helped to pave the way for the strong
response to the holiness ministry of Robert Pearsall Smith
which began that same year in England.

The National Committee in the South

        The year 1872 marked the first venture of the members
of the National Committee into the south.   The cause of Wesleyan perfection had suffered more in the south than in the
north during the immediate pre-war period.   The Methodist
Episcopal Church South, after the division of the Methodist
Church in 1844, looked upon the holiness papers and other
means of promotion for the doctrine such as the Tuesday
Meetings as tools of the Northern church; furthermore, the
close relationship between perfectionist teaching and the moral
issues concerning slave-holding scarcely lent popularity to
any advance of the doctrine in the Southern church.   The
anti-slavery cause had been a religious crusade.   The Wesleyan Methodists and the Free Methodists, now clearly allied
with the holiness cause, had stood firmly in the middle of
that agitation.   The whole movement was suspect. [101]

        The south too had been only slightly affected by the
Revival of 1858, in part, because that revival had been most
effective among the working men of the industrialized areas
of the country and the south shared few of those; in part, it
was also due to a general apathy against revivalism, itself,
which always was strongly moralistic, and by then, commonly
activistic. [102]   Nor could the Methodist Episcopal Church
South quickly forget what they considered to be undue efforts
by the Methodist Episcopal Church to take advantage of the
reconstruction period and the poverty of the southern church
to reestablish itself in the south at the cost of the latter. [103]
The National's evangelists preaching in the south reported
that the Methodist Episcopal Church South,

            Understood that we were there to make a raid upon
            the church for the purpose of enlarging our own
            territory ...; and that the Methodist Episcopal
            Church had loaned to the committee, not only its
            official sanction but also its money. [104]

        It was not surprising then that when the National Com-
mittee decided that some of its members would hold the last

of the five National Camps for 1872 in Knoxville, Tennessee
there was a raising of eyebrows in the north and rumblings
of discontent in the south. In the latter area some claimed
that the principal aim of the camp meeting was to "make
proselytes" for the northern church. Others felt that it was
"a grand electioneering trip...." The use of the term "National" in the name of the organization also misled some. [105]

In spite of all these concerns the National Camp Meeting Association's efforts produced numerous confessions to
conversions and sanctifications especially among the ministry
of the area. The Methodist Advocate, published at Atlanta,
Georgia, gave a favorable report on the meeting, noting that
doctrine was Wesleyan and everything was in "good order."
The following year the last National camp of the season was
again held at Knoxville. This time the committee was sure
enough of its grounds to invite Bishop Gilbert Haven of the
northern church to participate in the meetings. [106]

The revival of the preaching of entire sanctification
in the south was abetted in this same period by the establishment of new publications "to advance the cause of holiness."
The pace of the holiness revival would prove to be slower
than that in the north and the officials of the southern church
were less open to the holiness movement within the church.
Nevertheless, the aged Dr. Lovick Pierce, whose seventy
years in the Methodist ministry allowed him to reach back to
the very beginning of Methodism, linked hands with the new
movement. He reported to Inskip in 1875, that a new periodical on the same plan as the Christian Standard was out
with its first issue and already the "spring buds of holiness
are putting out, at the lowest points of sapped life."[107]

The National Committee and the
perfectionist churches

The two smaller Methodist bodies, the Wesleyan Methodists and the Free Methodists, who openly espoused Wesleyan holiness doctrine by incorporating articles concerning
it in their Discipline were not in a strong position to take
leadership in the expanding revival. The increase in articles
on the subject in their religious papers indicate that both
were influenced by the activities of the National Committee;
but during the post-war decades, the Wesleyans were de-
pleted by a severe loss in leadership and membership, due
to the return to the parent body of those who felt that the
purposes for the church's existence had been obviated by the

successful conclusion of the "war against slavery."[108] Those
who chose to continue the movement were concerned chiefly
with anti-secret society reform.[109] The Free Methodists,
organized in 1860, were busy developing and establishing their
work which was still in the formative stages. As already
noted, the Free Methodist Church was the first organized
church in history to specifically identify itself with the doctrine of Christian perfection as its founding. But the controversy which had surrounded its founding, and its popular
identification of the doctrine with the intense puritan ethic of
Finney and the western New York "burnt over" district, limited its influence in the general movement. In fact,[110] in
some circles the critics of the holiness movement used the
"Nazarite" affair in the Methodist Episcopal Church's Genesee
Conference in 1860 as a certain illustration of the devisive
nature of the holiness specialists within the church. Too
intimate an identification of the mainstream Methodist holiness movement with such a group would hardly have been
expedient for the National Committee.[111]

The holiness revival in Methodism: flow tide

         The participation of bishops, presiding elders, and
large numbers of Methodist laymen in the National Camp
meetings testified to a growing acceptance of the methods by
the organized church.[112] This acceptance was undoubtedly
widened by the ability of the National Association leaders to
avoid many of the extreme physical and emotional demonstra-
tions which had always been played up by critics of the camp
meeting movement. Commentaries on the services in the
Methodist Advocates were cast in increasingly favorable tones.
Typical of these is the guarded but positive language of the
report of Dr. Reid, editor of the Northwestern Christian
Advocate; of his observations on the closing service of the
first Midwestern National Camp Meeting held at Des Plaines,
Illinois, he wrote,

         Silence was a wonderful power with them; the vast
         assembly awaiting on God, just waiting. ... Not
         a word said, but every heart opened heavenward,
         and God pouring his blessing in. The results in
         bringing souls to Christ estimating no other good
         that was done, marks the meeting a signal success.
         It has evidently marked an era in the religious
         experience of Northwestern Methodism; and thus far
         there is in it great promise of good, and little
         promise of evil.[113]

An enthusiastic report to the <u>Philadelphia Home Journal</u> said:

> The whole Northwest is in a blaze of salvation. Holiness is the theme in every direction. . . . I have heard that ministers have gone home covered with sanctified power, and whole churches are at the altar seeking holiness. 114

In 1872, five years after the Vineland meeting, the president of the National Committee could report to the annual meeting of the Association in New York City that:

> Never before in the history of Christianity has there been so great and widespread an interest in this important subject as within the last four or five years. All denominations have been so aroused as to assure the most skeptical that this is truly the "work of God. "115

He rejoiced that not only the church in general, but the Methodist Church in particular had been largely won to the movement:

> The church in a degree, perhaps beyond what, all things considered, we would have expected, has given us countenance and appreciated our endeavor. 116

Less than ten years after the end of the Civil War the following facts about the holiness movement in America were evident: that the tide of revival was rising in America, that it was commonly, but not exclusively oriented toward Methodist Wesleyan perfectionism, that the National Camp Meeting Association Committee was playing the leadership role, and that those who had predicted schism for the church because of increased organization of the holiness party within it were obviously wrong. There was a genuine basis for Inskip's optimism for the cause.

The influence of the movement was also making itself felt at the administrative center of the church's life. Bishop Morris testified at a love-feast at the Urbana, Ohio National Camp Meeting in 1871:

> There are a number of things I praise God for. The first is, that I have lived to see a National Campmeeting in Ohio. 117

He later wrote about the Urbana Camp: "The final results

of this campmeeting will never be known fully till the great
day of reckoning."[118]

        The Methodist Episcopal General Conference of 1872
elected eight new bishops, six of them were friendly with
the holiness cause. Randolph S. Foster had been selected
by John McClintock, the first president of Drew University,
to head the theological studies of the new school; his theology
was pronouncedly Wesleyan; at the time of his election he
was serving as president of Drew. [119]   Stephen Merrill maintained an open and close relationship with the friends of holiness. [120]   Jesse T. Peck, the younger brother of George
Peck, the Methodist editor, had written one of the major de-
fenses of the doctrine of Christian perfection contributed
regularly to the Guide, and had participated in the National
camps as noted above.   He openly proposed that the church
should incorporate the "second blessing" view of the revival
into its doctrinal statement. [121]   Gilbert Haven, the fourth
of the holiness bishops elected that year, had defended the
activities of the National Committee during his editorship of
the Zion's Herald, the voice of New England Methodism. [122]
Thomas Bowman[123] was the fifth and William L. Harris, the
sixth; the latter joined Asa Mahan and Asbury Lowrey in a
special call to entire sanctification addressed to the ministers
and laymen of all denominations. [124]

The holiness revival in Methodism: ebb tide

        But even the groundswell of approbation for the move-
ment which helped to carry these men into ecclesiastical
power, did not silence the voice of the opposition.   John
Inskip's report to the National Association in 1872 recognized
the continuing conflict concerning the special promotion of
holiness within the church.   The doctrine of entire sanctification, he noted, had "in large measure" been put aside by
Methodism.   This fact accounted for the criticism and cen-
sure which the work of the National Committee had met.   In
the face of this misunderstanding and misrepresentation he
reminded the committee members that

            the vow taken at Vineland not to answer anything
            that might be alleged against us has been the oc-
            casion of much unfair dealing towards us; but it
            has saved the Church from the shame and dishonor
            of an acrimonious controversy. [125]

        The Vineland vow, of course did not prevent "acrimon-

ious controversy" in the church, for it applied only to non-
retaliation against attacks made upon members of the Association as persons.   The thrusts against the movement sometimes became ad hominum by nature, but, on the whole, they
were otherwise--first, doctrinal, and second, methodological.
Charges related to these two categories heightened the tensions
for the movement within its Methodist home.   In controversies
over doctrine, the movement ultimately established its broad
contention that the doctrinal positions it held were essentially
those which primitive Methodism had affirmed and which the
Methodism of their day continued to hold to in its official
utterances and exhortations. [126]   Bishops north and south declared the mission of the church to be the spreading of Scriptural holiness.   Even modern Methodism has not completely
ignored the traditional holiness emphasis of the church. [127]

But when the movement tried to establish the appropri-
ateness of its special methods for the promotion of holiness
within the increasingly bureaucratic structure of burgeoning
Methodism, they lost the day.   The intensity of the opposition,
which had refused to yield the field completely, even under
the more informal "irregularities" of the layman's movement
under the Palmers continued to increase in direct proportion
to the transfer of leadership to pastors who were more deeply
involved in the power structure of the church.   The critics
became especially vocal as the summer-camp evangelism
moved back into the churches after the close of the camp
meeting season.

The intense debates covering the propriety of holding
special meetings for the promotion of holiness again agitated
Methodist ministers' meetings, especially in New York City.
Unhappy critics maintained that every Methodist service was
a holiness meeting; proponents of the new measures, however,
contended that in reality this was no longer so; they insisted
that the backsliding of the church on this theme and the critical problems which she currently faced, mandated and justified even extraordinary agencies for the restoration of the
doctrine and the experience throughout the denomination. [128]

In 1873, Dr. Asbury Lowrey, pastor of Wesley Chapel
in Cincinnati, Ohio, invited John Inskip and William McDonald
to his church to hold a meeting "expressly for the promotion
of personal holiness."   Night after night capacity audiences
crowded the large church in a remote area of the town.   Even
concurrent nightly lectures in the city by Henry Ward Beecher
failed to diminish attendance at the holiness meetings.   In

spite of the popular success of the meeting, Lowrey came
under heavy criticism for his encouragement of those "special agencies." His reply to these objections in the Advocate of Christian Holiness for June 1873 is a classic example
of the many apologies which were made by the movement's
defenders from the time of the Palmers on. The propriety
of the methods of specialization utilized by the holiness reformers was the issue.

Lowrey's arguments centered in three basic points.
The first question at issue was, "Are specific and extraordin-
ary efforts needed at the present to revive personal holiness?"
Lowrey said:

> I unhesitatingly answer, yes, Nay more, I affirm
> that the conservation of our distinctive features,
> and the efficient perpetuity of our church, can only
> be secured by a diffusion of experimental holi-
> ness.... 129

This was the basic rationale for the movement; in that day
it was applied generally by Methodist to the Methodist Church,
but the continuing story will reveal that the interdenominational nature of the revival combined with the general hunger
in the churches for new spiritual power, gradually broadened
that theme to promote the revival of personal holiness in all
of Christendom as the only hope for a redeemed world.

Lowrey then turned to his second question: What is
the posture of affairs in the church? He listed six developments which he believed were militating against the future
usefulness of the church, a church which in more normal
times would have encouraged people into a life of Christian
holiness. These six in summary are (1) The expansion of
"ecclesiastical machinery." He warned that it threatened to
"break down with its own weight." The threat here was toward externality without spiritual depth. (2) The increased
wealth and popularity of the church. "We are numerous,
wealthy, educated, and damagingly respectable. From these
sources, influences are constantly springing adverse to holiness." He saw the tendency to "commute benevolent deeds
for heart purity,--to sink substance in the symbol, and exchange life for a name." (3) The neglect of holiness literature. "Very few of our own people now read Wesley, Fletcher, Clarke...." They were regarded as obsolete. (4) The
abandonment of the spiritual means of grace. In some localities "the class meetings, prayer meetings, bands, fasting,

family and secret prayer," were generally or totally given
up.   (5) The tolerance by the church of "respectable vices."
Papers were received on Sunday, the children of the church
went to dancing schools; dancing, games of chance, and even
drinking were tolerated in the homes of many in the church.
Visiting theaters, circuses, and horse races was common as
also was the participation in fairs, excursions and public fes-
tivities.   (5) The admission of large numbers of unconverted
members.

His concluding question was:

> If such is the true posture of affairs in our church
> is it probable that a general revival of personal
> holiness will ever take place without the use of
> special and extraordinary agencies?

Lowrey appealed to the church not to rule out this
holiness "irregularity." If the church should do so, he
warned,

> the brightest star of hope that has shown upon the
> church for a half a century will be struck from the
> heavens of Methodism. 130

In a contrary vein, an article in the Western Christian Advocate in the fall of 1875, entitled "Holiness Then and
Now," argued that special meetings for the promotion of holiness were "un-Wesleyan and should be suppressed." The
author contended that such meetings were "not exactly in
harmony with the old time-honored and well-tried Methodism."
Such effects, he said, were "incompatible with the spirit and
genius of Methodism, and altogether schismatical and revolutionary in its tendency."131

Inskip, editor of the Advocate of Christian Holiness,
replied that not only were such efforts fully in accord with
the practice and theology of Methodism, but that John Wesley,
himself, utilized similar measures when the testimony to the
experience of Christian perfection began to wane in his societies.   He made reference to Wesley's Journal entry for January 29, 1767 in which the latter noted:

> At five in the morning I began a course of sermons
> on Christian Perfection; if haply that thirst after
> it might return which was so general a few years
> ago.   Since that time how deeply have we grieved
> the Holy Spirit of God. 132

Inskip also argued that according to Tyerman's Life of Wesley, Methodism's founder, had organized special meetings
for the promotion of holiness and then had given them into
the charge of laymen in his absence.   The "band" meetings
and the "very select societies" were all meetings for the
special encouragement of Christian holiness; the rules for
such meetings, he pointed out, were carried in the Discipline
of the Methodist Episcopal Church until 1852. [133]

Phoebe Palmer's Death

In December 1874 at the height of the revival and in
the midst of the increasingly sharp conflict it was causing
in the Methodist Episcopal Church, Phoebe Palmer died.
After she and her husband had returned to America from their
evangelistic work in England ten years earlier, they continued
their holiness evangelism through the Tuesday Meetings, in
conventions, camps and in the churches assisted by the Lankfords.   Mrs. Palmer had accepted gracefully the organization
of the National Camp Meeting Association in 1867; recognizing
a new era in the movement, she blended her own ministry
with that of the new leadership.   She and her husband were
regular workers in the National camp meetings and consistently
promoted the work of the Association in the pages of the
Guide which she continued to edit until her death in December
of 1874.   Occasionally she had mildly rebuked the enthusiasm
of the reporters of the National Committee for their over-
zealous claims, [134] which, as indicated above, tended to be
too unconscious of the flow of history, and too enthusiastic
for "now" and the "tomorrow" which their efforts would in-
sure.   When the National had begun publication of its own
periodical, the Advocate of Christian Holiness, she had expressed regret that the resources and constituent readership
so vital to the holiness periodicals' survival had to be divided
by even friendly competition, but she had wished the new
venture every success. [135]

The pen-name, "Shepherdess," which she used in her
first writings, might aptly describe her religious activities
and informal, but influential, position in American Methodism
and the holiness movement.   Bishops and ministers were
part of the flock.   Twenty to thirty of them were regularly
in the congregations at the Tuesday Meetings.   She became
a spiritual guide to thousands more in the American churches
through her public ministry and her numerous books.   In the
Palmer's ministry in England and Scotland during the war

years, twenty thousand conversions and ten thousand sanctifications were recorded among people of all classes. Milton
Lorenzo Haney, a later leader in the movement, said that
to Phoebe Palmer, more than to any other single individual,
must be given the right to the title of founder of the modern
holiness movement. In granting such recognition to Mrs.
Palmer, he went on to say that it was nevertheless probable
that she would not have acknowledged all that was bound up
in the movement in his time. [136] Like all great leaders she
has been read variously by both friends and followers, on-
lookers and opponents. Her largeness of spirit and ecumenical viewpoint often did not suit the character or the times of
many who took up her concerns for the work of holiness in
the ongoing movement.

There is possibly some relationship between movements
which are centered in the perfection in Christian love and the
dominant positions they have often granted to the leadership
of women. [137] Undoubtedly, it was partly due to her feminine
persuasiveness that she was able to convince so many listen-
ers of the possibilities and values of the higher Christian
life after so many others failed to do so. But the religious
sentiments of Phoebe Palmer went considerably deeper than
the romanticism of the language of the mid-nineteenth century in which she expressed herself and by which others described her life and work would indicate. A double-page
spread of pictures in the Ladies Repository for February 1866
which shows a full page portrait of Phoebe Palmer seated
opposite a composite arrangement of the pictures of outstanding representatives of Methodist Church's first one hundred
years in America, symbolizes her influence in her day. [138]
Her sturdy chin and set features seem to express the cool
determination of a woman who for almost thirty years made
a simple gathering in a private home at a dull hour on a
weekday, a center of spiritual renewal in the face of inces-
sant criticism, neglect, gibes and ridicule. It was for Wesley to first bring the Protestant church at large to ask the
questions concerning the possibilities of practical holiness in
the Christian life; he said, "If there is grace for entire sanctification at the moment of death, why is not the same grace
available in life." He began to preach it and testified to
finding some genuine recipients of such grace in his lifetime;
it remained, however, for an American woman to introduce
into that Wesleyan theology the urgency of the revivalist call
for immediate decision and promise of perfection in love to
the masses. For her the "now" in the "if at death, why not
now" of Wesley, stood out in capital letters; she insisted that

present faith and entire consecration made Christian holiness
a possibility in grace for every Christian.   In writing of her
and her sister, Sarah, Bishop John P. Newman said that "no
two women of ... [the Methodist Episcopal Church] have left
a deeper ... impress upon their day and generation."[139]

The direct relationship between her application of
American revival methods to the promotion of Christian holiness and the questions which arose among friends and opponents who evaluated her efforts is illustrated in a summary
of her work by her friend, Dr. Asbury Lowrey upon her
death:

> Mrs. Palmer, we think, was strictly Wesleyan in
> her views and inculcations.   In order to lift indi-
> viduals over the bar of constitutional, habitual, or
> creed-bound unbelief, she would seem to lead them
> out, sometimes, to the very crest of presumption;
> but in such cases she always left the bridge of
> orthodoxy in good repair behind her....   They were
> seen by her keen insight to be necessary to suc-
> cess....   Indeed, every great revivalist has found
> it necessary to provoke action by cutting dull in-
> formalities, fossilized faith and perfuctory services
> at right angles.   Such exploits, considered hyper-
> critically, may easily be magnified into heresy and
> delusion; and yet, according to the verdict of his-
> tory, they are indispensable to success.[140]

When one attempts to explain the varying individual stances
taken towards the movement, in Methodism at least, he must
take into account the fact that the pros and cons may have
been determined by sympathy or antagonism toward revivalistic methods as much as toward the theology involved.

It is for this emphasis that the higher life movement
in all of Protestantism looks back to her life and work. De-
Witt Talmage recognized her interdenominational influences.
She had been a Methodist, he said, but denominational walls
could not contain her; some "caricatured" her higher life
evangelism, he observed, but, "she lived long enough to see
the whole Christian church waking up to this doctrine...."[141]
Asbury Lowrey's memorial in the Christian Advocate upon
her death, in the literary pattern of the day, is couched in
prose too flowery for the modern ear, but the closing sentence is solid and long since proven by subsequent history:
"Whoever promotes holiness in all this country, must build
upon the foundations of this holy woman."[142]

Continuing Controversy in Methodism

Not every one in Methodism was as enthusiastic as
Lowrey over Mrs. Palmer's work. By the time of her death
Dr. Daniel D. Whedon, 143 editor of the Methodist Quarterly
Review, had become the chief antagonist of the movement
which continued the special methods for holiness promotion
which she had fostered. He charged it with a theology of
"hyper-Wesleyanism." 144 In response to an objection by
George D. Watson, one of the movement's main advocates,
to a Quarterly Review article on holiness by Dr. J. O. A.
Clark, Whedon defended Clark's article as,

> Less perniciously divergent from Wesley than In-
> skip, McDonald, or this Dr. Watson. 145

In regard to the special methods utilized by the advocates of
holiness in the church, the holiness association, the holiness
periodical, the holiness prayer meeting, the holiness preacher.
Whedon charged that they "are all modern novelties. They
are not Wesleyan. We believe that a living Wesley would
never admit them into the system." 146 In an earlier controversy with Asbury Lowrey over Jonathan T. Crane's book,
Holiness the Birthright of All God's Children, Whedon repeated the original charges which Mattison had made against
the movement and the work of Phoebe Palmer in the debates
of 1857. The whole movement, he claimed, smacked of the
flavor of the enthusiastic George Bell. The "Nazarites" of
central New York were still fresh in his mind as an example
of the potential evil which could result from such holiness
propaganda as the Guide and the Standard of Holiness poured
out; he forecast that this movement like Bell's could lead to
nothing but disloyalty and division. 147

The controversy continued on into 1878. In March of
that same year William McDonald's editorial rejoinder to
Whedon's attack is one of the sharpest to be found anywhere
in the polemical writings of the proponents of holiness; the
personal inference and the biting irony of the reply to Dr.
Whedon pushed the non-retaliatory vow of the Vineland organizational meeting to the limits and probably beyond. McDonald
wrote,

> If Dr. Whedon is not the chief umpire in Methodism,
> he is a greatly mistaken man. Never did the oc-
> cupant of the fancied chair of St. Peter speak with
> greater constituted authority. Whenever he utters

his dictum, every Methodist preacher ... must
gracefully bow and silently submit. [148]

In his reply to Dr. Watson's tract against the position taken
by Dr. Clark in the Quarterly Review, Whedon was charged
with letting his "Shillalah" fall "without special care as to
whose head is broken." Whedon's views, McDonald continued,
had been rejected by "hundreds of our ablest and best ministers" as well as by a then recent action of the Wisconsin
Conference. [149]

The sharpest retort of all was his reference to the
efforts of certain ministers to excuse Whedon's alleged "un-
christian spirit" by attempting to

> Explain it on the ground that he is old and broken
> down and is not to be held to a strict account for
> what he has to say under such circumstances. [150]

The strong reaction of McDonald for the National Committee was probably prompted not only by Whedon's objections
to the work of the National Association, but because, although
the editor of one of the powerful papers in Methodism, Mc-
Donald claimed Whedon's theology of Methodist perfectionism
was pure "un-Wesleyan heresy" and "clear as mud."[151]

These exchanges not only demonstrate the depth of the
continuing controversy over the movement in the church, but
also its acrimonious spirit was prophetic of the extreme polarization which was taking place both in the National Association
and the institutional churches. There was a developing breakdown of communication between the growing movement and
the church structures. Within the next few years the strictures would be drawn sufficiently tight to give the more radical fringes of the movement a rationale for forsaking the
church structures to pioneer the narrow paths of schism
which finally became broad roads of separation. There would
be Methodists whose ties to the officialdom of the church were
not so warm and direct as those of the Palmers and the Inskips or even the McDonalds, and whose optimism for restoring the church to her holiness testimony would be considerably
less evident. Jones concludes,

> Well recommended in the church, early leaders
> became patriarchs in the holiness cause, ... but
> failed to father spiritual sons to lead a movement
> in the church. Despite their intentions, they were

unable to save Methodism from change, and unwittingly became agents of faction rather than fraternity
within its ranks.152

SUMMARY

        The formation of the National Camp Meeting Associa-
tion for the Promotion of Holiness in 1867, in many aspects,
was a very typical American action. The organization took
its place as one among many special groups within the nation
which were created by volunteer activists to propagandize
some particular concern, or to seek a desired reform. In
this context, the National Association was in the company of
such other evangelical reform organizations as the American
Bible Society, the Women's Christian Temperance Union, or
any other of the hundreds of reform movements which dot
and even clutter the social history of nineteenth century America. In its revivalistic activism, it undoubtedly shared in
the attitudes of suspicion, with which reforming movements
of any kind were commonly met by those who are not as
urgent about the issues as the reformers themselves may be.
Some of the persistent opposition in Methodism, to the work
of the National Committee, can probably be read in that light.
However, it was hard for the advocates of the holiness experience to refrain from regarding such hesitation to accept
their methods as anything but negativism toward perfectionist
teaching itself.

        Another sense in which the Association was also strongly
in step with a current mood, was in its strong sense of mission. Most of the reform efforts of such groups as the National Camp Meeting Association were deeply rooted in the
New England, American tradition which sought to bring a new
order to all society by means of the application of Christian
principles and law. As we have seen, this idea was deeply
ingrained in the national purpose. Although the National Association had as its immediate reformatory goal, the restoration of the experience of Christian holiness to the general
life of the Methodist churches, its ultimate sense of purpose
fully participated in that Puritan purpose, strengthened, as
it was, by the movement's inherent perfectionism. Its goal,
too, was the reformation of all society. The holiness evangelists hoped to accomplish this through a purified Methodist
Episcopal Church; that church, in turn, could give leadership
to a revival of holiness which would Christianize America; the
nation and the churches could then fulfill America's redemptive

mission to the whole world. The age of the Holy Spirit and
a new millenium would be ushered in. They were true Puritans.

But, as we have also indicated, more than that, they
were a new breed of pietists. It was already evident to the
National Committee, in the second National Camp Meeting at
Manheim, that their message had a much broader appeal than
to Methodism alone. They had caught hold of a new evangelistic method in the Palmer pattern. In combination with the
innately American institution of the camp meeting, it created
a new urgency in the promotion of Christian perfection. The
call for immediate consecration, immediate faith, and personal witness had a common appeal to an essential pietiem,
which had infused the Calvinistic as well as the Arminian
camps in America. The strength of that concern was demonstrated in the Evangelical Alliance meeting of 1873.

The appeal, therefore, of Asbury Lowrey, a member
of the National Committee, to the Methodist Episcopal Church
to not reject the Committee's special revival methods, was
not merely a response of a nineteenth century American pastor to his church and society; there was a much older and
broader tradition pressing through. He was speaking to problems, which others with concepts of the Christian faith very
similar to his own, had faced before him. He was reflect-
ing a Christian tradition of concern for a particular Christian approach to the world, the Christian's relationship to it,
and the most effective means for its redemption.

Finally, both its revivalistic formulation and its essential pietistic nature made the whole movement extremely experience centered. Its commitment to holiness primarily as
an experience facilitated the extension of the revival beyond
Methodism. It produced an interdenominationalism, mainly
grass-roots in character, which survived extreme variances
in creed and denominational polity. At the same time, it
laid the foundation for future conflict, not only within the
movement itself, but also between the movement and the
churches represented by its adherents. The success of the
revival, by the mid-seventies, created increasingly sharp
tensions between the members of the National Committee
and the Methodist Episcopal Church. More and more, the
Association with its subsidiary organizations and periodicals
was being regarded as an irregular agency. The strident
words between Daniel Whedon and William McDonald, at the
very zenith of the movement's success, plainly announced that
reality.

NOTES

1.   William A. Clebsch, From Sacred to Profane
America: the Role of Religion in American History (New
York: Harper and Row, 1968), p. 192.

2.   William Warren Sweet, Methodism in American History, p. 298, observes that "the four bloody years of the War
left their brutalizing effect upon society ... and exercised a
blighting effect upon the life of the nation for the years that
were to follow." Also see Boisen, op. cit., p. 128.

3.   Clebsch, op. cit., p. 199.

4.   Platt, op. cit., pp. vi, vii. Also see ibid.,
p. 231.

5.   Ibid.

6.   Gilbert Haven, Sermons, Speeches and Letters on
Slavery and Its War (Boston: Lee and Shephard, 1869), pp.
629-30. Out of such statements T. Smith, Revivalism and
Social Reform, p. 7, concluded that "revivalistic religion and
Christian Perfection lay at the fountainhead of our nation's
heritage of hope...." Clebsch, op. cit., p. 199, notes that
Father Isaac Hecker, famed as the center of the Americanism
Controversy in the Catholic Church, near the end of his life
in 1888 had written that Calvinism with its pessimism and
determinism was inadequate to support the American ideal.
On religious optimism also see Sperry, op. cit., p. 14.

7.   Marty, op. cit., p. 189. Also see Russell B.
Nye, The Almost Chosen People; Essays in the History of
American Ideas (n. p.: Michigan State University Press,
1966), chap. i, "The American Idea of Progress."

8.   Beauty of Holiness, VIII (April, 1857), 104.

9.   See Louis Gasper, The Fundamentalist Movement
(The Hague: Mouton and Co., 1963), pp. 7-8, 53-54.

10.   This development is the theme of T. Smith's
Revivalism and Social Reform. Also see Smith, Handy, and
Loetscher, op. cit., II, chap. xii, and the literature there
cited; S. Mead, The Lively Experiment, chap. vi.

11.   Anton Boisen in his classic study, Religion in
Crisis and Custom, indicates that religious concern is often

associated with social as well as personal crises with con-
structive results. War, however, he says, "seems to be an
exception to this principle." Prevailing reactions in war time
are "malignant"; Boisen, op. cit., p. 5. See also the whole
of "War as Social Crisis," ibid., pp. 95-107. On the Civil
War and the holiness revival see W. C. Muncy, Jr., Evangelism in the United States (Kansas City: Central Seminary
Press, 1945), p. 128.

    12.   Guide, XLVII (April, 1865), 91-93.

    13.   Ibid., XLVI (October, 1864), 93-94, reports on
the completion of Caughey's latest English campaign in which
3,300 converts were reported in nine months.

    14.   Guide, XLVII (May, 1865), 15, and ibid., XLVIII
(July 1865), 28-29, show typical lists.

    15.   McDonald and Searles, op. cit., p. 147.

    16.   Ibid., p. 148.

    17.   John S. Inskip, Methodism Explained and Defended
(Cincinnati, Ohio: H. S. and J. Applegate, 1851), p. 61.

    18.   Ibid., p. 60. Also see McDonald and Searles,
pp. 147-48. It is interesting to note that the very questions
which later became distinctive parts of his teaching on the
doctrine, at this period of his life he considered "questions
of but little consequence." See Inskip, op. cit., p. 61.

    19.   McDonald and Searles, op. cit., p. 150, as quoted
from Inskip's "Diary."

    20.   Ibid., p. 151.

    21.   Ibid., p. 152.

    22.   Ibid. For eight years after this religious experi-
ence, Inskip kept a full journal record of his activities; at
the top of each page printed in beautiful letters was the motto,
"I am, O Lord, wholly and forever thine!"; ibid., p. 160.

    23.   Ibid., pp. 154-55, as quoted from Inskip's "Diary."

    24.   Littell, op. cit., pp. 93ff., develops the thesis
that the rapid growth of the churches "was accompanied,

indeed in part accomplished, by the abandonment of the traditional standards of discipline."

    25.   McDonald and Searles, op. cit. , p. 157, as
quoted from Inskip's "Diary."

    26.   The Philadelphia Public Ledger (June 27, 1867).

    27.   McDonald and Searles, op. cit. , p. 118.

    28.   The Rev. Alfred Cookman, a member of the ad
hoc committee, called it "a bold move for the friends of
holiness." Ridgaway, op. cit. , p. 315.

    29.   McDonald, The Double Cure, pp. 5-6; McDonald
and Searles, op. cit. , pp. 185-88; Rose, op. cit. , pp. 50-53;
Autobiography of J. A. Wood (Chicage: Christian Witness
Co. , 1904), pp. 73-74; Adam Wallace, op. cit. , p. 202,
wrongly makes Wm B. Osborne the main instigator of the
movement; see Rose, op. cit. , p. 50.

    30.   Inskip noted in his "Diary" that "it is a new idea,
yet it forcibly impresses me." Quoted in McDonald and
Searles, op. cit. , p. 187.

    31.   George Roberts was a local preacher, physician,
and founder of the Historical Society of Baltimore; Simpson,
op. cit. , p. 759. Cookman was pastor to Bishop Matthew
Simpson and his family in pastorates in both Pittsburgh and
Philadelphia; Ridgaway, op. cit. , p. 47.

    32.   A term used frequently by Cookman and the move-
ment; it indicates the polarization in the churches on the
question.

    33.   McDonald and Searles, op. cit. , p. 190. The
terms "higher Christian life" and "life of holiness" or "victorious Christian life" were used interchangeably at these
early stages. Later with the birth of the Calvinistic holiness
movement attempts to distinguish between the Wesleyan movement and the former tended to use "higher Christian life" in
relation to the Calvinistic holiness movement and "holiness"
in relation to the Wesleyan camp.

    34.   Ibid.

    35.   Ibid. , p. 188; McDonald, Double Cure, p. 6.

Cookman, however, found less reaction than he had anticipated; see Ridgaway, op. cit. , p. 316.

36. Quoted by Daniel Steele, A Defense of Christian
Perfection or a Criticism of Dr. Mudge's Growth in Holiness
toward Perfection (New York: Hunt and Eaton, 1896), p. 14.
The holiness advocates also were encouraged by the Episcopal
Address to the General Conference of the Methodist Episcopal
Church in 1864 in which the Bishops prayed for "the outpouring of the Holy Ghost upon the Church, the nation, and the
world" as their only hope. They had exhorted: "Let faith
command it and it shall be." Journal of the General Conference of the M. E. Ch. , 1864 (New York: Carlton and Porter,
1864), p. 436.

37. One cannot help but be impressed with the expect-
ant optimism of the holiness proponents. Cookman wrote to
Inskip of his anticipation that Vineland Camp would begin a
revival of religion that "spreading North, South, East and
West, may wrap the nation, the continent, and the world in
a flame of devotion to Jesus"; Ridgaway, op. cit. , p. 316.
Wallace, in preparing for the printing of an account of the
National Camp at Landisville, Pa. in 1873, even prior to
the meeting, was "so confident that God would baptise the
assembled people with the Holy Ghost and fire sent down from
heaven that the plan of [his] ... prospective book embraced
the title, 'Pentecost Repeated. '..." The final notice of the
Vineland Camp in the Philadelphia Public Ledger (July 15,
1867), was cast in the same optimistic tones in phrases such
as "Grand Camp Meeting" and "the largest [camp meeting]
ever [to be] held in South Jersey."

38. The first stake had been driven for the development of the town only six years previously. The sale of
alcoholic beverages was prohibited; this undoubtedly contributed
to the choice of the town as the camp site. As a land promoter, Landis was happy to welcome national organizations
and their conventions to his development. "The Friends of
Progress Society," made up mainly of Spiritualists and a few
Quakers, an anti-Masonic group under Rev. Charles Blanch-
ard, and "women's rights" associations followed in the train
of the National Camp Meeting Association. The frequent
appearance of feminist leaders such as Mrs. M. E. Tillos-
ton, Spiritualist, Free Love advocate, and dress reformer,
who often walked the streets of Vineland in her trousers and
frock coat, stamped it as a "Free Love Town" only a few
years after the camp meeting there. See Vineland, N. J.

Centennial (Vineland Centennial Inc. , c. d. [ca. 1961]), pp.
16-24; Charles K. Landis, "The Settlement of Vineland in
N. J. ," Fraser's Magazine, XI (January, 1875), 126ff.; and
D. O. Kellog, Illustrated Vineland (n. p. : L. L. Buckminster
Printer, 1897). The last named provides descriptive materials on the life and layout of the town at the time of the
1867 camp.

39. McDonald and Searles, op. cit. , pp. 191-94;
Ridgaway, op. cit. , pp. 317-18.

40. See his letter as quoted by Ridgaway, op. cit. ,
p. 327. One should note the implications of this enthusiastic
reaction to the holiness camp meeting experience by the pastor
of the Spring Garden Methodist Episcopal Church in Philadelphia for any attempts to properly evaluate the tensions which
developed between many holiness Methodists and the regular
Methodist congregations pursuing their usual routine of religious service in the local church. The intensity of the
religious experience in the camp, oftentimes unjustly, made
the church services appear dead and lifeless.

41. McDonald and Searles, op. cit. , pp. 194-95; Advocate of Christian Holiness, III (July, 1872), 3-4; Ridgaway,
op. cit. , pp. 317-18; J. E. Searles, A Sermon Preached by
the Request of the National Camp Meeting at Pitman Grove,
N. J. , August 5, 1887 on the History of the Present Holiness
Revival (Boston: McDonald and Gill, 1887), pp. 4-5.

42. As stated by George Hughes in the Methodist Home
Journal (October 12, 1872) and quoted both in Ridgaway, op.
cit. , p. 323, and Searles, op. cit. , p. 12.

43. Ibid. , p. 10; McDonald and Searles, op. cit. , p.
194.

44. "Waiting for the Spirit to move" had traits of
Quakerism in it. Val B. Clear in "The Urbanization of a
Holiness Body," The City Church, IX (July-August, 1958),
8, illustrates the end to which it sometimes came; Church
of God (Anderson, Ind.) preachers sat on the front row of
camp benches, each with hand in Bible at his favorite text,
waiting for a chance to preach. This same Spirit-led order
of unstructured services was also adhered to in the Holiness
Church of California. Searles, op. cit. , p. 10, says this
arose out of the movement's emphasis on Spirit direction as
they believed it operated in the primitive, post-pentecostal
church.

45. McDonald and Searles, op. cit., p. 199. For a general description of the Mannheim meeting see the article from the Columbia, Pa. Daily Spy (July 20, 1868), quoted in ibid., pp. 201-202, and Ridgaway, op. cit., pp. 349-50. Lizzie R. Smith, a camp meeting minister, long active in the National Holiness Camps, described her experiences at Manheim in Leander L. Pickett, Faith Tonic I and II Combined. (Louisville, Ky.: Pentecostal Publishing Company, n. d.), pp. 34-42.

46. H. J. Bowman, compiler, Voices on Holiness from the Evangelical Association (Cleveland, Ohio: Publishing House of the Ev. Assoc., 1882), p. 205. The Living Epistle, the holiness periodical of the Evangelical Association, edited by Reuben Yeakel and Elisha A. Hoffman (September, 1871), p. 95, carried a report on the Easton, Pa. district camp meeting which noted that "A new camp-meeting spirit has been infused into the members...." The change was attributed to "Holiness" (emphasis theirs). Thirteen out of the seventeen ministers on the district had made a public confession "of having experienced this great salvation." Ibid. (1871), passim, reveals the growing influence of the movement on evangelicalism. Toward the end of the century official promotion of the doctrine flagged following a pattern parallel to that of the holiness emphasis in Methodism. An excellent summary of the movement in the Evangelical Association up to that turning point may be found in J. Wesley Corbin, "Christian Perfection and the Evangelical Association through 1875," Methodist History, VII (January, 1969), 28-44. Also see Raymond W. Albright, A History of the Evangelical Church (Harrisburg, Pa.: The Evangelical Press, 1942), pp. 268-78; W. Horn (comp.), Yearbook of the Evangelical Association (Cleveland, Ohio: Publishing House of the Evangelical Association, 1907), p. 48.

47. The holiness emphases in the Mennonite Brethren in Christ Church and other smaller Mennonite holiness bodies who affiliated with the movement developed out of these influences: Storms, op. cit., p. 201.

48. McDonald and Searles, op. cit., p. 201.

49. Ibid., p. 202.

50. Ibid., p. 197.

51. A correspondent for The Methodist (July 17, 1869),

as quoted by Ridgaway, op. cit., p. 360, reported that the
meeting had attracted natives of every state except Louisiana,
Florida, and Texas, as well as some Europeans; among the
latter was the English publisher, D. Morgan, Esq. One
hundred fifty ministers attended.

52. McDonald and Searles, op. cit., p. 203-204. Nye,
op. cit., pp. 164-207, speaks of "The American Sense of
Mission." That "the United States [was to] serve as an example to the rest of the world of God's plan" was part of the
nation's definition of its purpose.

53. Ibid.

54. Smith notes in his Revival and Social Reform that
Chas. Johnson, The Frontier Camp Meeting, Religious Harvest Time (Dallas: Southern Methodist University Press,
1955), discussed the decline of the frontier camp, while camps
in eastern urban centers were growing in number and importance. In the post-Civil War period a good railroad became
a prime consideration in the location of a camp. Special
rates were frequently provided by the rail lines for the campers. See Wallace, op. cit., pp. 12-13.

55. For typical discussions of the subject see Christian Advocate and Journal, XXXIII (August 26, 1858), 133;
Beauty, VIII (June, 1857), 161-63; ibid., VIII (August, 1857),
228-29.

56. In his Christian Nurture (Hartford, Conn.: n. n.,
1846), Bushnell proposed that the Christian education of children in the home and the church would be more effective in
producing Christians than the crisis conversion experiences
of the revivalists.

57. In 1868, in Philadelphia alone, the Methodists
announced fifteen area camp meetings for the summer. See
Philadelphia Public Ledger (July 9, 1868), "Local Religious
News."

58. Sweet, Revivalism, p. 166; the same, The American Churches, p. 56. After 1874, Chatauqua, one of the
oldest Methodist camps, became largely an educational institution.

59. Harper's Weekly, XVII (August 23, 1873), 742.
Also see "Amusement, Religion and Recreation Combined at

Chester Heights," Chester (Pa.) Times (July 26, 1883); James
F. Reisling, "Some Ocean Grove Observations," Christian
Advocate and Journal, LXXIII (September 22, 1898), 1542; the
latter reported that there were no "sinners or unsaved" at
Ocean Grove, N. J. camp, and that the holiness camp founded
by National Association leaders in 1869 was becoming "more
and more ... a Christian seaside resort and less a camp
meeting, ..." in spite of the fact that seventyeight holiness
meetings had been held during that season. For the history
of Ocean Grove, see Morris S. Daniels, The Story of Ocean
Grove (New York: Methodist Book Concern, 1919).

   60. R. Yeakel attributed "a great improvement in
holding and conducting camp meetings throughout the Evangelical Association and beyond her borders" to the influence of
the National camps; H. J. Bowman, op. cit. , p. 205. Gaddis, op. cit. , p. 445, claims that "the camp meeting from
the close of the Civil War on passed almost entirely under
perfectionist auspices...." It was through a camp meeting
that the Mennonite Brethren in Christ became a holiness denomination; see Huffman, op. cit. , pp. 148-49.

   61. Guide, LXIV (October, 1873), 117-18; ibid. , LX
(August, 1871), 62; ibid. , II (September, 1840), 70; ibid. ,
XLVIII (September, 1865), 87.

   62. Nye, op. cit. , pp. 256-304, "The American View
of Nature." Also see a more extended development of the
concept in American history in Hans Huth, Nature and the
American (Berkeley, Cal. : n. n. , 1957). Perry Miller, The
New England Mind (New York: n. n. , 1939), chap. viii, gives
a brief analysis of the Puritan and nature.

   63. In 1860, four out of five people lived in rural
areas; in 1870, three out of four. Historical Statistics of
the United States: Colonial Times to 1957 (Washington: Government Printing Office, 1961), p. 9.

   64. Advocate of Christian Holiness, III (July, 1872),
19.

   65. Zion's Herald, XXI (July 31, 1850), p. 1.

   66. Jones, op. cit. , p. 110.

   67. S. Mead, op. cit. , p. ix.

68. Christian Advocate and Journal, XXXIII (September 9, 1858), 141.

69. Jones, op. cit., p. 63. For an excellent interpretation of the significance of the place of the camp meeting within the holiness movement, see ibid., pp. 93-110. It is limited only by the restrictions of Jones' main thesis that the holiness institutions were shaped mainly to suit the nostalgia of rural immigrants to the city for situations similar to those they once knew "back home."

70. Beauty of Holiness, VIII (August, 1857), 253.

71. B. Rees, op. cit., p. 110. "The effect was tremendous. It was as if a great white lily had burst into full bloom in an instant"; ibid. Ridgaway, op. cit., p. 366.

72. B. Rees, op. cit., p. viii. Camp meeting commemtators usually referred to the place of music in the camps. In 1850 H. C. Atwater noted that one could learn there "the mighty power of congregational singing over the human heart, and what it would do ... if adopted in all ... churches." Zion's Herald, XXI (July 31, 1850), p. 1. In 1857 Rev. T. M. Eddy urged that "No man should be allowed to sing his fugue tunes, his opera music, or to flourish through his demi-semiquavers--No! We want good, old stirring tunes full of melody, full of soul--tunes in which the congregation can join," he concluded; Beauty, VIII (August, 1857), p. 228.

73. S. Mead, op. cit., pp. 52-58. One of the most famous camp meeting characters was "Camp Meetin' John Allen," the Rev. John Allen of Farmington, Maine. He attended 374 camps during his lifetime; he died in 1887, at the age of ninety-three at the Methodist Episcopal Church camp at East Livermore, Maine.

74. From the writer's personal experience at Beulah Park Camp Meeting, Allentown, Pa.

75. Wallace, op. cit., p. 215.

76. B. Rees, op. cit., p. 24.

77. Wallace, op. cit., p. 29. Clark and Smith, op. cit., pp. 173-180. Wallace, op. cit., p. 12, notes that at Manheim "rowdyism was met and on its own chosen field completely conquered."

78. Ibid. , p. 31.

79. C. S. Eby, "Wesley Grove National Camp Meeting," Earnest Christianity, I (October, 1875), 583. For typical variations in this schedule see ibid. , II (February, 1874), 48; also, Wallace, op. cit. , p. 28.

80. Wallace, op. cit. , p. 12. Also see Jones, op. cit. , p. 103.

81. Methodist, IX (August 4, 1897), 8-9, as quoted from the Waco, Texas Telegram. For another account of the same meeting see Jones, op. cit. , p. 398, taken from the Pentecostal Herald, IX (August 11, 1897), 4. Wallace, op. cit. , is the best description of all the aspects of a National Camp Meeting as seen by one in the movement.

82. Wm. B. Godbey, Bible Theology (Cincinnati, Ohio: Revivalist Office, 1911), p. 100.

83. T. Smith, Called Unto Holiness, pp. 63, 76, 130. Editor G. Hughes looked to the 1872 National Camps "to give the keynote that shall send its powerful vibrations through all our ranks." Advocate of Christian Holiness, III (July, 1872), p. 19.

84. T. Smith, Called Unto Holiness, p. 66. Daniel D. Williams in his article, "Tradition and Experience in American Theology," The Shaping of American Religion, Smith and Jamison, op. cit. , I, 454, says that "It was inevitable that pietists would discover in the camp meetings ... that the emotional patterns of the conversion experience could become the liturgy and sacrament of the religious fellowship."

85. McDonald and Searles, op. cit. , p. 207.

86. Ibid. , pp. 207-208.

87. Guide for 1871, passim. In 1872, the Guide began a systematic listing of the camp meetings.

88. McDonald and Searles, op. cit. , pp. 220ff.

89. For the full account of the Salt Lake meeting, see ibid. , pp. 263ff.; the Godbieites were one of three Mormon factions in Salt Lake at that time according to McDonald

and Searles, op. cit. , p. 265.   They, with the members of
the Reorganized Church of Jesus Christ of the Latter Day
Saints under Joseph Young, welcomed the evangelists to the
city.   Godbie was a "wealthy merchant," whose aims seemed
to be "political"; ibid.   Brigham Young, himself, appeared
friendly toward the party; ibid. , p. 264.

    90.   Ibid. , p. 271.

    91.   Ibid. , pp. 270-71, as quoted from the Christian
at Work.   It was pioneering work; Pierce had arrived only
a year before and the first Presbyterian church in the city
was not started until the month following the National Committee's meetings in the middle of June, 1871.

    92.   In 1871-1872 Inskip and his band traveled 20,000
miles, held 600 services, and claimed 1,200 converts and
3,000 Christians who sought entire sanctification.   Among the
latter was the industrialist, W. C. DePauw, an Indiana glass
manufacturer, who claimed the experience of sanctification in
one of Inskip's tabernacle meetings in Indianapolis, Indiana,
September 21, 1871.   DePauw became treasurer of the National Association.   He is best remembered through DePauw
University, a Methodist college in Greencastle, Indiana,
named in his honor.   McDonald and Searles, op. cit. , pp.
278-81.   Also see Michael F. O'Brien, "A Nineteenth Century Hoosier Business Man; Washington Charles DePauw"
(unpublished B. A. thesis, DePauw University, 1966).

    93.   See Guide and Advocate of Christian Holiness for
1871 and 1872, passim.   Also see Edward Davis, Illustrated
History of Douglas Camp Meeting (Boston: McDonald, Gill
and Co. , 1890), pp. 1-2.   Wallace, op. cit. , p. 63.   Holiness work in India centered in the work of Methodist missions
under James Mills Thoburn, missionary to India from 1859-
1908.   Later missionary bishop of India, Thoburn was directly
involved in the post-war holiness revival through the faith
missions work of William Taylor, a Methodist irregular in
missions, who was widely known for his independent work in
starting Methodist missions in India, Africa, and South America.   Taylor, later a Methodist missionary bishop, became
an active member of the National Camp Meeting Committee;
the holiness movement inside and outside of the Methodist
Episcopal Church was the main source of funds for his work
through what was known as "The Transit Fund. "   T. B.
Welch, M. D. , Vineland, N. J. , who gave his name to the famous nonfermented grape juice, was treasurer of the fund and

associate editor of Taylor's African News. See ibid., I (January, 1889), 1; William Taylor, The Story of My Life: an Account of What I Have Thought and Said and Done in My Ministry of More than Fifty-three Years in Christian Lands and
Among the Heathen (New York: Eaton and Mains, 1898); the
same, Four Years' Campaign in India (New York: Phillips
and Hunt, 1880 [originally published 1876]). Jones op. cit.,
pp. 151-59, has a good summary of Taylor's work and influence in the movement and Methodism. On Thoburn, see
Simpson, op. cit., 858-59; Webster's Biographical Dictionary
(Springfield, Mass.: G. and C. Merriam Co. Publishers,
1943), p. 1460.

94. Guide, LIX (May, 1871), 157. Among others
listed were layman Robert Pearsall Smith, Presbyterian from
Philadelphia; layman Charles Cullis, M.D., Boston; Rev. Dr.
Daniel Steele, Methodist, professor at Boston University; and
New England Baptist Evangelist A. B. Earle. Ibid.; Advocate of Christian Holiness, III (February, 1873), 185-86; a
letter from Boardman in ibid. (January, 1873), p. 159, also
refers to "one of the pillars of the Central Baptist Church of
Providence, and one of the trustees of Brown University,"
who was a believer in the holiness experience, together with
the holiness convention work in the Providence area in the
Congregational, Baptist, and Methodist churches.

95. Guide, XVI [New Series] (February, 1872), 58.

96. Advocate of Christian Holiness, III (February,
1873), 185.

97. Richard Fuller, "Personal Religion, Its Aids and
Hindrances," Schaff and Prime, op. cit., p. 335.

98. Ibid., pp. 335-36.

99. Supra, p. 6. Not all Pietism was quietistic, however; the beginnings of the social outreach of Protestantism
lay "in no small part" in Pietism. Stoeffler, op. cit., p. 4.

100. Schaff and Prime, op. cit., pp. 338-40. Jones,
op. cit., appendix C3, pp. 451-52, lists the membership of
the National Camp Meeting Committee for the years 1869,
1873, and 1894.

101. See Gaddis, op. cit., p. 426. Roy S. Nicholson,
Wesleyan Methodism in the South: Being the Story of Eighty-

Six Years of Reform and Religious Activities in the South as
Conducted by the American Wesleyans (Syracuse, N.Y.:
Wesleyan Methodist Publishing Association, 1933), pp. 1-113,
gives a full account of the opposition experienced by Wesleyans in the south prior to the Civil War. Wesleyans had also
been active in the Underground Railroad system, particularly
in Indiana and Michigan. McLeister, op. cit., pp. 424-25.

102.   Gaddis, loc. cit.

103.   See Jones' summary in, the same, op. cit., p.
53; Bishops Simpson, Janes, and Haven, all sympathetic to
the holiness cause, envisioned southern expansion after the
war. Alfred Cookman and Gilbert Haven after whom Cookman Institute in Jacksonville, Fla. and Haven Normal School
in Waynesborough, Ga. were named respectively, identified
the movement with the Negro cause and northern "carpetbag-
gers." See Simpson, op. cit., pp. 256, 380-381. Also see
Jervey, "Motives and Methods of the Methodist Episcopal
Church in the Period of Reconstruction," Methodist History,
IV, 17-25.

104.   Advocate of Christian Holiness, III (November,
1872), 108. "The Churches and Reconstruction," Olmstead,
op. cit., pp. 400-404.

105.   Ibid. (September, 1872), p. 69.

106.   Ibid. (November, 1872), 108-110. Also see Mc-
Donald and Searles, op. cit., p. 292. Haven was especially
rejected because of his close association with radical New
England movements; Jervey, loc. cit.

107.   Ibid. (September, 1872), 69; Christian Standard
and Home Journal, IX (November 27, 1875), 382. See also
Henry Clay Morrison, Life Sketches and Sermons (Louisville,
Ky.: Pentecostal Publishing Co., 1903), p. 33. Morrison
lists some of the early holiness leaders in the south as: Dr.
Lovick Pierce, Wm. B. Godbey, B. A. Cundiff, W. A. Dodge,
W. S. Grinstead, and J. S. Keen. For biographical notes on
Pierce see Simpson, op. cit., p. 717.

108.   McLeister, op. cit., pp. 86-89.

109.   Ibid., p. 85.

110.   The Free Methodists, who were noted especially

for their stringent standards of dress, were expressing the
direct instructions of both Wesley and B. T. Roberts, their
founder. The latter pointed out in The Free Methodist that
Wesley had laid down the rule that no ticket for admission
to a class meeting should be given " 'to any, until they have
left off superfluous ornaments. Allow no exempt case, not
even of a married woman. . . . Give no tickets to any that
wear high heads, enormous bonnets, ruffles, or rings.' "
"If this rule were carried out today, how many would they
[the Methodists] have in their love-feasts? Were they fanat-
ical then on the subject of dress, or are they backslidden
now? Times may change but God does not change" (emphasis
his). As quoted from ibid., in Pungent Truths, Being Extracts from the Writings of the Rev. Benjamin Titus Roberts,
A. M., while Editor of the Free Methodist from 1886-1890,
ed. William R. Rose (Chicago: The Free Methodist Publishing House, 1915), pp. 78-79; also see comment in ibid., p.
80, on not wearing a necktie. This became a prominent characteristic of male Free Methodist dress, especially among
the clergy. The degree to which times do change and "God"
with them is shown by the fact that a piled-up hair style undoubtedly quite similar to Wesley's "high heads" which kept
women out of the class meeting is currently the only one
commonly accepted by some of the very conservative holiness
and pentecostal sects today, and in the Free Methodist and
other larger holiness bodies, the average member's contemporary styles would also ban him.

111. Robert Pearsall Smith, the Philadelphia holiness
layman who led the holiness revival in Europe in the mid-
1870's, judged that the extremes which had been exercised
on both sides in the controversy had resulted in "one side,
taking the doctrine of full salvation, ... to be swept past the
tender, gentle, forbearing spirit of love into contentiousness
and separation; while the other side reacted into prejudice
against the experience of 'holiness.' " See the same, "The
Great Revival of 'Christian Perfection' as a Life in America,"
Earnest Christianity, II (1876), 46. See T. Smith's conclusions. Revivalism and Social Reform, pp. 132-33. The
Methodist Episcopal Church's Genesee Conference sought to
make amends for its part in the controversy when it restored
Roberts' ministerial parchments to his son, Benson Howard
Roberts, in 1910 at the conference's centenary celebration.
Roberts had died seventeen years previously. Marston, op.
cit., pp. 582-88.

112. Among these was Bishop Matthew Simpson.

Robert D. Clark, Simpson's biographer, discusses the bishop's personal struggles over the experience; The Life of
Matthew Simpson (New York: The Macmillan Co. , 1956),
pp. 175-77. Simpson counseled with Phoebe Palmer in 1852;
she urged him to no "longer let the tempter to hinder you
from laying hold upon the promise. . . . " Clark observes,
"Perhaps it was of signigicance to Methodism that the most
eloquent of the Bishops never discovered the satisfying spiritual condition of which she wrote." Ibid. , p. 176.

113.   McDonald and Searles, op. cit. , pp. 210-11.

114.   Ibid.

115.   Advocate of Christian Holiness, III (November,
1872), 111.

116.   Ibid.

117.   McDonald and Searles, op. cit. , p. 277.

118.   Ibid.

119.   Simpson, op. cit. , pp. 371-72.   Also see supra,
p. 50.

120.   Simpson, op. cit. , pp. 585-86.

121.   The Advocate of Christian Holiness was certain
that the bishop sympathized "most deeply with the work of
the National Committee. " In reporting on a visit by Peck
to the Thirty-first National Camp held at Clear Lake, Iowa,
the paper said, "If all our bishops would do as Bishop Peck
has done ... they would then be able to see for themselves
whether there was any peril to the church in this movement. "
Ibid. , IX (August, 1878), 188.

122.   Simpson, op. cit. , pp. 434-35.

123.   Simpson, op. cit. , p. 128.   Bishop Bowman was
still involved with the movement in 1901 when he signed the
call to the General Holiness Assembly at Chicage in 1901;
see S. B. Shaw, op. cit. , p. 13.

124.   See infra, p. 211; Simpson, op. cit. , pp. 430-
31.   Jones, op. cit. , p. 56-57, comments, "Having denounced
fanaticism and avoided schism, holiness believers had strong

representation in the church's progressive vanguard.   Their
year of majority had arrived." Note that Jones does not
list Harris among the sympathizers with the movement who
were elected in 1872.   In light of this joint action with Lowrey and Mahan, it seems he should be added to the list.
Divine Life (October, 1879), 61-67; ibid.   (March, 1880),
pp. 161-66.

125.   Advocate of Christian Holiness, III (November,
1872), 111.   Mrs. Hamline wrote to Phoebe Palmer in 1867
of the conflict over the holiness revival of the post-war period.   She observed that "Dr. Bannister ... is marked as an
advocate of 'Christian Perfection' ... [and] Dr. Kidder ...
is sinking deeper in the ocean of Salvation [sic].   But there
are those who stand exactly in the way, of the work of Holi-
ness--'Stumbling blocks, indeed.'" Letter of Mrs. L. Hamline to Phoebe Palmer from Evanston, Ill. , November 17,
1867, in manuscript collection of Drew University.

126.   T. Smith, Called Unto Holiness, p. 42.   Smith
contends here that "this, in part, explains the unanimity with
which Methodist officialdom professed loyalty to the doctrine
whole opposing measures to promote it." See L. L. Pickett,
Entire Sanctification from 1799 to 1901 (Louisville, Ky.:
Pickett Publishing Co. , 1901), for a summary of the doctrinal continuity of the movement with Wesley.   See Jones, op.
cit. , "Appendix C4: Official Methodist Pronouncements on
Holiness," pp. 454-56, for excerpts from numerous episcopal
addresses to the general conferences of both the Methodist
Episcopal Church and the Methodist Episcopal Church South
on the question.   Sweet, The Story of Religion in America,
pp. 405-406.

127.   Bishop John P. Newman's statement in the "Introduction" to Roche's biography of Sarah Lankford Palmer is
typical of many others: "For this purpose they were called
to be a Church.   To give pre-eminence to this central, subjective doctrine, was Wesley chosen by Providence ... and
the universal spread of these sentiments is now esteemed the
high mission of the Church which has survived him over a
hundred years." Roche, Sarah Lankford Palmer, pp. 8-9.
Kenneth W. Copeland, "The Magnificent Purpose," Asbury
Seminarian, XXVI (January, 1972), 31-33.

128.   Advocate of Christian Holiness, III (November,
1872), 150.   Ibid.   (December, 1872), 142.   Ibid.   (January,
1873), 160.   Perfect Love, or the Speeches of Rev. E. L.

Janes; Rev. H. Mattison, D.D.; Rev. D. Curry, D.D.; Rev.
J. M. Buckley and Rev. S. D. Brown in the New York
Preacher's Meeting in March and April 1867, upon the Subject of Sanctification ... (New York: N. Tibbals and Co.,
1868).

129. Advocate of Christian Holiness, III (June, 1873),
265.

130. Ibid., pp. 265-67.

131. Advocate of Christian Holiness, VI (October, 1875),
86.

132. Ibid.

133. Ibid. Also see Wm. McDonald, John Wesley and
His Doctrine (Boston: McDonald, Gill and Co., 1893), pp.
136ff. Simpson, op. cit., pp. 84-85. All of these were
essentially pietistic.

134. Supra, p. 111.

135. Guide, LX (August, 1871), 62.

136. M. L. Haney, The Inheritance Restored: or Plain
Truths on Bible Holiness (Chicago: Christian Witness Co.,
1904), p. 215.

137. In a more recent brief account of her life, Ernest
Wall compares and contrasts her life with that of Catherine
of Siena. Ernest Wall, "I Commend unto You Phoebe," Religion in Life, XXVI (Summer, 1957), 396-408.

138. The Ladies Repository, XXVI (February, 1866).

139. Roche, op. cit., p. 8.

140. Advocate of Christian Holiness, V (December,
1874), 136.

141. Guide, LXVII (January, 1875), 9.

142. Advocate of Christian Holiness, V (December,
1874), 137.

143. Simpson, op. cit., p. 936.

144. Methodist Quarterly Review, LX (January, 1878),
176.

145. Ibid.

146. Ibid. (October, 1878), 688ff. In this same article, Whedon says; "Many of us do not believe that Christian Perfection is a second special blessing 'gained instantaneously
by an act of faith.... ' " Ibid. , 696. He also attacked the
"altar terminology" of Phoebe Palmer; ibid. , 697.

147. Ibid. , LVI (October, 1874), pp. 662-81. Crane's
book, Holiness the Birthright of All God's Children (New
York: Nelson and Phillips, 1875), had been reviewed in the
Methodist Quarterly Review, LVI (July, 1874), 490-92. The
reviewer noted that the book seemed to support sanctification
of the believer at the time of his conversion. This was more
Zinzendorfian than Wesleyan.

148. "Methodist Quarterly Review," Advocate of Christian Holiness, IX (March, 1878), 64.

149. Ibid. , p. 65.

150. Ibid. , p. 65. In the Methodist Quarterly Review,
LVI (October, 1874), 662-63, Whedon defended his definition
of Wesleyan and Methodist doctrines which he had first outlined in Bibliotheca Sacra, XIX (April, 1862), 241-74. He
says the article still stood and had been republished in the
Advocate and Zion's Herald and was commended by McClintock
in Cyclopedia of Methodism as a standard statement of "our
Arminianism." He noted that part of the statement on Christian Perfection was included in the above. Whedon's statements on the topic were far too general to satisfy the holiness party in the church.

151. Ibid. , p. 64.

152. Jones, op. cit. , p. 89.

CHAPTER IV

FROM VINELAND AND MANHEIM TO BERLIN AND BRIGHTON:
THE EUROPEAN HOLINESS REVIVAL

THE BACKGROUND OF THE ENGLISH REVIVAL

The intercourse in religious revival movements between England and America presents an interesting study in
itself. From the revivalism of George Whitefield to that of
Billy Graham, there has not been a significant revival of
religion which has not crossed and sometimes recrossed the
Atlantic. The post-war revival of holiness evangelism by
the Palmers in England and Scotland after the American Revival of 1858 had done as much as anything else to prepare
the way for the great higher life conventions which were to
cause an explosion of that doctrine across England and the Continent in the 1870's. The revival meetings of James Caughey,
the Methodist holiness evangelist and the visits of American
evangelists, Charles Finney, Asa Mahan and William Boardman during the Second Evangelical Awakening,[1] also helped
to spread the dominantly Wesleyan perfectionist revivalism
from the American movement across the British Isles. As
noted above, the Palmers alone saw thousands of sanctifications recorded in their campaigns;[2] however, there was a
lack of any organized effort at that time to conserve the results of those meetings or to promote the doctrine in the
special manner popularized by the work of the National Camp
Association in America.

Some called the revival which ensued with the Palmer's
wartime ministry in the British Isles an Evangelical Alliance
Revival because of its ecumenical character;[3] although, as
has already been noted above, there was considerable opposition to the American evangelist within the official circles of
the Wesleyan Methodist Churches of the country, as well as

by the Camp Meeting or Primitive Methodists.[4] From 1860
to 1870, however, the mood in these churches was changing
providing another opportunity for the holiness revival to penetrate British Methodism with its message.

New holiness literature and periodicals complemented
the standard Wesleyan writings on the doctrine and experience;
they contributed to the growing religious expectancy which
finally issued in the dramatic responses to the appeals of
Dwight L. Moody and Ira D. Sankey and the American holiness evangelists, R. Pearsall Smith, William E. Boardman,
and Asa Mahan. The call for a new outpouring of the Holy
Spirit upon the churches came from as diverse sources as
Edward Golburn, the Dean of Norwich and William Arthur,
an influential leader in the Wesleyan Methodist Conferences.[5]

Initial Movements

Regular reports of the English religious scene began
to appear in the Guide to Holiness and the Advocate of Christian Holiness in the late 1872 editions. The Advocate's British correspondent in the December 1872 issue, noted the remarks of the retiring conference president to the members
of the conference:

> By what has recently come under my own notice,
> ... in proclaiming the truth on this point [entire
> sanctification], you will preach to appreciative and
> sympathizing audiences. I believe there is a re-
> vival and wide-spread yearning among our people
> for full salvation. ... Therefore, let this subject
> receive your special attention. You can hardly do
> the church any service equal to that of urging upon
> our people that they seek to be cleansed from all
> sin, to love God with all their heart ... [emphasis
> his].[6]

The King's Highway reported at the close of 1872 that
there was appearing a "movement of the evangelical churches
for united and earnest prayer arising chiefly from the influence of the Evangelical Alliance."[7] As a result, the last
conference of the Wesleyan Methodist Church had formed a
prayer union among its membership. The union appealed to
all who had "the purity of the church ... and the welfare of
soul at heart."[8] It was, in essence, a holiness association
on the pattern of the numerous similar groups which were

already rising all over the United States and Canada in the
wake of the well-publicized work of the National Camp Meeting Association. The members of the union received a card
reminding them to pray for certain specific results:

> For myself that I may be sanctified wholly and
> preserved blameless. For ministers that bearing
> the vessels of the Lord they may be clean. For
> Methodism, that it may rightly SPREAD SCRIPTURAL
> HOLINESS through the land. For all churches that
> the doctrine and experience of holiness may pre-
> vail among them. And for our TIMES that they
> may be marked by a CONTINUING REVIVAL OF
> RELIGION ensuing in the salvation of multitudes
> both at home, and abroad.... [9]

The patterns of the holiness revival dominated by
Methodist teaching and National Camp Meeting influences were
appearing in Wesley's homeland. To many it appeared to be
"carrying coals to Newcastle," but it was a fact, commonly
acknowledged, that the religious fires of Wesley's land and
his church had not been burning very brightly,[10] the almost
spontaneous gathering up of the spiritual hunger of evangelicals in all churches of the land into the desire for a deeper
Christian experience during these few years in the mid-seventies, is the strongest evidence of that.

The introduction of the idea of special meetings for
the promotion of holiness into the English religious scene
produced opposition equal to any that had been experienced
in America. W. G. Pascoe, the English correspondent who
most regularly reported to the American holiness journals on
the progress of the revival in the British Isles, wrote to the
Advocate of Christian Holiness in March 1873, that "there is
yet a large amount of prejudice against them." Even the
friends of the doctrine, he said, were reluctant to encourage
such special measures, "lest the charge of 'cliqueism' should
be brought against them...."[11]

In May of the same year, the Advocate carried a
private letter from the north of England which reported that,
"the two works of conversion and entire sanctification were
going on together...."[12] In June 1873, Pascoe again noted
that there was more mention of "entire sanctification in the
past six months than some ministers have heard in their
whole previous ministry"; nevertheless, he admitted that "the
few meetings held distinctly in the interest of holiness are

small...." The advocates, he said, had to move ahead "against the stream of prejudice which flows rapidly along."[13] The prejudice was diminishing, however, for even some established church parishes were using religious missions. Pascoe regarded these protracted meetings as "a remarkable proof of the mighty religious stir which is now affecting all religious circles,..." in spite of their promotion, at times, "of the confessional and other pernicious Romish teaching."[14]

Robert Pearsall and Hannah Whitall Smith

If the lay evangelists, Walter and Phoebe Palmer had represented the heart of the spiritual dynamic at work in popularizing the revival of Christian holiness in the Methodist and other churches in the United States another husband and wife team, Robert Pearsall and Hannah Whitall Smith, also laymen, represented the spark which finally ignited the holiness revival movement in England and throughout the continent of Europe.[15]

The Smiths were Quakers--her family from rural, and his from urban Philadelphia. They were the first among several evangelists of the Quaker faith who were to take a prominent part in the spreading holiness revival. In spite of their non-Methodist religious affiliations, they were, nevertheless, exponents of Wesleyan perfectionism; both had learned of the experience of entire sanctification in Methodist holiness meetings in Philadelphia and southern New Jersey where they lived.

Mrs. Smith had gone through a period of religious skepticism early in her married life in which she had seriously doubted her acceptance of the orthodox teachings of Christianity, particularly the doctrine of the atonement. Her rejection of this religious skepticism and her search for the "God [who was] making Himself manifest [to her] as an actual existence" are part of the story of the Revival of 1858. It was at one of the popular noon-day prayer meetings of that revival that she discovered God. Her description of her experience has a mystical ring which is illustrative of a theme which sounds its muted, but identifiable, note throughout the story of the movement. It readily suited an experience of inner devotion centered, as it was, so strongly in pursuit of the fullness of the Holy Spirit in the individual life. She said of that day in 1858:

> It was not that I felt myself to be a sinner needing
> salvation, or that I was troubled about my future
> destiny. It was not a personal question at all. It
> was simply and only that I had become aware of
> God, and that I felt I could not rest until I should
> know him.... All I wanted was to become acquainted
> with the God of whom I had suddenly become aware
> [emphasis mine]. 16

She did not claim to have become a Christian until
after a member of the Plymouth Brethren sect helped her to
believe that her new grasp of God and the joy which had ensued in her life were the result of her being "born of God."
She later described the certain conviction which followed that
moment of personal commitment:

> There it was--the grand central fact of God's love
> and forgiveness, and my soul was at rest about this
> forever. 17

Both because of this experience and the failure of her
reserved Quaker friends to understand the new-found enthusiasm she demonstrated in telling others of her spiritual discovery, she turned to members of the Plymouth Brethren sect
for continuing spiritual advice. Their simplistic approach to
belief and the Bible were, she confessed, a settling factor
in her life, but gradually their emphasis on the Calvinistic
doctrine of "election" began to raise questions in her mind
concerning their overall system of Christian doctrine. Perhaps her inbred Quaker latitudinarian instincts reacted against
a doctrine which was much too restrictive for them. The
warm relationships with the Plymouth Brethren began to cool. 18

It was not until she and her husband moved to Millville,
New Jersey, where he was to assist in the management of her
father's glass factory, that Hannah Whitall Smith claimed to
discover what she commonly called the "secret" of a happy
Christian life. One Saturday evening, as Mrs. Smith slipped
into a Methodist ladies prayer meeting, she heard a "factory
woman" testifying to her friends that previous to her sanctification the "whole horizon used to be filled with great big
Me." But that when she "got sight of Christ ... great big
Me wilted down to nothing."

Mrs. Smith acknowledged that these words brought a
"profound conviction" to her, and "that this must be real
Christianity, ... that it was, perhaps, the very thing I was

longing for." She said that the truth came to her as a discovery and without any definite crisis of spiritual experience. [19]
She began to testify to having found the secret of a happier
state of Christian experience which she later elaborated in
the book that very soon became and still remains one of the
great religious classics, The Christian's Secret of a Happy
Life. [20]   In those early years of discovery, she declared that
she had

> found that the gist of it was exactly what Paul meant
> when he said, "Not I but Christ," ... the victory I
> sought [she said] was to come by ceasing to live my
> own life and by letting the power of God "work in
> me to will and to do of his good pleasure...."
>   It is a Methodist doctrine, and I have been used
> to hearing Methodists much objected to on account
> of it, but it seems to be the only thing that can
> supply my needs, and I feel impelled to try it. [21]

In spite of considerable initial concern that his wife
had fallen into some dangerous heresy, Robert Pearsall Smith
gradually yielded to the convincing personal testimony and the
scriptural proof texts she provided for him in reply to his
questions concerning the experience.   He claimed the "blessing" in "true Methodist fashion" very soon thereafter at the
National Association's first camp at Vineland in July of 1867.
His wife describes his experience:

> Suddenly from head to foot he had been shaken by
> what seemed like a magnetic thrill of heavenly de-
> light, and floods of glory seemed to pour through
> him, soul and body, with the inward assurance that
> this was the longed-for Baptism of the Holy Spirit.
> The whole world seemed transformed to him, every
> leaf and blade of grass quivered with exquisite color,
> and heaven seemed to open out before him as a
> present blissful possession.   Everybody looked
> beautiful to him, for he seemed to see the Divine
> Spirit within each one without regard to their out-
> ward seemings.   This ecstacy lasted for several
> weeks.... [22]

Hannah confessed that for some time after observing her
husband's emotional experience, she was

> rather jealous that she did not receive a like bless-
> ing, for I felt that I needed it quite as much as he

did, and I renewed by efforts to obtain it. But
it was all in vain.... I became convinced at last
that the reason of this difference between my experience and that of some others was not that they
were peculiarly favoured by God above me, but
that their emotional nature received with these floods
of emotional delight, the same truths that I received
calmly, and with intellectual delight; the difference
being, not in the experiences but in the different
natures of the recipients of that experience. [23]

Regardless of intellectual or emotional variations, Mr.
and Mrs. Robert Pearsall Smith, of Millville, New Jersey,
had joined the holiness revival. They had discovered, what
Hannah, thereafter, commonly called, "the unselfishness of
God." The news of their enthusiastic witness to this new
experience rapidly spread across the movement in the United
States and Canada, but most significantly to England and
Europe. [24]

The Smiths' early English ministry

In 1873, Robert Pearsall Smith was informally introduced into the English evangelical circles, which were increasingly agitated on the question of the higher Christian
life. He was not there in response to any call for his religious services, but rather was traveling after a period of
severe sickness resulting from an accident which he had
suffered in 1871. [25] But the news of his espousal of the
"blessing" and his inability to resist testifying to it soon
deeply involved him in the already incipient tide of English
revival. The movement there was gradually overcoming its
opposition and building up strength for the unusual spiritual
response which Moody and Sankey experienced in their ministry on their first evangelistic tour of England in 1873. Informal meetings with Smith's English friends soon led to
more formal breakfast meetings, especially with the ministry
of the non-Methodist churches of England and the Established
Church. As a result, invitations multiplied for him to address groups seeking deeper life instruction. [26]

Initially, some English evangelicals were hesitant to
allow Mrs. Smith as free a range on the religious conference
speaking circuit as her husband; hints of her espousal of a
universalist view of eternal destiny had already begun to
steal across the Atlantic along with her much more widely
known reputation for evangelistic effectiveness. [27] It is most

remarkable that in spite of a long-standing commitment to a universalist view of the restitution of all things, not only was she widely used in the meetings, but soon she became known to English friends as "the angel of the churches."[28]

Hannah Whitall Smith's universalist tendencies not only did not restrict her English ministry, but even appeared to enlarge it. Her honest response to a chance remark at the home of Mrs. Cowper Temple, later Lady Mount Temple, opened up the door to the Smith's holiness evangelism among the English upper classes.

The incident occurred at an informal meeting of a group of evangelicals who were considering the endorsement of the Smiths for meetings among them. A passing funeral procession turned the group's conversation to the question of eternal destiny. The subject evoked an expression by Mrs. Smith of her basic belief in the final salvation of all men. Attracted by her candor in the face of the possible opposition it might arouse, Mrs. Temple invited the American woman evangelist to Broadlands, the family estate in Hampshire, formerly the estate of Lord Palmerston, Temple's stepfather. This relationship evinced strong support among the upper class of England for future holiness conferences and the subsequent work of the Smiths in England and Europe.[29]

The fact that her ministry and books continued to be influential in the holiness and higher life movement, in spite of her divergent views, is probably due to several factors: to her own attitude in the matter, to her personal effectiveness and winsomeness, and to the general disposition of a spiritual movement such as she was involved in to lay considerably more stress on experience and life style than on doctrinal rectitude. Or again, it may have been that her rock-ribbed Quaker character simply squelched much of the potential controversy. This clearly shows in a letter to her husband after he had successfully overcome pressure by a committee preparing for the Brighton Convention in 1874 to compromise the issue of her universalist views. The committee had agreed to invite her to attend, but wanted to restrict her public participation at the meeting. In reply to the invitation which finally came without the desired restrictions, she said:

> I am glad thee has got out of thy difficulty about thy heretical preaching wife with so little trouble.

But the idea of B_____ with shaky views of his
own, undertaking to excommunicate me. I really
do not think it was honest. I do not choose to
sail under false colours, and I am a thousand times
stronger in my views of restitution, every day I
live. If they let me alone in England I shall probably not say much about it, but if there is the least
hint of any compromise or underhanded secrecy on
my part, I shall blaze on in perfect conflagration....
So you must please bear this in mind, ye Lords
of Creation. Soberly, however, I do not feel at
all drawn to preach or to teach restitution over
there, and if the dear frightened Orthodox friends
do not make any fuss about it I shall not be likely
to. Their difficulties do not annoy me in the least.
I believe I actually enjoy being the victim of "odicum
theologicum." I guess there is something of the
war horse in my composition. 30

With the active help of the Smiths, the holiness forces
in England were coalescing and new allies were joining the
cause. Pascoe's own holiness journal, the King's Highway,
first published in 1873, was beginning to serve the English
movement in the same manner that Timothy Merritt's Guide
had done in the beginnings of the American revival. Robert
Pearsall Smith and William E. Boardman, who was now also
working on the English scene, seconded that initial effort in
1874 with their paper, The Christian's Pathway of Power.
This paper, under the editorship of Evan H. Hopkins, later
became the Life of Faith, voice of the Keswick movement. 31

By the fall of 1873, a now regular column on the
"Work of Holiness in England" in the Advocate of Christian
Holiness told the readers that Robert P. Smith is "doing a
good work in London in connection with the holiness movement, especially among the Calvinistic churches."32 Dr.
Charles Cullis of Boston, and the aged Asa Mahan, also,
were assisting Smith and Boardman by this time. A prominent London Baptist minister, Henry Varley,33 who had made
a public profession of his own entrance into the "rest of faith"
only a short time before, also became active in the movement. These non-Methodist men formed an effective force
for introducing the movement's message into circles which
may otherwise have arbitrarily denied it a sympathetic hearing. 34

The traditional official reserve which the British

Methodist bodies had shown to American holiness evangelists
such as Caughey and the Palmers now began to break down
under the expanding interest in spiritual revival. Holiness
meetings began to become a part of some official Methodist
conference gatherings; holiness associations were formed.
Smith was invited to bring his essentially Wesleyan message,
conditioned, as we have seen, by American revivalism, back
to its original home in special meetings with Methodist ministers of London and other urban centers. He was not un-
aware of whom he was addressing. At one such meeting
with Methodist clergymen, Smith reminded them that

> There were deep inward yearnings for an outpour-
> ing of the Spirit upon the universal Church. In
> the Establishment here and in the other denomina-
> tions in England and Scotland this was the promi-
> nent subject. There was not a church in this great
> city which has not the subject of consecration to
> God as the leading subject before its members and
> a very prominent subject in its ministry.

He then inquired,

> Should they as Methodists be behind them in this
> entire consecration? He expected to see the church
> of which John Wesley was the father in Christ rouse
> itself, and be more than it had been before....
> The great Establishment of England was getting into
> Methodist ways--holding after-meetings, singing in
> the power of the Spirit ... upon their knees; going
> round and talking to inquirers--they were close
> upon their heels; would they [the Methodists] con-
> tinue in the van in their great mission?[35]

Besides the reserved opposition of conservative forces
in the English churches which hesitated to commit themselves
too readily to these "new doctrines" flowing into England from
the camp meeting movement in the United States, there was
also outspoken questioning of Smith and Smith's message by
other critics. In the columns of the English Christian Standard. Mr. Grant, a newspaper man, wrote a series of sixteen articles attacking Robert Pearsall Smith. He quoted
John Wesley's teachings in contradiction to Smith's and charged
that the evangelist was a teacher of new doctrine, the possessor
of an experience greater than the Apostle Paul, and that he
must have reached absolute perfection. Reluctantly, Grant
admitted, however, that caught up by the growing momentum

of the English revival, "some of the holiest men of the land
have adopted these views which are yet 'altogether unscriptural and dangerous....' "36

The Broadlands and Oxford Conventions
for the Promotion of Holiness

The support of Lord and Lady Mount Temple and other
evangelicals prominent in English society provided a strong
base of operations for the evangelism of the Smiths. The
Temple's Broadlands estate was the scene of crucial meetings
in the promotion in England from July 17-23, 1874. "Union
Meetings for Consecration" held in Mildmay, Dublin, Manchester, and finally in Cambridge, had preceded these Broadlands meetings. The Broadlands meetings were held at the
request of some Cambridge students, who, influenced by the
Union Meeting at the University, wanted to spend time in
prayer and meditation in some secluded spot. Cowper Temple
opened up his 6000 acre estate to them, entertaining one hundred guests for the six days of a convention designed to suit
the students' purposes. At the conclusion of the conference,
Sir Arthur Blackwood, Earl of Chichester and president of
the Church Missionary Society, suggested that another, but
more extensive meeting for the promotion of holiness should
be held at Oxford during the summer vacation time. 37

The call for the Oxford Union Meeting for the Promotion of Scriptural Holiness went out on August 8, 1874.
The list of conveners for this special conference was much
more extensive and represented a much broader scope of
social, religious and political life than the list of the names
of the thirteen American Methodist ministers who sent out
the call to the first special holiness camp meeting at Vineland, New Jersey, only seven years earlier. The Oxford
list delineates the broadening patterns of the higher life
movement. In addition to the names of ministers prominent
in the promotion of holiness at that time in England, such
as William Arthur, William E. Boardman, and Henry Varley, the rising British Baptist evangelist, a fair representation of English society headed the list. Among them were
Sir Arthur Blackwood, Lord Farnham, Sir Thomas Bart,
Arthur Kinnard, M. P.; Stephenson A. Blackwood, Esq.;
Henry Kingscote, Esq.; and Charles Lloyd Braithwaite, Esq.
Among leading churchmen from England, France, and Germany, were the Very Rev. Dean of Canterbury, Theodore
Monod, son of the prominent French Free Church pastor,

Fred Monod; Paul Kover and Otto Stockmayer of Switzerland,
and from Germany, Theodor Jellinghaus and V. von Niebuhr
of Halle, whose father was one of the most influential diplo-
mats of the nineteenth century. [38]

The complexion of the company that gathered from the
first day's meetings at Oxford on August 29, paralleled that
of sponsors mentioned above. Many were from the English
upper classes. The revival of this period affected these
groups more than the former movements of 1864 had. A
foretaste of the international flavor of Brighton a year later
was provided by the twenty or thirty Continental pastors who
participated along with the ministers of both the established
and non-conformist churches of England. [39]

It is very probable that a careful comparison of the
obvious appeal of the holiness message to the complex social
and cultural pattern, portrayed by the groups which participated in the English holiness revival, with the conclusions
of sociologists of religion who have interpreted the American
holiness sect development in strongly sociological terms would
cast a note of caution into some of their conclusions. It
would appear that, granted the appeal of the movement to
the most basic religious desires, a poor man in America
may have responded to the holiness evangelist's call out of
the same existential impulses as did Lord Mount-Temple,
who obviously was not among "the disinherited." At least,
more tolerance must be allowed for such a possibility. The
appeal and the response, in both cases, probably arose out
of a common pietistic and Biblical orientation which strongly
permeated both English and American evangelical Protestantism.

Approximately one thousand, five hundred men and
women of all classes and denominations attended the ten-day
meeting. It was not uncommon to find most of them at the
very first early morning prayer and praise service, sharing
in prayer or testimony in the Methodist style, clergymen and
laymen declaring the spiritual joys already experienced or
eagerly anticipated before the meetings should end. W. G.
Pascoe reported to the Advocate of Christian Holiness, that
the Oxford meetings "more nearly approach to one of your
National Camp Meetings than anything we have hitherto seen
in England...."[40] The Rev. Evan H. Hopkins, one of the
fathers of the Keswick Conference, R. Pearsall Smith and
others recognized the continuity with the American revival
as well. Hopkins said, following the August 1874 meetings,

> We have attended many conferences, including a
> ten-day convention in America, the prototype of
> that at Oxford, but in most respects this excelled
> them all. It is the fruit and flower of those which
> have gone before--of those at Barnet and Mildmay,
> and Perth and other places at home, as well as at
> Manheim, and Vineland and Round Lake in the United
> States ... [emphasis mine]. 41

The Methodists were there in significant numbers, but
they stayed in the background so that there would be no suspicion that they were somehow executing a denominational
coup. Smith consistently declared, in his public addresses,
that the experience which he advocated was thoroughly Biblical and, therefore, non-denominational; at the same time he
rarely failed to speak of the debt which he felt the whole
Christian Church and especially he himself, owed to the "Holiness Methodists" for their clear proclamation of the possibilities of "the life of faith and Christian holiness." He was
now sharing their "depositum" with the whole European evangelical world. 42

The significance of such a meeting at the home of the
Tractarian movement in the Established Church, as well as
the place where the Wesleys and Whitefield had formed their
"holy club," was not lost on some. The Zion's Herald edi-
torialized that to the Methodists present,

> It must have been a suggestive spectacle to see
> old Oxford, the birthplace of Methodism, the scene
> of a great convention, composed of hundreds of
> Church of England clergymen, as well as represent-
> atives of other churches, entirely devoted, through
> a week or more to prayer, meditation, and consul-
> tation respecting "Scriptural holiness," the great
> theme which Wesley, almost alone, mediated within
> the University more than a century ago, ... 43

Inundated with a flow of enthusiastic public and private
correspondence and the personal reports of Smith and others
who returned to the United States at the end of the year,
William McDonald's excitement surfaced in the first editorial
of the Advocate for the year 1875,

> The witnesses to entire sanctification are now enu-
> merated by the thousands.... It promises even now
> to leaven the whole lump of Christianity. It is

> evident a new and progressive development of spir-
> itual religion is possessing and moving the churches.
> The Baptists, Presbyterians, Congregationalists,
> Quakers, Episcopalians, and most other ecclesiastic
> bodies, are ... directing attention to the higher
> privilege or obligation of Christians.

He then threw out the same challenge to American
Methodism which Smith had presented to British Methodism
in an effort to excite Wesley's descendants to renewed holiness emphasis and experience. He warned:

> Indeed some of these fellowships are getting to be
> so pronounced in the experience and so enthusiastic
> in the promotion of holiness, that we have had a
> little excusable apprehension that Methodism by her
> delinquencies and tardiness, not to say cold neglect
> and uncharitable opposition, might lose her God-
> given birthright. [44]

The Holiness Revival on the Continent

In late spring of 1875, just prior to a second large
convention for the promotion of holiness which was to meet
at the resort city of Brighton, on England's southeastern
coast in May of that year, Robert Pearsall Smith carried his
holiness evangelism to France, Germany, and Switzerland. [45]
Theodore Monod, who had attended the summer's convention
at Oxford, was anxious to see the revival spread among the
Free Churches of France. The response to the meetings
Smith held there indicated an active interest in the higher
life preaching among these French Protestants. [46] But nowhere did Smith receive such an enthusiastic reception as he
did on his German and Swiss tour. The doctrine and experience of Christian perfection were already being preached in
Germany prior to Smith's coming by a small, but vigorous,
German Methodist fellowship. Their cause was fed by the
ministry and writings of Dr. William Nast, the father of
German Methodism in America, and an active member of the
National Camp Meeting Association. [47] The year 1875 marked
the twenty-fifth anniversary of Methodism in Germany; in the
months preceding the evangelist's arrival, the Methodists already had been holding special holiness meetings. One of
these met at Ludwigsburg in the southern part of Germany.
A reporter said, "not one of the preachers reminded behind"
in seeking and claiming the experience. A similar meeting

was convened for the preachers in Switzerland. Evangelists
went to the Methodist stations in northern Germany, Preaching and singing full salvation."48 But, as in England, the
leadership for the breakthrough into the Established Churches
and other Free Churches had to come mainly from sources
other than Methodism.

Several of the ministers of the State Church in Germany had participated in the Oxford meeting in August of
1874. They returned home with the "blessing" and preached
the experience in spite of significant opposition. The interest
stirred by both proponents and opponents resulted in arrange-
ments for an alliance meeting for entire consecration at Bern.
On Smith's way to a similar meeting at Basel, one of the
main thrusts of the coming revival occurred at Berlin. There,
and in German lands in general, there was weariness with
the political pace surrounding the war of 1870 and its after-
math. The Established Church offered little personal religion
and the old Pietist cells were usually dormant in their interior quietism; the country was ripe for a transcendental appeal
such as Smith introduced.

Hermann Krummacher was one of the German representatives who responded to Philip Schaff's trip to Europe
to invite prominent European scholars and churchmen to the
1873 Evangelical Alliance meeting in New York. He described
German religious life to the delegates. Krummacher observed
that the signs of revival which had appeared in Germany in
1864-1870 among all classes of the nation had almost intensified with the outbreak of the Franco-Prussian War and its
nationalistic hopes. With the end of that conflict, however,
the hopes had not been realized, and the German nation was
moving ahead without Christianity. 49

August Tholuck, professor of theology at the University
of Halle, wrote in a paper read to the same assembly, at the
same time, in the same vein, that

> the unparalleled victory which God granted to the
> nation in the last war has not regenerated us in
> faith.... On the contrary the new epoch ... proves
> itself to be an ever proceeding dissolution of posi-
> tive faith and Christian interest.... 50

Pressed by such concerns prominent German theologians in Berlin, some of whom had attended the Oxford meetings, invited Smith to come to that city. 51 When the "Verein-

haus" built by the Pietists proved to be too small to accommo-
date the crowds which attended, the meetings moved to the
Military Church by permission of the Emperor and Court-
preacher Baur.   Four to five thousand people crowded into
the meetings day after day.   The message which had won
over so many adherents in England within the upper classes
and the Anglican Church, now brought an even more enthusiastic response from leaders of the established church in Germany as well as the pietistic elements within that church.
An observer reported that on the last Sunday night of the
meetings, the crowd stood "spellbound" as Smith made his
religious appeal through Dr. F. W. Beadecker, his inter-
preter. [52]

     Subsequently, the Secretary of State's house was made
available to the evangelist for a meeting with one hundred
and fifty of Berlin's scholars and statesmen.   Dr. Earl von
Hegel, son of the famed philosopher, president of the Brandenberg Consistorium, and Dr. Buchsel, [53] bishop of the German church, among them.   The Emperor thanked Smith by
letter for his ministry in the city.   On the Monday following
the close of the public services, Smith spoke to another group
of one hundred who had gathered at the American embassy
at the invitation of the ambassador, Bancroft Davis.   Smith
also ministered personally to Empress Augusta and her daughter, Luise, and Grand Duchess of Boston. [54]

     From Berlin, Smith and Pastor Ernest Gebhardt, [55]
who was singing for him in the services, moved on to Basel
for a week of camp meeting-style services, arranged for by
the Evangelical Alliance.   The meeting hall seated two thousand people, but it soon proved to be too crowded; a large
church was opened for the remainder of the services.   Five
thousand attended the day services.   Smith spoke six times
each day.

     At Stuttgart, an eight-day meeting was held with simi-
lar results.   Here the Lutherans were not ready to accept
the musical services of Pastor Gebhardt; they were prejudiced
against him because, as Methodist presiding elder in the
Wittenberg area, he had administered the sacraments in his
church.   However, Smith himself, who never sought to deny
his debt to the Methodists for his holiness teachings, was
enthusiastically received.   Services at Heidelberg, Karlsruhe
and Elberfeld followed.   In May 1875, he held the closing
meeting in Germany at Barmen with Theodor Christlieb, and
D. Fabri.   More than sixty German pastors followed him to

Brighton at the end of the month.   Among them was the respected D. G. Warneck, who with fifty other State Church
ministers had defended Smith's ministry in Germany; he later
remarked that at Brighton he had received "the strongest
impulses to his life of faith."[56]

The holiness movement and German Pietism

The most lasting effects of Smith's German ministry,
however, grew out of the impact of his preaching among the
old Pietist areas of southern Germany; students of the German Gemeinschaftsbewegung, such as Abdel Wentz, one-time
professor at Gettysburg Lutheran Seminary, maintain that this
modern German Pietist Movement represents a combination
of the staid strain of old German Pietism and the vigorous,
activistic strain of the American and English holiness movements.[57]   Conditioned by the waves of evangelism which
swept Germany at the beginning and the middle of the nineteenth century, traditional Pietism had already begun to move
away from its old separatistic, quietistic ways.   By Smith's
time, it was ready to hear a message which called for practical, positive, Christian holiness.   The response to the
revival and the new continuing Gemeinschaftsbewegung, are
ample proof that the rationalism of the century had not de-
stroyed the old Pietism.   The impact upon the German churches
was so significant that it is impossible to read the history of
the German evangelical church from that time to this without
understanding these origins of the movement.[58]

The German holiness movement took a different turn
from that found in the ongoing American and English movements.   Its converts formed conventicles within the Established or State Church in the old Pietistic tradition of small
group fellowships or churches within the church.   A scholarly
comparison of this tradition with that of the American movement at this point, also, might throw new light on the elements which enter into the dynamics of such movements vis-
a-vis the interpretations which rely chiefly on sociological
data.

These German groups had three main emphases: fellowship, which gave them their name "Gemeinschaftsbewegung,"
evangelization of the masses, and the promotion of the doctrine of entire sanctification.   The national movement finally
centered around the famous Gnadau Conference which first
met in 1888.   Jasper V. Oertzen who had been strongly influenced by Johann Wichern, the father of German Inner

Missions, was a leader of the movement. He served as head of the City Mission at Hamburg from 1873-1893, and was president of the Schleswig-Holstein Society for Inner Missions. Oertzen was presiding officer at the first three Gnadau Conferences.[59]

Another leader who left his impress on the movement was Theodor Christlieb, one of Smith's sponsors and professor of practical theology at Bonn. He began to agitate for evangelists in the church conferences and set up a school for evangelists at Bonn which emphasized lay training; lay participation became an important factor in the new holiness Pietistic movement.[60] A third prominent figure, Theodor Jellinghaus, was the theologian of the movement. His book, Complete Salvation in the Present, outlines the patterns of the movement's theology of Christian holiness; it was closer to Keswick's general terms than the more specific language which the American movement used to give theological definition to its concepts of entire sanctification. Jellinghaus, too, saw the value of the layman in evangelization; from 1885 to 1893 he instructed seventy-three laymen in his own house during devotional periods with his theological views and sent them out into the church.[61]

In 1890 a national organizational structure was formed under the name of Committee for the Cultivation of Christian Fellowship and Evangelical Piety, and a paper called Philadelphia was started with an initial subscription list of five thousand. Intense evangelization steadily increased the ranks; in 1901 the groups were legally registered as the German Philadelphia Society.[62]

By the second decade of the present century, these voluntary associations of Christians meeting in a particular community for spiritual edification, but without regular church connection, expanded their membership even further. Wurtemberg counted eight hundred societies, ranging in individual membership from two hundred to one thousand; Baden had one hundred fifty groups, all of old Pietist derivation. In Hessen and Hessen-Nassau, there were two hundred and fifty societies; in Palatinate, one hundred thirty; in the lower Rhine, one hundred; Wesphalia had four hundred societies, with twenty-five thousand members; Schleswig-Holstein, two hundred fifty; Saxony, two hundred seventy, which held over twenty-five thousand meetings in a year, published a paper for over thirty thousand subscribers and held conferences with attendances of three thousand people each; Berlin had

fifty; Pomerania, forty; West Prussia, sixty; Prussia, fifty;
other parts of Germany had a proportion varying in number
with the remaining remnants of Pietistic influence in the
particular area. In Denmark there were four hundred, sixty
two meeting houses.

Wentz also notes that the Christian Endeavor Societies,
the Young Men's Christian Associations, and the University
Christian Movements in Germany got almost all of their
strength from the new Pietist Movement. [63]

The movement in Germany was severely divided in
the second decade of the twentieth century when the Pentecostal movement began to promote its particular emphases
on the baptism of the Holy Ghost as evidenced by speaking
in tongues. Varying positions on the question were taken by
powerful leaders in the movement. More than doctrine and
experience were at issue; the strong separationist tendencies
of the incipient Pentecostal movement gradually led to a breakdown of the prevailing Pietist concept of a church within the
church and produced a church organization of distinct Pentecostal bodies much in the same pattern as the holiness and
pentecostal movements in the United States. [64]

This significant influence of the holiness movement
upon the German religious life has not generally been well
known to the American holiness movement. The involvement
of the ongoing holiness work in the Pietistic circles of the
State Churches makes it difficult to identify the movement's
total activities and influences; the nature of the organization,
also, was not conducive to a continued relationship between
the German holiness movement and the American. The Ger-
man-English language barrier also hindered any enduring
communication between the direct descendants of R. Pearsall
Smith's work in Germany and the American tradition. The
only consistent relationship of the American movement with
any segment of German holiness teaching was through its
development in German Methodism whose contacts with the
holiness advocates were kept alive through ecclesiastical
channels and church leaders, such as William Nast.

The Brighton Convention--Triumph and Tragedy

Robert Pearsall Smith returned from his triumphant
meetings on the Continent to immediately enter into the long
anticipated convention for the promotion of holiness which met

at Brighton on May 29, 1875. As that convention began,
Dwight L. Moody told his own London audiences that the
Brighton meeting was to be "perhaps the most important meeting ever gathered together."[65] He requested special prayer for
its success. If Oxford was the Vineland of the European movement, Brighton was its Manheim. In America the Vineland
appeal for a special promotion of holiness had gone out mainly
to Methodists who had already shown concern for the advancement of the teaching and experience. The initial response
proved to be so positive that the second efforts at Manheim
attracted a much broader spectrum of the American church
to the movement's message.[66] The experience in England
was remarkably similar. Those who had found the "blessing"
at Oxford had gone everywhere testifying to new spiritual
power and hope.

A German Methodist reported to the Guide:

> The doctrine of sanctification ... has found its way
> to the European continent and is awakening attention
> especially in the land of Zwingliius and Luther.
> Christians from Switzerland and Germany many
> attending the Oxford meetings conducted by E. [sic]
> Pearsall Smith, experienced the blessing of perfect
> love, and felt constrained to preach the doctrine
> and tell the experience in the Fatherland. The
> movement has thus found advocates in the Lutheran
> and Reformed Churches; and, what is most remark-
> able has been most heartily welcomed and endorsed
> by almost the entire religious press of Germany.... [67]

In Basel, Switzerland, a monthly magazine was published under the title of Des Christen Glaubensweg [The Christian's Way of Faith]. Indication of the positive publicity,
which such new journals provided for the incipient holiness
revival on the Continent, is provided by a "Correspondent
Krehbfel" who reported to the above mentioned journal that

> everywhere large numbers of professed Christians
> or heathen have been awakened, and a hungering
> and thirsting after practical holiness is the result.
> Many of these have had their longing desires satis-
> fied, by being filled with the Spirit in such a real
> manner as they had never thought possible in the
> present life. [68]

The editor of Earnest Christianity rejoiced in this new spread

of the holiness message which was reaching non-Methodist
churches in America and Europe. He observed that, "It is
no libel on others to say, that for many years, 'the people
called Methodists' were peculiar in ... that they made the
most strenuous efforts to build the churches in holiness."
But now, he continued, "Henry Varley is preaching in Canada
and the United States." McDonald and Inskip of the National
Camp Meeting movement had "been made a great blessing"
in a recent Canadian mission; the Canadian Camps at Grimsby
and Thousand Islands were "now to be numbered with the
Feasts of Tabernacles," and the Presbyterians, who "for
many years past have allowed the Methodists to monopolize
these special organizations ..." were holding a "grand camp."

The summary goes on to note that Moody's and Sankey's work is "too well known to dwell on," but at the same
time

> Messers. Pearsall [sic], Mahan, Boardman and
> others are permited to behold a work in England
> such as has hardly been witnessed during the pres-
> ent century; conferences are being held soley that
> ministers and others may understand the doctrine
> of holiness more clearly. Rev. Thornley Smith
> and other Wesleyan ministers are taking part in
> these holy convocations. Many of the evangelical
> party are very prominent....
> The Continent of Europe has caught the flame
> of spiritual power. A son of the well-known Fred
> Monod in France has become an itinerant preacher
> [T. Monod] and his business now is to travel through
> France and stir up zeal among the Protestant ranks.
> Conventions have been held in Germany and Switzer-
> land and great good has been done. [69]

Charles W. I. Christine, an English Methodist, summed up the hope which excited the English revival ranks
just prior to the Brighton Convention in May of 1875:

> We may confidently and calmly expect a wondrous
> outpouring of the hallowing Spirit at the Brighton
> Meetings. A thousand facts around tell us that
> with respect to our glorious theme "the winter is
> past, the rain is over and gone. The flowers ap-
> pear on the earth; the time of the singing of birds
> is come, and the voice of the turtle is heard in
> our land!"[70]

The numerous accounts of the time show that many
who anticipated Brighton and participated in it, shared Moody's
hopes for the gathering.   Whatever the contemporary actors
on the scene really expected to issue from the meeting, one
can only conjecture; unless one reads too much into their
predictions, undoubtedly, results shown by the ensuing history
did not fully meet their expections.   But it is certain that
the religious repercussions were far more reaching than often
has been recognized.

About eight thousand people traveled to Brighton, England that May of 1875, in response to the call of the sponsors.   Three wealthy "English gentlemen" had promised a
reserve fund of two thousand pounds to provide for the expenses of the meetings, but none of these funds were finally
required.   The town offered its three main meeting halls,
the Town Hall, the Corn Exchange, and the Dome, free of
charge to the sponsors of the meeting.   The center of organizational activities was the Royal Pavilion Apartments, which
were once the sporting place of George V and William IV;
when Victoria became queen they had been sold.[71]

The facilities were crowded from the seven o'clock
prayer meeting in the morning until the evening meetings in
the main halls.   The Smiths were the main speakers; to
some, Hannah Whitall Smith was an even more forceful presence than her husband.   Her daily Bible readings on various
spiritual themes, carried over from a type of service common to the National Camps in America, were the chief center
of interest.   She also conducted special services for the
women who were present.   An English newspaper correspondent noted that the crowds were so great at these Bible readings that she had to deliver them first in the Corn Exchange
and then in the Dome.   The more than six thousand people
in these and auditoriums, she observed, gave her "a congregation .... larger than Mr. Spurgeon's."   A reporter described the scene:

> Punctually to the moment, like Mr. Moody, she
> steps to the front of the platform, dressed in al-
> most eccentric Quaker simplicity, and then speaks
> for fifty minutes by the clock, without hesitating
> a moment.   Her freshness, her profound spiritual
> insight, are as remarkable as her surprising flu-
> ency.

Another reporter wrote:

By all she is recognized as the leading spirit of
the convention. Mrs. Smith has little of the feminine in her style of oratory.... Decision marks
every sentence she utters. The pathetic element
is almost wholly absent. As an expositor of the
Bible she is trenchant, and often powerful. [72]

For ten days the participants in the convention shared
in a kind of massive dialogue; in a quest for the experience
of Christian holiness taught by the Smiths, formal meetings
were commonly followed by smaller gatherings in which inquiry was made and questions answered on the "higher life"
and Christian holiness. Representatives of many Protestant
churches and sects in Europe and Britain, who came together
with the common understanding that doctrinal questions would
not be allowed to take center stage, had only the common
desire and pursuit of practical holiness. Laymen and ministers were involved on common terms. Frenchmen and Ger-
mans whose national interests still smarted from the wounds
of the Franco-Prussian War shared in frequent public testimony to common spiritual fellowship.

The prominence given to congregational singing represented another common feature with the American holiness
camp meeting. Pastor Gebhardt,[73] who wrote the hymn,
"Jesus erretet mich jetz" ("Jesus Saves Me Now") that bore
the revival throughout Germany, was there, and Theodore
Monod listened as his hymn of consecration, written at Broadlands, was sung. It became a favorite musical expression
of the theology and experience of the movement. [74]

The record of testimonies given in the course of the
meetings include that of J. Hudson Taylor, founder of the
China Inland Mission. He said that he had realized the reality of Christian life which was being promoted in the convention "about seven years" before. A Rev. M. Hesse of
Wurtemberg, Germany, told of his struggle involving theology,
which "was, that a certain quantity of sin was necessary, not
to orthodoxy, but to keep us humble.... Now he had learned
that as Jesus had pardoned his past sins, so he was willing
and able to keep him from sin in the future."[75] Elizabeth
Charles, author of "Chronicles of the Schoenberg Cotta Family," a story about Martin Luther summed up her view, and
apparently that of many others, when she predicted "that the
doctrine of sanctification by faith and the blessed experience
the doctrine brings are about to occupy the attention of Christians as they never have done before...." She felt that "no

qualified observer" could doubt that for a moment. "Nor
can we doubt," she said, "that a time will come when the
Conventions of Oxford and Brighton shall be historical as the
first great efforts [in the development of that movement]...."[76]

The significance of the European
holiness revival of 1873-1875

It would be easy to relegate such enthusiasm as Mrs.
Charles exhibited to the usual optimism of a revival atmosphere. However, when one reads the judgment of the scholarly, but rather prejudiced, Benjamin Warfield, concerning
the European holiness revival efforts of Robert Pearsall Smith
and his colleagues in the American holiness movement, he
can put into better perspective the obvious excitement which
infused the contemporary accounts. Warfield said that "there
is nothing more dramatic in the history of modern Christianity than the record of this 'Higher Life' Movement,"[77] even
though he himself, could find nothing in it except the same
old Methodist Pelagianism which he so consistently opposed.
And that is basically what Smith's message was--the message
which he and the others had imbibed out of their own experience in the American holiness movement, now adapted somewhat for their non-Methodist European audiences. It was
essentially the same call to Christian experience which Wesley's evangelists had preached to crowds of poor British
laborers a hundred years previously in the same places that
the Philadelphia Quaker layman was gathering together the
"lords and ladies" of the English upper classes, evangelicals
and ritualists of the Anglican Church, Lutheran and Reformed
theologians from Germany, and representative laymen and
pastors from most of the other churches of the day, for his
meetings for the "promotion of holiness." It was Phoebe
Palmer's and John Inskip's call for definite consecration,
definite faith, and definite witness--in short, a call to the
practical possibilities of a life of vital Christianity now, not
later. It was the proclamation of the new practical pietism
which the holiness revival represented.[78]

The participants at Brighton were conscious that they
were standing in some kind of enduring Christian tradition.
They testified that it was the truth of "our saviour and his
apostles, believed in by the godly of all ages."[79] The
Friend's Quarterly Examiner reported that

> the promoters of this movement are constant in
> their protest against being supposed to possess any

new truth. What is new in their teaching is simply
a vitalizing of the old--a making personal and definite that which has always been accepted as true,
but in too general a sense.
    It is making experimental that which we have
held doctrinally, that the whole vigour of our spiritual life consists; and this is the key to the rapid
spread of this movement for the promotion of Scriptural holiness ... [emphasis theirs].

This was the only explanation the Examiner could propose for
a meeting of eight thousand Christians "at which no doctrinal
questions were ... discussed, no resolutions passed, and no
fresh church organization attempted...."80 Mrs. Charles
said that it was the life, "which we all ought to be living,
not merely a few of us; which we ought to be living always,
and not merely now and then.... The tenses of the Christian are not mere narrative tenses. They are present and
perfect" [emphasis hers]. Quoting Coleridge, she said,

        To restore a common-place truth to its first un-
        common lustre, you need only to translate it into
        action [emphasis hers]. 81

    The implications of this last quote are very critical
to the understanding of what was happening. There was
something new, but we can only define that novelty by placing
it against the contemporary Victorian scene. An awareness
of the frame of mind of the Victorians, who heard the "higher
life" message, alone can explain why this activistic American
presentation, of what was essentially Wesleyan perfectionism,
burst upon the scene with such freshness--it was, in short,
a revival of hope in the midst of an "age of multiplied doubts
and shaken beliefs."82

    For the first time, in Walter Houghton's definitive
panorama of life in the Victorian age, we have a composite
picture of the dynamics of idealogical and sociological forces
which were tearing at the minds and lives of men and women
in England during the period of the revival. Houghton shows
that the dominant characteristics of the time were "transition"
and "doubt"--the transition of a "bourgeois industrial society"
and doubt "about the nature of man, society, and the universe."83 The pressure of unprecedented change and the
resultant uncertainty extended to every level of society; it
was "a large public living in an age of 'doubts, disputes,
distractions, fears....' "84 Matthew Arnold, in his essay on

"Bishop Butler and the Zeitgeist," declared that "amid that
breakup of traditional and conventional notions respecting
our life, its conduct, its sanctions," men were looking for
"some clear light and some sure stay."[85]

Houghton's description of the tensions the Victorians
faced in their religious life speaks even more directly to the
response given by the American holiness message and method.
He says that the common religious mood was marked by the
frustrations of "a daily sense of failure" under the hand of a
heavy Puritan theology with its sombre Deity.[86] There was
an almost universal sense that the church was not demonstra-
ting real Christianity. Wrapped up in the title of William
Wilberforce's "evangelical Bible," A Practical View of Prevailing Religious System of Professed Christians in the Higher
and Middle Classes, Contrasted with Real Christianity, was
the story of the age's sense of failure to demonstrate "Monday," as well as "Sunday" religion.[87] Ministers, generally
were caught up in the pressures of religious conformity and
were assailed by doubt and confusion. The answers which
they were attempting to provide for their equally disturbed
parishoners seemed to be totally inadequate.[88] Even the
liberal trend in men like Matthew Arnold may have prepared
the way for the revival appeal. He rejoiced that men could
now learn "what Christianity really is--simply a life of piety
and virtue."[89]

A general feeling of moral failure, existential loneliness, isolation, and nostalgia for a more sure past prevailed.
Bertrand Russell described it as "all the loneliness of human-
ity amid hostile forces ... concentrated upon the individual
soul."[90] The threats of the new "faith" in science and the
rising tide of Biblical criticism threatened the Biblical authority of the evangelical faith. The return to "Rome," whether
to the Anglo-Catholics or the Roman Catholics, worried them
as well.[91] All of these feelings undoubtedly contributed to
the confession of Canon T. D. Harford-Battersby, fellow grad-
uate student of Matthew Arnold, Lord Coleridge, and Arch-
bishop Fredrick Temple, and also later a leader in the Keswick conventions, to his own state of mind in 1873. He
wrote,

> At this moment I am feeling much inward struggle
> and questioning about this "higher Christian life"
> which is so much talked and written about....
> What I have been reading of the experience of
> others, Mr. Pearsall Smith and his excellent wife

and their wonderful boy, "Frank," has made me
utterly dissatisfied with myself and my state, I
feel I am dishonouring God and am wretched myself by living as I do; and that I must either go
backwards or forwards, reaching out towards the
light and the glory which my blessed Saviour holds
out to me, or falling back more and more into
worldliness and sin! [92]

Perhaps, for the first time then, one can begin to
comprehend what really lay behind the Examiner's conclusion
that the only explanation for the Brighton Convention was

that an earnest desire for increased personal holiness has been awakened in the Christian Church;
and to meet this desire there has arisen a fresh
setting forth of the truth concerning the Lord Jesus
Christ as a present, indwelling Saviour, living in
the soul and working there, "to will and to do of
His good pleasure. "[93]

It also gives us the interpretive context for the remarks of
Rev. J. B. Figgis in the Evangelical Magazine for September
1875; not agreeing fully with those who disclaimed any newness in the higher life revival, he attempted to articulate
the novelty which he sensed, but could not explicity identify.
"There is 'no small stir about this way,' " he said,

and this implies a certain amount of novelty and
(probably) of truth.   Some friends of the movement
have been a little too ready to disclaim the former....   But they are new to many, perhaps new
to most, new certainly to us; and glorious news--
they are "good news," a very "Gospel," only a
Gospel not merely for sinners, but for the saved....
and life is a continual triumph [emphasis his]. [94]

This articulation of new hope and joy comes through
to the researcher of the European holiness revival at every
turn.   To view it only as an adoption by the British, French,
German, and other participants of the inherent optimism of
the American movement provides only a partial explanation;
it must be contrasted with the picture of intense pessimism
which characterized the period to fully comprehend the newness which it represented to them.   The message answered
for many, apparently, the anxiety created by the frustrating
striving, which, Houghton says, was common in Victorian

religion. Figgis observed that "the old way used to be too
much of an effort--a way of self-control. This [new way]
is a way of faith...."95 The promise of a life of vital sanctification also promised an answer to the longing sense of
moral failure which also pervaded the English religious scene
in 1875. A witness to the new spiritual experiences he had
professed, as a result of the revivals, said that under his
old theology "the expectation ... was failure; success was
a surprise. The rule [he said] is reversed now; it [failure]
becomes the exception, and the exception [success] the rule."
The result was not a state of "sinlessness," but of "sunshine." The Victorians who heard Smith felt that they had
been freed from the heavy hand of a stern God. They professed a new joy in a relationship in which it was "possible
to walk with God, and to ... 'please' Him."96 In the midst
of a troubled society, the vigorous promotion of a faith relationship, which could produce sustained vitality in a Christian's life, spoke forcibly to the Pietistic Puritanism which
still infused much of English evangelicalism. It had also
spoken directly to the Pietistic remnants in Germany. The
result was "Brighton" and "Berlin" and the initiation of institutions and movements which have left a permanent impress upon
Protestant life ever since.

It was part of a "new era of American Pietism" which
Perry Miller, the able historian of American ideas, has identified with the rise of holiness literature such as Boardman's
Higher Christian Life just prior to the Civil War. Miller
claimed that this "new piety" was "no longer concerned with
doctrine," but rather, only with a "practical Christianity,"
purely of the heart. The extent to which it was received by
people of every class and creed, in both European and American Protestantism in the troubled 1870's, serves as a strong
reminder that, in spite of Miller's fear that it represented
"the ultimate reaches of the Revival's long efforts to elude
the trammels of metaphysics," it did speak to the heart.97
Many a Victorian was driven into himself as the ultimate
refuge from the change and doubt which threatened him from
every side. A religious experience which promised to bring
order, meaning, and hope in that center was attractive to
theologian and intellectual as well as pastor and parishoner.
The certainity and the immediateness of the holiness message
apparently represented a path to new purpose.98

The tragedy: the fall of
Robert Pearsall Smith

After Brighton, Smith and his followers were exuberant;

all Europe seemed to be at their feet. However, the continuing reports of the English revival in the Advocate of Christian Holiness, brought the announcement in September 1875 that,

> our brother R. P. Smith has been obliged because of failing health to return from his work in Europe to his home in Philadelphia....

The editor commented that,

> we have not been without fear that such a result would follow from what we could not but regard as an over pressure of his physical system just emerging from a serious breakdown.... May God very soon restore him to health and service as such laborers are greatly needed. [99]

The editor's hopes for a continued ministry for Robert Pearsall Smith in the holiness work were never realized. Smith and his wife were scheduled to speak at the first Keswick Convention to be held in July of 1875 following the Brighton Convention. When it suddenly was revealed that they would not attend, some explanation was necessary; stories concerning gross immorality and serious doctrinal deviations were spreading and threatening the whole higher life movement. Smith's friends issued a statement indicating that "in personal conversation" his friends had noted suggestions of doctrinal indiscretions which were "most unscriptural and dangerous...." They announced to their shocked followers that, "there had been conduct which although we were convinced that it was free from evil intention was yet such as to render action necessary on our part...." The action agreed upon was to ask Smith to refrain from all further public work. Smith apparently not only acquiesced in this decision but the statement continued that he "recognized with deep sorrow the unscriptural and dangerous character of the teaching of the conduct in question...." The explanation concluded with a reference to the recurrence of Smith's old illness of the brain which "rendered the immediate cessation from work an absolute necessity. [100]

For nearly ninety years the rumors and questions concerning Smith's "fall" persisted without any explanation beyond the above statement from the committee which had dismissed him from his work. The truth of the situation came out in 1965, when John Pollock discovered Smith's full confession of the whole matter in a letter to Cowper-Temple.

As Pollock has indicated, "the truth is pathetic rather than shocking...."[101] It appears now that it would have been much better for all concerned had Smith's friends been more forthright in their handling of the affair. At any rate, the pressure of the crisis proved to be too much for Smith, and the risks for the committee were too great; in a state of nervous prostration, he and his wife returned to America.

In all the currents which flowed around the Smiths during this controversy, Dr. Charles Cullis, Boston physician and lay evangelist, remained their staunchest friend. In August of 1876, he persuaded them to take up their public ministry again in a camp meeting; his hope was to restore them of their former usefulness. Mrs. Smith indicates that she and her husband had no personal feelings in the matter, and in agreeing to go, they were showing gratitude for the good intentions of an old friend. Nevertheless, they "hitched" themselves to "Dr. Cullis's team" and 'concluded the Lord would not be very angry with [them] under the circumstances [though it would serve them] right, if He should make the meeting a complete failure....''[102] But the meeting was in no sense a failure.

> There was just the same power and blessing as at Oxford or Brighton.... There was every sign of the continual presence of the Spirit. Souls were converted, backsliders restored, Christians sanctified, ... And Robert and I never worked more effectively. He had all his old power in preaching and leading meetings.... As for me, thee knows that I am not much given to tell of my own successes, but ... I shall have to tell thee that I was decidedly 'favored' as the Friends say.[103]

Dr. Cullis's hopes for restoration of Robert Pearsall's image of pulpit effectiveness seemed to be amply fulfilled as the fame of the meeting began to spread. Urgent invitations for Smith and his wife to hold public meetings in various places followed in increasing numbers. The Smith themselves, however, dashed the hopes to the ground forever, "without a longing thought, only too thankful to be released." The future course was set: "Henceforth home and homelife for us," they said. Both of them had "hated the adventure cordially";

> it was all a wearisome performance to us. We did it over an impassible gulf. The flood had come since the last time, and changed all things to us.

There was no interest, no enthusiasm. The meetings were a bore, the work was like a treadmill.
We counted the hours until we could get away and
hailed the moment of emancipation with unspeakable
joy. [104]

The incident baffled Hannah Smith; she was not sure
whether her lack of concern in the matter was due to such
an advance in grace that she was utterly indifferent to anything but the will of God, or that she had become "utterly
irreligious" and a "lazy fatalist." In spite of the doubts,
neither she nor her husband hesitated in their decision to
leave the scene of holiness evangelism forever. Later, she
said, "I was utterly unmoved; both Robert and I came away
more confirmed than ever in our feelings of entire relief
from everything of the kind. We are done! Somebody else
may do it now." [105]

As for the future, she personally testified that her
ever broadening views of "the limitless ocean of the love of
God that overflows all things" had thrown her "orthodoxy" to
the winds. The only certain conclusion which she could draw
from the perplexing events was the belief that God "means
us to be good human beings in this world, and nothing more." [106]
She spent the rest of her life doing just that. Her husband
still suffered from his physical affliction. Never as resolute
a person as his dynamic wife, he endured the rest of his
days in disappointment and remorse, but his name still echoes
through the mountain tops as well as the valleys of the history of the holiness revival and the holiness movement today.

The Institutionalization of the English Revival

The holiness movement in Europe was shaken by the
dissension over Smith, but not finally daunted. [107] Jack Ford
lists Wesleyan oriented groups which sprang up as a result
of the revival. In addition to his own Church of the Nazarene, he mentions Cliff College (1884), the Southport Convention (1885), The Faith Mission (1886), The Star Hall (1889),
The Pentecostal League (1891), The Salvation Army (1878),
The Holiness Church (ca. 1880), and the Independent Holiness
Movement (1907). [108]

But the continuing movement which sprang most directly
from the evangelism of the Smiths was the Keswick Convention.
The sudden return of the Smiths to America in 1875 precluded

their presence at the first convention for the promotion of
holiness held at Keswick, England. A decision was made to
go ahead with the meeting, nevertheless. Rev. H. W. Webb-
Peploe--later Prebendary--was called upon to take Smith's
place in the convention. He with men like Rev. Evan H. Hopkins; Robert Wilson, a Quaker; Canon Harford-Battersby,
vicar of St. John in Keswick; and Handley Moule, Principal
of Ridley Hall and later Bishop of Durham, determined the
early course of the Convention. Annual meetings "for the
Promotion of Scriptural Holiness" have been held to the present time. [109] Their on-going history represents the most
enduring form of what might properly be called the Calvinis-
tically or non-Methodistically oriented results of the holiness
revival. Its structure and purpose, in many ways, faithfully
reflects its Oxford-Brighton parentage.

Its purpose was the same. A letter from Canon T.
D. Harford-Battersby, the vicar of St. Johns in Keswick, to
another of its founders, the Quaker, Robert Wilson, proposed
that the promotion of "the full sanctification of believers" was
to be the object of the convention. [110]

The lack of pre-designed programs or even addresses,
yet the general sense of order and continuity which prevailed,
the tarrying for the mind of the Spirit, and prominence given
to the dialogue of testimony and congregational song, all were
common to the patterns which had already developed in the
meetings and conventions of the American movement and continue in much of the philosophy of the movement even to this
day. As has already been observed in the discussion above
on the American camp meeting, strong personalities who
guided the course of the "open ritual" of the gatherings, kept
order through a combination of their own personal ability,
charisma, semi- or offical position and the final appeal to
their sense of the "leadings of the Spirit."[111]

The higher life message of Keswick strongly influenced
evangelical religious organizations around the world through
such men as A. T. Pierson, Hudson Taylor, F. B. Meyer,
Theodore Monod, and Dr. Eugene Stock. The English evangelical community came under its continuing influence through
the ministers and laymen who gathered annually at Keswick
under the leadership of men like Webb-Peploe, Harford-Bat-
terersby, and Handley Moule, later Bishop of Durham. Similar higher life conferences standing in an informal relationship to Keswick through their teaching and speaking personel,
were begun in Europe and the United States; through F. B.

Meyer and others, the holiness message came back in full
circle to American Calvinistic publics, which the Methodist
based message often had not been able to penetrate. This
influence has remained a vital factor in American Evangelical life ever since, particularly through Dwight L. Moody,
as it reinforced his own earlier contacts with the movement.
Adoniram J. Gordon and Arthur T. Pierson, both active in
the evangelical student movements at the turn of the century
introduced the "Spirit-filled life" concepts into those groups.
How close to home it had come, has continually been shown
in the stream of polemic which has flowed between the closely
related Methodist and Calvinist wings of the movement since
that time. [112]

SUMMARY

A study of the European expansion of the revival has
been considered essential to the development of this thesis
basically because it gives us a view of the response to American holiness revivalism in a non-American context. This
European view of the movement, far removed from the American frontier, from all other distinctly American sociological
factors, and just as importantly, was largely removed from the
close involvement with American Methodism. The latter involvement, frequently has tended to make identification of the
issues in American perfectionist revivalism difficult. The
European revival history provides a unique interpretive control situation.

It may be that an analysis of the factors at work in
this non-American situation could be used much more widely
than they have been to achieve more accurate evaluations of
what was really occurring in the United States and Canada.
The close relationship, which seems to be evident, between
the effectiveness of the message and methods of the American movement and the prevailing circumstances of English
life, would appear to be an extremely important factor in the
interpretation of movement wherever it was active. The
response generated by its strongly perfectionist, pietistic
appeal, apparently was capable of arousing almost instant,
broad scale reaction in favor of experiential religion as the
only adequate answer to the dual threats of transitoriness
and doubt.

What was true of the revivalism in England, was also
true of its acceptance and influence in Germany and other

European countries. In Germany, in particular, it proved the basic nature of its appeal by reviving the old pietistic cells, while at the same time, attracting to itself men from all levels of society as well as Established churchmen. The disappointments in the religious life of the nation, after the success of the Franco-Prussian War and the dissatisfaction of increasing numbers of individuals with the answers of a sterile rationalism, provide us with a rationale for the amazing scenes in which the learned doctors of the church sang the simple revival chorus, "Jesus Saves Me Now," and testified to receiving the most powerful impulses of their spiritual lives.

Finally, the European story is important because of the numerous movements, which sprang from Smith's evangelism and that of others who continued his work; the basically pietistic impulses, strongly energized by the American movement's optimism and activism, shaped a new concept of the Christian life, not only for many in the Free Churches of England and Europe, but also for many in the evangelical elements of the Established Protestant Churches as well. New institutions, especially dedicated to the revival's holiness doctrines, came into being in England and Europe as they did in America. In the Germany and Switzerland of that day, the revival took up the "Inner Missions" movement and gave it a new dynamic, as an influential force within the State Churches.

NOTES

1. Supra, p. 61.

2. Advocate of Christian Holiness, III (January, 1873), 156; Palmer, Four Years, p. 105. Ibid. , p. 262, notes, "And thus the flame kindled when we were at Hamilton is spreading to Europe."

3. Ibid. , p. 105; Orr, op. cit. , p. 63.

4. Supra, pp. 59ff. The opposition of the Primitive Methodists was especially paradoxical; they themselves had been born in a revival movement sparked by Lorenzo Dow, an eccentric American Methodist evangelist of the early nineteenth century. "Crazy Dow," as he was known, ranged far and wide across the United States of his day like a "comet in the religious world." Many thought him more madman

than preacher, but the record of his accomplishments as the
first Methodist missionary to what was, in 1799, Lower Canada (now the Province of Quebec); his brief camp meeting
ministry in England which inspired Hugh Bourne and William
Clowes, the founders of Primitive Methodism; and his lesser
known achievements must modify and criticism of his strange
maverick life-style. See Joseph Riston, The Romance of
Primitive Methodism (London: Edwind Dalton, 1909), pp. 56-
58; Schaff-Herzog, op. cit., 111, 497.

    5. Edward Goulburn's Pursuit of Holiness (London:
Rivingtons, 1870), pp. 212ff., gives a classical statement of
the doctrine, paralleling the movement's theology of Christian perfection. William Arthur, a leading advocate of holiness promotion in the Wesleyan Methodist churches in England, published his Tongue of Fire in 1856; it was widely
read both in England and America in its time and continues
to exercise influence within holiness and higher-life ranks
today through constant reprints. Richard Poole's Center and
Circle of Evangelical Religion, or Perfect Love (London:
Jarrold and Sons, 1873), sold 10,000 copies in its first year.
Stephen Barabas, So Great Salvation: The History and Message of the Keswick Convention (Westwood, N.J.: Fleming
H. Revell, 1952), p. 16, lists the works of Upham and Mahan as also arousing interest in the experience of holiness;
but Barabas indicates that Boardman's Higher Christian Life
was most important. To these must be added all the works
of the Palmers, who were well known in England through
their Civil War period ministry, and the writings of Robert
and Hannah Smith. There was a strong desire-fulfillment
circle at work; Charles F. Harford, The Keswick Convention:
Its Message, Its Method, and Its Men (London: Marshall
Brothers, 1907), p. 124, gives Canon Harford-Battersby's
statement of the effect upon him of Hannah Whitall Smith's
account of her deceased college-age son who had professed
to receive a "second blessing" while a student at Princeton,
Frank, the Record of a Happy Life (Philadelphia: Printed
for Private Collection, 1873): "It would be impossible to
report the revolution in my religious thought and life effected
by that book. No book I have read has had anything like the
same effect. I suspect that today I should find nothing in it
of special import; but then it spoke with the voice of God to
my inmost condition" (emphasis mine).

    6. Advocate of Christian Holiness, III (December,
1872), 121.

7. Ibid. (January, 1873), 156, as quoted from the King's Highway.

8. Ibid.

9. Ibid.

10. Ibid., p. 155; ibid., IV (April, 1874), 231.

11. Ibid. (March, 1873); ibid. (June, 1873), p. 281.

12. Ibid. (May, 1873), p. 255.

13. Ibid. (June, 1873), p. 281.

14. Ibid., IV (April, 1874), 232. Also see Paulus Scharpff, History of Evangelism, Three Hundred Years of Evangelism in Germany, Great Britain, and the United States of America, Helga Henry (trans.) (Grand Rapids, Mich.: Wm. B. Eerdmans Publishing Co., 1966), pp. 192-93.

15. Warfield claims, "The whole whirlwind campaign conducted by Mr. Smith was simply a concerted 'drive' of American Perfectionism on the European stronghold"; see Warfield, Perfectionism, I, 513. Warfield seems to neglect the fact that Smith originally went to England only for his health and not a 'drive'; see Hannah Whitall Smith, The Unselfishness of God, and How I Discovered It: A Spiritual Autobiography (New York: Fleming H. Revell Co., 1903), p. 221; also, Logan Pearsall Smith (ed.), Philadelphia Quaker, the Letters of Hannah Whitall Smith (New York: Harcourt, Brace and Co., 1950), p. 15. As a young girl, Hannah had written to her cousin, Annie Whitall, "I think I would love to be a minister.... Would it not be grand, and then I could travel all over the world and do so much good...." Letter of Hannah Whitall to Annie Whitall, Philadelphia, February 17, 1850, as given in Philadelphia Quaker, p. 4. Other leading Quakers in the movement were Dr. Dougan Clark, one-time professor of theology at Earlham College, Richmond, Ind.; evangelist David Updegraff and evangelists Seth and Hulda Rees; Rees was one of the founders of the International Apostolic Holiness Union which later became the Pilgrim Holiness Church.

16. H. Smith, The Unselfishness of God, p. 172; see ibid., pp. 169ff., for her own account of her religious experience at this period.

17. Ibid. , p. 189.

18. Ibid. , pp. 195ff.

19. Ibid. , pp. 241-42. Also see H. Smith, Frank, the Record of a Happy Life, p. 37, and "Believing, Resting, Abiding. Experience of a Member of the Society of Friends," Guide, LII (July, 1867), 21-23. Garrison, op. cit. , pp. 119-30.

20. Her son, Logan Pearsall Smith, said in 1950, that the book had been translated into all the European languages and into some of the Oriental; more than one million copies had been sold; the same, op. cit. , p. v. However, the jacket of a 1952 paperbound edition by the original publisher, Fleming H. Revell Company, says that the "authorized edition had sold more than 2,000,000 copies"; it was originally published in 1870 and was one of the first Revell books; Hannah Whitall Smith, The Christian's Secret of a Happy Life (Westwood, N. J. : Fleming H. Revell Co. , 1952). L. Smith (ed.), Philadelphia Quaker, pp. viiff. , contains an excellent biographical note. Mrs. Smith used the circumstances under which she wrote the copy which eventually went into the book as a clear example of her belief that true religion was "an ordinary everyday walking in the path of duty" rather than "great ecstacies of inspiration. " She had become an ardent member and officer in the Women's Christian Temperance movement [see Frances E. Willard, Woman and Temperance: or the Woman's Christian Temperance Union (Chicage: Women's Temperance Publication Association, 1883), pp. 193-207]. her husband's doctor had ordered him to take wine at dinner for his illness. It was a great trial for her to see him drinking, so she offered to write an article for his holiness paper if he would give it up. The article was so well received that he insisted on a series which finally were compiled into the devotional classic. "These articles were dragged from me, so to speak, at the point of the bayonet, for I never wrote them in any month until the printers were clamouring for their copy. " Therefore she said that she could not say she wrote them out of any compelling feeling, but "to oblige my husband. " It was her duty, she had done it, and God had used it, she said, to be as helpful to thousands of people as any other book on "experimental religion" had proved to be; Strachey, op. cit. , pp. 252-53.

21. H. Smith, The Unselfishness of God, p. 243.

22. Ibid. , p. 288.

23. Ibid. , p. 289.

24. E. g. , Wallace, A Modern Pentecost, p. 12, "R.
Pearsall Smith and his excellent and laborious [sic] wife, who
at Manheim as never before, received a commission from
God which absorbed their being and proved an untold blessing
to all the churches through their abundant labors." Smith
took part in the evangelistic meetings of the National Association under Inskip in 1871 in California; Guide, LX (July,
1871), 27.

25. See supra, n. 13. Smith suffered a head injury
when he was thrown from a horse. His son, Logan Smith,
speaks differently of the story. See Logan Pearsall Smith,
Unforgotten Years (Boston: Little, Brown and Co. , 1939),
p. 61.

26. Christian Standard, VIII (No. 42), 333; also see
Pollock, op. cit. , pp. 18-19; A. T. Pierson, Forward Movements of the Last Half Century (New York: Funk and Wagnalls Co. , 1905), pp. 24ff. For the general picture of English Protestantism in this period see Schaff and Prime, op.
cit. , pp. 9ff.

27. L. Smith, Unforgotten Years, pp. 41-42. Mrs.
Smith defined her concept of "The Restitution of All things"
in the Unselfishness of God, pp. 199ff.; "There is to be a
final 'restitution of all things' when 'at the name of Jesus
every knee shall bow....' The how and when I could not see,
but the one essential fact was all I needed--somewhere and
somehow God was going to make everything right for all the
creatures he had created." Ibid. , p. 205. She became convinced of the belief very early in her life; she wavered in it
only briefly during her association with the Plymouth Brethren; she looked on it then as a "dreadful heresy, but later
on ... [she] learned even the blessed fact ... that we are
all, the heathen included, 'God's offspring.' ..." The doctrine came to her on a street car on Market Street in Philadelphia; it may have been, in part, a reaction to the rigid
Calvinism of her Plymouth Brethren advisors. Ibid. , pp.
83-85, 195ff. , 205-206.

28. Logan Smith (ed.), Philadelphia Quaker, p. iii.
The same, Unforgotten Years, p. 51.

29. H. Smith, The Unselfishness of God, pp. 221-22.
L. Smith, The Unforgotten Years, pp. 43-45.

30. Ibid. , p. 225.

31. A correspondent to the Advocate of Christian Holi-
ness reported from England that the King's Highway was "al-
ways Methodist in its approach"; whereas the Christian's
Pathway of Power "though giving a view of the doctrine which
Methodists cannot always endorse, has, without doubt, led
many, who would not have been reached by a Methodist organ,
into a closer walk with God." See Advocate of Christian
Holiness, V (November, 1875), 108. Also Walter B. Sloan,
These Sixty Years: The Story of the Keswick Convention
(London: Pickering and Inglis, 1935), p. 24.

32. Advocate of Christian Holiness, IV (September,
1873), 65; ibid. (July, 1873), 15.

33. Ibid. p. 15.

34. Mrs. W. E. Boardman says that 2,000 ministers
participated in the breakfast meetings held by Smith and
Boardman in the spring of 1873. The same, op. cit. , pp.
156-59. Pierson, op. cit. , pp. 18-19, said the breakfasts
were sponsored by Samuel Morley, Congregationalist and
member of Parliament.

35. Advocate of Christian Holiness, IV (May, 1874),
262. Also see Christian Standard and Home Journal, VIII
(December 19, 1874), 45.

36. Advocate of Christian Holiness, IV (January, 1874),
159, and preceding. See Pollock, op. cit. , p. 33; as quoted
from the Record, a Church of England paper: "Pearsall
Smithism ... [is] a new peril imported from America which
substitutes sentimentalism and visionary mysticism for solid
piety and Scriptural experimentalism founded on the word of
God." Pollock also notes, ibid. , that Lord Shaftesbury and
John Charles Ryle opposed the meetings; the latter claimed
that the difference between Moody and Brighton "is the difference between sunshine and fog." Note that Moody himself
hardly agreed with Ryle; see infra, p. 174.

37. Charles Harford, op. cit. , pp. 25-26. As a boy,
Logan Pearsall Smith was present at the Broadlands Estate
during the meetings. He says that Amanda Smith, the well-
known black woman holiness evangelist took part in the meetings; Smith also notes that Dante Gabriel Rossetti may also
have been there; he painted some of his pictures and wrote

some of his poems at Broadlands; Mrs. Cowper-Temple, "the queen of Evangelicals," as Smith calls her, was the patron of the Pre-Raphaelite school of artists; she was also the Egeria of Ruskin, who describes his first seeing her in Rome in 1840 in his Praeterita; L. Smith, Unforgotten Years, pp. 55-56, 51, 46.

38. Webster's Biographical Dictionary (Springfield, Mass.: G. & C. Merriam Co., Publishers, 1943), p. 1100.

39. Guide, XXIII [New Series] (May, 1875), 150; ibid. (June, 1875), 184; ibid. (August, 1875), 56.

40. Advocate of Christian Holiness, V (November, 1874), 113.

41. Evan Hopkins, "Preliminary Stages," Harford, op. cit., p. 30. The ten-day pattern of the American holiness camp meeting carried over in these meetings.

42. A full account of the proceedings is given in Account of the Union Meeting for the Promotion of Scriptural Holiness, Held at Oxford, Aug. 29 to Sept. 7, 1874 (Chicago: Fl. H. Revell, 1875). For further current accounts of the Oxford Convention see: The Christian Standard and Home Journal, VIII (November 7, 1874), 353; ibid. (November 14, 1874), 361; ibid. (November 21, 1874), 369; ibid. (December 5, 1874), 385. Advocate of Christian Holiness, V (December, 1874), 134-35; ibid. (November, 1874), 113. The Methodist Magazine, XVII (1874), 992ff.

43. Guide, XXIV [New Series] (February, 1876), 54. R. P. Smith reported to a Philadelphia preacher's meeting in December, 1874 that when the suggestion was made for the Oxford Meeting, one of those present had responded, "Yes, the very center of Ritualism is the place." Christian Standard and Home Journal, VIII (December 19, 1874), 405. Ritualism, a part of the Tractarian movement begun about 1833 to move the Anglican Church closer to Catholic creed, was the stage of that movement on the English church scene at the time of the holiness conventions. It sought to move the teachings of the Tractarians into the ritual or externals of the church; see Schaff-Herzog, op. cit., X, 49-55. It too was a perfectionist movement of its own stripe. See Walter E. Houghton, The Victorian Frame of Mind: 1830-1870 (New Haven: Yale University Press, 1957), pp. 230-31. Thus the holiness movement crossed its path and touched base

where some of its own initial impulses had been born in the
"Holy Club" of the Wesleys and Whitefield in the preceding
century.   Another Oxford Movement more closely related to
it than Ritualism was the later Buchmanite movement known
as the "Moral Re-armament Movement."   Scharpff, op. cit.,
pp. 277-78, says that Buchman's movement was actually inspired by a visit to Keswick in 1908 and a spiritual experience he had there.   Also see Sangster, Methodism Can Be
Born Again, pp. 52-64 for the parallels between Methodist
[and holiness] small-group patterns and practices and the
Oxford Movement's.

44.   Advocate of Christian Holiness, V (January, 1875),
163.

45.   See Smith's account in the Christian Standard and
Home Journal, VIII (December 19, 1874), 405.   Guide, XXIII
(January, 1875), 24-25, and Christian Advocate and Home
Journal, VIII (December 5, 1874), 389, give reports of con-
tinuing revival after the Oxford meetings.

46.   For an account of the Free Churches in Europe
at this time see Schaff and Prime, op. cit., pp. 76-77, 551.
Monod's account of his religious experience, including his
involvement in the Revival of 1858 while a law student in
America, is given in "Seven Weeks of Trust," quoted from
the Pathway of Power by the Advocate of Christian Holiness,
V (December, 1874), 139.   His father was Dr. Fredrick
Monod, a prominent French Free Church leader.

47.   Methodist membership in Germany in 1874 was
7,022.   See Paul F. Douglass, The Story of German Methodism, Biography of an Immigrant Soul (New York: Methodist
Book Concern, 1939), p. 127; ibid., chap. viii, gives the
history of early Methodist missions in Germany beginning in
1850.   This biography of Nast fails to recognize Nast's involvement in the National Camp Meeting Association.   It was
very signigicant for the movement, however, because through
Nast's great personal influence and his extensive holiness
writings, the revival's influences were consistently fed into
the life of both German Methodism in America and in Germany as well as to the United Brethren and Evangelical
Churches, both of which were German and Methodist-related.
See Advocate of Christian Holiness, VI (June, 1875), 17. A.
L. Drummond, German Protestantism Since Luther (London:
The Epworth Press, 1951), contains summaries of the re-
lation of Pietism, German Methodism, and R. P. Smith.

48. Ibid.

49. Hermann Krummacher, "Christian Life in Germany," Schaff and Prime, op. cit. , pp. 78-84.

50. August Tholuck, "Evangelical Theology in Germany," ibid. , pp. 85-89.

51. Smith's revivalism in Germany is summarized in:
Fr. Winkler, "Robert Pearsall Smith und der Perfectionismus,"
Friedrick D. Kropatscheck, Biblische Zeit- und Streitfragen
zur Afklärung der Gebildeten, Series ix (Berlin-Lichterfelde:
Edwin Runge, 1914), pp. 401-22; Advocate of Christian Holiness, VI (June, 1875), 17-18. Earnest Christianity, I (July,
1875), 444. Scharpff, op. cit. , pp. 220ff.

52. Earnest Christianity, I (July, 1875), 444, quoting
"a Berlin paper." Baedecker was known as the "German
George Müller of Bristol." Scharpff, op. cit. , p. 222.

53. Ibid. Buchsel is reported to have said on the
occasion, "Brethren, we have of late been throwing ourselves
with all our force into politics--secular politics, ecclesiastical
politics--but we have neglected the politics of the heart. Let
us listen to our brother's voice and practice these."

54. Ibid. Scharpff, op. cit. , p. 216.

55. Gebhardt was one of the pioneer German Methodists; he was noted for his contributions to the music of the
free church movement. See Douglass, op. cit. , pp. 120-21;
Scharpff, op. cit. , pp. 204, 220-21. Scharpff himself was
the son of German "holiness" Methodists; ibid. , ix. Also
see H. Brandenburg, "Heiligungsbewegung," Die Religion in
Geschichte und Gegenwart. Handwörterbuch für Theologie und
Religionswissenschaft (Tübingen: J. C. B. Mohr, 1859), III,
pp. 182ff. Hereafter referred to as RGG.

56. Advocate of Christian Holiness, VI (June, 1875),
17-18; Douglass, op. cit. , p. 120. Winkler, op. cit. , p. 415.

57. Abdel R. Wentz's Germany's Modern Pietistic
Movement (n. p. , n. n. , n. d.), is an excellent monograph on
the movement which developed out of the holiness revival;
see ibid. , p. 3: " ... In the seventies there came across
the Channel a second stream of influence [the first was the
mid-century impulse] which united with the remaining legacy

of the 17th and 18th century Pietism to bring about the mod-
ern Pietistic Movement. " Scharpff calls it "The Pietist Fel-
lowship Movement. " Scharpff, op. cit. , pp. 170, 203, and
RGG, II, 1366ff. , also discuss the movement. Also, L.
Tiesmeyer, "Was jederman von der christlichen Gemeinschafts-
bewegung in Deutschland wissen muss," RGG, II, 1751ff.
P. Fleisch, "Heiligungsbewegung," ibid. , II, 975ff.; ibid. ,
V, 586. The same, Die Moderne Gemeinschaftsbewegung in
Deutschland: ein Versuch dieselbe nach ihren Ursprung dar-
zustellen und zu würdigen. (Leipzig: H. G. Wallman, 1903).

58. Wentz, op. cit. , p. 2. Winkler, op. cit. , p. 402.

59. Ibid. , p. 4. H. Krummacher, "Christian Life
in Germany," Schaff and Prime, op. cit. , p. 81, defines
German "Inner Missions" as a society for combatting social
evils--gambling, drinking, prostitution, Sabbath desecration--
by direct social action. On Wichern see Scharpff, op. cit. ,
pp. 207-208, 232-33; RGG, II, 1367.

60. Wentz, op. cit. , p. 4; Scharpff, op. cit. , pp.
224-26. RGG, loc. cit.

61. Wentz, op. cit. , pp. 4-5. Scharpff, op. cit. ,
p. 219. Otto Stockmayer and Carl Rappard along with
Jellinghaus became the "theologischen Vertreter" of the movement, RGG, III, 182. For an article critical of the movement's claims see D. Gennrich, Wiedergeburt und Heiligung
mit Berzug suf die gegenwärtigen Strömungun des religiösen
Lebens (Leipzig: A. Deichert, 1908).

62. Wentz. op. cit. , p. 6. Scharpff, op. cit. , pp.
233-34.

63. Wentz, op. cit. , p. 8. RGG, II, 1367.

64. See H. Brandenburg, "Heiligungsbewegung," RGG,
III, 182ff. Paul Fleisch, "Pfingstbewegung," RGG, IV, 1153ff.
Brandenburg says that "die Einseitigkeit der Heiligungsbewegung fürhte im extremen Flügel zur Pfingstwegung." Wentz,
op. cit. , p. 2.

65. Record of the Convention for the Promotion of
Scriptural Holiness Held at Brighton, May 29 - June 7, 1875
(Brighton: W. J. Smith, n. d.), pp. 47, 319.

66. R. Smith wrote to J. Inskip from the Brighton

meeting: " ... The meeting was to Oxford, what Manheim
was to Vineland...."; Advocate of Christian Holiness, VI
(August, 1875), 37. By this time the National Association
had an agent in England publishing holiness tracts. See L.
R. Dunn, Holiness, What Is It? (London: F. E. Longley,
1875); Longley was the agent.

67.   Guide, XXII [New Series] (April, 1875), 20.

68.   Ibid.

69.   Earnest Christianity, I [New Series] (June, 1875),
282-83.

70.   Advocate of Christian Holiness, V (May, 1875),
284.

71.   Sunday School Times, XVII (June 26, 1875), 413:
"While Messers [sic] Moody and Sankey are gathering thousands in London to religious meetings, another American
evangelist, Mr. R. Pearsall Smith has collected nearly as
many thousands at Brighton." Other current reports may
be found in the Guide and the Advocate of Christian Holiness
issues following the convention. Most other accounts are
found in histories of the Keswick convention such as E. Hopkins, "Preliminary Stages," Harford, op. cit., pp. 32ff.;
Sloan, op. cit., pp. 18ff.; Barabas, op. cit., pp. 23ff.;
Pollock, op. cit.

72.   Advocate of Christian Holiness, V (August, 1875),
p. 36; also quoted by Sunday School Times, loc. cit.; both
are quoting unidentified English papers.

73.   Smith claimed that this was the only phrase he
knew in German at that time; Gebhardt picked it up as the
theme of the gospel song. The Guide, XXIII (August, 1875),
p. 55, gives the English translation of this song which became
the theme song of the European holiness movement. There
were seven verses. The chorus read:
             "Jesus saves me now.
             Jesus saves me now.
             Yes, Jesus saves me all the time--
             Jesus saves me now!"
Smith undoubtedly acquired this emphasis under the tutelage
of John Inskip in the American movement. At the Landisville National Camp Meeting, at the close of the first meeting, Inskip said to the audience, "Wait, the Lord is going

to save the people. Whisper it all around to one another,
'Jesus saves me now.' Tell it all over the ground." (Emphasis mine.) Also see Scharpff, op. cit. , pp. 220-21. Winkler, op. cit. , p. 419, n. 1.

74.   Gospel Hymns Consolidated, Embracing Numbers
1, 2, 3, and 4 ... for Use in Gospel Meetings and Other
Religious Services (Cincinnati, Ohio: The John Church Co. ,
1883), p. 268. Also see Brighton Convention Report, p. 23;
Pollock, op. cit. , p. 21. Harford, op. cit. , p. 28.

75.   Advocate of Christian Holiness, VI (September,
1875), 61-62.

76.   The Brighton Record, p. 429.

77.   As quoted by L. Smith, Unforgotten Years, pp.
59-60.

78.   In a rather negative fashion one of America's
foremost historians has supported our thesis: infra p. 183.

79.   The Brighton Record, p. 416.

80.   Ibid.

81.   Ibid. , pp. 424-25.

82.   Houghton, op. cit. , p. 10.   This work is critical
not only to this thesis, but to any effort to speak to the social currents of the Victorian Age, which Houghton generally
defines as 1830-1870.   His definition of 1870 as a critical
point of transition is especially significant for our discussion
of the revival.   All of the Victorian trends intensified from
that point on; ibid. , p. 14.

83.   Ibid. , pp. 1-22.

84.   Ibid. , p. xvi.

85.   As quoted by ibid. , p. 287, from Matthew Arnold,
Last Essays on Church and Religion (1877), p. 287.

86.   Houghton, op. cit. , p. 62.

87.   Ibid. , pp. 228, 405.   See especially 228-39.
Pierson, op. cit. , p. 15, notes that the successive waves of

religious excitement created by the Puseyite, Oxford, Cambridge, evangelical, and Plymouth Brethren movements had
left the second generation unsatisfied. "Their supposed religious standing and their lives of practical failure were in
startling contrast. "

88.   Ibid. , pp. 402-403.

89.   Ibid. , p. 49, as quoted from the New Republic,
pp. 51, 227-28.

90.   Ibid. , p. 87, n. 112, as quoted from Bertrand
Russell, "A Free Man's Worship," Selected Papers of Bertrand Russell (New York, n. n. , n. d.), pp. 11-12.

91.   Ibid. , pp. 96-102.

92.   Memoir of T. D. Harford-Battersby: By Two of
His Sons (London: Seely and Co. , 1890), p. 58.

93.   The Brighton Record, p. 416.

94.   Ibid. , p. 422.

95.   Ibid. , p. 423.

96.   Ibid. , p. 422.

97.   Perry Miller, The Life of the Mind in America
from the Revolution to the Civil War (New York: Harcourt,
Brace and World, Inc. , 1965), p. 93.

98.   Canon Harford-Battersby's remarks to the members of the Evangelical Union for the Diocese of Carlisle a
few weeks after the Oxford Convention in 1874 bear this out:
"There was a difference. There was a definiteness of purpose at these meetings, and a directness of aim in the
speakers.... That purpose was ... 'the promotion of Scriptural holiness.' The aim of the speakers therefore was to
bring about this result by an ordered scheme of teaching out
of the Holy Scriptures.... "; Account of the Union Meeting ...
at Oxford, pp. i-vii, as quoted from Barabas, op. cit. , pp.
22-23.

99.   Advocate of Christian Holiness, VI (September,
1875), 70.

100. Warfield, op. cit. , I, 505-508.

101. Pollock, op. cit. , pp. 34-37. For an account of
how the whole matter looked to his son, see L. Smith, Unforgotten Years, pp. 60-64.

102. L. Smith, Philadelphia Quaker, p. 31. Mrs.
Smith observed that the camp "ought not to have been called
a 'Convention for the promotion of holiness,' but a 'Convention for the promotion of Pearsall Smith.' " Also see the
same, Unforgotten Years, pp. 66-69.

103. L. Smith, Philadelphia Quaker, p. 31.

104. Ibid. , p. 33.

105. Ibid. , p. 32.

106. Ibid. , p. 34. Her son, Logan Smith, says that
"the experience confirmed in her the belief which she always
fervently preached, namely, that religion should be an affair,
not of the feelings, but of the will." L. Smith, Philadelphia
Quaker, p. xiii.

107. Ibid. , p. xvi. Smith died in 1898, "unhappy,
bitter, disappointed, his larger designs wrecked, although
during the short period of his noticeable work his influence
had been immense; nor did it perish with his unfortunate re-
tirement." Hannah continued to take an active interest in the
movement, answering the hundreds of letters which came to
her annually requesting spiritual advice. She participated at
times in the continuing Broadlands Conventions. The Smith's
English home became a center for such friends of their children as Roger Fry, Bernard Berenson, R. C. Tevelyan, the
Sidney Webbs and Bertrand Russell, whose first wife was
Alys Smith, Pearsall and Hannah's daughter. Mrs. Smith
died in 1911. Also see Strachey, op. cit. , p. 15, and L.
Smith, Unforgotten Years, p. 72. Barabas, op. cit. , p. 27;
Pollock, op. cit. , p. 36; Guide, XXIV (May, 1876), 150;
Advocate of Christian Holiness, VIII (May, 1877), 14-15; ibid.
(September, 1877), 214-15. Boardman and Mahan continued
their ministry; Divine Life, a magazine for the promotion of
holiness, edited jointly by Mahan and Asbury Lowrey, carried
accounts. McDonald and Searles, op. cit. , p. 317.

108. Ford, op. cit. , pp. 29-30. See also To the Uttermost: Commemorating the Diamond Jubilee of the South-

port Methodist Holiness Convention, 1885-1945 (London: The Epworth Press, 1945). I. R. Govan, Spirit Revival: Biography of J. G. Govan, Founder of Faith Mission (London: The Faith Mission, 1938).

109. The latest official history of the movement is Pollock, op. cit. Also see R. Duane Thompson, Keswick: Historical Origin and Doctrine of Holiness (Marion, Ind. : n. n. , 1963).

110. Harford, op. cit. , p. 62.

111. Pierson, op. cit. , p. 31; see supra, p. 115.

112. Robert Wilder was introduced to the holiness experience by a Salvation Army officer in Carlisle, England in 1891 at the age of twenty-eight while on his way to Keswick. His contacts there led to the founding of the Student Volunteers in Scotland and Great Britain; Pollock, op. cit. , p. 112. A. J. Gordon gave the opening message to the First International Convention of the Student Volunteer Movement; see the same, "The Holy Spirit in Missions," Report of the First Student Volunteer Movement for Foreign Missions Held at Cleveland, Ohio, U. S. A. , February 26, 27, 28 and March 1, 1891 (Boston: T. O. Metcalf and Co. , n. d.), pp. 7-20.

CHAPTER V

A TRADITION IN DILEMMA

THE REVIVAL IN THE GILDED AGE

The year 1875, which had proven to be so significant for the expansion of the influence of the American holiness movement to both England and the Continent, also ushered in one of the most dramatic periods of change for both the American nation and the American churches. Elements in the development of both of these, in the years immediately following, conditioned and altered the ongoing holiness revival movement. The very success of the revival efforts helped to produce increased tensions between the loosely organized holiness associations and the rapidly solidifying patterns of denominational bureaucracy. It was a critical period for the movement as well as a critical period for American religion in general. [1] Crucial forces were at work in every area and at every level of the nation's life. All of them had a share in shaping the future work of the holiness revival forces, now largely under the leadership of the National Camp Meeting Association.

The swift expansion of the economy, along with industrialization and the concomitant growth in the nation's wealth, merely helped to intensify those "backslidings" of the Methodist and other churches which had become one of the major concerns of the holiness reform movement. William Warren Sweet labels the increase in wealth, particularly from 1880 to the century's end, as "the most significant single influence in organized religion in the United States" during that time. [2] The Methodist Church through its rapidly increasing membership shared fully in the new wealth and the changes which it helped to produce within the churches. [3]

By 1875 the Methodists were swiftly becoming a mid-

dleclass church. They began to glory in the mass and beauty
of their buildings, in their political influence in local communities as well as in national affairs, and in their status
among other established churches in the religious community
of the nation. [4]   Bishop Matthew Simpson had been a close,
war-time adviser of President Lincoln. At the celebration
of the Centenary of American Methodism in 1866, the descendants of the church's pioneers in America rejoiced that they
were now recognized as equals by the other large churches
of the country. [5]   In fact, the triumph of Arminianism and a
renewing emphasis on Wesley's doctrine of perfection within
American revivalism, had put them in a place of leadership
which they were not hesitant to acknowledge. [6]

A third factor which strongly influenced the patterns
of development in the American churches during this era was
the rapid growth of the cities. [7]   The sources of the migration
which fed this urban expansion, were two-fold: the one involved large masses of people coming from Europe to America; the other less dramatic, but just as important, involved
the large numbers of people moving from America's rural
areas to its urban centers. The latter movement is especially
significant for the story of the development and institutionalization of the holiness movement. As Charles Jones has
shown, it was this rural class which formed the backbone of
the holiness churches and strongly shaped their institutional
patterns. [8]

Only a few leaders in the churches at the time were
really aware of the magnitude of the problem and what was
happening in the religious communities within the expanding
urban centers. Henry Ward Beecher expressed his concerns
in 1874 when he noted that, in,

> the average churches in New York and Brooklyn--,
> from Murray Hill downward ... it will be found
> that the aristocratic and prosperous elements have
> possession of them, and if the underclass, the poor
> and needy, go to them at all, they go sparsely, and
> not as to a home. [9]

Beecher was one of the few to note the trends so early in
their development. And Beecher's New York was not unique.
The situation was repeated in city after city in America. The
gap between the city churches with their new-found wealth,
their rented pews, their robed choirs, their professional mu-
sicians, their ritualistic worship, and their elaborate archi-
tecture, and the revivalistically oriented simple worship patterns

and the atmosphere of the country family church was not effectively bridged. Abell says that,

> even the Baptist and Methodist faiths, once religions
> of the poor, now displayed almost frantic solicitude
> for the spiritual welfare of the rich. [10]

The Methodists, among these rural immigrants, probably felt
these differences most keenly, for more than in any other
church, during this period, the city churches of that denomination accelerated their turn to liturgical patterns;[11] these
tendencies showed up even more starkly than they might have
in some other communions because of their direct contrast
with former patterns of Methodist induced freedom of expression, personal involvement, and even enthusiasm. Worship
in the established city churches seemed to be no part of the
religion the new city dweller had previously known; the name
on the church and the Discipline were the same, but little
else made him feel at home. [12]

A fourth factor at work in the growing alienation between any individual church members and the middle class
churches, was the type of minister which the newly-founded
seminaries of the church were supplying in increasing numbers. In those schools, the younger faculty members who
knew little of Wesley, began to wrestle with the problems
raised by their theological education. Consequently, the "holiness question," which had agitated the church for nearly a
hundred years, was often sloughed off as an irrelevant irri-
tant among much more interesting and important issues. This
tendency merely served to strengthen the conviction of the
advocates of the revival that new and foreign elements were
threatening original Wesleyanism within Methodism. This
tension fed the revival movements within that church as well
as other churches where German theology began to make its
influences felt in the schools and consequently in the ministry. [13]

A fifth factor, one which has commonly been over-
looked in assessing the changing Methodist reaction to the
holiness movement during this period, was the influx of an
unusually large number of new men into the total ministerial
force of the church. Bishop Matthew Simpson observed in
1875 that more than one-third of the total number of Methodist ministers then serving the church had had less than ten
years of experience. [14] The post-war expansion of the church,
much of it due to revivalism itself, had demanded an imme-

diate increase in the pastoral supply. Many of those new
men were neither indoctrinated in, nor interested in the issues which entered into the holiness controversy. Furthermore, the dynamic growth situation undoubtedly vaulted many
of them into positions of influence in all levels of the church's
structure much earlier than would have been so under more
normal growth patterns. The infusion of these new leaders
was hardly favorable to the puritan-pietist orientation of the
reforming movement.

The usual membership growth of the revival churches,
particularly of the Methodist Episcopal Church, during the
post-war years was a sixth factor which contributed to the
developing differences between the denominations and the revival forces. The very fact of the success of the general
revival efforts, the holiness revival among them, helped to
create a crisis of discipline in the churches. The enrollment of thousands of new converts in the churches' ranks
helped to overwhelm the regular patterns of Christian discipline and instruction. Many of the new members were sin-
cerely seeking to become mature Christians; on the other
hand, many were probably joining out of varying peer pressures. [15] They had little appreciation for the traditional
puritan-pietistic ethic and standards of the Christian life
which Methodism had commonly emphasized in its class meetings and Dicipline.

There was a concurrent, gradual relaxation of the
prohibitions against worldly amusements, fine dress, dancing,
etc.; revivalists had consistently inveighed against such involvements as totally incompatible with sincere Christian
commitment. In the holiness advocate's mind, the "worldly"
lives of thousands of church members who were enjoying the
social position which their growing wealth brought them bore
faint resemblance to the life-style of Bunyan's "Pilgrim,"
Wesley's "Methodist," or the revivalist's "seeker after holiness." [16] The roots of the protest went deep into the experiential tradition. Furthermore, the developing breakdown of
the class meeting in Methodism laid that church open, particularly, to the appeal of newly developed small groups who
offered the fellowship, discipline, and instruction which were
characteristic of that unique Wesleyan institution. The purposes and values of the class meeting in the Methodist structure were manifold. Bishop Simpson regarded these weekly
meetings as centers which uniquely incited Methodists to
"higher Christian experience," accustomed them to "religious
conversation and labor," developed "earnest and active Chris-

tian workers," brought young Christians into intimate dialogue
with more mature Christians, created "bonds of union" within
the church, personally involved every member in Christian
life, offered forums for the discussion of special topics, and
sought the overall goal of the cultivation of a "more vigorous
type of Christian piety."[17]

At the same time - 1875 - the Bishop had to admit
to all the world that regular attendance by the membership
of Methodist Episcopal Churches at this type of meeting was
no longer as common as it should be. In 1866, unable to
salvage its former patterns out of the ravages of the war,
the Methodist Episcopal Church South had already done away
with the mandatory requirements for class meetings attendance
among its members.[18] In the northern church, required
attendance continued until early in the twentieth century, but
as indicated in Bishop Simpson's remarks, its place in Methodism after the war continually waned.

The relationship between the fortunes of this institution
and holiness revivalism's reform concerns for the life of the
church were clearly shown in some comments by Nathan Bangs
on the class meeting during the Revival of 1858. In an article in the Christian Advocate, Bangs responded sharply to
the charges of some within the Methodist Church that the
stringent requirements of the class meeting were denying the
church its full share of the thousands of converts of the revival who were seeking a permanent church home. The pressure to relax the rules under such a pretext, he noted, merely
indicated that many of the "converts" who had purportedly
refused to join the Methodist Church out of their hesitancy
to participate in the spiritual exercises of the class meeting
were probably not really converted and should not be taken
into the church in any case.[19]

If one adds to this, Franklin Littell's judgement that,

> of the various institutions John Wesley introduced
> to plant and cultivate a living faith, none was so
> representative of his view of the Christian life as
> the Class meetings, and none was more character-
> istic of Methodism through the generations,[20]

one can understand why those holiness elements in the church
that claimed to be calling the church back to true Wesleyanism looked with dismay upon the declining influence of these
"schools of holiness" within that body. In a parallel development, the position of the class leader, with his responsibility

for the spiritual life on the members under the pastor was
lessening, and the power of the trustee, who frequently represented the influences of the new social and economic forces at work in the local churches, was increasing; it did not
give supporters of the class meeting any encouragement. [21]

A final factor which played an obvious role in the religious crisis of these decades, or one might more properly
say, showed the extent and nature of the crisis, was the
alienation of significant portions of the population from the
established patterns of orthodox Christian religion as demonstrated by the cults which rose around the same time.   In
1873 Russellism broke upon the American religious scene; in
1875 Helena P. Blavatsky organized her first Theosophical
Society in New York City; and in the same year, Mary Baker
Eddy was organizing her first Christian Science churches.
One cannot divorce the reality of the fractured religious and
social milieu which provided fertile soil for these cultic
movements from the pressures which were at work in the
total religious context of the developing holiness movement.
It was obviously a time of great religious dissatisfaction and
unrest, and, obviously as well, a time for new movements.

Wittingly or unwittingly caught up by such tensions, it
seemed to the holiness advocates that nothing but a revival
of Christian holiness, especially among the ministry, could
stem the tide of undisciplined worldliness which was sweeping
the church or save it from the onslaught of forces such as
German "higher criticism" and British "Darwinian evolution-
ism," both of which they insisted threatened their basic biblical assumptions.   Church fairs, dances, drunkeness, Sabbath-
breaking, card-playing, and other practices which were a part
of popular Christianity, they claimed, could only be remedied
by firm Christian discipline based in a total commitment of
all concerned to the final authority of God's will and Word
alone. [22]

The National Association in Tension with Methodism

Within this cultural complex, the increasing tempo of
the revivalism of John Inskip and his associates in the work
of the National Camp meeting Association for the Promotion
of Holiness greatly increased the potential for confrontation
which had existed within the movement and Methodism from
the Palmers' earliest efforts in the special promotion of the
experience.   The ability of Inskip and his cohorts to raise a

strong voice against the tendencies to compromise which they believed they discerned in the church and yet to maintain themselves in the general good graces of many of its most influential leaders is a testimony both to their own leadership and the basic integrity of their claims concerning the state of Methodism itself. In 1872, the Zion's Herald, a periodical generally sympathetic to the movement, had recognized that Inskip and McDonald had done an admirable job of "holding the horses." The paper warned that continuing opposition to the movement was unreasonable, and that unless its opponents relented, schism would be the inevitable consequence. 23

Conciliatory counsel such as that, however, did not deter continued opposition to the movement by others who were less enthusiastic for the special efforts to generate holiness reform in the church than the Herald was. In the mid-seventies, at the height of the National Association's effectiveness, an attack upon Inskip and the National Committee's publishing interests appeared in the New York Christian Advocate, the most prestigious voice in Methodism. 24 The paper charged that a ten thousand dollar holiness tract fund, for which Inskip was currently making an appeal, was really an attempt to secure funds which could be used to rescue the Association from its financial difficulties. The article represents a concise picture of the polity questions which were really predominant in the minds of many of those who eventually forced large segments of the holiness element within Methodism to leave the church and sometimes become its bitter critics. The article noted:

> When this new publishing movement started we chronicled it as a scheme fraught with methods if not purposes, directly hostile to the connectional interests of the Church.

It saw in this latest venture the verification of that prophecy, and that no sooner than had been anticipated. The writer charged further that,

> under the profession of Holiness--a doctrine justly precious to our people--a few men whose ministerial influence and position have been acquired under our itinerant system, ... have first, organized themselves into an association to choose their own time and place of service, and, next, have set themselves to the task of establishing a publishing system institution not recognized in our economy, but claiming the support of our pastors and people.

All of this represented a presence within the Church of "an irresponsible agency, the outcome of which will be another and mischievous secession.[25]

The closing prediction of potential schism over issues raised by the holiness question in these, the two oldest periodicals of the Methodist Episcopal Church, within a few years of each other, struck an ominous note for the future--the one predicted schism because of the way the movement was relating to the church and the other predicted the same because of the way some in the church were relating to the movement. This indicated that the problems which continued to arise within Methodism over the holiness revival were due not alone to doctrinal differences, but also to organizational tensions created by what many Methodists considered to be the irregularity of the National Committee's place within the church structure. The leaders of the National Association realized this. At every opportunity they publicized any activities of ecclesiastical leaders in the National Camps or any favorable comments by voices which were respected in the church on the movement or its concern for holiness.[26] These were commonly at hand.

In 1872, Luke Tyerman, the English Methodist biographer of Wesley, wrote to a friend:

> I shall be specially thankful if [the revival] helps to revive the glorious old Methodist doctrine of Christian Perfection, a doctrine of late years disastrously neglected but which is now ... obtaining more attention in the country [England] than it has done for more than the last twenty years.... All who are acquainted with Methodist history are well aware that Methodism has always prospered most when the doctrine of entire sanctification has been most popular [emphasis his].[27]

In the fall of 1879, Bishop William L. Harris of the Methodist Episcopal Church joined Asbury Lowrey, Asa Mahan, and Daniel Steele--all holiness leaders--in the publication of an "Address" which called for a revival of holiness among the ministers of all denominations. The next spring, a similar appeal to all Christian laymen appeared over the same signatures.[28] Statements at the Centenary Conference of 1884, just subsequent to Inskip's death at Ocean Grove, New Jersey, in March of that year, would have assured the leader of the movement again that the "inner leadings" which had "warmed" his heart at the thought of the first holiness

camp meeting at Vineland, New Jersey, had definitely been
in the "Divine will. " Bishop Merrill, elected in 1872, along
with Harris and other bishops favorable to holiness, declared
in the pastoral address at the hundredth anniversary of the
organization of the church in America:

> Take from Methodism these doctrines of experience
> ... or even the emphasis given them or everlay
> them with lifeless forms and ceremonies, or mar
> them by even human speculations concerning the
> mode of divine procedure in them, or confuse them
> by any conceivable departure from their simplicity
> so that they will only become doctrines in the creed,
> unverified in the soul as the very essence of sal-
> vation ... and the glory is departed forever. [29]

The bishop was ringing the changes of all the concerns of the
holiness advocates in the church. The threats to the promotion of the doctrine and the "glory" of the church, which he
voiced, had been part of the perfectionist revival's warnings
to the church since the beginnings of the movement in the
thirties. [30]

The bishop, in the same address, continued with the
statement that, "the mission of Methodism is to promote holiness," and that "this end and aim enters into all our organic
life.... [and] in all the borders of Methodism the doctrine
is preached and the experience of sanctification is urged. "[31]
His statement contained contradictory implications for the
future of the movement in the church. On the one hand, he
clearly declared the progress of the movement in awakening
the church to its holiness mission; on the other hand, he may
have been indicating that the regular organizations of the
church were now adequate to carry on the promotion of that
mission. The proponents realized that in spite of the revival
influence which everyone in the church recognized, either by
approbation or opposition, the battle was still far from over.

This would not have been so if the movement had been
moving on some kind of false premise which the church could
have readily dismissed, but it was not. Methodists everywhere in the church, from the Board of Bishops on down to
the laymen of the local churches, some of them not sympathetic to the holiness forces, still had a haunting fear that
all was not well. Bishop R. S. Foster's concern expressed
also on the occasion of the Methodist centennial, was not
atypical. Noting the numerous dangers that faced Methodism

in her centenary year, he said that they could all be summed
up in the one danger of a "fashionable church." "That there
should be signs of it in a hundred years from 'sail loft'
[seemed] ... almost the miracle of history."32

　　　Such expressions only served to confirm the fears of
holiness reformers. The movement increasingly presented
itself as the one last antidote which could counteract the poi-
son that the bishop sensed within Methodism's veins. The
appeal was a strong one, so strong that thousands left the
church when she seemed to reject the revival, while other
thousands continued the battle within the church, believing
that the holiness cause would be lost in all of Protestantism
if it were lost in Methodism. 33

The Rise of New Holiness Associations

　　　Contentions concerning the adequacy of the promotion
of holiness through regular means were hardly allowed by
these Methodists across the country who were organizing new
associations for holiness evangelism. Inspired by the successes of the National Association, similar associations sprang
up everywhere after 1870. 34 The leaders of the national organization were hard put to cope with these new elements in
the movement. After the second National Camp at Manheim
in 1868, they had brought their organization as tightly under
the Methodist organization as the structures allowed. The
result was that they had become so Methodist oriented that
they had been able to maintian a relatively acceptable position within the church. At the same time, however, their
ability to relate to the broader movement as it was developing outside of Methodism, was restricted to a proportionate
degree. 35

　　　Many of the new holiness organizations were very
loosely associated bands which cooperated around their common interest in promoting entire sanctification. The band
concept may have had its roots in two traditions. In the
degree in which they were Methodistic, they were related to
the bands which Wesley had organized in his societies in
England. Their major root, however, probably lay in the religious bands of the frontier. In sparsely settled communities
where there were not enough members of any one denomination to formally organize local churches, the band provided
a means in which a heterogeneous group of Christians could
gather together for a common religious purpose without re-

linquishing their regular denominational loyalties; there was
little need for either requirements of membership or discipline.[36] In many ways the Church of God concept of church
order was merely a step away from this elemental concept
of Christian fellowship.[37]

     The lack of discipline often evident among these lightly
organized indiscriminate groups of holiness zealots provided
ample ammunition for those who wanted to drive their fears
concerning extremism within the movement to their "logical"
ends. The movement recognized the problem. An article
in the Good Way, one of the prominent voices of the Missouri
holiness movement, attacked extremists who, it claimed, had
surfaced in some fringe elements there. Some taught that
"they should not sleep upon beds, but make their couch on
the ground ... eat crackers out of the dirt ... or go without food." The author claimed to have observed another,
who to demonstrate her humility, was "led" to "not eat at
the table with the unsanctified, not to visit her neighbors who
... [did] not profess sanctification."[38]

     What was read as fanaticism, however, was not al-
ways that. After a holiness meeting in a Missouri Methodist church, the opposition took the pulpit and referred to
the holiness evangelists as:

          a troupe of traveling gypsies, tramps, wild fanatics,
          and vagabonds ... guilty of all kinds of crime known
          to human depravity.[39]

The band was led by J. W. Caughlan, a Methodist Episcopal
minister, A. M. Kiergan, a minister of the Methodist Episcopal Church South, and Harry May, a Free Methodist minister. All were active in the Southwestern Holiness Association. The affiliation of two of these men with competitive
denominations may have added to the severe observations
made by the Methodist pastor who was suspicious of the
"gypsy band." This same Methodist minister[40] had objected
to his conference passing on the character of the Rev. M.
C. Robb, because he had "gone off with that gypsy band ...
that are working against the church." Defenders of Robb
pointed out to the conference that at the Des Plaines Camp
of the National Camp Meeting Association, Dr. C. H. Fowler,
president of Northwestern University and Dr. Raymond, head
of Garrett Biblical Institute, had been first to respond to the
holiness evangelists' appeals and they had been followed by
hundreds "who had pioneered the west for Methodism."[41] To

such differences in evaluation, the same reply may have been given which Dr. John Wesley Redfield used to respond to charges of excesses at the St. Charles, Illinois camp meeting in 1860; there was "full as much mercy," he thought, "for those who served God a little too hard as for those who did not serve him at all."[42]

Such tolerant judgment, however, could hardly be applied to the early Texas holiness movement. In searching out the beginnings of the holiness groups which preceded the rise of portions of the Church of the Nazarene there in the late years of the nineteenth century, Smith concluded that Hardin Wallace, one of the men most active in organizing holiness associations in the west in the early days of the movement, "accepted the ministry of preachers whom neither God nor man, seemingly, had ordained."[43] Such extreme positions as "salvation from sin is salvation from death," that "demons are God's servants sent into men to discipline them," and that holiness included "marital continence" so plagued the first association formed there that the regular Methodist ministry organized a competing association to save the cause from complete disruption.[44]

When one observes the lack of definitive organizational discipline among loosely related individuals who felt more loyalty to the promotion of an experience of entire sanctification than they did to any particular denomination, the marvel is probably not that there was fanaticism in evidence, but rather, that it was not more extensive. This tendency toward radicalism expedited the development of more effective holiness organizations; the majority of the advocates of the doctrine realized that otherwise the cause would suffer more severely at the hands of its professed friends than it would at the hands of its opponents.

The Early General Holiness Conventions

The holiness conventions of 1877

The rapid growth of the holiness movement in the west, as indicated by the organization of area associations and the vigorous opposition which its frontier components generated, was brought to the public attention of the eastern movement in the June 2, 1877 issue of the Christian Standard and Home Journal, in which Inskip printed a report of the Illinois work. It referred the publication of the Banner, a paper of the

Western Holiness Association in Illinois, edited by John P.
Brooks.[45] The Christian Standard suggested that closer
communications between the various elements of the movement were desirable.

In the same issue, Inskip put out initial feelers, seeking reaction to a proposal of Thomas Doty, editor of the
Cleveland, Ohio, Christian Harvester, for a general holiness
convention to be held at Urbana, Ohio in October 1877.

Inskip endorsed the idea, but felt that it should be
enlarged into "something rather more general and comprehensive ... a regular holiness conference embracing the
whole country." The purposes and nature of such a meeting
as shown in the exchanges of the men involved in the planning, reveal several significant things about this very primitive stage of organizational development; the diversity of the
movement was already showing; the men in the west generally
favored the name "convention" for the meeting; the eastern
leaders generally favored "conference." Inskip felt that "conference" was more in harmony with our denominational phraseology, ... and would be better understood ... by our people."[46]
The fact that Inskip thought first in the terms of the church
and "our people," the Methodist people, was indicative of a
prevailing attitude among the old eastern National Committee
leadership; such priorities were already meeting increasing
opposition from the western movements led by men less
closely related to the church either by their knowledge of its
leaders and history or by favorable experience.

The final decision was to use the word "conference"
for the meetings in spite of western usage and the protest
of the Rev. John A. Woods, one of the instigators of the
holiness camp meeting idea, that to call it a "Holiness Conference" might "stir up the old mad dog, humbug cry again,
'you will divide the church, and this thing will lead to a new
church organization.' "[47]

Doty's expressed aversion to the growing importance
of trustee boards in the Methodist Church surfaced during
the course of the planning for the convention. It demonstrates
the fear of ecclesiasticism felt by many in the western movement. Doty warned that the more wealthy members of the
congregation tended to dominate the membership of these
boards. He charged that their secular interests tended to
favor liberal goals and dilute the traditional power of the
class-leader and other lay spiritual directors of congregational

life. "Let us keep this out of the present movement, and out of the whole holiness movement ..."[48] Doty urged Inskip.

Doty's correspondence to the editor of the Christian Standard also carried another theme which became typical of succeeding national conventions, and indeed, of many segments of the later movement--a plea for an open and unstructured convention. He said,

> And while you provide something in the line of progress, please do not go largely into that. Give scope to the Holy Ghost, at the time and place of meeting, and, through messages that he shall then and there call out.[49]

This demand for non-structured meetings represented a degree of anti-ecclesiasticism, and political fear of yielding too much directive leadership to any single segment of the fluid movement; but beyond that, as the quote above indicates, it had a theological base in the very spiritual nature of the doctrine of the movement which taught that in everything the Holy Spirit must give leadership and whatever ritual of pre-planned program there was, everyone must be ready to yield to the program of the Spirit. The freedom on the camp meeting reinforced this theology and placed its heavy imprint upon the movement. Its extremes were to show up in the Church of God (Anderson, Ind.) and the Holiness Church of California.[50]

In the services of most of the holiness churches, this extreme did not become the pattern, but there has been a general concern for "the mind of the Spirit" in all services so that at any time human designs might be set aside for what the Lord was telling someone to do, whether it be the minister or a layman in the pew. To the ritualist, the results would frequently have represented chaos, and in some cases it may have been that, through abuse of this openness; nevertheless, it had the advantage of every open situation in intercommunication between individuals. There apparently was a development of personal fulfillment and community fulfillment in a fellowship in worship which would be the envy of those today who seek to emphasize the concept of the church as the people of God and encourage the individual priesthood of the believer. It grew out of the insistence in holiness preaching for sensitivity to the leadership of the Holy Spirit in the individual's life or the church's life. It was an attempt to create worship on the "Pentecostal" or

"Holy Ghost line," phrases commonly used by the members
of the movement as they sought to extrapolate holiness experience into a system of faith and order.

The anticipated hopes for the usefulness of such a
convention also illustrate conditions which enveloped the movement ten years after Vineland. J. P. Brooks felt that

> the prime business of the conference should be ...
> to secure ... a unification or, at least, an assim-
> ilation of all holiness agencies and plans, with a
> view to the more harmonious and more successful
> prosecution of our great holiness work. [51]

This same note ran through the suggestions of Inskip and
others. This desire for a united front in the promotion of
holiness evangelism became a fervent search for unity and
order which lay at the heart of each of the succeeding conventions. It was never fully achieved within that context.
Order finally was to come only with sect formation and other
institutionalization of the movement. [52]

Inskip suggested further that the proposed conference
could be of immense value as an occasion for the holiness
workers scattered across the nation to "compare notes" and
"communicate" with one another, to learn the condition of
the work and "determine upon the best measures to promote
it. "[53] Certain of the validity of the revival movement in
the church of its day, but themselves, unstructured, disor-
ganized, and uncertain about the next or proper moves, the
proponents of the revival were already setting patterns, just
ten years after Vineland, by which the revival would institu-
tionalize itself for its own perpetuation.

The proposed holiness "conference" finally became
two holiness "conferences," the one held at Cincinnati, Ohio
beginning November 26, 1877, and the other held at New
York City, beginning December 17, 1877. [54] Apparently,
some planning went into the conferences in spite of the fears
that it would be overstructured. The records of the proceedings contain pre-written addresses by a number of men who
were prominent in the movement at that time. Dr. William
Nast of the German Methodist Conferences in America, reported on the German and European holiness work: J. E.
Searles, one of the early historians of the movement, gave
a brief historical sketch of the holiness revival and the origins of the National Camp Meeting Association for the Pro-

motion of Holiness; C. W. Ketchum, the presiding elder of
the West Cincinnati District of the Methodist Episcopal Church,
read a paper prepared by C. A. Van Anda, then a Methodist
pastor at Rochester, New York.[55]

The significance of the conventions: the address of J. P. Brooks

        Two of the most significant implications of these first
conferences are found in a speech given by J. P. Brooks,
entitled, "What are the Chief Hindrances to the Progress of
the Work of Sanctification Among Believers."[56]   Brooks concluded that the hindrances to the movement were both external and internal.   The western editor's comments on exter-
ior obstacles were not designed to encourage unity in the
movement.   He observed that, in his opinion, the holiness
message was too closely tied to Methodism and, therefore,
too restricted.   This observation cut sharply across the
strong Methodist orientation of most of the leaders of the
original movement.   Brooks claimed that this sectarian emphasis was restricting the acceptance which the truth deserved;
other denominations, he claimed, were rejecting it, sight
unseen, as merely an effort to expand Methodism's borders
through an irregular, but very Methodistic organization.
Brooks went on to note that this suspicion was not a partic-
ularity of the denominations themselves, but rather a partic-
ularity of the sectarian spirit itself, which, he said, tends
to be "ever wary and suspicious."[57]   This indicated that
Brooks' ideas concerning the nature of the church, as an
open fellowship in the "Church of God' concept, already were
being shaped by his theology of holiness and his dedication
to its promotion.   Sects, by their very nature as sects, were
a hindrance to the spread of the doctrine; non-sectarianism and
the Church of God concept of church order were a natural
consequence.

        Brooks allowed that it was "lawful" for the Methodists
to reinforce the authority of the doctrine as it was propagated
in the Methodist Church, by referring to it as a Methodist
doctrine.   But he questioned the "expediency" of the approach
even in Methodism;

                it would seem wise ... to hold forth and enforce
                holiness as an altogether Catholic doctrine--Catho-
                lic because belonging in the sense of property to no
                one sect, but to all Catholic, because coming to

the people of God more from the general Gospel
than from the catechism, more from the Bible than
from the Discipline.

This catholic approach, he claimed, would provide the truth
"a more general welcome and cordial acceptance." It would
produce a "general holiness movement"[58]

In this appeal for a broader movement, Brooks had
laid down the gauntlet for a contest within the movement to
successfully incorporate into the American movement non-
Methodist people and the non-Methodist concepts which they
often brought with them. This, by its very nature, demanded
a greater non-sectarian emphasis on the part of the older
National Camp Meeting Association leaders at the very moment when they were coming under increasing criticism for
participating in an organization whose very existence was
threatened in its Methodist home.

The threat to the movement's future relationship with
Methodism was even more strongly intimated in a further
observation of Brooks on the situation the movement faced
in "wordly-minded" churches:

So long as there remains in the churches this un-
righteousness and darkness, and so long as carnal
counsels prevail in and rule over the churches, so
long will the doctrine of holiness be held aloof,
and so long will its witness be discountenanced and
proscribed. [59]

The approaching polarization of positions, both in significant portions of the Methodist Church and in the new revival forces, shows even more starkly in the aggressive position Brooks took toward the work of the evangelist. Holiness reform, he said, required:

open and unrestricted access to peoples and places.
Such access it has not had in the past; it has not
in the present. That it may have, hereafter, will
depend much upon the spirit of its champions, --
upon the wisdom and the courage shown ... on the
part of those who have been divinely commissioned
for its advocacy [emphasis his].

The question of access, he continued, was of "immense moment." The opposition to the work must not in any degree

deter those who "come under solemn vows to God in the guidance of this great reform." He maintained that there was
given to the evangelists of the movement a

> divine prerogative of making access, where it is
> not. Where entrance into new fields can be gotten
> without asking it ought to be taken. When entrance
> can only be gotten by the asking it ought to be asked.
> Where entrance has not been secured and cannot
> for the asking then should entrance be procured
> anyhow, independent of all considerations and all
> conditions but the command of God [emphasis his]. 60

        The appeal of this "divine prerogative" became the
rationale for the holiness evangelists in the churches for the
next twenty-five years. Without such aggressiveness the
movement would never have moved beyond Methodism, nor
would there have been much promise of a future in Methodism.
This aggressiveness was demonstrated in varying degrees of
intensity, depending upon the temper and perspective of the
individual evangelist. It created tensions between established
pastors and holiness evangelists which sparked much of the
controversy of this period. It appears in this developing
history that as long as the holiness movement largely restricted its evangelism to those people who were willing to
come to their special camps and the communities which opened
up their churches, generally Methodist, to them, the antagonism between the movement and the large mass of Methodist
pastors, to whom the movement was suspect, was kept at
a tolerable level; but when the free-ranging evangelists of the
early band organizations began to insist that the holiness
message had a right to be heard by every man, and sought
access to every community whether invited or not, a new
element of intensity and finality entered the conflict which
had always prevailed. Here were nineteenth century overtones of the ancient struggle in the early church between the
prophets, who felt they were Spirit-commissioned and the
bishops of established churches who sought to bring order to
the Christian community. It was a question of how much
openness a structure was able to tolerate, how many free
agents it could assimilate. The ancient prophet, because of
the lack of recourse within the social and religious structure
of the Constantinian Age, generally had to yield to the established order. 61 In the America of the latter nineteenth century, the separation of church and state, and voluntary church
membership opened up other alternatives to him. Brooks'
speech demonstrated that he knew this.

The intensifying presence of holiness proponents in
the local congregations made the holiness question an ever-
widening issue, one which every pastor had to face, not only
for his congregation, but for himself as well. When he had
been ordained to the Methodist ministry, he had promised
to go on to perfection; now the holiness movement challenged
him to perform his vows for his own soul's sake and the
sake of the church. Many men were not prepared to accept
these alternatives; their opposition combined with the nega-
tiveness of those in the church who were believers in the
Wesleyan doctrine of Christian perfection, but who were not
ready to allow any threat to the church's institutional life
from special instruments for its promotion, hastened the ultimate rejection by the church of these elements in the movement who felt that their holiness witness was being repressed
and that the institution's whole set of mind was irrevocably
against them.

The third major element of Brooks' address to the
1877 Convention was the recognition of hindrances to the
work which were generated by weaknesses in the movement
itself. He listed six of these; with the possible exception
of number four, they continued to show themselves again
and again in the future:

> (1) Imperfect teaching.... Every possessor
> of holiness is a competent and qualified witness,
> --- but not necessarily a competent and qualified
> teacher ... Public teaching ... by those who pos-
> sess no natural or gracious aptness as instructors
> ... whose teachings must hence be crude and im-
> perfect, perhaps essentially incorrect, [makes]
> the cause to suffer....
> (2) Unthorough experiences.... [Because of
> some people who are] regarded by the Church and
> the world as being representatives of holiness,
> while their lives are inconsistent and unholy, holi-
> ness stands compromised and loses influence....
> (3) A form of holiness that is unaggressive
> and inert.... The Church and community where
> such people live are impressed that holiness is a
> spiritless, forceless thing that has no inspiration
> of active well-doing in it....
> (4) Unedifying and misleading testimonies....
> Some say --- "I am not tempted" --- "I cannot
> sin" --- "I am infallibly saved, I cannot fall."
> All these testimonies are untrue, misleading and
> mischievous....

(5) A temptation to Church unaffiliation.
(6) Excessive and extravagant experiences.
(Extremes such as those listed above.) [62]

The weaknesses of the general conventions

If these first general holiness conventions demonstrated that the movement had a critical self-awareness of the difficulties it had to face both externally and internally, they also proved that the fears of these dangers were not sufficiently grave to force the already diverse elements within its borders to unite under one organizational framework. A committee appointed by the conference chairman, at the request of the Cincinnati Conference, John Inskip, which was

> to take into consideration the subject of combining in some way, in harmonious action, the various organizations interested in the holiness movement. . . .

could come to no other conclusion than to report the anticipated activities and plans of the various groups represented in the conference. [63] Failure at this critical point in this first effort at national unity, foretold similar lack of success in such efforts in 1880 at Jacksonville, in 1882 at Round Lake and at Chicago in 1885 and 1901.

This inability to come to joint decisions for future action, not only delayed the search for unity and order, but generally weakened the positive significance of these several general meetings held during these formative transitional years. The conventions listed above undoubtedly played a vital informal role in providing a continuing fellowship and a channel of direct communication between leaders of the movement which no other instrument could provide at that time. They also provided a forum which kept critical issues to the fore. But they were never legislative bodies and their committees, at best, were ad hoc groups, whose influence and vitality inevitably died with the convention which created them. In no case was the committee commonly appointed at each of the conventions to call another convention ever officially responsible for such. Each effort was a child of the pressures of the movement, even though the involvement of the same individuals provided considerable historical and organizational continuity.

By conscious design, the meetings were to be in the

pattern in which the movement felt most at home; the unstructured atmosphere of the holiness camp prevailed. Prayer,
preaching, inspiration were considered more important than
human organization. The Holy Spirit would lead in bringing
about what was best for the futherance of God's work at this
high level of national organization. The same men who often
worked arduously for organization and discipline at other levels, by resigning all activism to the Holy Spirit at this level, were admitting that the diversity in the movement could
be reconciled only in this way. Outside of a common dedication to holiness, the movement was seething with too many
variant factors in other areas to allow for a more definite
organization. [64]

It was genuinely a movement, and its composition was
complex. There were Methodists and others, thoroughly committed to the doctrine, yet just as thoroughly committed to
complete loyalty to their own sect; these hoped to work from
within their organizations to call, what they regarded as increasingly worldly churches, back to Christian purity and
power. There were also Methodists and others who were
rapidly being driven to the conclusion that the "old bottles"
were not pliable enough to tolerate their vital experience;
some of these had already begun to lead the exodus from the
old sects; out of the pure necessities of fellowship and order,
they created the primitive organizations which broke the trail
for the many thousands who eventually followed them out of
the established denominations, either out of force of ecclesiastical pressures, or out of individual desire. There was
also a third group involved who were members of established
holiness sects such as the Wesleyan Methodist Connection and
the Free Methodist Church. The latter church was especially
active within the movement during these fluid years; it was
young and aggressive and dedicated to a very radical standard of holiness and life. The former, although equally committed by its doctrines to the cause of Christian perfection
during most of the nineteenth century, was more interested
in social reform than in evangelism. Its organization was
very loose; the denominational pattern was not conducive to
any concerted appeal to the converts of the revival outside
of its own gates.

The fourth group, a group only in the sense of a
classification of those who shared a common religious condition, were the unchurched who had been converted to the cause.
Their only religious attachment was frequently to the holiness
evangelist who held the protracted meeting in the schoolhouse,

town hall, barn, or tent where they received their religious
experience. The tension between the evangelist and the local
pastors frequently legislated against his referring them to the
local church where he, himself, may have been denied place
or support for his holiness meetings.

The evangelist was usually committed to moving on to
the next center of revival or back to his secular or religious
work through which he supported himself. He could not stay.
It was the plight of these refugee converts that made the
conscientious evangelist feel that he was continually leaving
behind him a trail of religious orphans without adequate means
for fellowship and proper nurture; this constituted one of the
most influential rationales for the organization of holiness
churches. [65] These unchurched converts, in combination with
the evangelist, who was usually supported by holiness sympathizers in some organized church body, provided the combination for hundreds of holiness groups which developed by the
end of the century; they eventually turned away from the
churches to their own fellowships "on the holiness line."
This grass roots, localized origin of so much of the movement provided the most common cause for the diversity displayed throughout the movement's subsequent history; it also
accounts for the difficulty in ordering its forces in a more
consistent pattern.

By 1877, a tradition which had aroused a renewed
interest in Christian holiness within all Christian churches
by means of a specialized meeting for its promotion, a specialized theology for its attainment, a specialized terminology
for its expression, a specialized journal for its propagation;
and a specialized organization of evangelists for its leadership, was now ready for the ultimate step in this organized
promotion of the doctrine of Christian holiness--the organization of specialized holiness churches. In the world of 1877,
only a few men like J. P. Brooks were ready to openly admit that the next step in the promotion of holiness might involve such drastic measures. The straw man, often created
by the opponents of the special methods for polemical pur-
poses--separatism--was about to come to life.

SUMMARY

As the holiness revival, at the peak of its world-wide
influence in 1875, moved on into the last quarter of the nineteenth century, it was encompassed by social forces which

were taking America and the world through a period of change
at a giddy pace. The validity of Charles Jones's sociological
study of the National Association for the Promotion of Holiness within this cultural context cannot be questioned. However, it would appear that all such studies illuminate only
one series of facts in a very complex phenomenon.

This study has also sought to recognize that an understanding of the interplay between the movement and these con-
textual forces is essential to any proper analysis of its significance to the whole. However, as Stoeffler has suggested,
along with the sociological factors operative in the American
culture, one must take into account the concept of an enduring experiential tradition in the Christian Church.

The "oppositive" element in Stoeffler's definition of
Pietism, which was especially useful in interpreting the European Revival, is also helpful in understanding the same
period in the American revival. Particularly when applied
to American Methodism and the holiness movement, it helps
to define the changing religious emphases within Methodism
in regard to its own strongly pietistic, revivalistic heritage.
Had it not been that significant numbers of people were aware
of such trends, the movement obviously would not have emerged
as it did; nor, would the conflict within the churches have
been as intense and prolonged as it became. Basic religious
concerns must be considered in the interpretation of the movement at every period.

The issues were distinctly sharpened by the sociological forces at work in both church and society in general; but
there was something much deeper than that at stake--the
quality and nature of the Christian life and fellowship, as
understood within a long standing Christian tradition, were
being challenged. The elemental characteristics of experiential Christianity were scarcely focused more pointedly than
they were in those members of the National Committee and
the holiness advocates in other American revivalistic churches,
who constituted the leading edge of the revival after the Civil
War. The picture of the tendencies in American churches
and national life almost baited a direct response. Perhaps,
at no point in the history of the American churches, and
among no other group, is a recognition of this interpretive
factor more necessary or valid.

The conditions outlined at the beginning of the chapter
constituted a threat at every turn, to the basic Biblical,

puritan-pietism of the holiness movement. An individual
response to the holiness evangelists' call for a personal, inward conversion experience and a subsequent experience of
entire sanctification both claiming their authenticity from the
Word of God and personal inner assurance, was the foundation of all Christian relationships and the reality of the church
fellowship. In view of this, they felt that all that they believed was being mocked by the tendencies toward increasingly loose standards for church membership. These tendencies had allowed an influx into the churches of large numbers
of members who were not required to testify to a personal
experience of religion. When the fellowship had been sufficiently permeated with such members, the disciplinary powers
of the body were weakened to such an extent that they felt
that the church was no longer pure and, therefore, was in-
capable of maintaining either the individual priesthood of
each believer, or a vigorous corporate witness for the world's
redemption. Their position within the American churches
was strikingly similar to that of the Pietists and Puritans in
Germany and England within the Establishment Churches.

Moreover, the anxiety for the level of fellowship and
discipline was amplified by the collective effects of the growing urban churches upon these pietistic strivings. In large
group worship, the collective responses and the liturgical
trends, and, in large congregations, the need for increased
organization along business-like lines, all apparently left
many individuals of a pietistic bent highly dissatisfied. It
seemed to contradict the individuality, simplicity, and freedom of the experiential tradition. It was not the simplicity
of the Gospel.

The challenges which Biblical higher criticism and new
theories in the scientific world presented to the authority of
the Bible, as pure and simple Word for every man, as well
as for the life of the fellowship, seemed to endanger the
basis of their spiritual life. At the same time that these
were looked upon as destroying the Word by emasculating it,
it seemed to them that others such as the Mormons and the
Christian Scientists, were destroying it by adding to it their
own purportedly equally authoritative word. These threats
to the Bible also constituted a threat to both the preaching
and the devotion of these pietists, for it was the source of
both.

Finally, the holiness movement was concerned, beyond
all else, with the practical sanctification of the Christian life,

a characteristic of all pietistic movements, but especially
set aside by Wesley and the Methodists in their call to entire
sanctification as a possiblility in this life, a "second blessing."
In the view of the holiness people, the doctrine was being
set aside by the one church to whom God had trusted the responsibility for its promotion. There was a wide acceptance
of the revival of holiness in that church by the 1870's, but
not wide enough to overcome the growing tendencies toward
institutionalization, which the very success of the revival encouraged. There was increasing despair among loyal Methodists concerning the possibility of the recovery of the disciplinary standards which they believed necessary to the main-
tanance of the spiritual life of the church. In tension with
a rapidly changing church, and often pressed by radical disruption of their sense of community in other relationships
as well, many began to look to the institutionalization of the
one certainty they had--their commitment to the holiness revival.

NOTES

1. See Arthur M. Schlesinger, "A Critical Period
in American Religion, 1875-1900," Massachusetts Historical
Society, Proceedings, LXIV (1932), pp. 523-47; H. S. Smith
et al., American Christianity, II, 217. A recent and extensive review of the period is Paul A. Carter's Spiritual Crisis
of the Gilded Age.

2. Sweet, The Story of Religion in America, p. 495;
also see Sweet, Methodism in American History, pp. 332-68.

3. Ibid. Also see R. S. Foster, "State of the
Church," Christian Standard and Home Journal, XIX (June
6, 1885), 2. In 1864 the Methodist Church had 928,320 members and 1,580,559 in 1875; Matthew Simpson, A Hundred
Years of Methodism (New York: Nelson and Phillips, 1876),
pp. 185-86, 347.

4. Abel Stevens, The Centenary of American Methodism (New York: Carlton and Porter, 1865), pp. 201-211,
200, 233. Stevens said: "Its people, originally the poorest
in the land, have become, under its beneficent training, perhaps the wealthiest"; ibid., p. 225.

5. Simpson, A Hundred Years of Methodism, p. 208.

Ibid. , p. 340, notes that according to the 1870 census Methodism in the United States had one-third of the church buildings (21,337) and one-fifth of the church property values
($69,854,121). Six years later the M. E. Church alone had
church property valued at $80,893,181; Simpson, Cyclopedia,
p. 597.

6. Ibid. , pp. 333ff.

7. Henry F. May, Protestant Churches and Industrial
America (New York: Harper and Brothers, 1949), p. 119.
The Rise of the City, 1878-1898, ed. A. Schlesinger (Vol.
X, "History of American Life" Series; New York: The Mac-
millan Co. , 1933). In relation to Methodism, see A. Boisen,
op. cit. , pp. 130-31.

8. Supra, p. 114. Also see similar thesis in W. E.
Mann, op. cit.

9. As quoted in Herbert M. Morais, Deism in Eighteenth Century America (New York: Columbia University
Press, 1934), p. 20. Also see George Hedley, The Christian Heritage in America (New York: Macmillan Co. , 1946),
p. 143. Quoting the Methodist, the American Wesleyan
warned in 1880 that if the church wanted to be a power in
the future it had to befriend the "poor and almost friendless
young man [who] ... is a stranger in a strange city ...
lonely and homesick"; American Wesleyan, XXVIII (April 28,
1880), 5.

10. Aaron Abell, The Urban Impact on American Protestantism, 1865-1900 (Cambridge, Mass. : Harvard University Press, 1943), pp. 4, 6; also see Sweet, The American
Churches, p. 56.

11. Ibid.

12. Mann, op. cit. , p. 55. Abell, op. cit. , p. 6.
These conditions may have accounted for the lament of the
Bishops of the Methodist Episcopal Church in their Pastoral
Address to the 1880 General Conference: "The condition of
Methodism in our large cities has been a subject of discus-
sion, and its small relative advance has been contrasted
with its more rapid growth in rural populations. " As quoted
by Guide, LXXV (June, 1880), 178.

13. R. S. Foster, loc. cit.

14. Simpson, A Hundred Years, p. 205.

15. B. K. Kuiper, The Church in History (Grand Rapids, Mich.: Wm. B. Eerdmans Co., 1951), pp. 470-71; Foster, loc. cit. Littell, From State Church to Pluralism, pp. 140-42.

16. Ibid. Also see Simpson, A Hundred Years, p. 204. Two-fifths of the Methodist Church members had been added within the past ten years. The holiness churches themselves later faced similar problems as they developed more city congregations; see Val B. Clear, op. cit., pp. 2-3.

17. Simpson, Cyclopedia, p. 229. Also see John Atkinson, The Class Leader (New York: Nelson and Phillips, 1874); Chas. Keys, The Class Leader's Manual (New York: Carlton and Phillips, 1856); W. M. Prottsman, The Class Leader (St. Louis: Methodist Book Repository, 1856); L. Rosser, Class Meetings (Richmond: privately printed, 1855); W. J. Sasnett, "Theory of Methodist Class Meetings," Methodist Quarterly Review (So.), V, No. 2 (1851), 265-84.

18. Ibid. Also see George G. Smith, The Life and Times of George Foster Pierce with His Sketch of Lovick Pierce, D. D., His Father (Sparta, Ga.: Hancock Publishing co., 1888), p. 466, who says that "the regular class meetings had been suspended by the absence of their leaders...."

19. Nathan Bangs, "The Recent Revival," Christian Advocate and Journal, XXXIII (July 29, 1858), 117; also see ibid. (January 21, 1858), 9.

20. Franklin H. Littell, "Class Meeting," World Parish, IX (February, 1961), 15. Sangster, Methodism Can Be Born Again, p. 60, said that "the decay of the class meeting is a tragedy which the denominational historian will find it hard to exaggerate."

21. Sweet, History of Methodism, p. 341. Ibid., pp. 341-45, develops the thesis that the holiness movement arose mainly because of spiritual decline of the Methodist Church. Sangster said that when the fellowship of the class meeting was gone, "the hunger which the class deeply satisfied was still there, a hunger which could not be met in public worship or mass meetings. Finally it burst out in groups." Sangster, loc. cit.

22. G. Smith, op. cit. , p. 19.

23. Advocate of Bible Holiness, XIII (September, 1882),
p. 260, quoting an unidentified issue of the Zion's Herald.

24. As quoted by the Christian Standard and Home
Journal, VIII (November 27, 1875), 380. It is difficult to
reconcile a statement of John Inskip to his friends in ibid.
in which he says the finances of the Association "were never
in as good condition before" with a rather lengthy account of
his biographers, McDonald and Searles, about the financial
crisis which threatened to take the whole venture into bank-
ruptcy until Inskip with the financial support of one of his
converts, the wealthy Indiana glass manufacturer, Washington
DePauw, was made editor of both the Advocate and the Christian Standard and Home Journal. He weathered the difficulties; before his death in March of 1884 the stock of the company had been restored almost to par value, op. cit. , pp.
299-302. See a November 24, 1875 letter from Inskip to
Curry in the Daniel Curry file of the manuscript section of
the Drew University archives. In a handwritten note on Inskip's letter, probably Curry's, is the statement that the
attack was carried in the paper of which Curry was then
editor without his knowledge. Curry later spoke at Inskip's
funeral; he said that the latter's expression of the experience
of entire sanctification was "the most rational of any he had
ever heard"; McDonald and Searles, op. cit. , p. 367.

25. Christian Standard and Home Journal. loc. cit.

26. E. g. , a report in Divine Life (January, 1880) ,
p. 19, related that Alfred Carman, Bishop of the Methodist
Episcopal Church of Canada was "the first and most pro-
nounced witness and advocate of entire sanctification ..." at
the St. Clair, Ontario camp meeting; ibid. (May, 1880), pp.
207-209, gives an account of Carman's Christian experience.
Ibid. (October, 1879), pp. 61-67; ibid. (March, 1880), pp.
161-66.

27. "Letter of L. Tyerman to E. C. Estes from Stan-
hope House, Clapham Park, April 19, 1872," cited in Advocate of Christian Holiness, III (July, 1872).

28. Divine Life (October, 1879), 61-67; ibid. (March,
1880), 161-66.

29. Stephen M. Merrill, "Pastoral Address," Carroll,
Proceedings of the Methodist Centenial Conference, p. 319.

30. See <u>supra</u>, pp. 49, 50, 97-98, 105.

31. <u>Ibid.</u> , p. 320.

32. Cf. R. S. Foster, <u>Centenary Thoughts for Pew</u>
<u>and Pulpit</u> (New York: Phillips and Hunt, 1884), p. 166.

33. <u>Infra</u>, p. 272.

34. An illustrative but by no means comprehensive
list includes: Ohio Holiness Association (1870); The Nebraska
State Association (1871); The Western Holiness Association
(1871) centered in Illinois was instrumental in forming a number of other holiness associations under the leadership of
men like L. B. Kent and Hardin Wallace; Southern Ohio Holiness Association (1875); Iowa Holiness Association (1879)
long under the leadership of Isaiah Reid; Southwestern Association (1879); New England Association (1879) ; Indiana State
Association (1880), D. J. Warner, who later withdrew from
such associations because of his no-sectism, is listed as
first vice-president. Southern California and Arizona Holiness Association (1880); Kansas State Association (1884).
Since records were often poorly kept, and more than one
association may have taken the same state name, this summary, constructed mainly from periodical references, differs
in some dates with Jones, <u>op. cit.</u> , pp. 147-48.

35. <u>Supra</u>, p. 109.

36. See Simpson, <u>Cyclopedia</u>, pp. 85-86; W. E. Boardman began his ministry in such a band; Mrs. Boardman says
that it was the custom in that day [Sterling, Ill. , 1840] to
form what was called a "band composed of Christians of different denominations who united together to have services on
the Sabbath." Boardman, <u>op. cit.</u> , p. 39. B. T. Roberts
held his groups of followers together in such bands after
their expulsion from the Methodist Episcopal Church, hoping
that from these temporary organizations they could move back
into the church again. Marston, <u>op. cit.</u> , p. 227. For the
organization and activities of a typical band see Mrs. S. A.
Cooke, <u>The Handmaiden of the Lord or Wayside Sketches</u>
(Chicago: T. B. Arnold, 1896), <u>passim</u>. See <u>infra</u>, pp. 238ff.

37. See D. W. M'Laughlin, "Sectizing Holiness,"
<u>Good Way</u>, V (September 5, 1883), p. 2; M'Laughlin, favor-
able to the organization of independent holiness churches
warned that where such bands are not organized the holiness

work commonly went into dissolution or into the hands of the
Free Methodists. He called such bands "Embryo Churches."
Infra, pp. 257ff.

38. Good Way, III (October 15, 1881), 2.

39. Ibid.; also see ibid. (November 5, 1881), p. 1.

40. Ibid., p. 4.

41. Ibid.

42. As quoted by Marston, op. cit., p. 334, from
J. G. Terrill, The St. Charles Camp Meeting (Chicago: T.
B. Arnold, 1883), p. 13.

43. T. Smith, Called Unto Holiness, p. 31.

44. Ibid.; also see C. B. Jernigan, Pioneer Days of
the Holiness Movement in the Southwest (Kansas City, Mo.:
Pentecostal Nazarene Publishing House, 1919), pp. 150-57;
Macum Phelan, A History of the Expansion of Methodism in
Texas, 1867-1902 (Dallas, Tex.: Mathis, Van Nort and Co.,
1937), pp. 118-19. One of the most enlightening volumes on
religious fanaticisms including many related to the holiness
revival is Strachey, op. cit. Mrs. Smith says, ibid., p.
30, that her first introduction to fanaticisms other than that
which she got from her Quaker background, which she says
"was a good deal, came through the Methodist doctrine of
entire sanctification. That doctrine has been one of the
greatest blessings of my life, but it has also introduced me
into an emotional region where common sense has no chance
and where everything goes by feelings, voices and impres-
sions." See especially in reference to Texas revival, ibid.,
pp. 143-44, the account of "The Women's Commonwealth,"
a group of "sanctified women" in the Texas revival of 1876
led by Mrs. Martha Mac Whirter, who with other followers
were finally forsaken by their husbands and driven from town
because of their opposition to the denominations and organized
religion. They thereupon formed the "Women's Commonwealth," went into the hotel business and prospered, one of
them being elected to the local "board of trade." In 1904
they still existed in Washington state, surviving the death of
their founder. Hannah Smith was as objective an observer as
someone within the movement could be. She often chided herself for lack of religious feeling and emotion and her common
sense approach to her religious life. See supra, pp. 161-162.

45. "The Work in Illinois," Christian Standard and Home Journal, XI (June 2, 1877), 172.

46. Ibid.

47. "Holiness Conference," ibid.; ibid. (June 16, 1977), 188; ibid. (June 23, 1877), 197-98.

48. Ibid. (July 7, 1877), 213.

49. Ibid.

50. Supra p. 142, n. 44.

51. As quoted from the Banner of Holiness in the Christian Standard and Home Journal, XI (July 21, 1877), 228.

52. See Timothy L. Smith, "Congregation, State, and Denomination: The Forming of the American Religious Structure," William and Mary Quarterly, Third Series, XXV (April, 1968), p. 162; Smith speaks of the case with which the people of pioneer New England "fell easy prey to the emotionalism and egotism of the magnetic personalities whose teachings highlighted their sense of social and spiritual estrangement." The same may be said of the socially and religiously displaced converts of the revival.

53. Christian Standard and Home Journal, XI (June 2, 1877), p. 172.

54. See Proceedings of Holiness Conferences held at Cincinnati, November 26th, 1877 and at New York, December 17, 1877 (Philadelphia: National Publishing Association for the Promotion of Holiness [1878]), passim.

55. Ibid., p. 31.

56. Ibid., pp. 85-102.

57. Ibid., p. 96. Brooks developed these ideas further in the most systematic statement on ecclesiology which the movement ever produced, The Divine Church. A Treatise of the Origin, Constitution, Order, and Ordinances of the Church; Being a Vindication of the New Testament Ecclesia, and an Exposure of the Anti-Scriptural Character of the Modern Church of Sect (Columbia, Mo.: Herald Publishing House,

1891 [reprinted at Eldorado Springs, Mo.: Witt Printing Co., 1960]). See especially ibid., chap. xvi, pp. 267-83.

58. Ibid.

59. Proceedings of Holiness Conferences, p. 100.

60. Ibid., pp. 86-87.

61. See F. F. Bruce, The Spreading Flame: The Rise and Progress of Christianity (Grand Rapids, Mich.: Wm. B. Eerdmans Publishing Co., 1954), pp. 81-90.

62. Proceedings of Holiness Conferences, pp. 31, 111-12.

63. Ibid., p. 31.

64. E. g., differences on ordinances, millennialism, prudentials, church polity, divine healing.

65. The Methodists used the same rationale to justify Wesley's "societies." Simpson, Cyclopedia, p. 588, says, "This was done [organizing of societies] not because he designed to constitute any separate church, but because the converts came to him for instruction and longed for the fellowship of kindred spirits."

CHAPTER VI

IN SEARCH OF ORDER

It is not within the scope of this study to delineate
the details of the institutionalization of the revival's forces
which began about 1880. By that time, the revival, as a
movement within all of Protestantism, began to change its
character; thousands of Christians in the Methodist churches,
and others in all the churches which had become part of the
revivalistic pattern of denominational propagation, had responded in varying degrees to the perfectionist message of
the holiness evangelists. After 1880, the story became one
of gradual organization in the face of their increasingly sharp
struggle with those in the churches who reacted to this new
evangelism. It is a story even more complex than the general pattern of American religion after 1870, because of the
revival's unorganized nature and the involvement of hundreds
of ordinary laymen and pastors who engaged in the most
aggressive activities on behalf of their cause. This extensive, grass-roots activity makes the total impact of their
work difficult to assess. [1]

The history of these "bands" and "associations," which
formed the nucleus of the first holiness churches, is well
told in the works of Timothy Smith, Charles Jones, and Vincent Synan. [2] Smith and Jones, particularly, place the movement within the larger struggle for order in American society,
to which Robert Wiebe speaks in The Search for Order. [3] It
is Wiebe's thesis that the late nineteenth century saw the
breakdown and reordering of society; the process involved the
disruption of the "island communities, the earlier dominant
social unit, and the effort to create the newer social patterns
structured as a result of the unbroken acceleration of the
rural to urban migration. The gathering together of the holiness people into the institutional units which the movement
began to spawn after 1880, was part of what Wiebe describes
as a crisis precipitated by "a widespread loss of confidence

in the powers of the community," which led to attempts "to
preserve the society that had given their lives meaning."[4]

Within this context, the holiness churches which developed out of the revival are generally regarded as "trans-
plantations," or, attempts to recreate "village churches" in
the midst of the city, "churches identical to warmly remembered ones in town or country ... in a found attempt to create at least one bulwark against urban demoralization."[5] The
highly puritanical pietism of holiness religion was particularly
evident in the rural areas; its reaction to the "worldliness"
which it saw as a prevailing feature of the rapid social change
occurring in both church and community progressed concurrently with that change. It was accompanied by participation
in the common fears of the rapidly growing powers of the
industrial and political establishments; even in these realms,
as Wiebe points out, there was a call for "purity and unity."
The cry of the populists for "self determination" resulted
from those demands. [6]

The general purposes of this paper on revivalism and
holiness, however, speak more directly to another observation of Wiebe, that "the more [anxious the search for an-
swers] ..., the more serious society's predicament, the
more grandiose the visions of perfection following that single
correction."[7] It is possible, therefore, to see some of the
early efforts to orient the holiness revival after 1880 in this
light; as a perfectionist revival with perfectionist answers to
the problems of both individuals and society, its revivalism
and perfectionism strongly molded the nature of both the
problems, which the movement encountered in its search for
order, and the answers which the movement gave to those
problems. Perry Miller has identified the hermeneutical
principle that is involved here in his classical study of The
Life of the Mind in America; speaking to his development of
the evangelical basis of that mind, he said that in the nation's "religious mentality," by the end of the Civil War,
"the simple fact of the Revival was central. Whether it produced formal unity or created new churches was of less import than the omnipresence of the Revival."[8] The "omnipresence" of the revival in the "religious mentality" of the holiness converts, and, therefore, holiness advocated, is a critical factor in properly understanding what was occurring in
this period as well.

THE REVIVAL AND THE CHURCH QUESTION

It has already been pointed out in the summary of the
address of J. P. Brooks to the first conference of the general movement in 1877, that the special promotion of holiness
was raising trying issues, both external and internal to the
movement. At that early point, the difficulties of properly
relating the vigorous evangelism of the holiness revivalists
to the established structure of the churches, was a problem.
Holiness was a reformatory principle; how to most effectively
apply its purifying principles to the churches so that they
might in turn be restored to the hoped-for primitive holiness
and power, was by no means clear to them, and certainly
not to the churches. Furthermore, the question of how to
reconcile the tendencies to create divisions, both within the
churches and within the movement, seemingly inherent in
the movement itself, with the principles of perfect love which
were to make all the sanctified one, was all-present. This
question was seriously raised for some, by the inability of
the first conference to come to any kind of unified pattern
of organization for the future of the movement. 9 The flurry
of "church of God" thinking, even before 1880, indicates how
serious it had become.

Revivalism's Paradox

The tendency to divisiveness

The question of access for the holiness evangelists,
also raised by Brooks in 1877, pointed up the issue which
rapidly became the crucial problem between the organized
churches and the revival. Bands of holiness evangelists,
often representing several denominations, became increasingly
active and aggressive in their evangelism, as the intensity
of the holiness question and the growing response and reaction among the churches seemed to move along hand in hand.
These bands were loosely organized, and frequently unregu-
lated, except by the most simple peer pressure or a charismatic leader. Their very efforts to refrain from taking on
the nature of a second church--their members, in the early
period, were all members of some other regulated religious
body--prejudiced the groups against any tight internal control.
It allowed free spirits, who sometimes were escaping to the
group from discipline in some other religious society, or
were feeding their own sense of individuality, to readily find
a home and an outlet for their ambitions. Moreover, the

strong emphasis within the preaching of the movement, upon
the development of an obedience to the leadings of the Holy
Spirit, above the voice of any man or group of men, often
was used to reject the measure of peer discipline which was
exercised even in such informal organizations. [10]

That this created a problem both internally and externally for the movement, is indicated by the way in which it
was spoken to at the first gathering of the general movement
in 1877;[11] how serious a matter it was for some, was indicated also by the reaction which even the minimal efforts of
the next convention at Jacksonville to regulate members created. [12]   It was mentioned consistently thereafter in the conventions which followed. [13]   Inskip, McDonald, Walter Palmer, George Hughes, and the many others in the leadership
of the disciplined Methodist mainstream of the movement in
the Palmer tradition, refuted, both by argument and example,
the charges that such problems were inevitably inherent in
the movement; but, as has been indicated, even they, with
the strong support of high ecclesiastical authorities, had been
constantly reminded of the tendencies of side effects to schism.
By the 1870's, they too, were increasingly being attacked as
irregulars because of their expanding numbers of cohorts in
special holiness promotion through holiness associations and,
especially, through the numerous holiness papers which sup-
plemented the effectiveness of the Guide and the Advocate of
Christian Holiness. [14]

In the light of these facts, it is not difficult to see
why the holiness bands and the holiness evangelists, at the
local levels of the church, progressively agitated those pastors and members who were totally unsympathetic to, or un-
interested in, their work; but it also agitated others who
were in general sympathy with the doctrines, but not in sufficient degree to encourage its promotion to the disruption
of the churches. [15]   The result of these tensions was this:
that the opposition to the revival continued to increase, in
spite of the fact that the holiness evangelist was getting a
wider and wider hearing in more and more communities, as
the laymen and small-town pastor took the regular promulgation of the doctrine into any place which would invite them--
and just as often, into any place which would not--the opposition to the revival increased. [16]   The end result was that
by 1880, thirteen years after the post-war phase of the revival had begun, at the Vineland National Camp Meeting, the
contest within the Methodist Church over the Holiness question, which Bishop Hamline had eagerly looked forward to,

was forcing difficult decisions concerning church loyalties
upon not only many Methodists, but upon many non-Methodists
as well.

The sense of unity

It was against this background of growing strife, resulting from the aggressive efforts of the holiness associations and bands to win the churches to their holiness reform,
that their equally perfectionist statements concerning Christian unity sounded so contradictory to some. The basic origin of the Christian unity theme, undoubtedly, developed
mainly as a natural consequence of their Biblical orientation. [17]
The logical relationship of their sanctification concept to the
removal of those selfish prejudices and personal interests,
which were commonly regarded as the source of individual
differences, introduced the practical problem into every life
situation. Perfection in love, as preached by the movement,
was certainly foreign to such self-centeredness, whether in
men or in churches. It will be seen that its implications,
when driven to their logical ends by some men within the
early movement, raised serious questions within the revival's
rank concerning the very nature of the church itself, and the
pattern of denominationalism, which had grown out of the voluntaristic organization of the American churches.

The force of the rhetoric which was common to the
unity theme within the holiness revival could be illustrated
by the record of almost every holiness meeting which is
available to the researcher. But it was probably the rhetoric
of the National Committee itself and of the other dominant
sources of influence in the fluid movement--the holiness per-
iodicals--which provided the most valid examples of the perfectionist ultraism inherent in the holiness message. At the
Landisville, Pennsylvania National Holiness Camp Meeting in
1873, John Inskip, the recognized leader of the general movement until his death in 1884, said to those who had gathered
for the first service of the camp:

> We come here not so much to argue as to assert,
> demonstrate, proclaim, and announce the truth as
> it is in Christ Jesus.... This is not fair, you
> say. Yes, it is fair. You get this blessing and
> we'll take your creed, whatever it may be, that is
> we'll find then that there is very little difference
> between us.... This is the lazy way to fight. Any
> of us can be tripped up if we go into speculative

questions. Let us keep to the fundamental idea
[emphasis mine]. 18

At the same camp, Dr. Edgar M. Levy, long-time
Baptist participant in the movement, gave a typical statement
of the optimism which was generated on the unity theme by
the "Beulah Land" experiences of the fellowshipping holiness
community. He said that after all previous efforts to achieve
Christian unity had been thwarted because of the "impossibil-
ity of creating uniformity in the expression of belief in the
constitution of the church, and in the administration of the
ordinaces," now,

> at last we have discovered the basis for Christian
> unity. The sanctification of the believers of every
> name, create unity in the great Christian brother-
> hood, such as no creed has ever been able to ac-
> complish. Here ... we have ... an exhibition of
> Christian unity as thrills one's soul to behold. A
> unity not in ordinances; a unity not in church govern-
> ment; a unity not in forms of worship; a unity not
> in mere letter of creed--but in ... the baptism of
> the Holy Spirit. As it is the nature of sin to sep-
> arate, disintegrate, and repel, it is the nature of
> holiness to unite and adjust and harmonize [empha-
> sis mine]. 19

The implications of revivalism for church unity

The paradox which the holiness evangelists and converts of the revival faced in the schism-unity syndrome,
which so strongly fastened itself upon the consciousness of
the movement, was certainly not foreign to American revivalism as a tradition. The tension between the polarizing and
the unifying tendencies in revival efforts was ever present.
Revivalism, with its impatient call for immediate decision in
the areas of the most deep-seated loyalties, had always caused
divisions within religious communities; it became a commonplace in the nation's religious history. Perry Miller says
that, in fact, it was virtually bound "to do so." The divisions in New England after the First Great Awakening, the
Presbyterian schisms, the secession of the Cumberland Presbytery, and the establishment of the Disciples of Christ--all
testify to that, he said. 20

On the other hand, witnesses are replete in the history of the holiness revival and American revivalism, in

general, that the sense of oneness which the members of diverse religious communities enjoyed in the revival atmosphere
exceeded that to be found in any other religious situation.
The example of the Cane Ridge camp meeting, where Methodists, Baptists, and Presbyterians had worked together as
one body of Christians, became an example of the fact for
all future time. It was "a mighty symbol of concordance...."21
Robert Baird had forthrightly adopted this apparent paradox
of "unity in diversity" to provide a rationale to his European
readers for the "scandal" which the numerous American sects
represented to them under the American voluntaristic system. 22
It became part of the American mind.

It especially fixed itself in revivalistic thought, because in the revival meeting it often came closest to reality;
there as they worked together in their highest calling, the
oneness was felt more poignantly than at most other times
in the relationships between the churches. It was in revivals that the dream of unity was moved along most directly.
It was there that most men, even as early as the period
when the holiness revival began, located the hope of its ultimate realization.   The Christian Spectator wrote in 1832,
that in the fellowship of the revival,

> we find a principle of affinity, which, just in pro-
> portion as the widespread medium of spiritual emo-
> tion becomes purified, will draw all classes of
> Christians nearer still nearer, until the practical
> ends even of external unity shall be fulfilled. 23

The interdenominational realities, and the strong future anti-
cipations of greater unity, and less and less sectarian feeling, found in the pre-Civil War holiness movement, have
already been noted. 24   It, too, was part of a general hope
for the future of the churches.   William Starr, a somewhat
controversial Congregational pastor in Elgin, Illinois, wrote
just before the War:

> The union for which I look and long, is to be
> brought about by a certain change of views among
> Christians; not by their coming to a common doc-
> trinal basis ... [but by] inplicit faith in the Lord
> Jesus Christ, ... proven not by their agreeing to
> what dogma you attribute Christ, but 'by their
> fruits' ..." [emphasis his]. 25

The unity which holiness advocates professed in their

meetings, and the unity among the heterogeneous groups, which the holiness evangelistic bands represented, seemed to them to seal the certain promise that the eschatology of the revival's hoped-for unity was at the threshold of actuality. This mentality persisted generally in holiness ranks; the absence of grass-roots character which Miller noted in most of the associated religious efforts engaged in among the denominations before the Civil War, definitely was not lacking among these post-war bands of men and women from all revivalistic churches. 26

Perfectionism and the promise of unity

In fact, the application of the holiness ideology to the revival dream of one church acting redemptively in the work of the evangelization of society, seemed to them to show the way at last to achieving the goal. This reinforcement of one of the basic rationales of American revivalism by the dynamics of the unifying, adjusting, and harmonizing powers which men such as Levy claimed for the Spirit-baptizing experience they were proclaiming, demonstrates once again the manner in which the perfectionist tended to modify the basic elements, which were characteristic of revivalism as it had developed by the period the new perfectionism arose in the third decade of the nineteenth century. Its ultraistic tendencies had already led it into deeper life evangelism; into new and more aggressive methods of revivalism; and, through its call to complete consecration of the individual, to a life of holiness, into an intensification of the puritanical moralism, advocated by the preaching of such revivalists as Finney. These same tendencies now naturally led some pioneers in the movement into more radical concepts of ecclesiology than the vast majority of holiness people were willing to accept.

The continuing mood of optimism

The problem was further intensified by the fact that at the same time that the movement believed that it had found a new principle which would move the churches on rapidly to the unity which the revival tradition had always held out to them, the churches, as ecclesiastical structures, they felt, were increasingly rejecting both their methods and their message. 27 Moreover, in their minds, the churches were ignoring the Spirit of God who was testifying to his intentions for the age, not only by the spread of what they saw as the most extensive holiness revival in church history, but also by

"wonderfully" unifying, adjusting, and integrating all of history for the reformation of the world.

In the same year that Josiah Strong made his penetrat-
ing analysis of the mission of the American nation and its
churches, just prior to the turn of the century, William Jones,
one of the movement's evangelists, published a book which
illustrates the mood which helped to produce the apocalyptic
atmosphere within, which the movement regarded as its mission. In From Elim to Carmel, Jones, speaking to questions
not commonly touched upon in holiness literature, discussed
the churches' responsibility to the "turbil stream of immi-
gration" which was emptying "its ever-increasing flood" upon
the nation's shores, as well as to the millions of the illiter-
ate and imbruted ex-slaves," and the "fetid Indians that still
linger in squalor and filth upon our Western borders." These
grave obligations and the degenerative spiritual inclinations
in the life of the churches raised, he said, the all important
question as to whether or not the church would "be true to
God in the whole broad realm of Christian thought and Christian activity?" He believed it would, and contemplated "the
near approach of [that] ultimate victory" with "inexpressible
pleasure." He continued,

> The tremor of the invisible forces that now pervades
> all lands and thrills and agitates all peoples, is the
> product of that spirit that is inherent in the gospel.
> The impulse to a better life is manifest everywhere;
> it throbs in the heart of all peoples. Everywhere
> the struggle of all peoples is toward light.... Na-
> tion is calling to nation; ... and the muffled tread
> of the gathering throng, startles conservatism from
> its death of sleep. Thrones are crumbling, and
> crowns are falling like stars in an apocalyptic vi-
> sion. Empires of spiritual oppression are dissolv-
> ing into light....

In the projection of railroads into the heart of Africa, he
heard the "footsteps of Jehovah ... in his omnipotent tramp
to his final conquest." Like the engineer who had carefully
tunneled into the rocks at Hell's Gate, set his explosive
charges, and then "loosed the electric spark that converted
the potential energy into actual energy," so,

> God is tunneling the world and packing it with his
> truth.
> When the church gets ready, when the world is

> filled with pure Christian thought, when the minis-
> try shall believe in the Holy Ghost, and accept his
> fiery baptism, ... the Father will let slip one spark
> of the Pentecostal fire.... [28]

and the whole earth will become the Kingdom of God. It was
with such rhetoric of "crumbling thrones," "falling crowns,"
"dissolving empires," and the explosive potential of "one
spark of Pentecostal fire," ringing in their ears, that the
holiness leaders faced the question of the nature of the church.
That some should propose new answers to the questions raised,
is not surprising. The combination was a powerful one; its
elements were basic to the mood, and must be kept in mind
when one attempts to explain the cast of the perfectionist
mind as the period of organization began to set in about 1880.

The Radical Holiness Reformers

        The import of the earliest secessions from the estab-
lished churches over the holiness question, can be illustrated
in the answers to the church question given by the men who
were most prominent in leading the groups of early schis-
matics. These commonly became known to the movement and
to its opponents in the churches as "the come-outers." A
brief review of the contribution of three of these men will
illustrate why this period of sect formation deserves more
attention than it has commonly received. These leaders were
Daniel S. Warner,[29] founder of the Church of God (Anderson,
Indiana); John P. Brooks,[30] leader in the independent movement in Missouri, out of which the Church of God (Holiness)
rose; and James F. Washburn,[31] leader, with his wife, Josephine, of the Southern California and Arizona Holiness Association, out of which the Holiness Church was ultimately organized. In the past, the historians of the movement have
lent significance to these earliest holiness secessionist movements, mainly, because their rural puritan-pietism, and their
often undisciplined and enthusiastic, evangelistic bands were
a source of embarrassment to the leaders of the mainstream
Methodist holiness movement.[32] These leaders were already
hard put to defend their loyalty to the discipline of the church
as well as the relevance of their special concern for holiness
promotion in a church gradually shifting away from Wesleyan
perfectionism and New Testament standards of life. Criticized by the more conservative element in the movement for
their "compromises" in life-style and their failure to cast
their reform efforts within a more radical framework in

relation to church loyalty versus movement loyalty, it was
difficult for these mainstream Methodists to appreciate any
aspect of "come-outism."[33] The history of the church question, within the institutionalization of the main forces of the
movement, can largely be written around the way in which
the National Association leadership controlled the successive
general holiness conventions and successfully blocked the efforts of the radical reformers to bring their concepts of the
kind of reform, which the holiness revival implied, before
the larger public in any official way. By the time that the
last convention was held in Chicago in 1901, the incipient
patterns for the organization of the strong center of the movement were more to the liking of a National Association leadership, by then, considerably more liberal themselves, in their
views of church loyalty and the holiness question, because of
the increasing rejection of the movement within the churches.[34]

    The significance of this radical movement, however,
should no longer be relegated so completely to so negative
a context; when one develops the fuller inplications of what
is only hinted at in Smith's statement that D. S. Warner
"carried the non-sectarian traditions of the holiness revival
to such extremes that he rejected entirely the idea of an organized denomination,"[35] he finds the interesting fact that
their participation in the holiness revival had raised, for such
men as Warner, deeper issues than the immediate, practical
questions of church membership. In each of the three examples that will be considered, the individual, after being challenged by his respective church on the issue of holiness evangelism, sought to apply the logic of Christian perfectionism,
with all the ultraistic inclinations of the perfectionist mentality, to the church question.

Daniel S. Warner and the Church of God movement

    The first to propose such radical applications of the
revival's promise of unity among all true Christian believers
was Daniel Sidney Warner. Warner was born in Wayne
County, Ohio in 1842. He served for a time in the Union
Army. After the war, he attended Oberlin College for a
brief period and later Vermillion College in Hayesville, Ohio,
then under Presbyterian auspices. Converted as a young
man, under no particular denominational influence, he left
his profession as a school teacher in 1867 to prepare to enter the ministry. He preached his first sermon in a Methodist protracted meeting in a schoolhouse not far from where

he lived; but finally he cast his lot with the Church of God
(Winebrennerian), a small sect formed out of the German
Reformed Churches of Pennsylvania after they had rejected
the revivalism of John Winebrenner.   They claimed to hold
no creed except the Bible, repudiated sectarianism, baptized
by immersion, and practiced the ordinance of foot washing as
well as the Lord's Supper.   Undoubtedly, many of Warner's
later concepts on the church question in relation to the holiness movement were strongly influenced by his ten years of
ministry with that church. [36]

          Warner's introduction to the holiness movement and
his personal profession of the experience of entire sanctification came like Inskip's, mainly, through the influence of his
wife.   While visiting some relatives of hers in Upper Sand-
usky, Ohio, she had claimed the experience in a holiness
band meeting.   The band was in contact with National Association evangelists.   Another important influence upon him
was his association with a Baptist minister who was active
in the Ohio Holiness Alliance, R. C. R. Dunbar. [37]   Warner
immediately plunged into holiness evangelism within the Winebrennerian churches.   His attempts to promulgate his newly
found "light" within his own church produced one of the first
examples of the familiar pattern by which many of the holiness proponents, especially those who were active ministers,
were separated from the established churches.   He had served
the Winebrennerians for ten years.   Less than three months
after he began to preach entire sanctification, he was presented with charges by the church for his holiness advocacy,
but after trial was allowed to retain a restricted license to
preach; after a brief stay on a new pastorate, he resigned
from those duties to become a full-time holiness evangelist,
continuing to work within his own denomination.   On January
30, 1878, he was charged and tried again for "dividing the
church"; the charges were sustained and his license withheld. [38]

The Church of God concept

          How strongly his basic ideas on the relationship of
holiness and the nature of the church were cast by the sectarianism which he felt had rejected him and his message,
is indicated by an entry in his diary in March of the same
year, in which he said:

> On the 31st of last January, the Lord showed me
> that holiness could never prosper upon sectarian
> soil, encumbered by human creeds, and party names,

and he gave me a new commission to join holiness
and all truth together and build up the apostolical
[sic] church of the living God [emphasis mine]. 39

January 31st was one day after he had been ejected from the
Winebrennerian ministry. As will be seen below, the truth
to which Warner related the truths of holiness, as he understood them in the American holiness revival tradition, especially in the fuller development of his thought, proved to be
adaptations of some of the fundamental concepts of the church
and its reformation, as developed in the classic tradition of
Joachim of Fiore. 40   The result was a remarkable system
for the final reformation of the Christian church, built upon
Biblical proof texts, the dispensational view of history in the
ideological patterns of Joachim, modified at times by the
dispensationalism contemporary with his times and the free application of the Old Testament and New Testament prophecies
by types and symbols to the church and her history. The
whole was integrated by Warner's concept of the holiness revival
as an instrument of the church's final reformation, final because of its universal extent and the ability of its purifying
message to destroy the last element of sin in the church--
sectarianism. In this "Age of the Spirit," the one "invisible"
church which was hidden away in the mass of denominational
members, much as the true church had been hidden away
within the Catholic Church from the time of Constantine to
Luther, could be called out one by one, as through entire
sanctification, they were cleansed from the "mildew" of sectarianism, to represent the one, visible Church of God. 41

In September of 1868, about a year after Warner was
licensed to preach, he purchased a copy of William Henry
Starr's Discourses on the Nature of Faith. Starr, himself
somewhat of an irregular among his fellow Congregational
ministers in Illinois, felt that he was being ill-treated by the
church establishment which was forcing him into an uncom-
fortable conformity to its demands. Strong statements in
his book protested against the sectarianism which he felt was
stifling his freedom to preach as he would. Sometime before 1880, Warner wrote a note on one of the pages of his
copy of Starr's book; it followed a strong exhortation by Starr
for men to rise up against sectarianism and bring to the
world the reality of a "holy and united church." Warner responded to his appeals in the following annotation:

If this holy man, perceiving only the eavil [sic] of
division is thus moved to cry out, what must be

> the guilt of one who sees both the eavil [sic] and
> remedy and yet will close his mouth and see the
> world go to ruin. [42]

The call to the reformation movement which Warner began to
announce, as the central theme of his holiness evangelism,
was already apparently ringing in his own ears.

Warner's earliest extensive treatment of his views of
radical holiness reform are found in three consecutive chapters of his first book, Bible Proofs of the Second Work of
Grace ... Including a Description of the Great Holiness Crisis of the Present Age, by the Prophets. In these chapters,
Hebrews 12:25-29 is utilized as the key for an interpretation
of what he considered to be the Old Testament's prophetic
description of the "great work of holiness" of his day. He
said that the Holy Spirit had given him that Scriptural key
on "the 30th of August, 1879 ... in a special manner...."[43]
In the double shaking spoken of in the Scripture passage,
Warner saw a shaking of the world first and then, secondly,
of the church. In the restoration that the prophets promised
to fallen Israel, which he saw as a type of the church, the
latter would enjoy not only the glories of the primitive church,
but was to exceed them, "that preceded the dark age of cap-
tivity."[44] He said the warnings of Ezekiel to the pastors
applied to the pastors of the sectarian churches

> I will seek out my sheep and will deliver them out
> of all places (sectarian coops) where they have been
> scattered (into several hundred parties) in the cloudy
> and dark day.... The perfect reign of the Mes-
> siah ... is to succeed the dark days of party con-
> fusion. [45]

The passages surrounding Ezekiel's vision of the valley of dry bones provided a picture of the fallen Catholic
church in the type of "Mt. Seir," and the chapters following
the vision pictured the Protestant sects which were patterned
after the Roman sectarian error. The resurrection of the
dry bones was a prophetic picture for him of the ordering
of the true church out of this "Babylon of confusion" through
the effective working of entire sanctification, preached by the
holiness revivalists until the "true Israel" would be unified
again as indicated by Ezekiel's parable of the "one stick of
Judah." Sectism, because it resisted this unity, was represented as Gog and Magog. They create "war in the camp
and a general commotion in the heavens and the earth." In

all of this Warner believed that there seemed to be "a reference to the primitive power of the Church and its restoration
again after the lapse of the 'years of many generations' of
darkness." It would come through "the sin consuming flames
of the Sanctifier, the baptism of the Holy Ghost," which cor-
responded with "the shaking of the Church." Warner appealed
to the widespread stir created by the holiness revival as a
fulfillment of this great struggle; its universality indicated
that this holiness reform was different from those which had
preceded it. [46]

He reinforced his anti-sectarian logic by arguments
proposed both outside and inside the movement. William
Starr's protest against his treatment at the hands of sects
obviously had a strong influence upon him. [47] Within the
movement, he drew on the copious supply of statements on
holiness as a unifying experience which appeared regularly
in the holiness journals. Citing proof for his position from
an article by Thomas Doty in the Christian Harvester which
admitted that there was "not one word in the Bible favorable
to denominations or sects ... ; that "denominations are directly or indirectly the result of sin remaining in the great
body of professors"; and that "thorough and widespread holiness would soon destroy denominations"; (emphasis his)[48]
he refuted Doty's qualification of these statements in allowing
that reform cannot come "until holiness more widely prevails."
Warner would have none of such delay. His perfectionism
carried strong tones of the holiness advocates involved in the
abolitionist movements of the pre-Civil War period: "But
for the love of truth I am constrained to differ with the position that sects are a present necessity. They originated
from sin in the church; and shall we admit that the fruit of
sin is necessary under any circumstances?"[49] The nature
of the radical holiness reform proposed by those men must
be seen then, in significant measure, as a valid consequence
of their perfectionism brought to the support of their essentially pietistic revivalism, fortified by the rural milieu.

Having put forth these arguments, Warner called for
each sanctified individual to reject sectarianism in his own
heart and leave his denomination "to join the only holy Church
of the Bible, not bound together by rigid articles of faith,
but perfectly united in love, under the primitive glory of the
Sanctifier, continuing steadfastly in the Apostles's doctrine
and fellowship, and taking captive the world for Jesus."[50]
Warner concluded his arguments with the restatement of his
conviction that "the great holiness reform" could not go for-

ward until "every vestige of denominational distinction" had
been consecrated and done away with, and God had perfected
into "one indeed and in truth--all the sanctified" (emphasis
his).

> It will then be discovered who for Jesus will be,
> And who are in Babylon the saints then will see;
> The time of division then will fully be known,
> Between the pure kingdom and defiled Babylon.
>   (emphasis his.)[51]

About ten years after Warner had published the substance of his new thinking on the church question in relationship with the holiness revival, he began to record a much
fuller treatment of his views; they were cast in a much more
apocalyptic mood and showed obvious reaction to the Adventist teaching of Uriah Smith, which must have come to his
attention between the writing of the first and second books.[52]
His efforts to explicate the basis of his reform message now
included, not only the apocalypticism of Revelation, but also
involved a mild attempt at countering the date-setting of the
Adventists, who obviously loomed large in his thinking at the
time, along with some projections of his own.[53] But on the
whole, the later work is an enlargement of the three chapters
of the Proofs.

The dominant theme, however, was the strong primitivism which was present in all holiness concepts of the
church. The original Pentecost experience and the church
which lived close to that period were looked upon as the models of the pure church. In Warner's mind, "the real presence of God in his church is the substance and joyful realization of that which his abode in the tabernacle and temple
was but a faint type, ..." this was "the peculiar heritage
of the present dispensation."[54] Both in individual Christians
and collectively, "the Holy Spirit now comes and dwells in
the true sanctuary of the church of the living God."[55] Warner's perfectionism came to the fore as he continued that
the "Spirit" could not dwell among a divided people,

> therefore, the confused and disintegrated factions
> of sectism cannot be the temple of God.... No
> one of them is a church, nor do all together con-
> stitute that holy temple; but the "spiritual house"
> of God is made up of the spiritual. In other words
> the church of the living God includes all saved in
> Christ.[56]

The "Spirit" was working in his time through the holiness
revival to cleanse the church from

> all rubbish of creeds, traditions and inventions of
> sectism which the dark ages of the past have heaped
> upon her....
>   But all this wood, hay, and stubble, the fire
> of holiness is consuming, and the temple of God
> appears in view again in primitive glory.[57]

He then described the "Heroic Age" of the church which lay
back "over the 1,260 years of utter night that extend far beyond, even into the third century." He saw it as "one,"
"visible," holy," "universal" church with an order formed
by the God, "who really organizes the church himself."[58]

But the church as a whole fell, in the Constantinian
Age, from its pristine state; as a result, in the third century, "the living church retired gradually within the lonely
sanctuary of a few solitary hearts." And there it continued
as a "Church in the Wilderness" during the creedal church's
"Great Apostasy," for the 1,260 years until the sixteenth
century Reformation. That reign of Catholicism was the dark
night of the church and the visible church became the "great
whore."[59]

The restitution of the church began with the Reformers,
but only progressed spasmodically, because whenever a truly
spiritual reformation was begun such as that of the reformers
themselves, or of Wesley, or of another, a creedal sect was
formed and the true church that was gathering was again divided. The Protestant sects became images of the Catholic
Church before them, as they perpetuated its doctrines and
services--e. g., the rite of sprinkling, infant baptism, confirmation, etc. The organization of the sects was the disorganization of the church of God. In the fall of Babylon,
depicted by John the Revelator, he saw the fall of the Protestant churches. The loss of holiness caused the downfall
of the church.[60]

Now, in the new holiness revival, he declared, God
was again restoring to the church her original holiness. During all the dark ages of the fallen church, it had been a "mystery," hidden in the "book written within and on the back-
side, sealed with seven seals," which "no man in heaven or
earth could open." But the "Lion of the Tribe of Judah" took
the book and opened it; it was the plan of "salvation and

redemption," it was the cleansing of the sanctuary by "holiness and truth, ... [which] burn the false religions of the world and restore the true worship of God as in the days of yore--as it existed in apostolic times."[61] Another note, written by Warner sometime before 1880, in the pages of his copy of Starr's Discourses, indicated that the progressive revelation of the "mystery" was already in his thinking. In response to one of Starr's strongly anti-sectarian comments, Warner wrote,

> It is evident from the above remarks that the author
> was fully awake to the eavils [sic] of divisions but
> had not discovered the remedy for the eavil [sic]
> --which is to use the universal name, "Church of
> God."[62]

The mystery was at last revealed.

It is impossible to review these two works of Warner's together with the contents of a rather complete journal which he kept during this period, without being impressed with the fact that in the expression of his concepts of the Biblical truth as he saw it, there were propositions obviously imprinted with classical Anabaptist views of the church and church reform. If one compares them with the views of the church held by the sixteenth century reformers as outlined by Franklin Littell in his Origins of Sectarian Protestantism --an ironic title to introduce into the interpretation of a group which preached the end of all sectarianism--he can see apparent crossovers from the older tradition to the one under consideration. However, one must always keep foremost, a principle, also stated by Littell, "that Christianity is a historical religion with a sacred book in which all reforms seek their inspiration and confirmation. Since the norm provided by the book was itself diverse, it was, in turn, selectively applied in the light of the real problems of the age."[63]

That caution applies to the review of Warner's relation to the classical tradition. He, too, claimed that he had received these truths by inspiration of the Spirit and the Word, and was applying them "in light of the real problems" of his age. Nevertheless, one can still say that Warner's system was expressed in many conceptual patterns which show the strong influence of classical Anabaptism. Through him they were introduced into the holiness movement at this early period of its institutional development. As indicated in the

outline of his teaching already given above, his development
of the church as the dwelling place of the Spirit, the baptism
of believers only, the centrality of the Word of God in the
midst of the congregation as the "universal law," the strong
sense of mission as a reformer, the strongly apocalyptical
tone, and even the retention of the rite of foot washing as
an ordinance of the church--all may be closely identified with
the Anabaptist tradition. [64]

These were all strongly Biblical; their application in
reform movements throughout all church history proves that.
In Warner's case, however, there is good reason to conclude
that the identification of thought between him and the radical
sixteenth century tradition, is a result of more than their
common Biblical source and the fact that both were in conflict with the prevailing church structures in their day.

That the Winebrennerian Church of God must have encouraged some of Warner's earliest thinking, not only in the
area of his expansion of their "church of God" concept under
the aegis of his consequent holiness perfectionism, but also
in the fact that the Winebrennerian Church drew heavily upon
"free church" principles in its separation from the German
Reformed Church. In its polity and practice there were elements of Anabaptist ideology such as foot washing, the believer's church, the concept of the fall of the church from
its "Heroic Age," and consequently its own strong primitivism.
It was especially exposed to such ideology by its geography,
for it had shaped its own structures of independency, surrounded by the large concentrations of Mennonite and other
"peace church" groups of east central Pennsylvania, northern
Ohio, and Indiana. [65]

Warner's own contacts with earlier Anabaptist concepts of the nature of the church and its reformation, probably came from more direct association than his former
church relationships, however. Warner had ample opportunity
to know their teachings, as they were practiced and preserved
by their descendants in America. His diary mentions meetings with the Dunkards and other "peace groups," and that
he preached for them. But most important of all, at one
point in his religious quest, after he was ejected from the
Winebrennerian ministry, he had associated for a short time
with the Northern Indiana Eldership of the Church of God.
This group had dissociated themselves from the Winebrennerians because of the refusal of the latter to deny membership
to those who belonged to secret orders. [66]

As a member of the Northern Indiana Eldership, Warner took part in union talks with a Mennonite association
known as the United Mennonite Church. His diary records
that he and they had met in Hawpatch, Indiana, September
24 - 26, 1879, and their hearts were "wonderfully knit together in love."[67] On December 5, 1879, as he was "pushing" his book, Bible Proofs, to completion, he left to attend
the joint meeting of the committees on union, which were to
draw up an agreement for merger of the two groups. But
at the joint convention, resolutions for union were agreed
upon. They provided for union as soon as it could be con-
summated, a common recognition of the Word of God as the
true basis of Christian union, and the provision for bringing
all points of difference to "the truth as it is in Christ Jesus"
in the belief that it could be "ascertained" and that all were
"morally bound to learn and abide its decision."[68]

The fact that Warner's group and the United Mennonites
never did consummate the merger, is not of consequence to
our purpose here. But it is consequential that, in addition
to the impact of others upon his thinking, that during the
period in which he was writing his first defense of the "Church
of God" idea, he had spent several days of serious discussion
with a Mennonite group about the nature of the church and
church union. The import for the history of the holiness
movement is that the "come-outer" movement, at least as
associated with men like Warner, had some contacts with
strong traditions of the church behind it. As Littell said,
they were "selectively applied," for the time,[69] but their
goal of the restoration of the true church in its primitive
holiness was one. It was another demonstration of the manner
in which the perfectionist movement tended to be modified by,
and to modify a tradition with which it interacted.

Fully dedicated to his new reform ideas, Warner attempted to persuade the Indiana Holiness Association, which
he had served as a vice-president, to modify its membership
statement on church membership to allow men like himself
to continue to participate in the activities of the association;
Warner was already in contest with men like Thomas Doty,
and especially with the Free Methodists who, under B. T.
Roberts, were avidly trying to rally their own reform movement to a single denominational loyalty. Warner's suggestions
were rejected.[70]

Warner had proposed that the association's rules which
provided that it should "consist of members of various Christian

organizations and seek to work in harmony with all these
societies," should be changed to read: "It shall consist of
and seek to cooperate with, all true Christians everywhere."
It is probable that both sides had essentially polarized their
positions before the meeting. [71]

He and his friends who accompanied him to the meeting in Terre Haute, he said, "were positively denied membership on the ground of not adhering to any sect." Consequently,
they declared, "we wish to announce to all that we wish to
cooperate with all Christians, as such in saving souls--but
forever withdraw from all organisms that uphold and endorse
sects and denominations in the body of Christ."[72] This point
marked the final organizational separation of Warner and his
followers from the mainstream National Association movement. It was not until recent years that the Church of God
provided a rationale for organization of its work which
allowed for identification again with the present components of the Christian Holiness Association. The latter is
the direct successor of the National Association from which
Warner and his friends "forever" withdrew in 1881. [73]

The attractiveness of Warner's approach to holiness
evangelism, for many people, is demonstrated by the fact
that the Church of God, (Anderson, Indiana) which grew around
his revivalism became the third largest of the holiness groups. [74]
The appeal lay largely in the simple alternatives which his
democratic structures provided for people who were increasingly fearful of, what they regarded as, a complex ecclesiasticism. That ecclesiasticism, they believed, was threatening the religious simplicity which, in the Church of God order, they attributed to the primitive church and pure religion.
They sought to maintain that simplicity in the midst of the
rapid social change of the last two decades of the nineteenth
century. Warner's promise of a group, gathered together
under the guidance and instruction of the sanctifying Spirit,
free of denominational and sectarian trammels, as he pictured
them, combined with a reformatory, eschatological thrust,
carried a certain populist magnetism. It continued to demonstrate its democratic effectiveness as the church of God concept was even more widely used among the Pentecostal sects
in the next century, especially in the black pentecostal movements. [75] To many it offered the simplest form of organization by which an informal revival group could conceive of
themselves and the church. This may have been its most
obvious Anabaptist characteristic. These features obviously
provided one answer to the call for a broader movement by

those who were not Methodists and those to whom Methodism
was secondary to the revival.   The Church of God came to
represent a more equal balance of Methodists and non-Methodists in its early constituency than the other holiness bodies
of similar size. [76]

John P. Brooks and the church of God
concept

John P. Brooks was an Illinois Methodist minister.
He was closely associated with the activities of the Western
Holiness Association, formed in 1871, following a holiness
movement revival in the state.   Brooks' voice, in the early
stages of the movement's search for order, was widely heard
through the Banner of Holiness, the official voice of the Western Association, published at Bloomington, Illinois.   In 1882 he
was tried by the Illinois Conference on charges relating to
alleged slanderous articles in the Banner.   He was acquitted. [77]
Soon thereafter, be became deeply involved in the movements
toward independency among the associations of the rural,
more conservative holiness converts of the area.   Many of
the groups had been particularly aggressive in their holiness
evangelism.   In no other area of the movement was the revival more wracked with extremisms of every kind.   The
agitation ultimately centered in the Southwestern Holiness
Association, active in Missouri and Kansas. [78]

Because of the accusations of its enemies and the
fears of its friends, that the undisciplined nature of some of
the evangelistic bands was damaging the reputation of the
whole movement; a holiness convention was called by the
western leaders at Jacksonville, Illinois, in December, 1880. [79]
Its purpose was to try to answer the charges of their detractors, that the movement "had no administrative authority
over those who compose its own body of workers." [80]   The
National Association's leadership, possibly reinforced by the
Free Methodists who were present, controlled the proceedings to the extent that the convention urged that all holiness evangelists should be members of "some Evangelical Church...." [81]
The strength which the independent movement had already
gained at this early date is demonstrated, however, in the
fact that the above statement was qualified by the exception
of those individuals who had been "expelled for the teaching
of holiness." [82]   The tensions within the convention are best
illustrated by the tenor of the addresses presented by men
who represented each of the two main factions, the conservative and the radical.   John W. Caughlan, at that time editor

of the Good Way, the paper of the Southwestern Association,
reviewed the history of the holiness work in the Association's
area, beginning in 1872. He concluded with the observation
that the work had had permanent results

> only in those places where a regular Holiness Band
> is organized. In those places where out of regard
> to ecclesiastical influences, such organizations have
> been omitted, the holiness work has come to naught.
> Those who work for Christ have to consecrate the
> Church, and go forward." Loyalty to Christ is the
> first duty [emphasis his]. 83

Thomas K. Doty, a Wesleyan Methodist, associated
with a loose connection of churches, rather than a more
highly organized denomination, made equally strong stabs at
"denominationalism." Although urging the representatives
at the convention to work in their church, if they were in a
church, he quickly set the priorities of loyalty for the holiness evangelists, by saying,

> Bring everything in your church work to bear on
> the work of holiness. While you do this, you must
> be saved from the church. You must use your
> church meetings to promote this work.

According to the transcribed record of the address, a voice
broke into his remarks with the question, "But what if they
will not allow you?" Doty replied:

> If they turn you out of the synagogue, I have no
> objection. I don't believe in this denominational
> idea as God's idea. He permits it and so must
> we.... The time will come when these denomina-
> tions will all crumble; and the sooner the better,
> if we can build on a better basis. 84

In contrast with the more radical calls of men like
Caughlan and Doty, M. L. Haney, one of the more irenic
holiness evangelists, cautioned against any tendency to follow
"the come-outers, who insist on the silly dogma of no-churchism, and favor the disorganization of all Christian forces."
He also warned against those who "have desired and advocated
the organization of a distinctively Holiness church." He said
that the holiness movement had always been "designed of God
to spread scriptural holiness in existing churches, and thus
fit them to subjugate the world to Christ."85

The New Testament Church

The confusion over the church question demonstrated,
in the record of proceedings of the Jacksonville Convention,
illustrates the milieu within which the church of God or New
Testament church idea, as it was at first known, began to
develop within the ranks of the Southwestern Holiness Association. C. E. Cowan, in his history of the Church of God
(Holiness), indicates that the concept was generated more or
less out of the pragmatic answers which the independents,
separated from their former churches and not yet certain of
how to reorganize, gave to the situation in which they found
themselves.[86] That answer began to be hammered out in
the pages of the Good Way soon after the conclusion of the
Western Union Holiness Convention; it finally led to the formation of the early independent Holiness Churches after 1882.[87]

It was not until 1887, when John P. Brooks became the
editor of the Good Way, the paper then representing the independent movement, that he began to develop his treatise on
the church of God ideas which had been generated within the
movement.[88] The Divine Church, which he published in 1891,
in many ways, stands in stark contrast with Warner's presen-
tations, in either his initial development in the Bible Proofs,
or the more extensive development in The Cleansing of the
Sanctuary. Warner's work is that of reformer, proclaiming
the message from God in strong Biblical terms. Brooks'
effort is what he claims for it in its sub-title--a treatise, a
systematic rationale for a system of congregational organization which had already developed.[89] The atmosphere of
Brooks' work is one of theological defense; the work of the
scholar, the preface indicated that he realized that his ideas
would not be well received, but he offered them with the
hope that in the process of time, reasonable men would accept them and act upon them.[90] The atmosphere of Warner's
work, as we have already indicated, is apocalyptic, proclama-
tory, and urgent--the reform was already begun and every
sanctified member of the sectarian bodies was called to a revivalistic response.[91] The expositions of the editor of the
Good Way were an attempt to inject some kind of order into
disorder which had arisen out of the extreme independency
of the western radical movement. Warner's ideas had become the basis for the eastern movement from the beginning.
The work of Brooks was an attempt to explain a group of
people who had already worked out a church of God congregational system for themselves out of a disarray of extremism
and individuality; the thinking of Warner offered a comprehen-

sive idea to which the individual committed himself before he
came into the fellowship.[92] The difference between the nature of the two men's works in their attempts to answer the
question of church order in the holiness revival, with the
concepts of the church of God idea, probably is best shown
in their continuing impact upon the holiness revival and its
institutionalization. The Church of God (Anderson) became
a worldwide movement and one of the larger bodies within
the revival's ranks; the Independent Churches, to whom Brooks
was speaking, had already set a pattern of local congrega-
tionalism and individuality. Together with the conservatism
and even extremism in which the western movement was born,
it has greatly restricted the growth and apparent appeal to
the movement in general.

Warner's influence upon the Independent Holiness Churches

        The basic concepts of the ideal church of God as pro-
posed by both men are remarkably similar. The parallels
are particularly striking in the outlines by each of them in
the pattern of the New Testament Church in its Old Testament
types,[93] of the essential characteristics of the pristine New
Testament Church,[94] of the nature of the fall of the church
from its original purity,[95] the evaluation of the intervening
period of sectarian rule,[96] the subsequent failure of the Protestant reforming movements to retain the purity of their reform because of sectarian organization,[97] and the necessity
and dynamic of the holiness movement as the hoped for agent
for the final destruction of sectarianism, and the establishment of the fully visible church of God.[98] The question naturally arises as to what influence Warner, who was publicly
proclaiming his views in some systematic rationale for some
time before Brooks, may have had on the early development
of the idea among the Independent Churches. Warner's concepts not only helped to set the pattern for the New Testament Church idea, but may have even been the reason for
its adoption in the early 1880's. It appears, from the discussion which follows, that one can properly conclude that the
fact of direct contacts between Warner and Brooks, during
the early period of Warner's reform efforts, and the concurrent beginnings of the agitation of the church of God question in Brooks' area, can be established.   If they had not
met previously in the common dedication to the work of holiness associations related to the National Association, they
did meet and spent four days together as representatives to
the 1880 Western Union Holiness Convention. Both men were

prominent in the activities of that convention. Brooks served
on the committee which drew up the official report for the
convention; Warner was appointed to the committee responsible for the planning of any succeeding conventions. Warner
was brought prominently to the attention of the convention as
one of its main speakers; he may have been introduced as
representing the Church of God; his registration was in that
name. It is difficult to believe that his thinking on the church
question, already published in his Bible Proofs, but not referred to in his public address to the convention, was not
discussed. The church question was the foremost one on
everyone's mind. [99]

There is evidence, both circumstantial and actual,
that his views injected themselves into the accelerated discussions of the church question among the western independents, in the years immediately following the 1880 meeting.
The proceedings of the Jacksonville convention, as published
with the roll of registrants, showed Warner and two others
registered as members of the Church of God. [100] Ordinarily,
this might not have been noteworthy to those who read the
proceedings, except that the church name probably was not
as familiar to them as were the names of the other churches
represented; moreover, in combination with the publication
of Warner's address and his appointment to help to arrange
for future conventions, attention was called to him as one of
the recognized leaders among others who had been at the
forefront for a much longer time. [101] These are all strong
indicators that both he and his views on the question which
was pressing itself most urgently upon every one in the movement at the time, were brought to the attention of this area
of the movement.

Such reasoning must modify, to some extent, Cowan's
claim, noted above, that the western independents came to
their views on the "New Testament Church" based on the
"two outstanding ideas ... --Holiness and the church." They
had come to these beliefs, they reasoned, out of their search
of the Scriptures and the practical exigencies of their lack
of organization. [102] A significant number of the most prominent leaders in the Southwestern Association and the Independent movement were at the Jacksonville Convention in
1880. Although some of them left the Association at a later
date, because of disagreement with its "come-outer" tendencies, they all were deeply involved in the discussions on the
church of God question. These included Rev. John H. Allen,
Methodist Episcopal; Justice Morris, Methodist Protestant;

Rev. J. W. Caughlan, Methodist Episcopal; Rev. Isaiah Reid, Presbyterian; Rev. W. B. M. Colt, Free Methodist; and Rev. A. M. Kiergan, Methodist Episcopal Church South.[103] Kiergan's presence at Jacksonville with Warner is especially significant to the establishing of possible connections between Warner's and Brooks's concepts of the church of God. It was Kiergan who was the central figure in encouraging independency and defending the church of God or New Testament church idea in the movement. It was he who reminisced thirty-seven years later that the Southwestern Association's ideas had developed "without any conscious understanding of the New Testament polity of the church."[104]

The initiation of Warner's own holiness publishing career as associate editor for the holiness page of the Herald of Gospel Freedom, the official paper of the Northern Indiana Eldership of the Church of God, and his editorship of the newly-established Gospel Trumpet, soon thereafter, spread his early views widely throughout the movement.[105] His widespread views were further publicized by the general reaction to his withdrawal from the organizations of the movement in 1881. Discussions of his "come-outism" and of his rationale for denying "no-churchism" filled the movement's journals.[106]

Definite evidence that the line of reasoning, outlined above, is not entirely circumstantial, is provided by an article by F. H. Sumpter, entitled "One Church," which appeared in the Good Way for June 3, 1883.[107] The publication date was only one day after Sumpter, with eight others, had been ordained to the ministry of the Southwestern Association at Centralia, Missouri, by a presbytery headed by Isaiah Reid.[108] On the same day that the article appeared, Reid, a Presbyterian pastor in Nevada, Iowa, until he was expelled by the Iowa Synod for his holiness evangelism, preached the sermon for the dedication of the church building which had been erected by the Centralia organization.[109] It was the first of a number of such churches that quickly followed.[110] It is striking that in his article, Sumpter makes reference to Warner's church of God thinking in support of his contention. Consequently, he declared that the time had "fully come for that part of the church of God that has the light on Bible holiness and is determined to walk in it to unite into independent organizations."[111] In combination with the circumstances outlined above, this represents strong evidence that Warner's ideas were under consideration within the inner circle of men who made the first steps toward the Independent Churches in that area.

In conclusion, it appears that Warner must be considered not only as the originator of the church of God concept,
as modified by the preaching of the holiness revival, and
around which the Anderson, Indiana group gathered, but he
must also be regarded as a direct contributor to the rise
of the church of God concept around which the independency
movement in the Southwestern Holiness Association rallied
just a few years later.   The latter development came through
the familiarity of the prominent leaders in that movement
with Warner and his ideas at the time of their earliest efforts
to establish some kind of New Testament order in their des-
organized ranks.   These conclusions do not negate the reality
of the Biblical and pragmatic context in which these early
leaders later placed the struggle which resulted in their adoption of the New Testament Church of God church order;[112]
but they do indicate again, that no movement, especially no
Christian movement, can divorce itself from history.   The
continuity of tradition is always there even within those churches
who make the strongest appeals to the essentially Biblical
sources of their life and order.   In the light of the above
contentions, the question arises as to why Brooks nowhere
in his extensive treatise refers to Warner by name, in spite
of their agreement upon the implications which they saw in
the holiness movement for the church question.   The answer
probably lies, in part, in the fact that, contrary to the in-
tervention of Warner's ideology at a critical point in the organization of the New Testament Church movement, he himself was not personally involved with that movement.   But
more probably, the reason that no credit was given to his
views among the Missouri and Kansas Church of God groups,
after the early period, is due to the strong mutual antagonism
which developed between the two movements as their evangelistic efforts crossed paths.   Warner's reports on his evangelism in Mississippi in 1889 contain numerous, strong recrim-
inations against the "Straight Holiness" people of Scott, Kansas and their paper, the Good Way, then under Brooks'
editorship.[113]   Warner regarded their work as the chief hindrance to his own work there.   This sharp contest between
the two groups was taking place at the same time at which
Brooks was writing The Divine Church; it was highly unlikely
that he would refer directly to Warner under those circumstances.   It also explains why there has been little contact
between the two groups at any time since then.

James F. Washburn: churches "on
the holiness line"

The question of the nature of the New Testament

Church, as it was raised among the first groups of converts
of the holiness revival in California, surfaced in the Southern California and Arizona Holiness Association. The
Association had been organized at Artesia, California
on July 1, 1880 out of the revivalism of Rev. Hardin
Wallace, an aged minister of the Methodist Episcopal
Church, and veteran holiness evangelist. Rev. Harry Ashcraft, a young evangelist of the Free Methodist Church, and
James Jayns, a Methodist Gospel singer, assisted Wallace. 114
All were from Illinois. Mr. and Mrs. James F. Washburn,
living at that time in the Azusa Valley of California, became
the prominent leaders in the holiness evangelism of the Association in the Los Angeles area.

Under their leadership, the organization of the revival's adherents within new holiness structures followed the
common pattern. The converts of the revival, first of all,
gathered together into bands which gradually assumed the
nature of a simple church fellowship, with standards for
membership and standards of discipline for their workers.
The purchase, or renting of places for their meetings, the
increasingly organized activity, brought the groups intensified
opposition from pastors who were not sympathetic with the
movement. 115   The opposition tended to expand the activities
of the bands and associations, and thus one feeding on the
other, the most ardent advocates of radical action eventually
turned their semi-formal, interdenominational associations
into full-fledged churches; they provided basic statements of
faith and rules for order. These included a provision for
the ordination of a ministry and the administration of the
sacraments. 116   The conservation of the fruits of their revival efforts is the most common reason given for the moves
to final organization. "A few of us ... heard the bleating
of the starving, dying sheep.... And before high heaven we
promised the Lord in the oaken groves of Santa Barbara that
we would feed the sheep."117

The Pentecost, the official journal of the Southern
California and Arizona Holiness Association, provided a contemporary account of the evolution of one of the first Holiness churches. Of the organization of the Downey, California
"Holiness" church, he said,

> Some members of the Baptist denomination having
> professed that God had sanctified them wholly were
> tried by their churches and excluded from the mem-
> bership because they would not recant.... Some

Methodists had withdrawn from the M. E. Church
South and others felt that they could no longer support preachers who were opposing the holiness
movement and preaching against sanctification....
Some of them were visited by the pastor and urged
to withdraw from the Holiness Band or leave the
Methodist Church. Some of them told them to
drop their names from the roll. Their names were
dropped as in the case above, sometimes without
the consent of the one whose name was dropped.
    The Downey Band was at first composed alto-
gether of those who held membership in some Christian denomination or sect, but in this respect has
undergone a gradual change until now only one or
two members have their name on any other church
book....
    In the year 1884 the Downey Band appointed a
committee of five to draw up a constitution and
by-laws to be submitted to the Band for its adoption. In August 1884 the committee made their
report and submitted ... a constitution and by-laws
very much like that of the Holiness Church at San
Bernardino.... The word "Band" was retained in
the name to avoid expense ... the words "or church"
were added. The name is "Downey Holiness Band
or Church." It is "free and independent" subject
to no ecclesiastical control. [118]

    The Downey California Church was not the first to be
organized out of the Southern California Holiness Association.
The chapels at Azusa, Pomona, Downey, San Bernardino and
Santa Barbara erected by the Holiness Bands for regular services on "the Pentecost line" in 1882 and 1883 were actually
churches. [119] At first they held their meetings Sunday afternoon and Tuesday evening, but finally as unchurched converts
joined the denominationally attached band members, they began to meet during the same hours as the denominational
meetings. "It was soon made evident the Lord should have
the best hours in the day for holiness."[120]

The "Holiness" church of California

    The unique contribution which the California group
made to the work of the radical reformers represented another application of the perfectionist impulses of the revival
at work in the undisciplined formative years. It did not
involve the breadth of concept which had swept Warner into

what he proclaimed as the final reformation of the church,
nor were its principles ever developed in a lengthy treatise
such as Brooks had provided for the New Testament Church
groups which grew out of the Southwestern Association.
Washburn had not attended college as both Brooks and Warner
had.   His approach to the church question was more pragmatic than either of theirs had been.   The statement above,
tracing the history of the organization of the Downey church,
illustrates that pragmatism.

However, Washburn's ideas, like those of the other
two men under consideration, did not develop in isolation.
In fact, there was very little isolation within the diverse
movement; the constant flow of periodical literature and its
peripatetic evangelists who circulated continuously among the
local groups and in the general camp meetings, provided a
complex, yet efficient network of communication.   Washburn
was in direct contact with the areas in which the Independent
Churches were developing in the mid-west.   As we have
noted, Wallace and Ashcraft were from Illinois; they continued
their contacts with the California movement.   Moreover, there
were family ties which took prominent members of the California
movement back to the same area. [121]   His views on the church
question were carried by the papers of the Independent Church
movement.   The fact that such links existed between California
and Illinois, and the fact of the links which have already been
shown between that area and Warner and his reform movement, seem to indicate that this early period of church organization, between 1800 and 1885, should be studied in the
light of these relationships--possibly they constituted components parts of a single movement in spite of their geographical separation. [122]

The best outlines of the reasoning by which the first
"come-outers" justified their decisions for leaving the churches
and creating new holiness band-churches of their own are
provided by another Washburn who was active in the California
Association--B. A. Washburn.   His most extensive treatment
of the church question was given in his book, Holiness Links,
published in 1887.   Washburn defended their separation from
the denominational churches because "the sanctified" were no
longer tolerated in their congregations.   Since, in most cases,
the sheer disparity of numbers between them and the "sinners made it impossible for the "saints" to purify the local
churches, he recommended, therefore, that the latter should
organize themselves into independent churches in which they
could set in order a congregation more amenable to their holiness interests. [123]

In the same book, Washburn answered questions concerning that new order. It was very primitive at first and
extremely congregational. Elders were elected by the congregation for no more than a year and frequently, for briefer
periods; the only ordination that was required was "the baptism of fire." If one received that experience, he was "ordained enough." "The men, women and children" were free
to take part in the services "as led by the Spirit." No one
was given a special commission to preach at any particular
service. The use of musical instruments was relegated to
the Old Testament dispensation and had no place in the congregation of "the saints." Washburn said that it was "high
noon-tide" then, and in the dispensation of the Holy Ghost,
"every sanctified soul" was "a harp of a thousand strings"
and the "baptism of fire" had set "them all going." He saw
such small holiness band-churches, as places where "the
poorest of the poor" could have the Gospel preached to them.
The plainness of their service, of the churches and their life-
style, they believed, helped to guarantee that.[124]

The basic, practical conclusions on the implications
of the holiness revival for the future of church order had been
outlined in two letters which were sent by B. A. Washburn
and James Swing, of the California Association, to the General Holiness Assembly which met in Chicago, at the Park
Avenue Methodist Church from May 20 to May 26, 1885.[125]
Other than in their unique concept of the basis for membership required by the California independents discussed below,
they represented a concise statement of the rationale by which
all of the radical reformers explained their separatist actions.
Both documents were denied any formal hearing at the convention. They were labeled by the National Association forces, who continued to exercise discipline over the movement
as a whole through the general conventions, as "a perfect
charge of dynamite come-outism."[126]

When one compares the reasoning of these men with
the conclusions of the convention as interpreted by the National Association's journal, he can see why the charge was
made against them by the main group of loyal Methodists
who represented the heart of the movement. The Christian
Standard and Home Journal said that the convention had denied that the holiness people had any right "to sever connection with the Church even if the Spirit of holiness did not
prevail in the congregation."[127] On the other hand, James
Swing and B. A. Washburn contended that many of the converts had no church home. "They [could not] endorse the

the modes and customs of the religious denominations around
them." Many of them had been "turned out" of their congregations because they had joined the holiness associations; their
zeal became a "living rebuke" to the churches. These, they
continued, had been joined by large numbers of others whom
the revival had won who never joined any denomination; "This
is the people's movement and is as broad as the universe."
Furthermore, the holiness people have the right to "set things
in order" without consulting or receiving the approval of any
other denomination.

Their independent churches, they said, were essential
not only to sustain the spiritual life of holiness people who
often found little food or fellowship in the larger churches,
but also to check the growing ecclesiasticism which all of
these groups feared. "Many small independent churches,"
he said, "prevent pride of denominational glory and give poor
people a chance." Finally, he appealed again to the obvious
"success" of their efforts as a sign of divine blessing upon
them. In light of the prevailing circumstances, he asked the
Assembly to "declare to the world that the permanent salvation of souls is vastly more important than methods regular
or irregular. Speak out," he said, "voice freedom over the
earth by declaring in favor of 'Independent Holiness Churches
with pentecost sanctification as a basis for membership...."[128]

Entire sanctification: a new basis
for church membership

This concluding appeal of B. A. Washburn to the
Chicago Holiness Assembly identifies the unique results of
another application of the perfectionist impulses of the revival to the church question. The "Holiness" churches in
California were to be fellowships of the "entirely sanctified."
In most other aspects of their organization, they demonstrated
many of the prominent characteristics of the congregations
which had formed around the church of God concept in the
other two areas under review. Most prominent among these
was their attempt to restore the purity of the church within
local congregations gathered by the Spirit around the Word
of God, as previously outlined. They were responsible only
to the direction of the Spirit in the congregation. The emphasis in the California groups upon such leadership was
probably the most extreme of any of these three reform
groups. Complete disorder was checked by the recognition
that personal impulses had to somehow come under the teaching of the Scripture as generally accepted by the congregation. [129]

The strong emphasis of all the holiness people upon
the centrality of Spirit guidance in the worship of the congregation, and, in the radical groups under consideration, in
church polity as well, created classic situations for the oper-
ation of what Franklin Littell saw as one of the pivotal points
of Free Church concern.   In his discussion of the origin of
the Anabaptist believers churches, he noted that "among the
Anabaptists the Bible was opened in the congregation and the
Spirit gave guidance to interpret the meaning of the Word."
He said that this resulted in their claim to the right to change
their minds about truth.   "The same attitude was taken to
church law and structures: the Spirit, and not the letter
ruled.   But the Spirit was the one who gave order, not atom-
ism and anarchy."[130]

This professed openness to the Spirit in the midst of
the congregation, in the holiness context described above,
provides one with useful insight into the dynamics of the radical holiness reform movements.   Such a context helps to account for the "pentecost sanctification" basis for church membership proposed by James Washburn "in the early eighties."[131]
As was true of the discovery of the basic thought of the other
two movements, Washburn's reflections on the nature of the
church carried him back across the centuries, past the history of the sectarian origins of the churches which were now
rejecting holiness as he believed, to what he saw as the pure
life of the New Testament Church.   But, Washburn envisioned
that church, not only as a group of true Christians, but as
a group of entirely sanctified Christians.   He had brought the
"second blessing" revivalism message into the ordering of the
restored church of the Holy Ghost dispensation in which he
and all holiness people believed they were living.   The church
was to be once more a visible gathered company of the
"saints"--and "saints," for Washburn, meant those who were
entirely sanctified Christians.   The result was an effort to re-
gain the purity of the congregation by demanding the highest
standard of Christian profession ever proposed for church membership.[132]

Like Warner and Kiergan, Washburn attributed this
new insight to the direct inspiration of the Spirit's unveiling
of Biblical truth.   In what he believed to be "a vision, revelation direct from Jesus Christ," he claimed that John the
Revelator's picture of the spiritual deficiencies of the "Seven
Churches of Asia" flashed as a "panorama" before his eyes.
It was further revealed to him, that each deficiency in those
churches which, for him, were representative of the denom-

inations of his time, had developed because of a lack of holiness in their membership. They too had consisted of mixtures of sinful people who had rejected holiness, and God had demanded repentance and sanctification as remedy for their sin. He finally concluded that God was revealing to him the pattern for the restoration of apostolic purity and order, for

> the Spirit, at the same moment seemed to speak
> in audible words, saying: "What God required at
> the beginning, will he require at the end. [133]

It became obvious to him that "through this clear revelation" ... it had been made quite clear that the establishing of the New Testament or Christ's Church was founded on Holiness or Sanctification." This light of Divine Revelation," he said, "spread rapidly, as a forest fire...."[134]

On this "holiness line," the Holiness Church of California was ultimately organized out of Washburn's Southern California and Arizona Holiness Association bands. In 1946, having failed to experience any significant growth under this radical organizational basis, it merged with the Pilgrim Holiness Church. In that merger, its churches abandoned Washburn's concept and took up the Pilgrim's requirement of conversion and a willingness to pursue holiness as the standard church fellowship. The latter represented the common pattern for membership in the holiness churches. [135]

The Mainstream's Rejection of the "Come-Outers"

Regardless of the fact that the three early holiness separatists movements which have been reviewed above, represented a classic example in American church history of efforts to apply the doctrine of the Holy Spirit to the questions of church order in the Free Church tradition, the results constituted too much of an irregularity for the Methodist mainstream holiness movement. B. A. Washburn's independency was undoubtedly a much greater issue to the 1885 General Holiness Assembly than his "pentecost sanctification" requirement for local church membership. Methodism could tolerate almost anything easier than it could tolerate independent, irregular methods which conflicted, in any significant degree, with its own tightly knit structures. The whole movement learned the reality of that fact by the end of the century, according to Charles Ferguson's recent history of Methodism. [136]

The independent movements of the 1880's constituted
an unbearable embarrassment to the leaders of the moderate
holiness center who were pursuing their own holiness reform
almost exclusively in terms of their Methodist loyalist context. The torment of these men, whose optimistic hope for
the perfection of the churches was irrevocably related to the
success of the Methodist churches as holiness churches, became increasingly evident as the pressures, which had created
the radical reform groups, intensified in the next two decades.
In 1890, the Guide's editor, George Hughes, remembering
the happier days of the Palmer movement in Methodism,
chided the independents for their "voluntary" withdrawal from
"the several churches" or "the sects," as they called them.
He deplored "the spirit of 'COME-OUTISM' " which had seized
these "friends of holiness." He wrote plaintively,

> In doing this they have wounded the cause of holi-
> ness in the house of its friends, and they have
> done serious harm in making the allotment harder
> on those who determine to remain in the Church of
> their choice.   That is not acting on the golden rule,
> we think. 137

Looking back from a twentieth-century vantage point,
it appears that the reformers were merely ahead of their
time. They were acting out of the exigencies of the moment
in an attempt to discover an answer to their relationship
with the universal church. With the possible exception of
Warner, they recognized that they were reacting as pragma-
tists--although Biblical pragmatists. 138   They felt that they
had been rejected by churches, which, for them, no longer
represented believers churches and especially not holiness
churches. They brought into play all the conscious or unconscious influences from historical Christian traditions which
had been infused into their thinking and experience.

The goal they were seeking was to try to establish
new believers' fellowships, in which the doctrines and life
style that they adhered to, could be nourished, and above
all, propagated. Their efforts to express the universality
of the church in their "church of God" and their "church of
the saints" concepts, the attempt to express the equality of
the worth and contribution of each member, their strong emphasis on the separateness and holiness of the fellowship,
and their impelling sense of mission were not new. They
were well known as the Free Church tradition. 139 What
made their efforts somewhat unique was the holiness her-

meneutic by which they interpreted that tradition in their
contemporary application of it. Their perfectionist tendencies
and the special concern for the primacy of freedom in the
Holy Spirit strongly reinforced the basic elements of the
tradition. Their efforts marked the final interaction between
revivalism and perfectionism within the framework of the
movement. In this instance, it was not the message or the
method of its propagation, but the manner of its perpetuation
within the church structures which was in view. They were
proving Sperry's contention that

> it is in the bodies which inherit the Reformation
> passion for a church purged from worldliness and
> purified after the primitive pattern that we find in
> America those schisms and sub-schisms of the
> more evangelical types of Protestantism.

Sperry continued,

> Here is the truth of most of our excessive denom-
> inations. [140]

Although the answers at which they arrived were rejected by the main body of holiness people at the time, and
eventually modified by the groups themselves, these early
separatists, with their radical demands for a place within
the structure of the American denomination, were merely
the pioneers of a pattern which was repeatedly followed by
others within the movement over the next fifteen years. [141]
Among the later group were many who had to defend themselves against the same charges of "come-outism" which had
been directed against the earlier group. [142] By the time of
the denunciation of the movement's raison d'être--its special
promotion of the doctrine of Christian holiness--in the episcopal address to the Methodist Episcopal Church South in
1894, the die had been cast for many who had once stoutly resisted the early separatist tendencies. [143] They had probably
learned from the bitter experience of the first independent
movement. The leaders of the later movements were often
men of broader experience, both within their denomination
and the holiness revival. They set the course of their own
independency within patterns more acceptable to the Methodistic orientation of the movement. These new organizations
provided church homes for the majority of those adherents
of the revival who did not choose to stay within the established churches. [144] "A strange silence shrouded the subject
of holiness" in the churches which they left, for it seems that

with their separation, not only the controversy over the doctrine, but the zeal in its proclamation waned. The lure,
which the call to perfection still carried, was demonstrated
in the success of the evangelism of the new holiness churches.
That evangelism, together with that of the pentecostal sects
which also sprang from the revival's milieu, eventually attracted a constituency which approximated that of world-wide
Methodism itself.[145]

SUMMARY

Pressed by the rapidly changing patterns of life in
their post-war communities and churches, many of the converts of the holiness revival turned to the incipient institutions
of the movement to find identity and community. These holiness bands or associations shared in the sense of unity, which
had become common among members of American evangelical
churches who met and worked together in joint evangelism.
Out of those experiences, revivalists had boldly spoken of a
coming day when the revival would eventuate in one united
church. In the restoration, they said, a true, spiritual
brotherhood would subsume the differences among what to
them were the obviously deficient denominations. The visible
unity of the church would be restored.

The rhetoric of the holiness partisans concerning the
unity which the general acceptance of the holiness experience
would bring among the churches, was stronger than the rhetoric on Christian unity in any other segment of the American
revival. Faced with opposition in their own churches, which,
they felt, were progressively falling away from the puritan-
pietism life style, which the Holiness advocates commonly
recognized as an integral part of genuine Christian witness,
they adopted new strategies. They applied the combined
teleology of the logic of their message of perfectionism and
their doctrines of present purification by the Holy Spirit to
the questions of their church relations and the nature of the
church itself.

That logical union, reinforced by the vitality of the
idealistic dreams represented by the expansive mood of America's belief in her manifest destiny, resulted in a challenge
to the holiness movement and the American "sects" to fulfill the revival's promise of a pure, unified, visible church.
A small group of radical pioneers began to call for a radical
reformation of the churches. In the real perfection in love

which they believed the Holy Spirit had made possible for
every Christian now, they saw the potential for the restoration of the perfection of the primitive church of Pentecost,
in which the "saints" and the "sanctified" would gather together once again in undivided Christian witness. The divine
patterns of that church, they felt, had been obscured by the
accumulation of human creeds and ecclesiasticism. Out of
their own commitment to perfectionism, they proclaimed that
God had revealed the mystery of the restoration of his true
church; it was to be a church of God, pure and one, com-
prised of people who were freed from selfish partisanship
by entire sanctification by faith. For them, the holiness
revival was the testimony to this new "age of the Spirit."

It was a bold new dream, made even bolder by the
growing negative reaction of the churches to the perfectionist's
optimistic claims. There was little hope, therefore, that
the denominations would accept the ultimate conclusions of
the radical application of that perfectionism to their own
structure. Moreover, most segments of the holiness movement, itself, were equally unprepared to accept the radical
reformer's conclusions. They were genuinely dedicated to
Methodism's own commitment to order and organization. Beginning with Methodism, though admittedly increasingly reluctant Methodism, they continued to hope to usher in the
long anticipated reformation of the many churches into one
great holiness crusade.

The rapid deterioration of relations between the movement and the churches within a decade after the separation
of the radicals from the churches forced many moderates
in the movement to take their own reluctant steps toward
"come-outism." The process was almost identical with that
which they had so roundly condemned previously. By 1900,
they too, apparently felt that the holiness revival's aggressive
zeal to usher in a new day of hope for the world, in the
"age of the Spirit," could not survive among the established
churches. In that measure, they were acknowledging that
the radicals had been right; to survive in the future, they
agreed the promotion of the dream had to be carried on in
structures which were more congenial to its own character
and ends.

The result was the generation, within a twenty year
period at the close of the nineteenth century, of the largest
group of new church organizations which America had ever
produced in so short a time. Most of them did not accept

the "church of God" order, which the radical holiness reformers called for in one way or another. The largest number of revival converts clustered around churches with more
moderate Wesleyan concepts of church fellowship. The moderates too, preached the message of "holiness--now," but
accepted into their fellowship, not only "the sanctified," but
also those who promised "to follow after holiness." Most of
their original constituencies were drawn from the holiness
sympathizers in Methodist bodies. The positive nature of
the response of many others--Methodists and non-Methodists--
to the anti-ecclesiastical populism of the "churches of God"
and the "churches of the saints," which the mainstream rejected, was demonstrated by the fact that the boldest reform
movement of them all became one of the more significant
segments of the twentieth century holiness movement.

Whether by one new organization or another, however,
and whether by separating from the churches of their own
volition, or by being forced into schism, thousands of individuals left the established denominations and carried much
of the active promotion of America's perfectionist dreams
along with them. Whatever force Wesleyan perfectionism
exercised in American life, thereafter, lay almost exclusively
within the hands of the holiness churches and the interdenominational agencies the movement had generated. Until recently when new interests in their message developed as a
part of the regenerating interest in the work of the Holy
Spirit in the churches, their place among the Christian churches
was largely forgotten. The fact of that regeneration and the
continuing vitality shown by the holiness movements, testifies
to the enduring contribution of the nineteenth century revival
which produced them. In the midst of one of the most trying periods of history, it carried its aggressive promotion
of Wesleyan perfectionism to America and the world. It
cast the message in the urgent, unrelenting patterns of the
"immediacy" of the American revival tradition. Its perfectionism, set in the mold of the American revival tradition, promised hope and optimism--"now," and its faith promised purity
and perfect love--"now." That the dreams faded within the
established churches did not detract from the fact that the
movement had been the significant bearer of the idealistic
dreams of the American nation and had created an enduring
experiential tradition in the Protestant churches--a new pietism.

NOTES

1. This can best be seen by following the activities
of the various associations in their periodicals referred to
throughout this paper. More readily available sources which
illustrate the type of personnel who made up such bands and
their band activities are Josephine F. Washburn, History and
Reminiscences of Holiness Church Work in Southern California
and Arizona (South Pasadena, Cal.: Record Press [1912]);
or Sarah A. Cooke, op. cit. The work of the numerous individual evangelists who were continually carrying on informal
evangelism wherever "the Spirit led them" can be reviewed
in the work of the black Methodist evangelist Amanda Smith,
An Autobiography (Chicago: Meyer and Brothers, Publishers,
1893); or Jennie Smith, From Baca to Beulah (Philadelphia:
Garrigues Brothers, 1880).

2. T. Smith, Called Unto Holiness, pp. 27-242; C.
Jones, Perfectionist Persuasion, pp. 194-234; Vinson Synan,
The Holiness-Pentecostal Movement in the United States
(Grand Rapids, Mich.: William B. Eerdmans Publishing
Co. , 1971), pp. 44-76.

3. Robert Wiebe, The Search for Order: American
Society, 1877-1920, Vol. V of "Making of America," American Century Series (New York: Hill and Wang, 1967).

4. Ibid. , pp. xiii, 12, 27, 44; also see Mann, op.
cit. , pp. 154-55. Paul Kramer and Fredrick L. Holborn
(eds.), The City in American Life: A Historical Anthology
(New York: G. P. Putnam's Sons, 1970), pp. 263-64.

5. Ibid. , 247. T. Smith, Called Unto Holiness, p.
29. Val Clear, op. cit. , p. 3.

6. Wiebe, op. cit. , p. 44. C. Jones, op. cit. ,
pp. 146-47; T. Smith, Called Unto Holiness, p. 28; Hudson,
op. cit. , p. 307, notes that during this period, the Green-
back and the Farmer's Alliance movements of the 1870's
and 1880's were soon followed by the Populists of the 1890's.
His statement that the eastern papers described the agrarian
protesters as "dangerous characters," may throw some light
on the reaction of the National's leaders to the rural reformers of the holiness movement. Hudson claims that "the evangelical religion of the rural and village churches of the Mid-
west and South ... was implicated in the farm revolt and contributed to its continuing impetus." The "relationship" between the two, he says, "has recieved little study."

7. Wiebe, op. cit., p. 62.

8. Perry Miller, op. cit., p. 23.

9. The committee appointed at the 1877 Holiness
Conference in Cincinnati to achieve "harmonious action" among
the participants in their holiness promotion could only produce a report of the future plans of each of them; Proceedings of Holiness Conferences, pp. 31, 111-12.

10. A. M. Kiergan, Historical Sketches of the Revival of True Holiness and Local Church Polity from 1865-
1916 (n. p. : Published by the Board of Publication of the
Church Advocate and Good Way [1972]), p. 40. "A Survey
of the Field," A Survey of the Field and Strictures Thereon,
by J. P. Brooks reviewed by T. J. Bryant (n. p. : n. n.
[1882]), pp. 4-9. The "Survey of the Field," had appeared
as an editorial in the Central Christian Advocate, one of the
many Methodist "Advocates"; it was a sharp attack upon the
holiness movement in the Illinois area for what the editor
claimed were the large numbers of people involved in it
whose lives "were not up to the common standards of Christian morals" and who were "lacking in the spirit of Christ...."
Those individuals, he said, were "captious, arrogant, ready
in finding fault, wanting in Christian courtesy, [and] over-
anxious, apparently, to assert and show their disregard for
proper authority"; ibid., p. 3. J. P. Brooks, editor of the
Banner, charged that the attack was an attack on the doctrines
of entire sanctification which the movement was propagating;
that there were irregularities among some, he could not
deny, but he claimed that they were due to the fact that people
in the holiness associations were human and subject to the
problems which had faced all Christian revivals of religion.
He claimed, however, that the western holiness movement
was subject to fewer such faults than some others; ibid.,
pp. 9-14. That Bryant was probably the less prejudiced of
the two may be indicated by the fact that he was generally
a friend of the movement. Only a year before he wrote his
review, he had said that "Nobler and purer men than Hardin Wallace, M. L. Haney and L. B. Kent are not to be
found in or out of Illinois," and that in spite of fanaticism in
"the work at Williamsville" the holiness people on the whole
were just as true to their professions of religion as were
those who made no claim to such an experience; Good Way,
III (November 12, 1881), 4. The Good Way, III (October 15,
1881), 7, carried an advertisement of five sermons by Bryant in support of the movement and its central doctrine.
Also see supra, p. 214.

11.   Proceedings of Holiness Conferences, pp. 100-102.

12.   "The Holiness Movement an Error," Good Way,
IV (November, 1884), 2.   "Address of General Western
Union Holiness Convention, to the Friends of Holiness, ..."
Proceedings of the Western Union Holiness Convention Held
at Jacksonville, Ill., December 15th-19th, 1880 (Bloomington,
Ill.: Published by Western Holiness Association, 1881), p.
81.

13.   "The Holiness Convention: Round Lake, N.Y.,"
Advocate of Bible Holiness, XIII (August, 1882), p. 227.
The report of the convention was signed by "J. S. Inskip,
President" and "J. N. Short, Secretary"; Short later was a
dominant figure in the unions which created the Church of
the Nazarene.   For the 1885 Chicago Assembly's "Declara-
tion of Principles," see Guide, LXXVI (July, 1885), 26-28.

14.   See "That Illinois Conference Report," Advocate
of Christian Holiness, X (December, 1879), 283-84.   The
paper noted that when every Methodist minister became a
preacher of perfect love as the conference recommended,
there would be "no further need of 'Associations,' 'Evangelists,' or 'periodicals,' for the special promotion of holiness; ..."

15.   E. g., T. J. Bryant mentioned above and particularly the friends of the movement among the church's hier-
archy.

16.   One of the main divisions of the Western Convention "Address" was titled "Aggression"; Proceedings of the
Western Union Holiness Convention, p. 82; their "aim," they
said, was "pushing the whole truth of God upon the attention
of the whole population around them." (Emphasis theirs.)
Some of the best examples of both the extreme aggressiveness
and the extreme reaction are found in Kiergan, op. cit.,
pp. 11-34 et passim.

17.   The strong statement on Christian unity in the
prayer of Christ, in John 17, which carried great import
for the whole Christian Church carried a special import for
them because it immediately followed a statement on sanctification which was widely used in the teaching of the movement.

18.   Wallace, op. cit., p. 15.

19.   Ibid. , p. 144.

20.   Miller, op. cit. , pp. 22-23.

21.   Ibid. , p. 43.

22.   Ibid. , pp. 46-47.

23.   Ibid. , p. 46.

24.   Supra, pp. 37-40.

25.   William H. Starr, Discourses on the Nature of
Faith and Kindred Subjects (Chicago: D. B. Cook and Co. ,
1857), p. 35.   Starr was particularly put out with the denominational establishment because of what he considered to
be their shabby treatment of him at his ordination.   "It is
thought there is more liberty at the West than at the East,"
he wrote.   "With the people perhaps it is so.   Yet with the
ministry, I should think it the reverse.... But the handle
of our pap-spoon is at the East, and so we have to turn our
faces that way to get the bowl to our mouths.   This makes
us wonderfully orthodox. " This book was apparently one of
the most influential books in the development of the views of
Daniel S. Warner's "church of God" concepts; infra, p. 248.
It may also be significant that it was written in Illinois and
probably well known there where the independency movement
of the Southwestern Holiness Association, a movement ideo-
logically related to Warner's, began.

26.   E. g. , Daniel Sidney Warner, Bible Proofs of the
Second Work of Grace or Entire Sanctification as a Distinct
Experience, Subsequent to Justification, Established by the
United Testimony of Several Hundred Texts, Including a
Description of the Great Holiness Crisis of the Present Age,
by the Prophets (Goshen, Ind. : E. U. Mennonite Publishing
Society, 1880), p. 397, said, "I have ... heard the charge
that these holiness bands are a 'conglomeration of all sects,'
etc.   Well here is a striking evidence of the Divinity [sic]
of the whole movement.   What but the power of God could
join into such loving bands of union ... elements from the
various disintegrated and selfish parties of Israel.... " Only
"the all resolvent and utilizing virtues of holiness" could
accomplish it, he concluded.   The largely rural Southwestern
Holiness Association said the same thing: "We do not ...
aim to labor only on denominational lines, but to secure in
the different tribes of our common Israel 'the unity of the

Spirit in the bonds of peace' and bring about the desire of
the redeemer's heart 'that they may be one.'" Clarence E.
Cowan, A History of the Church of God (Holiness) (Overland
Park, Kan.: Herald and Banner Press, 1949), p. 18, as
quoted from the Good Way (October 16, 1880). Also see
Kiergan, op. cit., p. 10.

27.   See supra, pp. 134-36.

28.   William Jones, From Elim to Carmel (Boston:
Christian Witness Co., 1885), pp. 78-81. Also see Clebsch,
op. cit., p. 202; Hudson, Religion in America, pp. 320ff.
The holiness people were reading the Zeitgeist and placing
their movement within it. James Buckley, editor of the
New York Christian Advocate, said in 1898, ibid., LXXIII,
No. 2, 65, that "the number of believers who look for the
speedy fulfillment of all that is meant in the dispensation of
the Holy Ghost is rapidly increasing." In June of the same
year Wm. B. Godbey, one of the movement's most prominent evangelists, declared that the holiness movement was
"the last call of the Gospel age." Its acceptance would "give
the Church power and glory such as she had never known."
Guide, CII (June, 1898), 179.

29.   A discussion of the work of Warner and the two
other men listed here follows below. Warner's work is most
fully outlined in A. L. Byers, Birth of a Reformation: Or
the Life and Labors of Daniel S. Warner (Anderson, Ind.:
Gospel Trumpet Co., 1921); it is especially useful for the
long passages from Warner's diary. Other accounts of Warner's life and work are found in Charles Ewing Brown, When
the Trumpet Sounded: A History of the Church of God Reformation Movement (Anderson, Ind.: The Warner Press,
1951) and John W. V. Smith, Heralds of a Brighter Day:
Biographical Sketches of Early Leaders in the Church of God
Reformation Movement (Anderson, Ind.: Gospel Trumpet
Co., 1955).

30.   Brooks is best known for his treatise on the
church and church order, The Divine Church, previously
cited in chap. v. Until he joined the Independent Church
movement, he was a member of the Central Illinois Conference of the Methodist Episcopal Church.

31.   Washburn's work is best told in Josephine M.
Washburn, op. cit., and the Pentecost Magazine where most

of the material in the book was originally printed; also see
mostly from the same source, L. A. Clark (ed.), Truths of
Interest: Bible Doctrine and Experience as Advocated by
"The Holiness Church" (El Monte, Cal.: The Standard Bearer
Publishing House, 1939).

32. T. Smith, Called Unto Holiness, pp. 28-33, 160.

33. S. B. Shaw, long active in the movement in the
Michigan Holiness Association and editor of the Michigan
Holiness Record, was one of their most vocal critics. Shaw
reported on a National Association camp in Lansing, Michigan. He admitted that "the preaching was good as far as it
went." But he thought "the teaching and the explanations regarding consecration were not sufficiently definite." He also
decried the National's use of gate fees and renting of tenting
space for "unreasonable rates"; Michigan Holiness Record,
II (June, 1884), 21. The National's workers present at the
camp were Wm. McDonald, George D. Watson, John A.
Wood, E. I. D. Pepper, and Dougan Clark. "All of them
seem honest," he noted, "and some of them [were] dear,
good men of God who are in sympathy with our radical holiness work"; ibid. Also see T. Smith, Called Unto Holiness,
p. 33. The Free Methodists generally worked actively in
the expanding movement, but they too had criticism for the
National's Methodist leadership at times; see "An Unkind In-
sinuation," Advocate of Bible Holiness, XIII (September,
1882), 263. Also see Christian Standard and Home Journal,
XIX (February 21, 1885), 5.

34. E. g., George Hughes' editorial, "An Awful Drift,"
Guide, CII (March, 1898), 82-83; the same, Holiness Yearbook: 1893, as cited by Peters, op. cit., p. 147.

35. T. Smith, Called Unto Holiness, p. 28.

36. A. L. Byers, op. cit., pp. 30-42; Brown, op.
cit., pp. 42-54; J. W. V. Smith, op. cit., pp. 20-25. John
Winebrenner, "History of the Church of God," History of All
Religious Denominations in the United States: Containing
Authentic Accounts of the Rise and Progress, Faith and Prac-
tice, Localities and Statistics of the Different Persuasions ...
(Harrisburg, Pa.: Published by John Winebrenner, V. D.
M., 1848); the same, Doctrinal and Practice Sermons (Le-
banon, Pa.: Published by Authority of the General Elder-
ship of the Church of God, 1868).

37. Byers, op. cit., pp. 103-109; Brown, op. cit.,
pp. 62-68; J. W. V. Smith, op. cit., pp. 17-20.

38. Byers, op. cit., pp. 132-33, 154-56; Brown, op.
cit., pp. 68-72.

39. As quoted from Warner's journal for March 7,
1878 in Brown, op. cit., pp. 71-72.

40. In their efforts to develop a rationale for their
movements and their place within the Christian Church, Warner and the other radicals under discussion exhibited a classic
illustration of a persistent Christian tradition which may be
traced back to Joachim of Fiore (ca. 1145-1202). Joachim,
out of his study of the Scriptures and in his earnestness for
reform of the church as he knew it, divided the history of
the church into seven periods, dominant among which were
the Constantinian fall and restitution of the church under a
new Constantine in the end time. His further division of
history into the dispensations (status) of the Father, Son,
and Spirit with the "age of the Spirit" as the greatest and
last is especially represented in its long passage through men
and movements in subsequent church history. It recurs in
the concept of the "Holy Ghost and last Dispensation" which,
as we have seen, was so important to the holiness movement
and particularly to the perfectionism of the radical reformers.
They saw their age as corresponding with the end time, which
Joachim, in his scheme, had seen as the time "when the
Spirit and Life" would be in the church in "the time of the
eternal Gospel." It was the time as well of the battle against
evil in the person of the "last and worst anti-Christ, in Gog."
Victory over Gog, in turn would usher in "the final judgement
and the great Sabbath of consummation...." S. M. Deutsch,
"Joachim of Fiore and the 'Everlasting Gospel,'" Schaff-
Herzog, op. cit., pp. 184-85. Franklin Littell has shown
how these ideas constantly surfaced in the Anabaptist groups
of the Reformation period. Joachim's "thought has influenced
the underground of Christian dissent ever since, ..." Littell
says. Its influence or recurrence in basic but adapted forms
is indicated in the discussion which follows. See Littell, The
Anabaptist View of the Church, pp. 51-53. Also see Brown,
op. cit., pp. 24-35.

41. Warner, Bible Proofs, pp. 415-19.

42. Starr, op. cit., p. 231.

43.   Warner, Bible Proofs, p. 367.

44.   Ibid. , pp. 367-73.

45.   Ibid. , p. 376.

46.   Ibid. , pp. 375-85; "The 'seven months' that are
required to bury Gog and cleanse the Church, it is probable,
is prophetic time--'a day for a year'--making 210 years; but
whether the Wesleyan reformation, or the present more general movement be the point to reckon from, I am unable to
say." Ibid. , p. 386.   Although Warner at times speculated
cautiously with dates as he did here, he rarely pressed his
conclusions.

47.   According to his inscription in his copy of Starr's
Discourses in the Warner Collection of Anderson School of
Theology Library, Anderson, Indiana, Warner purchased the
book in 1868 at the start of his ministry.   It is the only
source he identifies outside of the holiness periodicals cited
below.   See ibid. , pp. 420, 422-25, 430-31.

48.   Warner, Bible Proofs, p. 419.

49.   Ibid. , p. 420, as quoted from Starr.

50.   Ibid. , p. 429.   Immediately preceding this passage, Warner specifically claims that he is not "advocating
the no-church theory that we hear of in the west...."

51.   Ibid. , p. 436.

52.   D. S. Warner and H. M. Riggle, The Cleansing
of the Sanctuary: Or The Church of God in Type and Anti-
type, and in Prophecy and Revelation, (Moundsville, W. Va. :
The Gospel Trumpet Publishing Co. , 1903).   Warner was
especially concerned because Adventist theology applied the
"cleansing of the sanctuary" concept, which he had applied
to the holiness reform of the day, to "a cleansing in heaven
... to begin in 1844." Ibid. , p. 38 et passim.

53.   Ibid. , p. 389.

54.   Ibid. , pp. 225-26.

55.   Ibid. , pp. 227-28.

56.   Ibid. , p. 229.

57.   Ibid. , pp. 229-30.

58.   Ibid. , pp. 230-35, 283, 291-315.   The "Heroic Age" is a term used by Littell for the early church prior to the Constantinian fall.   The Anabaptist View, p. 57 et passim.

59.   Ibid. , pp. 237, 298-335, 349.

60.   Ibid. , pp. 375-79.   He saw the second "beast" of Rev. 13 as the type of the Reformation sects; the first "beast" represented, for him, the Catholic Church.   His most recent fulfillment of the type was applied to the sectarian spirit of the Free Methodists under B. T. Roberts.   He said that they began to shout, "We're free, we're free!"   But when they organized, they became "as dead spiritually as their mother. "

61.   Ibid. , pp. 435-36, 448ff.; see Littell, The Anabaptist View, p. 52.   Here was the "eschatological accent" which Littell saw in the Anabaptist movement.   Like them, Warner and the other radical reformers, and indeed the movement as a whole, looked on "themselves as the secret meaning and bearers of the New Age...." Ibid. , pp. 76-77. Just prior to these passages Warner had described the final battle of Gog and Magog as a struggle between the sects and the true church of God, which the holiness revival was calling together out of all denominations; ibid. , pp. 411ff.

62.   Handwritten note on p. 221 of Warner's copy of Starr's Discourses.

63.   Littell, The Anabaptist View, p. 77.

64.   Charles Ewing Brown, Church of God (Anderson, Ind.) historian, emphasized the links with this tradition and others such as Pietism; see the same, When the Trumpet Sounded, pp. 30-35; the same, When Souls Awaken: An Interpretation of Radical Christianity (Anderson, Ind.: Gospel Trumpet Co. , 1954), pp. 34-37.

65.   Winebrenner, Doctrinal and Practical Sermons, pp. 37, 88, 119-20, 177-83, 211, 266-67, 283, 285-90, 333-70; the same, The Religious Denominations, pp. 173-82.

66.   Byers, op. cit. , pp. 124, 190-91; 177-79.   Brown,
When the Trumpet Sounded, pp. 72-73.

67.   Byers, op. cit. , p. 191.

68.   Ibid. , pp. 193-94.

69.   The Evangelical Mennonite Publishing House at
Goshen, Indiana published Warner's Bible Proofs.

70.   Byers, op. cit. , p. 261; the date was April 22,
1881.   In the same year the first Church of God congregation
was established at Beaver Dam, Indiana; ibid. , p. 269.

71.   Ibid.

72.   Ibid.

73.   Supra, p. 107.   The Church of God (Anderson,
Ind.) has not officially joined the Christian Holiness Association, but does have members of its official family who participate in its activities and serve on some of its committees.

74.   Present membership is reported as 150,198.   The
Church of the Nazarene reports 383,284 and The Salvation
Army 326,934; Year Book of American Churches with Information on Religious Bodies in Canada, Issued 1972, ed. Constant H. Jacquet, Jr. (40th issue; Nashville, Tenn. : Abingdon Press, 1972), pp. 234, 92.

75.   Among the churches of the Churches of God which
followed was the Church of God (Cleveland, Tenn.).   According to Brown, A. J. Tomlinson, founder of the southern
church, may have been involved in the Church of God movement of Warner in his earliest ministry; he also purportedly
took the Church of God name from the Warner group's use
of it.   Brown, When the Trumpet Sounded, pp. 362-63, xii.
It adopted the name Church of God in 1907.

76.   Val Clear, "The Church of God: A Study in Social
Adaptation" (Unpublished Ph. D. dissertation, University of
Chicago, 1963), p. 117, as cited by Ralph Eugene Price,
"The American Holiness Movement, 1830-1910" (Unpublished
B. D. thesis, Anderson School of Theology, Anderson, Ind. ,
1957), pp. 2-3.   Clear, in a detailed study of the early Gos-
pel Trumpet, examined the published letters to the editor and
found that of 99 persons mentioning the group from which they

came, 44 came from non-Methodist groups and 45 came from
Methodist denominations.

77.   Advocate of Bible Holiness, XIII (May, 1882),
157.   Also see ibid.   (February, 1882), p.   62; apparently
Brooks had considered resigning his editorship of the Banner
to become editor of the Free Methodist.   McDonald, editor
of the Advocate, wrote: "We are fully persuaded that the
interests of Holiness in the West will be conserved by this
decision."   The Good Way, III (November 8, 1882), p.   4,
reported that he joined the Free Methodists, but there is no
further record of this.

78.   Kiergan, op. cit. , pp. 31, 51-57.   These involved
some of the first evidences of the "tongues" phenomenon in
the holiness movement's context; ibid. , p.   31.   Charges of
"free lovism" and other moral irregularities were rampant.
Kiergan denies that these were tolerated in the Independent
Church movement, and that the fact that they did exist more
widely in the undisciplined holiness associations was one of
the reasons he and others pressed for the organization of
local holiness congregations; ibid. , pp. 40-42.   Also see
Byers, op. cit. , pp. 365-67.   Bryant, op. cit. , pp. 4-6.

79.   The conveners of the convention were careful to
explain that they were not planning to "give law to the work."
However, one of the main topics placed on the agenda was
the consideration of "Teachers--the proper kinds; preserva-
tion of the work from the damaging influence of those who
have proven themselves unfit; ..."   Proceedings of the Western Union Holiness Convention, pp. 2-3; also see Good Way,
VI (November 1, 1884), 2.   The   Bible Standard, a Wesleyan
Methodist holiness periodical, reported that the delegates to
the convention were determined that the "work of holiness
shall go forward. in spite of the interdiction of preachers,
Churches or Conferences"; Ibid. , XIII (January, 1881), p.
30.   Also see Peters, op. cit. , p. 136.

80.   Bryant, op. cit. , p. 5.

81.   Proceedings of the Western Union Holiness Convention, p. 81.

82.   Ibid.

83.   J. W. Caughlan, "Some Account of the Holiness
Work in Missouri and West," ibid. , p. 21.   Kiergan in his

reminiscences written many years later makes much of this statement as a critical point in the independency movement; see Kiergan, op. cit. , pp. 28-29. It is of more than passing interest to the development of the independency movement that Kiergan in this same passage attributed the origin of the key phrase, "consecrating the church," to a "Sister M. E. Scott," a Baptist holiness evangelist who was active with the Southwestern Association at that time. She had caused "a furor," he said, "among the ultra inter-holiness folks [interdenominational holiness groups] in Illinois some years before by saying she had 'consecrated her church.' " She was active in the Missouri work as early as 1880; ibid.

84. Thomas K. Doty, "Right and Wise Methods of Promoting Holiness," Proceedings of the Western Union Holiness Convention, p. 23. Nowhere does the confusion of the movement at this early stage of its effort to find its place for the future within the prevailing pattern of the revival churches show itself more than in Doty's speech. He concluded: "Sometimes you hardly know what to do;...." Ibid. , p. 26.

85. M. L. Haney, "Current Errors among Teachers of Holiness," ibid. , pp. 44, 43-49.

86. Cowan, op. cit. , pp. 20-21; Kiergan, op. cit. , p. 38.

87. See, e. g. , Good Way, III (October 15, 1881); ibid. (November 12, 1881); ibid. , IV (March 4, 1882); ibid. (April 1, 1882); ibid. (September 23, 1882); ibid. (October 21, 1882); ibid. (November 18, 1882); ibid. , V (June 2, 1883). Also see infra, pp. 263ff.

88. Cowan, op. cit. , pp. 43, 48.

89. Brooks, op. cit.

90. Ibid. , "Preface. "

91. Warner, Bible Proofs, pp. 431-32, made his appeals personal; the "enormous sin [of sectarianism] must be answered for by individual adherents to ... sects.... The divisions of the church are caused by ... deposits of the enemy, which exist in the hearts and practices of individual members, involving their responsibility and requiring their personal purgation.... These facts make your duty plain" (emphasis his).

92. It appears that the individual who was most influential in the pragmatic development of the movement which
Brooks undertook to explicate in his treatise was A. M. Kiergan. The first churches were organized around six principles
which Kiergan had outlined in a series of unpublished articles
early in 1882. They show the simple pattern of organization
common to these early movements: "(1) This congregation
shall be called 'The church at ____.' (2) 'The Church at
____' takes the Word of God as its confession of faith and
rule of conduct and agrees to live and teach by that alone.
(3) The bond of union between 'The Church at ____' and any
and all other congregations of 'the church' shall be simply
the unity of the Spirit and God shed abroad in the heart.
(4) Let offenders be dealt with or disposed of by admonition,
or if incorrigible, simply by withdrawal from the fellowship,
according to directions laid down in the New Testament. (5)
'The Church at ____' shall exercise its coherent right to 'ordain elders' by the laying on of hands of the presbytery. (6)
The temporal affairs of the church shall be administered by
'deacons' chosen by the congregation." The similarity of
this pattern with basic Baptist or other congregational organization of the local church may have been due to direct influences from Baptist, Congregational, and Disciples groups who
were prominently associated with Kiergan and the Southwestern
Association. A. B. Earle, New England Baptist holiness
evangelist, had held holiness revivals among the Baptists in
Missouri which brought about the eventual separation of small
groups of "holiness Baptists" from their churches. These
people did not find a congenial home in the Methodist churches.
Their association with Kiergan and the other independents apparently was very close. Many joined the independent movement. Their concepts of church organization must have contributed directly to Kiergan's thinking on congregational organization. Moreover, one of the six men who marked the beginning of the main "come-outer" movement with their agreement in March, 1881 to leave their churches was a Dr. J.
W. Blosser of Macon, Missouri, a Congregationalist minister.
See Kiergan, op. cit., pp. 3-5, 29, 32, 39.

93. Brooks, op. cit., pp. 1-17. Warner and Riggle,
op. cit., p. 98 et passim.

94. Brooks, op. cit., pp. 63-92. Warner and Riggle, op. cit., pp. 230ff.

95. Brooks, op. cit., pp. 32-36. Warner and Riggle, op. cit., pp. 317-23.

96. Brooks, op. cit., pp. 36-39. Warner and Riggle, op. cit., pp. 323-33.

97. Brooks, op. cit., pp. 39-42, 242-66. Warner
and Riggle, op. cit., pp. 375-90.

98. Brooks, op. cit., pp. 267-83. Warner and Riggle, op. cit., pp. 435-43.

99. Kiergan, op. cit., pp. 28-29; Proceedings of
Western Union Holiness Convention, pp. 18-26, 44, 81-83.

100. Ibid., p. 12.

101. Ibid., pp. 13, 16.

102. Kiergan. op. cit., pp. 44; Cowan, op. cit., p. 26.

103. Proceedings of the Western Union Holiness Convention, pp. 7-12.

104. Cowan, op. cit., pp. 20-21; Kiergan, op. cit.,
pp. 34-42.

105. Byers, op. cit., pp. 178-81, 237-41, 259-60.

106. Ibid., pp. 263-66. Warner's separation from the
Northern Indiana Eldership of the Church of God in October
of 1881 caused a widespread stir in the holiness press; ibid.,
pp. 266, 272. Warner recognized that he was receiving considerable attention at this period; at the beginning of 1882,
he wrote: "Nearly all the professed holiness periodicals have
been hauling barrels of water and pouring on the altar of
God's truth...." See articles from the Gospel Trumpet in
reply to some of these as quoted in papers; Ibid., pp. 275-89.

107. F. H. Sumpter, "One Church," Good Way, V
(June 2, 1883). Sumpter was one of the six original "come-
outers" who took part in the March, 1881 meeting at Macon,
Missouri. Kiergan, op. cit., p. 39.

108. Good Way, V (June 9, 1883); Kiergan, op. cit.,
pp. 44-49, gives a complete account of the events. He is
in error on the date, however; he gave it as May, 1883 instead of June; ibid. Cowan, op. cit., pp. 26-27.

109. Kiergan, loc. cit. Cowan, loc. cit. Good Way,

III (November 12, 1881), p. 4.

110.   Kiergan, loc. cit.

111.   Sumpter, loc. cit.   An article by J. H. Allen,
another of the prominent leaders in the early holiness work
in Missouri, appeared in the same periodical later in the
year entitled "Sectism Doomed." It requested the editor to
publish a letter by D. W. McLaughlin which offered the holiness people an alternative to either the undesirable "come-
outism" or Free Methodism, which he looked upon as an attempt to "patch up or resuscitate dying Methodism...." Good
Way, V (September 23, 1882), p. 2.   The significance for
the present argument is that McLaughlin was writing for
Warner's Gospel Trumpet in defense of Warner's ideas at
the same time; see Byers, op. cit., pp. 286-88.

112.   Kiergan, op. cit., pp. 1-51, and Brooks, op.
cit., pp. 266-75.

113.   See accounts from Warner's journal for his claims
that the "Fort Scott creed" people, as he called them actually
stirred up mobs against him; Byers, op. cit., pp. 370-71,
366; also see ibid., pp. 368-69 for his charges against their
moral conduct and ethics.   It should be remembered that the
Missouri independency movement created absolute autonomy
for the local congregation and the discipline which was exercised depended completely on its local administration; that
varied greatly among these churches.   See Kiergan, op. cit.,
p. 41.   Byers, op. cit., p. 285, also cites an article from
the Gospel Trumpet (ca. 1381) in which Warner said that under pressure from M. L. Haney and L. B. Kent, Brooks
had failed to put "radical truth" in the Banner.   Warner called
the former "temporizers" and said Brooks had yielded and
backslid "from Holy Ghost power."   This hardly encouraged
warm relationships between the men or the movements.

114.   Washburn, op. cit., p. 7; Clark, op. cit., p. 1.

115.   Ibid., p. 2; Washburn, op. cit., pp. 10, 19, 24.

116.   Clark, op. cit., p. 2.

117.   B. A. Washburn, Holiness Links (Los Angeles:
Pentecost Office, 1887), pp. 155-56.

118.   George E. Butler, "Holiness in Downey," Pentecost,
I (February 28, 1886), 8; Clark, op. cit., pp. 3-5.

119. The first formal organization was that at San Bernardino in 1884 by James Swing, a leader in the early years of the Association; Clark, op. cit. , p. 2; also see B. A. Washburn, Holiness Links, pp. 189-200, for rules and policy adopted by these congregations.

120. Ibid. , p. 155. Clark, op. cit. , p. 4.

121. Dennis Rogers, Holiness Pioneering (Hemet, Calif. , 1944), p. 13.

122. This may be true in spite of their differences and antagonisms. Their common goal for a method of applying the holiness revival's message to local church organization and their simultaneous and not unrelated rise make such common study profitable.

123. B. A. Washburn, op. cit. , p. 155.

124. Ibid. , pp. 165-81.

125. Ibid. , p. 184.

126. B. A. Washburn, op. cit. , pp. 184ff. , gives the contents of James W. Swing's letter to the 1885 convention. Washburn's letter is published in the Good Way, VII (May 23, 1885), 1. Cowan, op. cit. , pp. 24-25, gives it from that source. Both, however, were widely broadcast across the movement by their publication in the Good Way and the Banner of Holiness; B. A. Washburn, op. cit. , p. 184. Brooks, editor of the Banner, was the one who tried to force the letters to the floor of the convention. According to Kiergan in spite of Brooks' statement that he would be heard "if he had to get on a goodsbox in front of the door," and the support of L. B. Kent against the ruling of the chair against the hearing of the California documents, the "communication was pigeon-holed in the chairman's pocket"; Kiergan, op. cit. , p. 63. Kiergan also points up the opposing points of view in quotes from two men; E. Davis, "a Methodist preacher from Massachusetts, rock-ribbed sectarian, said: 'What do we want better than we had? What we want is not machinery so it will run better. ' Bro. Doty replied to the above remarks, that 'We are not here to bind hands or hearts, but to give our brethren something that will do them good and help them in their work. ' " Kiergan, op. cit. , p. 62. Kiergan's account, though written late in life, is the best account we have of the inner workings of the convention; ibid. , pp. 64-65. Kiergan had been elected as Secretary of the Chicago

292 The Holiness Revival

Assembly, but did not serve because of his duties as a reporter for the Good Way; ibid. , p. 62. The conclusion of
the independents was that they had attended "a National prayer
meeting. " Loc. cit. The official report of the proceedings
is given in Proceedings of the Gen. Hol. Assembly, Held in
the Park Ave. M. E. Ch. , Chicago, May 20-26, 1885 (Grand
Rapids, Mich. : S. B. Shaw, 1885). The Guide through its
editor, George Hughes, reported that in the Assembly "there
was a disposition on the part of a few to discuss 'come-outism'; this was decidedly checked and on the whole there was
a great unity of spirit and action. " Ibid. , LXXVI (July,
1885), 26.

127. Christian Standard and Home Journal, XIX (June
6, 1885), 8.

128. B. A. Washburn, op. cit. , pp. 174-210.

129. Supra, p. 142, n. 44; also see Washburn, op.
cit. , p. 139; Swing and James Washburn never talked about
who was to preach. They waited for the Spirit. L. B.
Kent, as late as 1900, reported on a meeting of the Holiness
Church which he attended: "Aiming to have the meetings
Pentecostal, formal order and ordering were unknown, and
free-speaking, prophesying and testimony, were quite in ex-
cess of preaching and not a few of the Lord's handmaidens
spoke and prophesied to edification, exhortation, and comfort. "
Ibid. , p. 278. Kent was still president of the Illinois Holiness Association at that time. This freedom of, or from,
liturgy was typical of the movement, although not commonly
in this extreme. It arose both out of the movement's teaching on the Holy Spirit's leadership of the individual and the
freedom of the camp meeting atmosphere which was so dominant in shaping all the holiness churches, even the bodies
which had first left Methodism--the Free Methodists and the
Wesleyan Methodists. E. g. , see David B. Updegraff's remarks on the programming at Mountain Lake Park Camp
Meeting, Maryland: "The meetings are remarkably free of
pre-arrangement and programme. " Dougan Clark and Joseph
Smith, op. cit. , p. 175. Churches like the Holiness Churches
gradually brought more order to their services; see Josephine
Washburn, op. cit. , p. 359. The most complete single collection of source material on the "Pentecostal order" as
used by this church is in Clark, op. cit. , pp. 44-48.

130. Littell, "Concerns of the Believer's Church," The
Chicago Theological Seminary Register, LVIII (December, 1967),
p. 14.

131. Josephine Washburn, op. cit. , pp. 58-59; Pentecost, I (February 5, 1886), 2; Clark, op. cit. , pp. 39-40.

132. Ibid. For the Holiness Churches' explanation of
the church relationship of those who were not entirely sanctified, see J. W. Swing, "The Relation of Justified People to
Christ's Holy Church"; in summary he likens it to the citizen who was undergoing naturalization, he did not have full
rights until he was finally declared a citizen; this happened
for the Christian when he was finally sanctified; Pentecost,
XXI (September 28, 1905), 1, quoting from a pamphlet of
Swing's originally printed in 1889.

133. Josephine Washburn, op. cit. , p. 58; Clark, op.
cit. , p. 53-68.

134. Ibid. , p. 59.

135. Ibid. , pp. 112, 132-34, 146, 276, 241; Manual of
the Pilgrim Holiness Church, Revised by the International
Conference of 1966, Edited by the Committee (Indianapolis,
Ind. : The Pilgrim Publishing House [1966]), p. 14.

136. Organizing to Beat the Devil (Garden City, N. Y. :
Doubleday and Co. , Inc. , 1971), p. 277; Ferguson said,
"Holiness was one thing, but disturbance was another"; pp.
282-83; T. Smith, Revivalism and Social Reform, p. 132;
the same, Called Unto Holiness, pp. 52-53.

137. "No Schism in the Body," Guide, LXXXV (April,
1890), 122.

138. The exception of Warner is made because his reform concepts seemed to involve a much broader scope of
thinking than the other two men under discussion. This was
possibly why he was the only one to specifically call his
movement a reform movement. The others frankly admitted
their pragmatism; supra, pp. 261ff. , 266ff.

139. Littell, Register, pp. 15-18.

140. Sperry, op. cit. , p. 76. Peters, op. cit. , p.
190, says, "It is sometimes assumed that the movement was
primarily an expression of an economically and culturally
submerged group finding in the high promises of religion
compensation for their poverty in other areas. It may be
possible to illustrate this thesis by examples from later periods. But the post-Civil War revival of holiness cannot be

so explained.   Economic and social factors undoubtedly played
a part.   But the more basic motivation for those who were
active in the holiness movement within the Methodist Church
must be sought for in the realm of theology and psychological
predisposition."   The period at which this paper concludes
probably marks the beginning of the "later period" Peters
referred to.

141.   Synan said, "Never before in the history of the
nation had so many churches been founded in so short a
time"; op. cit. , p. 53.   Also see T. Smith, Called Unto Holiness, p. 36; "A dozen denominations ... set sail in the nar-
rows between 'anarchy' and ecclesiasticism."

142.   E. g. , Phineas Bresee, founder of the Church of
the Nazarene, asked in The Nazarene, IV (June 28, 1900),
3, why there was a Salvation Army, why a Keswick Movement "filling already so largely the minds of people interested in a better spiritual life in Europe and America?   Simply, because of the failure of Methodism to continue to preach
the pure Pauline doctrines of entire sanctification by a second
definite work of grace....   Why the Church of the Nazarene?
Simply because Methodism will not brook holiness revivals,
and be an agency for the distinctive work of sanctification.
It is no child's play to go out under the blue sky, without
means and agencies and try to create them."   He said that
anyone would prefer to work with existing agencies than to
have to go out "single handed, mistrusted, misunderstood,
and misrepresented.   Nothing but dire necessity would compel
any man to do.   [sic]"   In ibid.   (July 26, 1900), p. 1, he
noted that the logic against establishing new churches has always been the same: "All are unnecessary, unwise, uncalled
for; if only the promoter [would] have had the superior wisdom which 'we' possess, they would have found a better way."
This he said was applied to Luther, the Independents in Great
Britain, the Free Churches of Scotland, the Friends and the
Methodists; also see ibid.   (August 2, 1900), p. 1, "Whether
a man leaves his fellowship or not is entirely up to his own
situation"; ibid.   (November 8, 1900, p. 1, "All the churches
were new once, and we are unable to see what difference it
makes whether a church is one year old or a thousand."

143.   The bishops in their address observed: "But there
has sprung up among us a party with holiness as a watchword; they have holiness associations, holiness meetings, holiness preachers, holiness evangelists, and holiness property....

We do not question the sincerity and zeal of these brethren; we desire the church to profit by their earnest preaching and godly example; but we deplore their teaching and methods in so far as they claim a monopoly of the experience, practice, and advocacy of holiness, and separate themselves from the body of ministers and disciples"; as quoted by Synan, op. cit. , pp. 50-51.   Also see Peters, op. cit. , p. 148; T. Smith, Called Unto Holiness, p. 41; Jones, op. cit. , p. 456.

144.   Of the new holiness churches which eventually were organized out of the revival, The Church of the Naza- rene, under Bresee rapidly gathered together the largest number of holiness adherents.   See infra, p. 285, n. 74; the the second largest was the Pilgrim Holiness Church which grew by a series of mergers out of the Apostolic Holiness Union and Prayer League started by Martin Wells Knapp and Seth Cook Rees in Cincinnati, Ohio in 1897.   In 1968, at its merger with the Wesleyan Methodist Church, in their joint formation of The Wesleyan Church, it reported a member- ship in the United States and overseas of 56,607; Minutes of the Twenty-Sixth International Conference of The Pilgrim Holi- ness Church: June 25, 1968, Anderson, Indiana (Marion, Ind. :   The Wesleyan Publishing House, 1968), p. 31.

145.   Ferguson, op. cit. , pp. 283-85.   Synan, op. cit. , pp. 213-15.

BIBLIOGRAPHY

PRIMARY SOURCES

UNPUBLISHED MATERIAL

Inskip, John S. "Letter" to Daniel Currey, November 24, 1875. Currey Folder. Drew University Archives Manuscript Collection.

Merritt, Timothy. "Autobiographical Note." Merritt Folder. Drew University Archives Manuscript Collection.

Palmer, Walter and Phoebe. Nineteen "Letters" to Walter and Phoebe Palmer. Palmer Folder. Drew University Archives Manuscript Collection.

_____. "Letters." Catalog Nos. 460, 461. New York Methodist Historical Society Collection.

_____. "Letters." Inventory No. 439. Methodist Episcopal Church Records Collection. New York Public Library Manuscript Collection.

Taylor, William. "Letter" to Dr. and Mrs. Palmer, January 25, 1867. Taylor Folder. Drew University Archives Manuscript Collection.

Wesleyan Methodist Church. Original "Record of the Wesleyan Convention," held at Utica, N.Y., 1843. Archives of The Wesleyan Church, Marion, Indiana.

PERIODICALS

Advocate of Christian Holiness. 1870-1882.

African News. 1889.

American Wesleyan.   1860-1880.

Beauty of Holiness.   1857, 1860.

Biblical Repository and Review.   1848.

Bibliotheca Sacra and Biblical Repository.   1860, 1865, 1866.

Chester Times (Pa.).   1883.

Christian Standard and Home Journal.   1874-1877.

Congregational Quarterly.   1876.

Divine Life and International Expositor of Scriptural Holiness.
     1879, 1886.

Earnest Christianity.   1873, 1875.

Fraser's Magazine.   1875.

God's Revivalist and Bible Advocate.   1901.

Good Way.   1881-1886.

Guide to Christian Perfection (Guide to Holiness).   1839-1901.

Harper's Weekly.   1873.

Ladies Repository.   1860-1870.

Living Epistle.   1866, 1871, 1886, 1888.

Methodist Quarterly Review.   1841-1878.

Methodist Quarterly Review (So.).   1851.

Michigan Holiness Record.   1883-1885.

Nazarene Messenger.   1910.

New York Christian Advocate and Journal.   1855-1885.

Pentecost Magazine.   1886-1900.

Pentecostal Herald.   1899.

Philadelphia Public Ledger.   1867-1868.

Sunday School Times.   1875.

Zion's Herald and Wesleyan Journal.   1837-1860.

BOOKS AND ARTICLES

Abbott, Jacob. "The Higher Christian Life," Bibliotheca
    Sacra and Biblical Repository, XVII (July, 1860), 508-535.

Account of the Union Meeting for the Promotion of Scriptural
    Holiness, Held at Oxford, Aug. 29 to Sept. 7, 1874. Chi-
    cago: F. H. Revell, 1875.

Agnew, Milton S.   Manual of Salvationism.   N. p. : The Sal-
    vation Army, 1968.

Aitken, W. Hay.   The Highway of Holiness: Helps to the
    Spiritual Life.   London: J. F. Shaw, n. d.

Akers, Lewis, R.   God's Specific for Sin. N. p. : n. n. , n. d.

Alexander, James Waddell.   Forty Years' Familiar Letters
    of James W. Alexander: Constituting with Notes, a Mem-
    oir of His Life.   2 vols.   Edited by John Hall.   New
    York: Scribner, 1860.

_____. The New York Pulpit in the Revival of 1858: A
    Memorial Volume of Sermons.   New York: Sheldon, Blake-
    man and Co. , 1858.

_____. The Revival and Its Lessons.   New York: Anson
    D. F. Randolf, 1859.

Allis, Matilda.   Holiness Briefs.   Fort Scott, Kan. : Mon-
    itor Publishing House, 1889.

Alsop, Christine Majolier.   Memorials of Christine Majolier
    Alsop.   Compiled by Martha Braithwaite.   Philadelphia:
    H. Longstreth, 1882.

American Almanac: 1885.   Edited by R. Ainsworth Spofford.
    New York: The American News Co. , 1885.

The American Christian Record: Containing the History,

Confession of Faith and Statistics of Each Religious Denomination in the United States and Europe. New York: W.
R. C. Clark and Meeker, 1860.

Arnold, J. M. Selections from the Autobiography of Rev. M.
Arnold, D. D. and from His Editorial Writings on the Doctrine of Sanctification. Compiled and arranged by M. A.
Boughton. Ann Arbor, Mich. : Endex Publishing House,
1885.

Arthur, William. The Tongue of Fire: Or the True Power
of Christianity. New York: Harper and Brothers, 1880.

Atkinson, John. The Class Leader. New York: Nelson and
Phillips, 1874.

Atwood, Anthony. The Abiding Comforter: A Necessity to
Joyful Piety and Eminent Usefulness. Philadelphia: Adam
Wallace, 1874.

_____. Causes of the Marvelous Success of Methodism in
This Country within the Past Century. Philadelphia: National Publishing Association for the Promotion of Holiness,
1884.

Ayars, J. E. The Holiness Revival of the Past Century:
Commerative of the National Camp Meeting Association,
Its Work and the Philadelphia Friday Meeting with Chron-
ological Notes from the Writer's Journal--Supplementary.
Philadelphia: J. E. A. , 1913.

Baker, Sheridan. Living Waters: Being Bible Expositions
and Addresses Given at Different Camp Meetings and to
Ministers and Christian Workers on Various Other Occa-
sions. Introduced with the Author's Experiences in Spreading Holiness. 3d. ed. , corrected and enlarged. New York:
Phillips and Hunt, 1888.

_____. A Peculiar People: Being Expositions, Addresses
and Posthumous Papers by Sheridan Baker. Edited by G.
F. Oliver. Introd. by Bishop Isaac W. Joyce. Boston:
McDonald, Gill and Co. , 1890.

Bangs, Nathan. The Necessity, Nature and Fruits of Entire
Sanctification. New York: Phillips and Hunt, 1851.

_____. Prospects and Responsibilities of the Methodist
Episcopal Church. New York: Lane and Scott, 1850.

Barchwitz-Krauser, Oscar van. Six Years with William Tay-
    lor in South America. Boston: McDonald, Gill, Office
    of the Christian Witness, 1885.

Belman, J. C.   The Great Revival at Roberts Park M. E.
    Church and Other Churches. Indianapolis: Journal Co. ,
    1881.

Bennett, William W.   A Narrative of the Great Revival Which
    Prevailed in the Southern Armies.   Philadelphia: Claxton,
    Remsen and Haffelfinger, 1877.

Binney, Amos.   The Theological Compend.   Cincinnati: O. :
    Swormstead, 1858.

Boardman, Henry A.   The Higher Life of Sanctification as
    Tried by the Word of God.   Philadelphia: Presbyterian
    Board of Publication, 1877.

Boardman, William Edwin.   Faith Work under Dr. Cullis in
    Boston.   Boston: Willard Tract Repository, 1874.

_____. The Higher Christian Life.   Boston: Henry Hoyt,
    1858.

_____. In the Power of the Spirit.   Boston: Willard
    Tract Repository, 1875.

Boardman, Mrs. William Edwin.   Life and Labors of the
    Rev. W. E. Boardman.   New York: D. Appleton and Co. ,
    1887.

Boland, J. M.   The Problem of Methodism: Being a Review
    of the Residue Theory of Regeneration and the Second
    Change Theory of Sanctification and the Philosophy of
    Christian Perfection.   Nashville, Tenn. : Publishing House
    of the M. E. Church South, for the Author, 1888.

Booth, Catherine.   Aggressive Christianity.   Boston: Mc-
    Donald, Gill and Co. , 1883.

_____. Godliness: Being Reports of a Series of Addresses.
    Boston: McDonald, Gill and Co. , 1893.

_____. Popular Christianity.   Boston: McDonald, Gill
    and Co. , 1888.

Bowman, H. J. (comp.). Voices on Holiness from the Evangelical Association. Cleveland: Published for the Author
at the Publishing House of the Evangelical Association,
1882.

Boynton, J. Sanctification Practical: A Book for the Times.
New York: Foster and Palmer, 1867.

Bristol, Sherlock. Paracletos: Or the Baptism of the Holy
Spirit. New York: F. H. Revell, 1892.

Brooks, John P. The Divine Church: A Treatise on the
Origin, Constitution, Order and Ordinances of the Church;
Being a Vindication of the New Testament Ecclesia, and
an Exposure of the Anti-Scriptural Character of the Modern
Church of Sect. Columbia, Mo.: Herald Publishing House,
Printers and Binders, 1891.

Brooks, John R. Scriptural Sanctification: An Attempted
Solution of Holiness Problem. Nashville, Tenn.: Publishing House of the M. E. Church South, 1899.

Brown, H. D. Personal Memories of the Ministry of Dr.
Phineas F. Bresee. Seattle, Wash.: H. D. Brown, 1930.

Brown, James Baldwin. The Higher Life: Its Reality, Experience and Destiny. London: Henry S. King and Co.,
1875.

Byers, A. L. Birth of a Reformation: Or the Life and
Labors of Daniel S. Warner. Anderson, Ind.: Gospel
Trumpet Co., 1921.

Caldwell, Merritt. The Philosopny of Christian Perfection.
Philadelphia: Sorin and Ball, 1848.

Carradine, Beverly. Beulah Land. Boston: The Christian
Witness Co., 1904.

_____. Sanctification. Cincinnati: God's Revivalist Of-
fice, 1890.

Carter, Russell Kelso. The Atonement for Sin and Sickness:
Or a Full Salvation for Soul and Body. Boston: Willard
Tract Repository, 1884.

_____. "Faith Healing" Reviewed after Twenty Years.
Boston: The Christian Witness Co., 1897.

Caughey, James. Arrows from My Quiver: Pointed with
    the Steel of Truth and Sent Winged by Faith and Love.
    New York: W. C. Palmer, Jr. Publisher, 1867.

_____. Conflicts with Skepticism. Boston: George C.
    Rand and Avery, 1860.

_____. Earnest Christianity Illustrated: Or Selections
    from the Journal of the Rev. James Caughey. Boston:
    J. P. Magee, 1854.

_____. Methodism in Earnest: Being the History of a
    Great Revival in Great Britain. Selected and arranged
    from "Caughey's Letters" by Rev. R. W. Allen and edited
    by Dan Wise. Boston: C. H. Pierce, 1850.

Cheever, Henry T. "Life and Writings of Madame Guyon,"
    Biblical Repository and Review, IV (October, 1848), 608-
    644.

Clark, Dougan. From Elim to Carmel. Boston: The Chris-
    tian Witness Co. , 1895.

_____. The Holy Ghost Dispensation. Chicago: Associa-
    tion of Friends, 1892.

_____. The Offices of the Holy Spirit. Philadelphia: The
    National Association for the Promotion of Holiness, 1879.

Clark, Dougan, and Smith, Joseph. H. David Updegraff and
    His Work. Cincinnati, O. : Published for Joseph H. Smith
    by Martin Wells Knapp, Revivalist Office, 1895.

Clark, L. A. (ed.). Truths of Interest: Origin and Distinc-
    tive Teachings of the "Holiness Church." El Monte, Cal. :
    Standard Bearer Publishing House, 1939.

Conant, Wm. C. Narratives of Remarkable Conversions and
    Revival Incidents. New York: Derby and Jackson, 1858.

Constitution and Bylaws of the Churches of Christ in Chris-
    tian Union. 1968 Edition. Circleville, O. : The Advocate
    Publishing House.

Cooke, Sarah A. The Handmaiden of the Lord: Or Wayside
    Sketches. Introd. by. L. B. Kent. Chicago: T. B.
    Arnold, 1896.

Cookman, Alfred. The Higher Christian Life. Boston:
Christian Witness Co. , 1900.

Cowen, Clarence Eugene. A History of the Church of God
(Holiness). Overland Park, Kan. : Herald and Banner
Press, 1949.

Crane, J. T. Popular Amusements. Cincinnati, O. : Hitchcock and Walden, 1869.

_____. Holiness the Birthright of All God's Children.
New York: Nelson and Phillips, 1875.

Cullis, Charles. History of the Consumptives Home, No. 11
Willard Street and Other Institutions Connected with a Work
of Faith. Being the Five Annual Reports. Boston: A.
Williams and Co. , 1869.

Curnick, Edward T. A Catechism of Christian Perfection.
Chicago: The Christian Witness Co. , 1885.

Danforth, Samuel A. Spreading Scriptural Holiness. Chicago: Christian Witness Co. , 1913.

Daniels, Morris S. The Story of Ocean Grove: Related in
the Year of Its Golden Jubilee, 1869-1919. New York:
Methodist Book Concern, 1919.

Davies, Edward. The Believer's Hand-Book on Holiness for
Christians of Every Name. Reading, Mass. : Published
by the Author, 1877.

_____. The Bishop of Africa: Or Life of William Tay-
lor, D. D. , with an Account of the Congo Country and Mission. Published for the Benefit of the Building and Transit Fund of William Taylor's Mission. Reading, Mass. :
Holiness Book Concern, 1885.

_____. Frances Ridley Havergal. Reading, Mass. : Holi-
ness Book Concern, 1885.

_____. The Gift of the Holy Ghost: The Believer's Priv-
ilege. Reading, Mass. : Rev. E. Davis, 1877.

_____. He Leadeth Me. New York: Nelson and Phillips,
1873.

_____. History of Silver Lake Camp Meeting. Reading,
Mass.: Holiness Book Concern, 1899.

_____. Illustrated History of Douglas Camp Meeting.
Boston: McDonald, Gill and Co., 1890.

Degen, H. V. The Promise of the Father. Boston: Henry
V. Degen, 1859.

Dodsworth, Jeremiah. The Better Land: Or the Christian
Emigrant's Guide to Heaven. Columbia, S. C.: L. L.
Pickett, 1857.

Doty, Thomas K. Lessons in Holiness. Cleveland, O.:
Published by the Author, 1881.

_____. The Two-Fold Gift of the Holy Spirit. Chicago:
T. B. Arnold, 1891.

Dunn, Lewis Romaine. The Gospel in the Book of Numbers.
New York: Hunt and Eaton, 1889.

_____. Holiness--What Is It? London: F. E. Longley,
1875.

_____. A Manual of Holiness and a Review of Dr. James
B. Mudge. Cincinnati, O.: Cranston and Curtis, 1895.

_____. Relations of the Holy Spirit to the Work of Entire
Holiness. New York: W. C. Palmer, 1883.

_____. Sermons on the Higher Life. Cincinnati, O.:
Walden and Stowe, 1882.

Earle, A. B. Bringing in the Sheaves. Boston: James H.
Earle, 1870.

_____. The Rest of Faith. Boston: James H. Earle,
1876.

Fairchild, James H. "The Doctrine of Sanctification at Oberlin," Congregational Quarterly, LXX (April, 1876), 237-
259.

Fenélon, Francois de Salignac de La Mothe. Christian Perfection. New York: Harper and Brothers, 1947.

Fenélon, Guyon and Lacombe. Spiritual Progress. New
York: Dodd, Mead and Co. , n. d.

Ferguson, Mamie Payne. T. P. Ferguson, the Love Slave
of Jesus Christ and His People and the Founder of Peniel
Missions. Los Angeles: n. p. , n. d.

Figgis, J. B. Christ and Full Salvation. Cincinnati, O. :
Cranston and Curtis, 1893.

Finney, Charles Grandison. Memoirs of Rev. Charles G.
Finney Written by Himself. New York: Fleming H. Revell Co. , 1908. (Originally published in 1876.)

_____. Power from on High. London: The Victory
Press, 1957.

_____. Revivals of Religion. New York: Fleming H.
Revell Co. , n. d.

_____. Sermons on Gospel Themes. New York: Flem-
ing H. Revell Co. , 1876.

_____. Sermons on Important Subjects. New York: John
S. Taylor, 1836.

_____. Views on Sanctification. Oberlin, O. : James
Steele, 1840.

Fisch, George. Nine Months in the United States during the
Crisis. London: J. Nisbet, 1863.

Fish, Henry Clay. Primitive Piety Revived: Or the Aggressive Power of the Christian Church. A Premium Essay.
Boston: Congregational Board of Publication, 1855.

Fiske, Daniel T. "New England Theology," Bibliotheca
Sacra and Biblical Repository, XXII (July, 1865).

Foster, Randolph S. Nature and Blessedness of Christian
Purity. Introd. by Bishop Janes. New York: Lane and
Scott, 1851.

Franklin, S. A Critical View of Wesleyan Perfection. Cincinnati, O. : Methodist Book Concern, 1875.

Fraternal Camp Meeting Sermons Preached by Ministers of

the Various Branches of Methodism at the Round Lake
Camp Meeting, New York, July 1874, with an Account of
the Fraternal Meeting. Phonographically reported by S.
M. Stiles and J. G. Patterson. New York: Nelson and
Phillips, 1875.

The Free Methodist Yearbook: 1968. Winona Lake, Ind. :
The Free Methodist Publishing House, 1968.

Garrison, S. Olin. Forty Witnesses, Covering the Whole
Range of Christian Experience. Freeport, Pa. : The
Fountain Press, 1955. (Reprint of the 1888 edition).

Gibson, William. The Year of Grace: A History of the Revival in Ireland, A. D. 1859. Boston: Gould and Lincoln,
1860.

Godbey, William B. Autobiography of Rev. William B. Godbey. Cincinnati, O. : God's Revivalist Office, 1909.

_____. Happy Nonagenarian. Zarapheth, N. J. : Pillar
of Fire, 1919.

_____. Holiness Clergy Bureau. Greensboro, N. C. :
Apostolic Messenger Office, n. d.

_____. Holiness or Hell. Louisville, Ky. : Pentecostal
Publishing Co. , 1899.

_____. Psychology and Pneumatology. Cincinnati, O. :
God's Revivalist Office, n. d.

_____. Woman Preacher. Atlanta, Ga. : Office of the
Way of Faith, 1891.

Gordon, Adoniram J. Ecce Venit: Behold He Cometh. New
York: Fleming H. Revell, 1889.

_____. How Christ Came to the Church: The Pastor's
Dream, A Spiritual Autobiography. Philadelphia: American Baptist Publishing Society, 1895.

_____. The Holy Spirit in Missions. Harrisburg, Pa. :
The Christian Alliance Publishing Co. , n. d.

_____. Yet Speaking: A Collection of Addresses by A.
J. Gordon. New York: Fleming H. Revell Co. , 1897.

Gorham, B. W. God's Method with Man. Boston: Published
by the Author, 1885.

Goulburn, Edward M. The Pursuit of Holiness, 2nd ed.
London: Rivington, 1870.

Govan, I. R. Spirit of Revival: Biography of J. G. Govan,
Founder of the Faith Mission. London: The Faith Mission, 1938.

Guyon, Jeanne Marie (Bouvier de La Mothe). Sweet Smell-
ing Myrrh: The Autobiography of Madame Guyon. Edited
by Abbie C. Morrow, Cincinnati, O.: God's Revivalist
Office, n. d.

Haney, Milton Lorenzo, The Inheritance Restored: Or Plain
Truths on Bible Holiness. Chicago: Christian Witness
Co., 1904.

_____. Pentecostal Possibilities: Or Story of My Life.
Chicago: Christian Witness Co., 1906.

Canon Harford-Battersby and the Keswick Convention. Edited
by two of his sons. London: Seely and Co., n. d.

Harford, Charles F. (ed.). The Keswick Convention: Its
Message, Its Method and Its Men. London: Marshall
Bros., 1907.

Hart, Edward P. Reminisences of Early Free Methodism.
Chicago: Free Methodist Publishing House, 1903.

Haven, Gilbert. Sermons, Speeches and Letters on Slavery
and Its War. Boston: Lee and Shepherd, 1869.

Haygood, Atticus G. (ed.). Bishop Pierce's Sermons and
Addresses: With a Few Special Discourses by Dr. Pierce.
Nashville, Tenn.: Southern Methodist Publishing House,
1886.

Haynes, B. F. Fact, Faith and Fire. Nashville, Tenn.:
B. F. Haynes Publishing Co., 1900.

Hazen, E. A. Salvation to the Uttermost. Lansing, Mich.:
Darius D. Thorpe, 1892.

The Heavenly Recruit Association: Its History, Articles of

Faith, and Proceedings of Conference Held at Reading,
Pa., January 25, 26, 27, and 28, 1892.

Hermiz, Thomas. What We Teach: A Summary of the Doctrines of the Churches of Christ in Christian Union. Cir-
cleville, O.: The Advocate Publishing House, 1965.

Hills, Aaron Merritt. Scriptural Holiness and Keswick Teaching Compared. Manchester: Star Hall Publishing Co.,
1900.

Hoke, Jacob. Holiness: Or the Higher Christian Life. Dayton, O.: United Brethren Printing Establishment, 1870.

Holiness Miscellany: Essays of Adam Clarke, Richard Watson; Experiences of Bishop Foster, George Peck, Alfred
Cookman, J. A. Wood, Edgar Levy, and Daniel Steele.
Philadelphia: National Publication Association for the Promotion of Holiness, 1882.

Horner, R. C. Notes on Boland: Or Mr. Wesley and the
Second Work of Grace. Boston: McDonald, Gill and Co.,
1893.

Hughes, George. The Beloved Physician, Walter C. Palmer,
M. D.: His Sunlit Journey to the Celestial City. Introd.
by F. G. Hibbard. New York: Palmer and Hughes, 1884.

_____. Days of Power in the Forest Temple: A Review
of the Wonderful Work of God at Fourteen National Campmeetings from 1867 to 1872. With an Introduction by Bishop
Haven. Boston: John Bent and Co., 1873.

_____. The Double Cure: Or Echoes from the National
Campmeetings. Boston: The Christian Witness Co., 1894.

_____. Fragrant Memories of the Tuesday Meeting and
the Guide to Holiness and Their Fifty Years' Work for
Jesus. New York: Palmer and Hughes, 1886.

_____. Ministerial Life Pictures. With an introduction
by Alfred Cookman. Philadelphia: Methodist Home Journal Press Establishment, 1869.

Hughes, John Wesley. Autobiography. Louisville, Ky.:
Pentecostal Publishing Co., 1923.

Hunt, John. Entire Sanctification: Its Nature, the Way of
    Its Attainment, Motives for Its Pursuit. London: John
    Mason, 1860.

Huntington, DeWitt Clinton. What Is It to Be Holy?: Or the
    Theory of Entire Sanctification. Rochester: Benton and
    Andrews, 1869.

Inskip, John S. Methodism Explained and Defended. Cincin-
    nati, O.: H. J. and J. Applegate, 1851.

_____ (comp.). Songs of Triumph Adapted to Prayer
    Meetings, Camp Meetings and All Other Seasons of Re-
    ligious Worship. Philadelphia: National Publishing Asso-
    ciation for the Promotion of Holiness, 1882.

Janes, Edmund S. Sermons on the Death of Nathan Bangs.
    New York: Carlton and Porter, 1862.

Jernigan, Charles Brougher. Pioneer Days of the Holiness
    Movement in the Southwest. Kansas City, Mo.: Pente-
    costal Nazarene Publishing House, 1919.

Jones, J. William. Christ in the Camp: Or Religion in
    Lee's Army. Richmond, 1877.

Jones, William. Elim to Carmel. Boston: Christian Wit-
    ness Co., 1885.

Journal of the General Conference of the Methodist Episcopal
    Church. New York: Carlton and Porter, 1864.

Journals of the General Conference of the Methodist Episcopal
    Church: 1848-1856. New York: Carlton and Porter,
    1856.

Keen, Mary J. Memorial Papers: Or the Record of a
    Spirit-filled Life. Cincinnati, O.: M. W. Knapp, 1899.

Keen, S. A. Salvation Papers. Cincinnati, O.: Revivalist
    Office, 1896.

Keys, Charles C. The Class Leader's Manual. New York:
    Carlton and Phillips, 1856.

Kiergan, A. M. Historical Sketches of the Revival of True

310 The Holiness Revival

Holiness and Local Church Polity from 1865-1916. N. p. : Published by the Board of Publication of the Church Advocate and Good Way, [1972].

Kimbrough, Mary D. His Way with Me: Life Story and Poems. Overland Park, Kan. : The Herald and Banner Press, 1967.

Kring, James A. Trumpet Blasts to the Unsaved. College Mound, Mo. : Herald Printing, 1907.

Landis, Charles K. The Founder's Own Story of the Founding of Vineland, N. J. Published by the Vineland Historical and Antiquarian Society. Vineland, N. J. : The Vineland Printing House, 1903.

_____. "The Settlement of Vineland in N. J. ," Fraser's Magazine, XI [New Series] (January, 1875), 129ff.

Lee, Luther. Wesleyan Manual: A Defense of the Organization of the Wesleyan Methodist Connection. Syracuse, N. Y. : Samuel Lee Publisher, 1862.

Lowrey, Asbury. Possibilities of Grace. Chicago: Christian Witness Co. , 1884.

McDonald, William. John Wesley and His Doctrine. Boston: McDonald, Gill and Co. , 1893.

_____. Life Sketches of Rev. Alfred Cookman. Cincinnati, O. : The Freedman's Aid and Southern Education Society, 1900.

_____. Marquis de Renty: Or Holiness Exemplified by a Roman Catholic ... to Which Is Appended ... Some Account of Madame Guyon and F. W. Faber. Philadelphia: National Publishing Association for the Promotion of Holiness, 1881.

_____ and Hartsough, L. Beulah Songs: A Choice Collection of Popular Hymns and Music, New and Old Especially Adapted Camp Meetings, Prayer and Conference Meetings, Family Worship, and All Other Assemblies Where Jesus Is Praised. Philadelphia: National Publishing Association for the Promotion of Holiness, 1881.

_____ and Searles, John E. The Life of Rev. John S.

Inskip, President of the National Association for the Promotion of Holiness.   Chicago: The Christian Witness Co. ,
1885.

McLaughlin, G. A. Old Wine in New Bottles.   Chicago:
Christian Witness Co. , 1897.

McLean, A. and Eaton, J. W. (eds.).   Penuel: Or Face
to Face With God. New York: W. C. Palmer, Jr. , 1869.

Mahan, Asa. Autobiography. London: T. Woolmer, 1882.

_____. The Baptism of the Holy Ghost.   New York: W.
C. Palmer, Jr. , 1870.

_____. Out of Darkness into Light: Or the Hidden Life
Made Manifest.   Louisville, Ky. : Pickett Publishing Co. ,
n. d. (Originally published in 1876.)

_____. Scripture Doctrine of Christian Perfection.   Bos-
ton: D. S. King, 1839.

Manual of the Pilgrim Holiness Church: Revised by the International Conference of 1966.   Edited by the Committee.
Indianapolis, Ind. : The Pilgrim Publishing House, [1966].

Marvin, E. M. The Doctrinal Integrity of Methodism.   St.
Louis, Mo. : Advocate Publishing Co. , 1878.

Mead, Amos P. Manna in the Wilderness: Or the Grove
and Its Altar, Offerings, and Thrilling Incidents, Containing a History of the Origin and Rise of Camp Meetings
and a Defense of This Remarkable Means of Grace; Also
an Account of the Wyoming Camp Meeting, Together With
Sketches of Sermons and Preachers.   With an introduction
by J. B. Wakely of New York.   Philadelphia: Perkinpine
and Higgins, 1860.

Merrill, Stephen M.   The Aspects of Christian Experience.
New York: Walden and Stowe, 1882.

_____. Sanctification: Right Views and Other Views.
Cincinnati, O. : Jennings and Pye, 1901.

Merritt, Timothy. The Christian's Manual. New York:
Published by N. Bangs and J. Emory for the Methodist
Episcopal Church, 1827.

Meyer, Fredrick Brotherton. The Soul's Pure Intention.
Samuel Bagster and Sons, 1907.

Miley, John. Treatise on Class Meetings. Cincinnati, O.:
Poe and Hitchcock, 1866.

Miller, H. E. Reply to F. B. Meyer. Boston: Christian
Witness Co., 1898.

Minutes of Several Conversations Between The Rev. Thomas
Coke, L. L.D., The Rev. Francis Asbury and Others ...
in the Year 1784. Composing a Form of Discipline for
the Ministers ... of the Methodist Episcopal Church in
America. Philadelphia: Chas. Cist, 1785.

Minutes of the Twenty-Sixth International Conference of the
Pilgrim Holiness Church: June 25, 1968, Anderson, Indiana. Marion, Ind. The Wesleyan Publishing House,
1968.

Moberly, George. The Administration of the Holy Spirit in
the Body of Christ. London: J. Parker and Co., 1868.

Moody, Dwight Lyman. Power from on High. London: Morgan and Scott, n. d.

_____. Secret Power. Chicago: Fleming H. Revell Co.,
1881.

Morell, James Fletcher. A Perfect Christian and How He
Became So. New York: Phillips and Hunt, 1881.

Morrison, Henry Clay. Life Sketches and Sermons. Louisville, Ky.: Pentecostal Publishing Co., 1903.

_____. Open Letters to the Bishops, Ministers and Mem-
bers of the Methodist Episcopal Church South. Louisville,
Ky.: Pentecostal Publishing Co., n. d.

_____. Some Chapters of My Life Story. Louisville, Ky.:
Pentecostal Publishing Co., 1941.

Moule, Handley Carr Glyn. The Cross and the Spirit. London: Pickering and Inglis, Ltd., n. d.

_____. Veni Creator. London: Hodder and Stoughton,
1892.

Mudge, James. Growth in Holiness Toward Perfection: Or Progressive Sanctification. New York: Hunt and Eaton, 1895.

_____. The Perfect Life in Exposition and Doctrine: A Restatement. With an introduction by Rev. Wm. F. Warren. New York: Eaton and Mains, 1911.

Murray, Andrew. Holy in Christ. New York: F. H. Revell Co. , 1887.

_____. The Two Covenants and the Second Blessing. New York: Fleming H. Revell, 1898-99.

National Association for the Promotion of Holiness. (Booklet for 1907-1908.) Chicago: The Christian Witness Co. , [1908].

Nelson Thomas H. Life and Labors of Rev. Vivian A. Dake, Organizer and Leader of the Pentecost Bands: Embracing and Account of His Travels in America, Europe and Africa with Selections from His Sketches, Poems and Songs. Chicago: T. B. Arnold, 1894.

Osborn, Lucy Reed Drake. Heavenly Pearls Set in a Life: A Record of Experiences and Labors in America, India and Australia. New York: Fleming H. Revell Co. , 1893.

_____. Pioneer Days of Ocean Grove. New York: Printed for the Author by Methodist Book concern, n. d.

Palmer Phoebe. Faith and Its Effects: Or Fragments from My Portfolio. New York: Published for the Author at 200 Mulberry St. , 1854.

_____. Four Years in the Old World: Comprising the Travels, Incidents and Evangelistic Labors of Dr. and Mrs. Palmer in England, Ireland, Scotland, and Wales. New York: Foster and Palmer, Jr. , 1867.

_____. Incidental Illustrations of the Economy of Salvation, Its Doctrines and Duties. Boston: Henry V. Degen, 1860.

_____. (ed.). Pioneer Experiences: Or the Gift of Power Received by Faith and Confirmed by the Testimony of Eighty Living Ministers of Various Denominations. Introduction by Rev. Bishop Janes. New York: W. C. Palmer, Jr. Office for Works on the Higher Christian Life, [1868].

_____. A Present for My Friend on Entire Devotion to God. New York: Published for the Author, 1853.

_____. The Promise of the Father: Or a Neglected Specialty of the Last Days. New York: Foster and Palmer, 1866.

_____. Some Account of the Recent Revival in the North of England and Glasgow. Manchester: W. Bremner, [1859].

_____. Sweet Mary. London: Simpkin Marshall and Co., 1862.

_____. The Way of Holiness. New York: Palmer and Hughes, 1867.

Palmer, Walter Clark. Life and Letters of Leonidas L. Hamline, D. D. New York: Carlton and Porter, 1866.

Parker, Theodore. Autobiography, Poems, Prayers. Edited with notes by Rufus Leighton; vol xiii; his Works. Centenary ed. : Boston: American Unitarian Association, 1910.

Pearse, Mark Guy. Thoughts on Holiness. Chicago: The Christian Witness Co. , 1884.

_____. The Christian's Secret of Holiness. Boston: Ira Bradley and Co. , 1886.

Peck, George. The Scripture Doctrine of Christian Perfection Stated and Defended. New York: Lane and P. P. Sanford, 1842.

Peck, George B. Steps and Studies: An Inquiry Concerning the Gift of the Holy Spirit. Boston: H. Gannett, 1884.

Peck, Jesse T. The Central Idea of Christianity. Boston: H. V. Degen, 1856.

Pepper, E. I. D. (ed.). Memorial of Rev. John S. Inskip. Philadelphia: National Publishing Association for the Promotion of Holiness, [1884].

Perfect Love: Or the Speeches of Rev. E. L. Janes, Rev. Hiram Mattison, D. D. , Rev. D. Currey, D. D. , Rev. J. M. Buckley, and Rev. S. D. Brown, in the New York Preachers Meeting in March and April 1867 upon the Subject of Sanctification: also Bishop Janes' Sermons of Sin and Salvation. New York: N. Tibbals and Co. , 1868.

Phonographic Report of the Debates and Addresses together with the Essays and Resolutions of the New England Methodist Centenary Convention Held in Boston, June 5-7, 1866. Boston: B. B. Russell Co. , 1866.

Pickett, Leander Lycurgus. Entire Sanctification from 1799-1901. Louisville, Ky. : Pickett Publishing Co. , 1901.

_____. Faith Tonic I and II Combined. Louisville, Ky. : Pentecostal Publishing Co. , n. d.

_____. A Plea for the Present Holiness Movement. Louisville, Ky. : Pickett Publishing Co. , 1896.

Platt, Smith N. Christ and Adornments. Cincinnati, O. : American Reform Tract and Book Society, 1858.

_____. Christian Holiness: Its Philosophy, Theory and Experience. Brooklyn: The Hope Publishing Co. , 1882.

_____. Christian Separation from the World: ... With Especial Reference to Popular Amusements. With an introductory letter by Theodore L. Cuyler. Winsted, [Conn.]: Printed at the Winsted Herald Office, 1868.

_____. The Gift of Power: Or the Special Influences of the Holy Spirit: The Need of the Church. New York: Carlton and Porter, 1856.

Pomeroy, B. Visons from Modern Mounts: Namely, Vineland, Manheim, Round Lake, Hamilton, Oakington, Canton, with Other Selections. Albany: Van Benthuysen Printing House, 1871.

Poole, Richard. The Center and Circle of Evangelical Religion: Or Perfect Love. London: Jarrold and Sons, 1873.

The Present State of the Methodist Church: A Symposium. Edited by George R. Crooks. Syracuse, N. Y. : Northern Christian Advocate Office, 1891.

Prime, S. Iraneus. The Power of Prayer, Illustrated in the
    Wonderful Displays of Divine Grace at the Fulton Street
    and Other Meetings. New York: Sheldon Blakeman and
    Co. , 1859.

Proceedings of Holiness Conferences Held at Cincinnati, Nov-
    ember 26th, 1877, and at New York, December 17th, 1877.
    Philadelphia: National Publishing Association for the Pro-
    motion of Holiness, [1878].

Proceedings of the Western Union Holiness Convention Held
    at Jacksonville, Ill. , December 15th-19th, 1880. Bloom-
    ington, Ill. : Published by Western Holiness Association,
    1881.

Prottsman, William. The Class Leader. St. Louis, Mo. :
    Methodist Book Repository, 1856.

Quaker Sesqui-centennial: 1818-1962. Damascus, O. : The
    Friends Church Ohio Yearly Meeting, 1962.

Record of the Convention for the Promotion of Scriptural
    Holiness Held at Brighton, May 29 to June 7, 1875.
    Brighton: W. J. Smith, n. d.

Rees, Byron J. Halleluyahs from Portsmouth Camp Meeting
    Number Three: A Report of the Camp Meeting Held at
    Portsmouth, Rhode Island, July 29 to August 8, 1898.
    Springfield, Mass. : Christian Unity Publishing Co. , 1898.

_____. Hulda, the Pentecostal Prophetess. Philadelphia:
    Christian Standard Co. , Ltd. , 1898.

Rees, Seth Cook. The Ideal Pentecostal Church. Cincinnati,
    O. : God's Revivalist Office, 1897.

Report of the First Student Volunteer Movement for Foreign
    Missions Held at Cleveland, Ohio, U. S. A. , February 26,
    27, 28, and March 1, 1891. Boston: T. O. Metcalf and
    Co. , [1891].

Ridgaway, Henry B. The Life of Rev. Alfred Cookman: With
    Some Account of His Father, the Rev. George Crimston
    Cookman. Introduction by the Rev. R. S. Foster. New
    York: Harper and Brothers, 1873.

Roberts, Benjamin Titus. Holiness Teachings. North Chili,
    N. Y. : "Earnest Christian" Publishing House, 1893.

_____. Pungent Truths: Being Extracts from the Writings of the Rev. Benjamin Titus Roberts while Editor of the Free Methodist from 1886-1890. Compiled and edited by Wm. B. Rose. Chicago: The Free Methodist Publishing House, 1915.

_____. Why Another Sect: Containing a Review of the Articles by Bishop Simpson and Others on the Free Methodist Church. Rochester, N. Y. : "The Earnest Christian" Publishing House, 1879.

Roche, John A. The Life of Mrs. Sarah A. Lankford Palmer Who for Sixty Years Was the Able Teacher of Entire Holiness. Introduction by John P. Newman, Bishop of the Methodist Episcopal Church. New York: George Hughes and Co. , 1898.

Rogers, Dennis, Holiness Pioneering in the Southland. Hemet, Cal. : n. n. 1944.

Rosser, Leonidas. Class Meetings. Richmond: Privately printed, 1855.

_____. A Reply to the Problem of Methodism. Nashville, Tenn. : Printed for the Author, 1899.

Sage, Charles H. Autobiography of Charles H. Sage. Edited by Wm. B. Olmstead. Chicago: Free Methodist Publishing House, 1903.

Schaff, Philip and Prime, S. Iranaeus (eds.). History, Essays, Orations, and Other Documents of the Sixth General Conference of the Evangelical Alliance Held in New York, October 2-12, 1873. New York: Harper and Brothers Publishers, 1874.

Searles, J. E. A Sermon Preached by the Request of the National Camp Meeting at Pitman Grove, N. J. , August 5, 1887 on the History of the Present Holiness Revival. Boston: McDonald, Gill and Co. , 1887.

See, Isaac, M. The Rest of Faith. New York: W. C. Palmer, 1871.

Shaw, S. B. (ed.). Echoes of the General Holiness Assembly Held in Chicago, May 3-13, 1901. Chicago: S. B. Shaw, [1901].

_____. (ed.). Proceedings of the General Holiness As-
sembly, Held in the Park Avenue M. E. Church in Chicago, May 20-26, 1885.   Grand Rapids, Mich. :   S. B.
Shaw, [1885].

_____. Old Time Religion: Including an Account of the
Greatest Revivals Since Pentecostal Days, and Telling How
to Bring About an Old Time Revival.   Chicago: S. B.
Shaw Publisher, 1904.

Simpson, A. B.   Christ Our Sanctifier.   Harrisburg, Pa. :
Christian Publications, Inc. , 1947.

_____. The Four-fold Gospel.   New York: Christian
Alliance Publishing Co. , 1890.

_____. Wholly Sanctified.   New York: Christian Alliance
Publishing Co. , 1893.

Smith, Amanda.   An Autobiography: The Story of the Lord's
Dealings with Mrs. Amanda Smith, the Colored Evangelist;
Containing the Account of Her Life Work of Faith, and
Her Travels in America, England, Ireland, Scotland, India,
and Africa as an Independent Missionary.   Chicago: Meyer
and Bros. , Publishers, 1893.

Smith, George G.   The Life and Times of George Foster
Pierce with His Sketch of Lovick Pierce, D. D. , His Father.
Sparta, Ga. : Hancock Publishing Co. , 1888.

Smith, Hannah Whitall.   The Christian's Secret of a Happy
Life.   Westwood, N. J. : Fleming H. Revell Co. , 1952.
(Originally published in 1870.)

_____. Difficulties of Life.   New York: H. M. Caldwell,
1897.

_____. Frank: The Record of a Happy Life.   Philadel-
phia: Printed for Private Collection, 1873.

_____. The Open Secret.   New York: Fleming H. Re-
vell Co. , 1885.

_____. Philadelphia Quaker: The Letters of Hannah Whit-
all Smith.   Edited by Logan Pearsall Smith.   New York:
Harcourt and Brace and Co. , 1950.

_____. Religious Fanaticism: Extracts from the Papers of Hannah Whitall Smith. Edited with an Introduction by Ray Strachey [Rachel Costelloe] Consisting of an Account of the Author of these Papers and of the Times in which She lived; together with a Description of the Various Religious Sects and Communities of America during the Early and Middle Years of the Nineteenth Century. London: Faber and Gwyer, Ltd. , 1928.

_____. The Unselfishness of God, and How I Discovered It: A Spiritual Autobiography. New York: Fleming H. Revell Co. , 1903.

Smith, Jennie. From Baca to Beulah. Philadelphia: Guarigues Brothers, 1880.

Smith, Logan Pearsall. Unforgotten Years. Boston: Little, Brown and Co. , 1939.

Smith, Robert Pearsall. Holiness Through Faith: Light on the Way of Holiness. Boston: Willard Street Tract Repository, 1870.

_____. Walking in the Light: Words of Counsel to Those Who Have Entered into "The Rest of Faith." Boston: Willard Tract Repository, 1872.

Spener, P. J. Das geistliche Priesterthum. English Translation in H. E. Jacobs A Summary of Christian Faith. Philadelphia: General Council Board of Publications, 1905. pp. 58-595.

Star Hall Convention. Addresses on Holiness Delivered at the Star Hall Convention. Manchester, November 9-16, 1890. Ed. Isabella S. Leonard. London: S. W. Partridge and Co., 1890.

Starr, William H. Discourses on the Nature of Faith and Kindred Subjects. Chicago: D. B. Cook and Co. , 1857.

Steele, Daniel. Antinomianism Revived: Or The Theology of the So-called Plymouth Brethren Examined and Refuted. Toronto: Wm. Briggs, 1887.

_____. A Defense of Christian Perfection: Or a Criticism of Dr. Mudge's Growth in Holiness towards Perfection. New York: Hunt and Eaton, 1896.

_____. Love Enthroned. Boston: Christian Witness Co. ,
1875.

_____. Milestone Papers. New York: Phillips and Hunt,
1878.

Stevens, Abel. Life and Times of Nathan Bangs. New York:
Carlton and Porter, 1863.

"A Survey of the Field and Strictures Thereon" by J. P.
Brooks. Reviewed by T. J. Bryant. N. p. : n. n. , n. d.

Taylor, B. S. Full Salvation. Des Moines, Ia. : Northwestern Holiness Publishing Co. , 1886.

Taylor, William. Four Years Campaign in India. New York:
Phillips and Hunt, 1880.

_____. Seven Years' Street Preaching in San Francisco
California. New York: Phillips and Hunt, [1856].

_____. The Story of My Life: An Account of What I Have
Thought, Said, and Done in My Ministry of More than
Fifty-three Years in Christian Lands and among the Hea-
then. New York: Eaton and Mains, 1898.

Ten Years by the Sea: Annual Report of the Ocean Grove
Camp Meeting Association. Philadelphia: Published by
order of the Association, 1890.

Thoburn, J. M. The Church of Pentecost. Cincinnati, O. :
Jennings and Pye, 1901.

Torrey, R. A. The Baptism with the Holy Spirit. New
York: Fleming H. Revell Co. , 1895.

_____. How to Obtain the Fullness of Power in Christian
Life and Service. New York: Fleming H. Revell, 1897.

Tucker, F. de L. Booth. The Life of Catherine Booth, the
Mother of the Salvation Army. 2 Vols. New York: Fleming H. Revell Co. , 1892.

Tyng, Stephen H. Christ Is All. New York: Robt. Carter
and Bros. , 1849.

U. S. Bureau of the Census. Historical Statistics of the

United States, Colonial Times to 1957. Prepared by the Bureau of the Census with the cooperation of the Social Science Research Council. Washington, D. C. : Government Printing Office, 1960. (Statistical Abstract Supplement.)

Van Cott, Maggie N. The Harvest and the Reaper: Reminiscences of Revival Work. New York: N. Tibbals and Sons. , Publishers, 1876.

Vincent, H. History of the Camp-meeting and Grounds at Wesley Grove Martha's Vineyard, for the Years Ending with the Meeting of 1869, with Glances at the Earlier Years. Boston: Lee and Shepard, 1870.

Wallace, Adam (ed.). A Modern Pentecost: Embracing a Record of the Sixteenth National Campmeeting for the Promotion of Holiness Held at Landisville, Pa. , July 23 to August 1st, 1873. Philadelphia: Methodist Home Journal Publishing House, 1873.

Warner, Daniel Sidney. Bible Proofs of the Second Work of Grace: Or Entire Sanctification as a Distinct Experience Subsequent to Justification, Established by the United Testimony of Several Hundred Texts; Including a Description of the Great Holiness Crisis of the Present Age, by the Prophets. Goshen, Ind. : E. U. Mennonite Publishing Society, 1880.

_____. The Church of God: Or What Is the Church and What Is Not? Moundsville, W. Va. : Gospel Trumpet Co. , [1902].

_____. and Riggle, H. M. The Cleansing of the Sanctuary: Or the Church of God in Type, and in Prophecy and Revelation. Moundsville, W. Va. : The Gospel Trumpet Publishing Co. , 1903.

Washburn, B. A. Holiness Links. Los Angeles: Pentecost Office, 1887.

Washburn, Josephine F. History and Reminiscences of Holiness Church Work in Southern California and Arizona. South Pasadena, Cal. : Record Press, [1912].

Wesley, John. Explanatory Notes Upon the New Testament. London: Epworth Press, 1950.

_____ . Plain Account of Christian Perfection. Boston:
The Christian Witness Co. , n. d.

_____ . The Scripture Way of Salvation. Waukesha, Wis. :
Metropolitan Church Association, n. d.

_____ . Works, Ed. Thomas Jackson. 14 vols. Grand
Rapids, Mich. : Zondervan Publishing House, 1958. (Photo
offset reprint of the authorized ed; London: Wesleyan Conference Office, 1872.)

Wheatley, Richard. The Life and Letters of Mrs. Phoebe
Palmer. New York: W. C. Palmer, Jr. , 1876.

Whedon, Daniel A. Entire Sanctification: John Wesley's
View. New York: Hunt and Eaton, n. d.

Willard, Frances E. Woman and Temperance: Or the Work
and Workers of the Woman's Christian Temperance Union.
Chicago: Woman's Temperance Publication Association,
1883.

Winebrenner, John. Doctrinal and Practical Sermons. Le-
banon, Pa. : Published by the Authority of the General
eldership of the Church of God. , 1868.

_____ . History of All Religious Denominations: Containing Authentic Accounts of the Rise and Progress, Faith
and Practice, Localities, and Statistics of the Different
Persuasions.... Harrisburg, Pa. , Published by John
Winebrenner, V. D. M. , 1848.

Wonders of Grace: Or Instances of the Mighty Cleansing
Power of Jesus' Blood. Compiled by Rev. A. Sims, Edi-
tor of The Radical Christian (Kelvin, Ontario). Toronto:
Wm. Lightfoot, n. d.

Wood, John A. Autobiography. Chicago: Christian Witness
Co. , 1904.

_____ . Christian Perfection as Taught by John Wesley.
Boston: McDonald, Gill and Co. , 1885.

_____ . Perfect Love. Chicago: Christian Witness Co. ,
1880.

Yearbook of American Churches with Information on Religious

Bodies in Canada.   Edited by Costant Jacquet, Jr. 40th
issue. Nashville, Tenn. : Abingdon Press, 1972.

Yearbook of the Evangelical Association.   Compiled by W.
Horn.   Cleveland, O. :   Publishing House of the Evangelical Association, 1907.

                        SECONDARY SOURCES

UNPUBLISHED MATERIALS

Behney, J. B.   "Conservatism and Liberalism in the Late
    19th Century in American Protestantism."   Unpublished
    Doctoral dissertation, Yale University, 1941.

Clear, Valorous Bernard.   "The Church of God: A Study in
    Social Adaptation."   Unpublished Ph. D. thesis, University
    of Chicago, 1954.

Emmons, Irvin.   "A History of Revivalism in America Since
    the Civil War."   Unpublished Th. M. thesis.   Princeton
    Theological Seminary, 1944.

Forrest, Aubrey Leland.   "A Study of the Development of the
    Basic Doctrine and Institutional Patterns in the Church of
    God (Anderson, Ind.)."   Unpublished Ph. D. Dissertation,
    University of Southern California, 1948.

Gaddis, Merrill Elmer.   "Christian Perfectionism in Amer-
    ica."   Unpublished Ph. D. dissertation, University of Chi-
    cago, 1929.

Hughes, Howard Raymond.   "The History of Delanco Camp
    Meeting Association."   Unpublished Th. M. thesis, Eastern
    Baptist Seminary, 1961.

Jones, Charles E.   "Perfectionist Persuasion: A Social Pro-
    file of the National Holiness Movement within American
    Methodism, 1867-1936."   Unpublished Ph. D. thesis, Uni-
    versity of Wisconsin, 1968.

Knapp, John Franklin.   "The Doctrine of Holiness in the
    Light of Early Theological and Philosophical Conceptions."
    Unpublished M. A. thesis, University of Cincinnati, 1924.

O'Brien, Michael F.   "A Nineteenth Century Hoosier Busi-

ness Man: Washington Charles DePauw. " Unpublished
B. A. thesis, DePauw University, 1966.

Rader, Paul A.   "A Study of the Doctrine of Sanctification
in the Life and Thought of Charles G. Finney." Unpublished B. D. thesis, Asbury Theological Seminary, 1959.

Roberts, Arthur Owen.   "The Concepts of Perfection in the
History of the Quaker Movement. " Unpublished B. D.
thesis, Nazarene Theological Seminary, 1951.

Schwab, Ralph K.   "The History of the Doctrine of Christian
Perfection in the Evangelical Association. " Unpublished
Ph. D. dissertation, University of Chicago, 1922.

Smith, Willard Garfield.   "The History of the Church-Con-
trolled Colleges in the Wesleyan Methodist Church. " Unpublished Ph. D. thesis, School of Education of New York
University, 1951.

Sproul, Jerry.   "The Methodist Class Meeting: A Study in
Its Development, Dynamics, Distinctions, Demise, and
Denouement. " Unpublished Master's thesis, Asbury Theo-
logical Seminary, 1957.

Thompson, Claude H.   "The Witness of American Methodism
to the Historical Doctrine of Christian Perfection. " Unpublished Ph. D. thesis, Drew University, 1949.

Walton, Herbert.   "The Pillars of Methodism: A Historical
Study of the Class System of the Methodist Church in
America. " Unpublished Th. M. thesis, Princeton Theologi-
cal Seminary, 1958.

Wesche, Percival A.   "The Revival of Camp Meetings by the
Holiness Groups. " Unpublished M. A. thesis, University
of Chicago, 1945.

PUBLISHED BOOKS AND ARTICLES

Abell, Aaron I.   The Urban Impact on American Protestantism: 1865-1900.   Cambridge, Mass. : Harvard University
Press, 1943.

Acornley, J. H.   A History of the Primitive Methodist Church
in the United States of America.   Fall River, Mass. : Rev.
N. W. Marrhuga, 1909.

Albright, Raymond W. A History of the Evangelical Church.
Harrisburg, Pa.: The Evangelical Press, 1942.

Anderson, William K. Protestantism: A Symposium. Nashville, Tenn.: Commission on Courses of Study, the Methodist Church, 1944.

Arnett, W. M. "Current Theological Emphases in the American Holiness Tradition." Mennonite Quarterly Review,
XXXV (April, 1961), 120-129.

Arnold, W. E. A History of Methodism in Kentucky. Louisville, Ky.: Herald Press, 1936.

Asbury Theological Seminary Fortieth Anniversary Committee. The Doctrinal Distinctives of Asbury Theological
Seminary. Edited by Harold B. Kuhn. Wilmore, Ky.:
n. n., 1963

Atkins, Glenn C. Religion in Our Times. New York: Round
Table Press, 1932.

Atkinson, J. Baines. The Beauty of Holiness. New York:
Philosophical Library, 1963.

Bach, Marcus. Report to Protestants. New York: Bobbs
Merrill Co., 1948.

Bainton, Roland. Christian Unity and Religion in New England. Boston: Beacon Press, 1964.

Baird, Robert. Religion in the United States of America.
New York: Arno Press and the New York Times, 1969.
(Originally printed in 1844.)

Baker, Eric. The Faith of A Methodist. New York: Abingdon Press, 1958.

Barabas, Steven. So Great Salvation: The History and Message of the Keswick Convention. Westwood, N. J.: Fleming H. Revell, 1952.

Barnes, G. H. The Anti-Salvery Impulse: 1830-1844. New
York: Appleton-Century-Crofts, Inc., 1933.

Bebb, E. Douglas. A Man with a Concern. London: Epworth Press, 1950.

Beet, Joseph Agar. Holiness as Understood by the Writers
of the Bible. New York: Phillips and Hunt, 1889.

_____. Holiness Symbolical and Real. London: Robert
Culley, 1910.

Begbie, Harold. Life of William Booth, the Founder of the
Salvation Army. 2 vols. London: Macmillan and Co. ,
1920.

Bemensderfer, James O. Pietism and Its Influence upon the
Evangelical United Brethren Church. Annville, Pa. n.n.,
1966.

Bishop, Edward. Blood and Fire: The Story of General
William Booth and the Salvation Army. London: Long-
mans, 1964.

Boisen, Anton T. Religion in Crisis and Custom: A Sociological and Psychological Study. New York: Harper Brothers, 1955.

Bossard, James H. The Churches of Allentown: A Study in
Statistics. Allentown, Pa. : Jacks the Printer, 1918.

Bouyer, Louis. The Spirit and Forms of Protestantism.
Westminster, Md. : The Newman Press, 1961.

Bowen, Elias. History of the Origin of the Free Methodist
Church. Rochester, N. Y. : B. T. Roberts, 1871.

Boyd, Robert. The Wonderful Career of Moody and Sankey
in Great Britain and America. New York: Henry S.
Goodspeed and Co. , 1875.

Brandenberg, H. "Heiligungsbewegung," Die Religion in
Geschichte und Gegenwart: Handwörterbuch für Theologie
und Religionswissenschaft. Tübingen: J. C. B. Mohr,
1959. Ill, 182ff.

Brash, John. Our Lovefeast and Testimonies to the Christian's Full Salvation. London: Woolmer, 1887.

Brauer, Jerald C. Protestantism in America. Philadelphia:
The Westminster Press, 1953.

Brickley, Donald Paul. Man of the Morning: The Life and Work of Phineas F. Bresee. Kansas City, Mo.: Nazarene Publishing House, 1960.

Bronkema, Ralph. The Essence of Puritanism. Goes, Holland: Oosterban and Lecointre, n. d.

Brown, Charles Ewing. When the Trumpet Sounded: A History of the Church of God Reformation Movement. Anderson, Ind.: Warner Press, 1951.

Bruce, F. F. The Spreading Flame: The Rise and Progress of Christianity. Grand Rapids, Mich.: Wm. B. Eerdmans Co., 1954.

Bucke, Emory, et al. The History of American Methodism. 3 vols. New York: Abingdon Press, 1964.

Buckley, James M. A History of Methodism in the United States 2 vols. New York: Harper Brothers, 1898.

Burr, Nelson R. A Critical Bibliography of Religion in America. In collaboration with the editors, James Ward Smith and S. Leland Jamison. Vol. IV; "Religion in American Life." No. 5 of Princeton Studies in American Civilization; Princeton, N. J.: Princeton University Press, 1961.

Bury, John B. The Idea of Progress: An Inquiry into Its Origin and Growth. Introduction by Charles A. Beard. London: Macmillan, 1928. (Reprinted in 1955: New York: Dover Publications, Inc.)

Calliet, Emile, Pascal: The Emergence of Genius. New York: Harper and Brothers, 1961.

Campbell, Joseph E. The Pentecostal Holiness Church, 1898-1948: Its Background and History. Franklin Springs, Ga.: Publishing House of the Pentecostal Holiness Church, 1951.

Cannon, Wm. R. The Theology of John Wesley, with Special Reference to the Doctrine of Justification. New York: Abingdon Press, 1946.

Carroll, H. K. (ed.). Proceedings, Sermons, Essays, and Addresses of the Centennial Methodist Conference Held in Mt. Vernon Place Methodist Episcopal Church, Baltimore,

Md., December 9-17, 1884. New York: Cranston and
Stowe, 1885.

_____. The Religious Forces of the United States, Enum-
erated, Classified and Described on the Basis of the Government Census in 1890. New York: The Christian Literature Co., (1893).

Carter, Paul A. The Spiritual Crisis of the Gilded Age.
DeKalb, Ill.: Northern Illinois University Press, 1971.

Cell, George Croft. The Rediscovery of John Wesley. New
York: Abingdon-Cokesbury Press, 1946.

Chiles, Robert E. "Methodist Apostasy: From Free Grace
to Free Will." Religion in Life, XXVII (Summer 1958),
438-449.

_____. Theological Transition in American Methodism:
1790-1935. Abingdon Press, 1965.

Church, Leslie F. The Early Methodist People. London:
Epworth Press, 1949.

Clark, Elmer T. The Small Sects in America. Rev. ed.;
New York: Abingdon Press, 1949.

Clark, Robert D. The Life of Matthew Simpson. New York:
The Macmillan Co., 1956.

Clear, Valorous Bernard. "The Urbanization of a Holiness
Body." City Church, IX (July-August, 1958), pp. 2ff.

Clebsch, Wm. A. From Sacred to Profane America: The
Role of Religion in American History. New York: Harper and Rowe, 1969.

Climenhaga, A. W. History of the Brethren in Christ Church.
Napanee, Ind.: E. U. Publishing House, 1942.

Cobbins, Otho. History of the Church of Christ (Holiness)
U. S. A.: 1895-1964. New York: Vantage Press, 1965.

Cole, Charles C., Jr. The Social Ideas of the Northern
Evangelists: 1826-1860. New York: Columbia University
Press, 1954.

Collier, Richard. The General Next to God: The Story of William Booth and the Salvation Army. New York: Dutton, 1965.

Copeland, Kenneth W. "The Magnificent Purpose." Asbury Seminarian, XXVI (January, 1972), 31-33.

Corbin, J. Wesley. "Christian Perfection and the Evangelical Association through 1875." Methodist History, VII (January, 1969), 28-44.

Cox, Leo George. John Wesley's Concept of Perfection. Kansas City, Mo.: Beacon Hill Press, 1964.

Cross, Whitney R. The Burned-Over District: The Social and Intellectual History of Enthusiastic Religion in Western New York, 1800-1850. Ithaca, N.Y.: Cornell University Press, 1950.

Cumming, J. Elder. "An Exposition of Recent Teaching on Holiness." Expository Times. V (1893-94), 164-168.

Daniel, Harrison W. "A Brief Account of the Methodist Episcopal Church South in the Confederacy." Methodist History, VI (January, 1968).

Day, Richard Ellsworth. Man of Like Passions: A Dramatic Biography of Charles Grandison Finney. Grand Rapids, Mich.: Zondervan Publishing House, n.d.

Dayton, Donald W. The American Holiness Movement: A Bibliographic Introduction. Wilmore, Ky.: Asbury Theological Seminary, 1971.

DeVoist, S. G. History of the East Michigan Conference of the Free Methodist Church. Owosso, Mich.: Time Printing Co., 1925.

Douglas, W. M. Andrew Murray and His Message: One of God's Choice Saints. Fort Washington, Pa.: Christian Crusade, 1957.

Douglass, Paul F. The Story of German Methodism: Biography of an Immigrant Soul. With an introduction by Bishop John L. Nuelson. New York: Methodist Book Concern, 1939.

Drummond, L. R. German Protestantism Since Luther.
London: The Epworth Press, 1951.

Farish, Hunter D. The Circuit Rider Dismounts: A Social
History of Southern Methodism, 1865-1900. Richmond,
Va. : Dietz Press, 1938.

Ferguson, Charles W. Organizing to Beat the Devil. Garden City, N. Y. : Doubleday and Co. , Inc. , 1972.

Fleisch, Paul. Die Moderne Gemeinschaftsbewegung in
Deutschland. Ein Versuch dieselbe nach ihren Ursprüngen
darzustellen und zu würdigen. Leipzig: H. G. Wallman,
1903.

_____. "Pfingstbewegung. " Die Religion in Geschichte
und Gegenwart: Handwörterbuch für Theologie und Religionswissenschaft. Tübingen: J. C. B. Mohr, 1959.
IV, 1153ff.

Fleming, Walter L. "The Religious and Hospitable Rite of
Feet Washing. " The Sewanee Review, XVI No. 1, 1-13.

Flew, Newton R. The Idea of Perfection in Christian Theology: Historical Study of the Christian Ideal for the Present Life. London: Oxford University Press, 1934.

Ford, Jack. In the Steps of John Wesley: The Church of
the Nazarene in Britain. Kansas City, Mo. : Nazarene
Publishing House, 1968.

Foss, Martin. The Idea of Perfection in the Western World.
Princeton, N. J. : Princeton University Press, 1946.

Foster, F. H. A Genetic History of New England Theology.
Chicago: University of Chicago Press, 1907.

Foster, John O. "The First Des Plaines Camp Meeting,
Des Plaines, Ill. : August, 1860. " Journal of the Illinois
State Historical Society, XXIV (January, 1932).

Freemantle, Anne (ed.). The Protestant Mystics. London:
Weidenfeld and Nicolson, 1964.

Garrison, W. E. The March of Faith: The Story of Religion in America Since 1865. New York: Harper and
Brothers, 1933.

Gasper, Louis. The Fundamentalist Movement. The Hague:
Mouton and Co. , 1963.

Gaustad, Edwin S. The Great Awakening in New England.
New York: Harper and Brothers, 1957.

_____. Historical Atlas of Religion in America. New
York: Harper and Row, 1962.

_____. A Religious History of America. New York:
Harper and Row, 1966.

Girvin, E. A. Phineas F. Bresee, A Prince in Israel: A
Biography. Kansas City, Mo. : Pentecostal Nazarene
Publishing House, 1916.

Goen C. C. "The Methodist Age in American Church History. " Religion in Life, XXXIV (1965), 562-572.

_____. Revival and Separatism in New England: 1740-
1800. New Haven: Yale University Press, 1962.

Gospel Hymns Consolidated: Embracing Numbers 1, 2, 3,
and 4 ... for Use in Gospel Meetings and other Religious
Services. Cincinnati: O. : The John Church Co. , 1883.

Green John Brazier. John Wesley and William Law. London: The Epworth Press, 1945.

Hall, Clarence W. Samuel Logan Brengle, Portrait of a
Prophet. New York: Salvationist Publishing Co. , n. d.

Handlin, Oscar. The Uprooted: The Epic Story of Great
Migrations that Made the American People. New York:
Grosset and Dunlap, 1951.

Handy, R. T. "The Protestant Quest for a Christian America: 1830-1930. " Church History, XXI (1953-54), 11-13.

_____. American Christianity: An Historical Representa-
tion with Representative Documents. Edited by R. T.
Handy, L. H. Loetscher and H. Shelton Smith. 2 vols.
New York: Chas. Scribner's Sons, 1960-1963.

_____. A Christian America: Protestant Hope and His-
torical Realities. New York: Oxford University Press,
1971.

Harkness, Georgia E. The Fellowship of the Holy Spirit.
Nashville, Tenn. : Abingdon Press, 1966.

_____ . The Methodist Church in Social Thought and Action. New York: Abingdon Press, 1964.

Haroutunian, Jos. Piety vs. Moralism: The Passing of New
England Theology. New York: Henry Holt and Co. , 1932.

Hay, Fanny A. , Cargo, Ruth E. , Freeman, Harlan. A History of Adrian College: The Story of a Noble Devotion.
Adrian, Mich. : Adrian College Press, 1945.

Hedley, George. The Christian Heritage in America. New
York: Macmillan Co. , 1946.

Henry, George W. History of the Jumpers: Or Shouting
Genuine and Spurious; a History of the Outward Demon-
strations of the Spirit. Waukesha, Wis. : Metropolitan
Church Association, 1909.

Hertzberg, A. , Marty, Martin E. , Moody, Jos. W. The
Outbursts that Await Us. New York: Macmillan, 1963.

Hilson, James B. History of the South Carolina Conference
of the Wesleyan Methodist Church of America: 55 Years
of Wesleyan Methodism in South Carolina. Winona Lake,
Ind. : Light and Life Press, 1950.

Hobbhouse, Stephen. Wm. Law and 18th Century Quakerism.
London: George Allen and Unwin, Ltd. , 1927.

Hogue, Wilson T. History of the Free Methodist Church of
North America. 2 vols. Chicago: The Free Methodist
Publishing House, 1915.

Holdrich, Joseph. The Life of Wilbur Fisk, D. D. , First
President of Wesleyan University. New York: Harper and
Brothers, 1842.

Holt, John B. "Holiness Religion: Cultural Shock and Re-
organization. " American Social Review, V (1940), 740-
747.

Hopkins, Chas. H. History of the Y. M. C. A. in North America. New York: Association Press, 1951.

Houghton, Walter Edwards. The Victorian Frame of Mind:
1830-1870. New Haven, Conn.: Yale University Press,
1957.

Howard, Ivan. "Wesley vs. Phoebe Palmer: An Extended
Controversy." Wesleyan Theological Journal, VI (Spring,
1971), 31-40.

Hudson, Winthrop. American Protestantism. Chicago: University of Chicago Press, 1961.

_____. Religion in America. New York: Chas. Scrib-
ner and Sons, 1965.

Huffman, Jasper Abraham (ed.). History of the Mennonite
Brethern in Christ Church. New Carlisle, O.: Bethel
Publishing Co., 1920.

Inge, W. R. Mysticism in Religion. Chicago: University
of Chicago Press, 1948.

Inventory of the Church Archives in the City of New York.
"The Methodist Church." New York: The Historical
Records Survey, 1940.

Jackson, Samuel, et al. (eds.). The New Schaff-Herzog Encyclopedia of Religious Knowledge. 12 vols. New York:
Funk and Wagnalls, 1909.

James, Wm. The Varieties of Religious Experience: A
Study in Human Nature; Being the Gifford Lectures on
Natural Religion Delivered in Edinburgh in 1901-1902.
New York: Modern Library, 1902.

Jervey, Edward D. "LaRoy Sunderland, Zion's Watchman."
Methodist History, VI (April, 1968), 16-32.

_____. "Motives and Methods of the Methodist Episcopal
Church in the Period of Reconstruction." Methodist History, IV (July, 1966), 17-25.

Johnson, Carles A. The Frontier Camp Meeting: Religious
Harvest Time. Dallas: Southern Methodist University
Press, 1955.

Johnson, James E. "Charles G. Finney and a Theology of Revivalism." Church History, XXXVIII (September, 1969).

Katzenbach, Friedrich W. Die Erweckungsbewegung: Stud-
ien zur Geschichte ihrer Entstehung und ersten Zubereitung
in Deutschland. Neuendettlesau: Freimundverlag, 1957.

Kellog, D. O. Illustrated Vineland. Vineland, N. J. : L.
L. Buckminster, Printer, 1897.

Knox, Ronald A. Enthusiasm: A Chapter in the History of
Religion with Reference to the XVII and XVIII Centuries.
New York: Oxford University Press, 1961.

Kramer, Paul and Holborn, Fredrick L. The City in American Life: A Historical Anthology. New York: G. P.
Putnam's Sons, 1970.

Latourette, K. S. The Great Century in America, Australia
and Africa. Vol V. "A History of the Expansion of Christianity." New York: Harper and Brothers, 1944.

Lee, Umphrey. The Historic Backgrounds of Early Methodist
Enthusiasm. New York: Columbia University Press, 1931.

Lindström, Harald. Wesley and Sanctification: A Study in
the Doctrine of Salvation. Translated by H. S. Harvey.
London: Epworth Press, 1946.

Littell, Franklin H. The Anabaptist View of the Church: A
Study in the Origins of Sectarian Protestantism. Second
ed. ; revised and enlarged: Boston: Star King Press,
1958.

_____. "The Concerns of the Believer's Church." The
Chicago Theological Seminary Register, LVIII (December,
1967), 12-21.

_____. From State Church to Pluralism: A Protestant
Interpretation of Religion in American History. New York:
Macmillan Co., 1971.

_____. "The Methodist Class Meeting as an Instrument
of Discipline, I: The Early Phase." World Parish, IX
(February, 1961), 14-24.

_____. "Some Free Church Remarks on the Concept of
the Body of Christ." K. E. Skydsgaard, et al. , The
Church as the Body of Christ. Vol I. "The Cardinal
O'Hara Series." Robert S. Pelton (ed.). Studies and

Research in Christian Theology at Notre Dame University. Notre Dame, Ind. : University of Notre Dame Press, 1963.

McCutchan, Robert G. Our Hymnody: A Manual of the Methodist Hymnal. 2nd ed. New York: Abingdon Press, 1937.

MacGregor, G. H. C. "An Exposition of Recent Teachings on Holiness." Expository Times, V (1893-94), 28-31.

McKelvey, Blake. The Urbanization of America: 1860-1915. New Brunswick, N. J. : Rutgers University Press, 1963.

McLeister, Ira Ford. History of the Wesleyan Methodist Church of America. 3rd ed. revised by R. S. Nicholson. Marion Ind.: Wesley Press, 1959.

McLoughlin, Wm. , Jr. Modern Revivalism: Charles Grandison Finney to Billy Graham. New York: Ronald Press Co. , 1959.

McNeill, John T. Modern Christian Movements. Philadelphia: Westminster Press, 1954.

Mann, W. E. Sect, Cult, and Church in Alberta. Toronto: University of Toronto Press, 1955.

Marston, L. R. From Age to Age a Living Witness: An Historical Interpretation of Free Methodism's First Century. Winona Lake, Ind. : Light and Life Press, 1960.

Martin, Joel. The Wesleyan Manual: Or History of Wesleyan Methodism. Syracuse, N. Y. : Wesleyan Methodist Publishing House, 1889.

Marty, Martin E. Righteous Empire: The Protestant Experience in America. New York: Dial Press, 1970.

May, Henry Farnham. Protestant Churches in Industrial America. New York: Harper and Brothers, 1949.

Mayer, F. E. The Religious Bodies of America. St. Louis, Mo. : Concordia, 1956.

Mead, Sidney Earl. Nathaniel William Taylor, 1798-1858: A Connecticut Liberal. Chicago: The University of Chicago Press, 1942.

_____ . The Lively Experiment: The Shaping of Christianity in America. New York: Harper and Row Publishers, 1963.

Mead, Frank S. Handbook of Denominations in the United
States. New York: Abingdon Press, 1965.

Miller, Perry. The Life of the Mind in America from the
Revolution to the Civil War. New York: Harcourt, Brace
and World, Inc. , 1965.

Morais, Herbert M. Deism in Eighteenth Century America.
New York: Columbia University Press, 1934.

Morento, J. L. Sociometry Reader. Glencoe, Ill. : Free
Press, 1960.

Morrow, Ralph E. Northern Methodism and Reconstruction.
East Lansing, Mich. : Michigan State University Press,
1941.

Mudge, James. History of the New England Conferences of
the Methodist Episcopal Church. Boston: Published by
the Conference, 1910.

Muncy, W. C., Jr. Evangelism in the United States. Kansas City, Mo. : Central Seminary Press, 1945.

Nagler, A. W. Pietism and Methodism. Nashville, Tenn. :
Publishing House Episcopal Church South, 1918.

The Nature of the Holy Life: Four Papers from the Anabap-
tist and Wesleyan Tradition Seminar, December 10, 1960.
(Reprint from the Mennonite Quarterly Review, XXXV
(April, 1961).

Neill, Stephen Charles and Weber, Hans-Ruedi (eds.). The
Layman in Christian History: A Project of the Department on the Laity of the World Council of Churches. Philadelphia: The Wesminster Press, 1963.

Neve, J. L. Churches and Sects of Christendom. Blair,
Neb. : Lutheran Publishing House, 1952.

Newby, J. Edwin. Teachings of Evangelical Friends as Gleaned
from George Fox's Journal and Friends' Disciplines. N. p.
Messages given to Central Yearly Meeting, 1952.

Nicholson, Roy Stephen. Wesleyan Methodism in the South:
Being the Story of Eighty-Six Years of Reform and Religious Activities in the South as Conducted by American
Wesleyans. Syracuse, N. Y. : Wesleyan Methodist Publishing Association, 1933.

Niebuhr, Helmut Richard. The Kingdom of God in America.
Chicago: Willet, Clark and Co. , 1937.

_____. The Social Sources of the Denominations. New
York: Henry Holt and Co. , 1929. (Reprinted; New York:
Meridian Books, Inc. , 1957.)

Noble, W. E. P. A Century of Gospel Work: A History of
the Growth of Evangelical Religion in the U. S. (1776-1876).
Philadelphia: H. C. Watts and Co. , 1876.

Nordhoff, Charles. Communistic Societies of the United
States. New York: Hillary House Publishers, Ltd. , 1961.

Nye, Russell E. This Almost Chosen People: Essays in the
History of American Ideas. N. p. : Michigan State University Press, 1966.

Olmstead, Clifton E. History of Religion in the United States.
Englewood Cliffs, N. J. : Prentice-Hall, 1960.

Orr, James E. The Second Evangelical Awakening. London:
Marshall, Morgan and Scott, 1955.

_____. The Second Evangelical Awakening in America.
London: Marshall, Morgan and Scott, 1952.

_____. The Second Evangelical Awakening in Britain.
London: Marshall, Morgan and Scott, 1949.

Osborn, Ronald E. The Spirit of American Christianity. New
York: Harper and Brothers Publishers, 1958.

Peters, John L. Christian Perfection and American Methodism. New York: Abingdon Press, 1956.

Phelan, Macum. A History of Early Methodism in Texas:
1817-1866. Nashville, Tenn. : Cokesbury Press, 1924.

_____. A History of the Expansion of Methodism in Texas,
1867-1902: Being a Continuation of the History of Early

Methodism in Texas. Dallas, Tex.: Mathis, Van Nort
and Co., 1937.

Pierson, Arthur T. Forward Movements of the Last Half
Century. New York: Funk and Wagnalls Co., 1905.

Pollock, John Charles. The Keswick Story: The Authorized
History of the Keswick Convention. London: Hodder and
Stoughton, 1964.

_____. Moody: A Biographical Portrait of the Pacesetter
in Modern Mass Evangelism. New York: Macmillan, 1963.

Pollock, Norman. The Populist Response to Industial America:
Midwest Populist Thought. Cambridge, Mass.: Harvard
University Press, 1962.

Porter, James. Revivals of Religion Showing Their Theory,
Means, Obstruction, Importance, and Perversions. New
York: Nelson and Phillips, 1878.

Potts, J. H. Pastor and People: Methodism in the Field.
New York: Phillips and Hunt, 1879.

Preece, Harold and Kraft, Celia. Dew on Jordan. New York:
E. P. Dutton and Co., 1946.

Prescott, Wm. Ray. The Fathers Still Speak: A History of
Michigan Methodism. Lansing, Mich.: Michigan Printing
Service, 1941.

Rhodes, Arnold B. (ed.). The Church Faces the Isms. New
York: Abingdon Press, 1958.

Richardson, E. C. et al. (comp. and ed.). An Alphabetical
Subject Index and Index Encyclopedia to Periodical Articles
on Religion, 1890-1899. New York: Chas. Scribner and
Sons, 1907.

Riston, Joseph. The Romance of Primitive Methodism. London: The Primitive Methodist Publishing House, 1909.

Roberts, Philip I. F. B. Meyer: Preacher, Teacher,
Man of God. By Chester A. Mann, pseud. New York:
Fleming H. Revell, 1929.

Rose, Delbert A. A Theology of Christian Experience:

Interpreting the Historic Wesleyan Message. Minneapolis,
Minn.: Bethany Fellowship, Inc., 1965.

Rosenbaum, Max and Berger, Milton. (eds.). Group Psychotherapy and Group Function. New York: Basic Books,
1963.

Salisbury, W. Seward. Religion in American Culture: A
Sociological Interpretation. Homewood, Ill.: The Dorsey
Press, 1964.

Sangster, Wm. E. "The Church's One Privation." Religion
in Life, XVIII (Winter, 1949), 493-502.

_____. Methodism Can Be Born Again. New York: The
Methodist Book Concern, 1938.

_____. The Path to Perfection: An Examination and Re-
statement of John Wesley's Doctrine of Christian Perfection. London: Epworth Press, 1943.

_____. The Pure in Heart: A Study in Christian Sanctity.
New York: Abingdon Press, 1954.

_____. "Wesley and Sanctification." London Quarterly
and Holborn Review. CLXXI (July, 1946), 214-221.

Sasnett, W. J. "Theory of Methodist Class Meetings,"
Methodist Quarterly Review (So.), V (1851), 265-284.

Scharpff, Paulus. The History of Evangelism: Three Hundred Years of Evangelism in Germany, Great Britain and
the United States of America. Translated by Helga Ben-
der Henry. Grand Rapids, Mich.: Wm. B. Eerdmans
Publishing Co., 1966.

Schilling, S. Paul. Methodism and Society in Theological
Perspective. Vol. III of "Methodism in Society." New
York: Abingdon Press, 1960.

Schlesinger, Arthur M. "A Critical Period in American Religion: 1875-1900." Massachusetts Historical Society
Proceedings, LXIV (1932), 523-547.

_____. (ed.). The Rise of the City: 1878-1898. New
York: Macmillan, 1933.

Schwab, Ralph K.   The History of the Doctrine of Christian
    Perfection in the Evangelical Association.   Menasha, Wis. :
    George Banta Publishing Co. , 1922.

Scott, Leland H.   Methodist Theology in America in the Nine-
    teenth Century.   Published by the Microcard Foundation
    for the American Theological Library Association, 1954.

Simpson, Matthew (ed.).   A Cyclopedia of Methodism.   Phil-
    adelphia: Everts and Stewart, 1878.

_____.   A Hundred Years of Methodism.   New York: Nel-
    son and Phillips, 1876.

Sloan, Walter B.   These Sixty Years: The Story of the Kes-
    wick Convention.   London: Pickering and Inglis, [1935].

Smith, James Ward and Jamison A. Leland (eds.).   Religious
    Perspectives in American Culture.   Vol. II of "Religion
    in American Life."   No 5 of Princeton Studies in American
    Civilization.   Princeton, N. J. :   Princeton University Press,
    1961.

_____.   The Shaping of American Religion.   Vol. I of
    "Religion in American Life."   No. 5 of Princeton Studies
    in American Civilization.   Princeton, N. J. :   Princeton
    University Press, 1961.

Smith, John W. V.   Heralds of a Brighter Day: Biographical
    Sketches of Early Leaders in the   Church of God Reforma-
    tion Movement.   Anderson, Ind. :   Gospel Trumpet Co. ,
    1955.

Smith, Joseph H.   Things Behind and Things Before in the
    Holiness Movement.   Chicago: Evangelistic Institute Press,
    1916.

Smith, Timothy L.   Called unto Holiness: The Story of the
    Nazarenes, The Formative Years.   Kansas City, Mo. :
    Nazarene Publishing Co. , 1962.

_____.   "Congregation, State, and Denomination: The
    Forming of the American Religious Structure."   William
    and Mary Quarterly, XXV (April, 1968), 156-176.

_____.   "Historic Waves of Religious Interest in America."
    Annals of the American Academy of Political and Social Sci-
    ence.   No. 332 (1960), pp. 9-19.

_____. Revivalism and Social Reform in Mid-Nineteenth
Century America. New York: Abingdon Press, 1957.

Sperry, Willard L. Religion in America. Cambridge: University Press, 1946.

Stark, Rodney and Clock, Charles Y. Patterns of Religious
Commitment; Vol I; American Piety: The Nature of Religious Commitment. Berkeley and Los Angeles: University of California Press, 1969.

Starkey, Lycurgus, Jr. The Work of the Holy Spirit. New
York: Abingdon Press, 1962.

Stevens Abel. History of the Methodist Episcopal Church
in the United States of America. 4 vols. New York:
Carlton and Lanahan, 1864.

Stoeffler, F. Earnest. The Rise of Evangelical Pietism.
Leiden: E. J. Brill, 1971.

Storms, Everck. History of the United Missionary Church.
Elkhart, Ind. : Bethel Publishing Co. , 1958.

Strong, Josiah. The New Era: Or the Coming Kingdom.
New York: Baker and Taylor. , 1893.

Sweet, William Warren. The American Churches: An Interpretation. New York: Cokesbury Press, 1947.

_____. Methodism in American History. Revision of
of 1953 ed. New York: Abingdon Press, 1961.

_____. Our American Churches: Studies in Christian
Faith. Edited by Henry H. Meyer. New York: The
Methodist Book Concern, 1924.

_____. Revivalism in America: Its Origin, Growth and
Decline. New York: Charles Scribner's Sons, 1944.

_____. The Story of Religion in America. New York:
Harper and Brothers, 1950.

Synan, Vincent. The Holiness-Pentecostal Movement in the
United States. Grand Rapids, Mich. : Wm. B. Eerdmans
Publishing Co., 1971.

Tappert, T. G. "Orthodoxism, Pietism, and Rationalism:

1580-1830." Christian Social Responsibility. Edited by
Harold C. Letts. Philadelphia: Muhlenberg Press, 1957.

Taylor, Mendell B. Exploring Evangelism. Kansas City,
Mo.: Beacon Hill, 1964.

Taylor, W. S. "Perfectionism in Psychology and in Theology." Canadian Journal of Theology, IV (July, 1959),
170-179.

Tenny, Mary Alice. Blueprint for a Christian World: An
Analysis of the Wesleyan Way. Winona Lake, Ind.: Light
and Life Press, 1953.

Terrill, Joseph Goodwin. The Life of Rev. John Wesley
Redfield, M.D. Chicago: Free Methodist Publishing House,
1899.

_____. The St. Charles Campmeeting. Chicago: T. B.
Arnold, 1883.

Thompson, A. E. A. B. Simpson: His Life and Work.
Revised ed. Harrisburg, Pa.: Christian Publications,
1960.

Thompson, R. Duane. Keswick: Historical Origin and Doctrine of Holiness. Marion, Ind.: n.n., 1963.

Thompson, Robert Ellis. A History of the Presbyterian
Churches in the United States. New York: Chas. Scribner's Sons, 1895.

Troeltsch, Ernest. The Social Teachings of the Christian
Churches. Translated by Olive Wyon, with introductory
notes by Chas. Gore. New York: Macmillan Co., 1931.
(Reprinted; New York: Harper, 1960. With an introduction by H. Richard Niebuhr.)

Turner, George Allen. The More Excellent Way: The Scriptural Basis of the Wesleyan Message. Winona Lake, Ind.:
Light and Life Press, 1951.

Tyler, Alice Felt. Freedoms Ferment: Phases of American
Social History from the Colonial Period to the Outbreak of
the Civil War. Minneapolis: University of Minneapolis
Press, 1944. (New York: Harper Torchbooks, 1962.)

Van Duesen, Henry P.   "Third Force in Christendom." Life
    (June, 9, 1958), pp. 113-124.

Vineland N. J. Centennial.   Vineland, N. J. :   Vineland Centen-
    nial, Inc. n. d.

The Vineland Historical Magazine.   Edited by Elena J. Dar-
    ling.   Vineland, N. J. :   Vineland Historical and Antiquarian
    Society, 1961.

Wall, Ernest.   "I Commend unto You Phoebe."   Religion in
    Life, XXVI (Summer, 1957), 396-408.

Warfield Benjamin B.   Perfectionism.   2 vols.   New York:
    Oxford University Press, 1931-1932.

Warren, Austin.   New England Saints.   Ann Arbor. ;   Univer-
    sity of Michigan Press, 1956.

Watson Bernard D.   A Hundred Years' War: The Salvation
    Army, 1865-1965.   London: Hodder and Stoughton, 1964.

Watson, Richard.   The Life of Rev. John Wesley, A. M. ,
    Sometime Fellow of Lincoln College, Oxford, and Founder
    of the Methodist Societies.   New York: Lane and Tippett,
    1847.

Weber, Max.   The Sociology of Religion.   Translated by E.
    Fischoff.   London: Methuen, 1965.

Webster's Biographical Dictionary.   Springfield, Mass. :   G.
    and C. Merriam Co. Publishers, 1943.

Wentz, Abdel R.   Germany's Modern Pietistic Movement.
    N. p. n. n. , n. d.

Wesley, John.   Christian Perfection as Believed and Taught
    by John Wesley.   Edited and with introduction by Thomas
    S. Kepler.   Cleveland, O. :   World Publishing Co. , 1954.

_____ . The Message of the Wesleys: A Reader of In-
    struction and Devotion.   Compiled and with an introduction
    by Phillip S. Watson.   New York: Macmillan Co. , 1964.

Wheatley, Richard.   The Life and Letters of Mrs. Phoebe
    Palmer.   New York: W. C. Palmer, Jr. , 1876.

Wiebe, Robert. The Search for Order: American Society, 1877-1920. Vol. V of "Making of America: American Century Series." New York: Hill and Wang, 1967.

Wilcox, Leslie D. Be Ye Holy: A Study of the Teaching of Scripture Relative to Entire Sanctification with a Sketch of the History and Literature of the Holiness Movement. Cincinnati, O.: Revivalist Press, 1965.

Wilson, George. "An Exposition of Recent Teaching on Holiness." Expository Times, No. 5 (1893-94), pp. 108-111.

Wilson, George. Methodist Theology vs. Methodist Theologians. Cincinnati, O.: Jennings and Pye, 1904.

Winkler, Fr. "Robert Pearsall Smith und der Perfektionismus." Friedrich D. Kopatschek, Biblische Zeit und Streitfragen zur Aufklärung der Gebildeten. Series ix. Berlin-Lichterfelde: Edwin Runge, 1915.

Wittke, Carl F. William Nast, Patriarch of German Methodism. Detroit: Wayne State University Press, 1959.

Wolf, Richard C. "The Middle Period, 1800-1870: The Matrix of Modern American Christianity." Religion in Life, XXII (1952-53), 72-84.

Worcester, Paul W. The Master Key: The Story of the Hephzibah Faith Missionary Association. Kansas City, Mo.: Nazarene Publishing House, 1966.

Yates, Arthur S. The Doctrine of Assurance. London: The Epworth Press, 1952.

Yocum, Dale M. (ed.). The New Testament Church. Church of God (Holiness) Unification Commission. Overland Park, Kan.: Witt Printing Co., n.d.

INDEX

345